VOICES FROM THE FRONT LINES
THE PANDEMIC AND THE HUMANITIES

Perspectives in Health Humanities

UC Health Humanities Press publishes scholarship produced or reviewed under the auspices of the University of California Health Humanities Consortium, a multi-campus collaborative of faculty, students, and trainees in the humanities, medicine, and health sciences. Our series invites scholars from the humanities and healthcare professions to share narratives and analysis on health, healing, and the contexts of our beliefs and practices that impact biomedical inquiry.

General Editor

Brian Dolan, PhD, Professor, Department of Humanities and Social Sciences, University of California, San Francisco (UCSF)

Other Titles in this Series

Heart Murmurs: What Patients Teach Their Doctors
Edited by Sharon Dobie, MD (2014)

Humanitas: Readings in the Development of the Medical Humanities
Edited by Brian Dolan (2015)

Follow the Money: Funding Research in a Large Academic Health Center
Henry R. Bourne and Eric B. Vermillion (2016)

Soul Stories: Voices from the Margins
Josephine Ensign (2018)

Fixing Women: The Birth of Obstetrics and Gynecology in Britain and America
Marcia D. Nichols (2021)

Autobiography of a Sea Creature: Healing the Trauma of Infant Surgery
Wendy P. Williams (2023)

Medical Humanities, Cultural Humility, and Social Justice
Edited by Dalia Magaña, Christina Lux, and Ignacio López-Calvo (2023)

www.UCHealthHumanitiesPress.com

This series is made possible by the generous support of the Dean of the School of Medicine at UCSF, the UCSF Library, and a Multicampus Research Program Grant from the University of California Office of the President. Grant ID MR-15-328363 and Grant ID M23PR5992.

VOICES FROM THE FRONT LINES
THE PANDEMIC AND THE HUMANITIES

Edited by Katherine Ratzan Peeler and Richard M. Ratzan

© 2024 University of California Health Humanities Press

University of California
Center for Health Humanities
Department of Humanities and Social Sciences
UCSF (Box 0850)
490 Illinois Street, Floor 7
San Francisco, CA 94143-0850

Cover Art (detail on front cover, full image on back cover):
Justin Fiala, 2022, *Self Portrait: Intubated and Cannulated*. Oil on canvas. 36" x 48"
Image courtesy of the author.

Book design by Virtuoso Press

Library of Congress Control Number (LCCN): 2024930792

ISBN (print): 979-8-9899229-0-1
ISBN (ePUB): 979-8-9899229-1-8

Printed in USA

Contents

Acknowledgments	x
Acronyms and Glossary	xii
List of Images	xiv
Introduction	1

Part I: Care

Emily Rubin, MD, JD, MS
Waiting for the Rubber to Hit the Road: Ethical Frameworks
and Clinical Realities During the COVID-19 Pandemic — 9

Audrey Shafer, MD
Essential — 24

Angel Taddei, Paramedic and Fire Captain
Frontline Experiences from a Paramedic on the US-Mexico
Border — 28

Peter Canning, Paramedic, RN, MFA
COVID-19: A Paramedic's View — 33

Chase Baldwin Samsel, MD
This crisis! It's Always Been a Crisis — 41

C. Nicholas Cuneo, MD, MPH and
Rebeca Cázares-Adame, MD, MPH
Across a Border, a Pandemic Unfolds 49

Janet M. Shapiro, MD
Coronavirus Disease 2019: Who Has My Back? 60

Elizabeth P. Clayborne, MD, MA
Divergent Roles: Pregnant Mother, ER Physician, and Human 63

Pascale Audain, MSN, RN, CCRN
The Bedside and Beyond 68

Katherine R. Peeler, MD, MA
On the Front Lines, but of What Battle? 72

Stacy R. Nigliazzo, MSN, RN, CEN
The Tempest 76

Deadria Clarke, RRT
A Breath of COVID Air: Insights from a Respiratory Therapist 82

Matthew S. O'Donnell, DMin, ThM, MDiv
Healing Wounds, Practicing Compassion 86

Bradley A. Dreifuss, MD
Are You Listening? COVID-19 Realities and Reflections from an Emergency Medicine Physician 94

Kelly Pabilonia, LCSW
View from the Emergency Department Social Worker 103

Robin S. Goldman, MD, MPH
Reflections from My Time as a Hotel Doctor – How a Navajo Community Inspired Me During the Pandemic 109

Part II: Support

Joseph R. Betancourt, MD, MPH
Dispatches from the First COVID Surge: The Creation of the
Spanish Language Care Group   115

Robert A. Duncan, MD, MPH
A Pandemic Memoir, in Parallax   123

James E. Odom Jr., MBA, CHESP, CMIP, T-CHEST
COVID-19 from the Environmental Services Perspective   139

Margaret Rea, PhD and Michael S. Wilkes, MD, PhD, MPH
Health Professionalism, Trainees, and Moral Imperative   142

Michael SD Agus, MD
Adaptation, Compromise, and Resilience: COVID in a
Pediatric Intensive Care Unit   153

Jeffrey P. Burns, MD, MPH
The Transformational Effect of the Pandemic on Medical
Knowledge Exchange: From Webinar-to-Bedside   159

Tim Lahey, MD, MMSc, HEC-C
We are Demons, a Blind Old Woman, a Nurse Who Does Nails,
We are Musicians   164

Eric Jones, RRT
Anomalous: Respiratory Care Delivered During, and Redefined
By, COVID-19   170

David Hellerstein, MD
Tripping the Pandemic   173

Victor A. Lopez-Carmen, MPH
Hunkpati at Harvard: Stories of an Indigenous Medical Student
During the COVID-19 Pandemic   189

Part III: The Humanities

Justin Fiala, MD
Reflections on "Self Portrait: Intubated and Cannulated"   198

Fady Joudah, MD
Corona Radiata   201

Anne Hudson Jones, PhD
How I Learned about the 1918 Flu and Why It Matters   207

Peter Pereira, MD
Quarantine Dreams   214
Other People's Lawns   215
Bulldog   215

Richard M. Ratzan, MD
On Wearing Masks   216

Amalie Flynn, PhD, MFA
Whispers   249

Ieva Jusionyte, PhD, Paramedic
The Virus and the Border: Reflections on the Experiences of Emergency Responders in Southern Arizona   252

Sandeep Jauhar, MD, PhD
In a Pandemic, Do Doctors Still Have a Duty to Treat?   261

David Orentlicher, MD, JD
COVID-19 and the Physician's Duty to Treat   264

Fiona Woollard, PhD
Doing vs Allowing Harm and The Freedom Objection to Mask-Mandates and Other Anti-COVID-19 Regulations   271

Jack Coulehan, MD, MPH
Prayer to St. Roch, Patron of Plague Sufferers   281

Craig D. Blinderman, MD, MA
The Great Matter of Life and Death (or Morning in Kilauea)   283

Sheri Fink, MD, PhD
Early Pandemic Reporting from New York City: A Journalist's Reflections   285
'Code Blue': A Brooklyn I.C.U. Fights for Each Life in a Coronavirus Surge   286

Richard Donze, DO, MPH
Spiked Cetus   295

Pracha Peter Eamranond, MD, MPH, ALM
Digital Health Revolution   297

Kenneth V. Iserson, MD, MBA
Family Legends: Physicians and Pandemics Across Millennia   313

Ryan Christopher Jones
On Witnessing: Photojournalism and Visualized Trauma   329
Photographs from the sacrament of last rites in Boston hospitals, Spring 2020   334

Acknowledgments

"A labor of love." While hackneyed, there is no other phrase that better describes this project. I (KRP) was dubious about asking people who were already over-committed, stressed, and burned out to contribute work for this book. But here we are, four years and 45 contributors later. Some authors have been published before, and for others, this represents their first public writing. Some writers (including me) needed more than a year to finalize their pieces because it was so emotionally complicated and draining to get the words right. Throughout, I was amazed at everyone's patience with, and commitment to, this project. It has been an incredible honor to be trusted with your words and art. Thank you. Of note, all authors here are writing in their individual voices and not as representatives of their various institutions.

Time and space to work on this project were graciously provided by The Edmond and Lily Safra Center for Ethics at Harvard University and the Harvard Medical School Center for Bioethics where I was a joint fellow-in-residence from 2022-2023. My co-fellows at both centers served as excellent listeners about this book (and a different book underway) as it proceeded ever onward. Additionally, I would like to thank Michael Agus for taking a leap of faith in hiring me seven years ago and continually supporting my unique interests, and Bob Truog and Ed Hundert for guiding me through HMS and the world of bioethics and teaching. The students I teach at Harvard have taught me much more than they realize, and this book is better because of their influence.

Generous funding for this project was provided by the Committee for the Provostial Fund for the Arts and Humanities at Harvard University. Speaking of provosts, I had the great fortune to meet and befriend Willy Lensch, who provided much food for thought during our many hours together in our bioethics seminar.

It has been an immense pleasure working with our editor, Brian Dolan, of the University of California Health Humanities Press and his colleagues at Virtuoso Press. Thank you for your patience as we pulled this all together! We would also like to thank Michael Grey who helped jump start this project and was a wonderful source of ideas for contributors and the varied perspectives they could bring to this book.

Sithya Lach is the unsung hero of this book. Sithya's fiercely intelligent, thoughtful, and detail-oriented approach to organizing and copyediting these essays, poems and images was invaluable. Thank you from the bottom of our hearts for all your work on this book. This could not have been done without you.

This book is dedicated, in part, to Paul Farmer. It is impossible to put into words the influence Paul had on my life, despite the fact that our paths only crossed formally a handful of times. More than twenty years ago, his book, *Infections and Inequalities*, set me on the career and life path I still follow today. Paul's book led me to Arthur Kleinman, my sage and kind mentor during my masters in medical anthropology, and to Physicians for Human Rights, my partner in advocacy for the last two decades. But mostly Paul's book led me to Paul. I will leave the reader to read more about him as many others have eloquently written about the magnanimity that was Paul.

My husband, Crandall Peeler, and amazing two children, Arlo and Noa Peeler, deserve special thanks. I love my family so much, and as they know all too well, I also really love my work. Thank you for understanding me and supporting me and reminding me that it is ok to love work but not ok to miss vacation for it.

As I write this, I am sitting in my father's home office in Cape Cod. Surrounding me are framed conference posters I remember adorning our halls as a kid: "Art & Medicine 1985: Diagnosing the Canvas, April 12-13, 1985" and "Dying Before Their Time: A Conference on the Medical Humanities, Early Death and AIDS, April 15-16, 1988." Both conferences were held at University of Connecticut School of Medicine, and both were organized by my father. My father's intertwining of medicine and writing and art were what I understood medicine to be. My father was the writer and studier, and my mother was the storyteller. I would accompany her to clinic some days, and she knew every patient, their backstory, their parents' travails in trying to get their children care, and everything else about them without even looking at the chart. It was incredible and awesome in the truest sense. I did not appreciate the incredible role models that raised me until I was in my 20s, but I am forever grateful for that childhood and for the years I have had since I opened my eyes.

Acronyms and Glossary

AIDS – acquired immunodeficiency syndrome
Attending – a physician who has completed her medical training and is responsible for the overall care of a patient
ARDS – acute respiratory distress syndrome
BiPAP – bilevel positive airway pressure; a mode of respiratory support involving a mask that delivers breaths to a patient, generally considered a higher level of support than CPAP
BCU – biocontainment unit; a specialized unit in a hospital that has an environment, policies, and procedures in place to take care of patients with highly contagious diseases
CDC – Centers for Disease Control and Prevention
Code – the short-hand term referring to a resuscitation effort of someone in cardiac and/or respiratory arrest
COVID-19 – coronavirus disease 2019
CPAP – continuous positive airway pressure; a mode of respiratory support involving a mask that provides a continuous level of pressure to a patient's airway, making it easier to breathe
CPR – cardiopulmonary resuscitation; CPR most often refers to performing chest compressions in attempts to restart someone's heart but also includes certain medications that assist with resuscitation
Doff – to take off an article of clothing (such as a medical gown)
Don – to put on an article of clothing (such as a medical gown)
ECMO – extracorporeal membrane oxygenation; a mode of cardiac and/or respiratory support involving bypassing the heart and/or lungs via a mechanical pump and gas exchange system
ED – Emergency Department
ER – Emergency Room
EMS – Emergency Medical Services
EMT – Emergency Medical Technician
Extubation – removing a breathing tube from a patient's trachea
FDA – US Food and Drug Administration
Fellow – a physician in training in a subspeciality (i.e. has finished residency but is pursuing additional training in a more specialized field so is not yet an attending)
H1N1 – a strain of influenza virus (sometimes referred to as swine flu) that has periodically caused influenza pandemics, most famously in the 1918 influenza pandemic and more recently in 2009

HIV – human immunodeficiency virus
ICU – intensive care unit
Intern – a physician in the first year of residency training
Intubation – the process of placing a breathing tube into a patient's trachea
IV – intravenous
MERS/MERS-CoV – Middle East respiratory syndrome caused by MERS-coronavirus (CoV)
MI – myocardial infarction
MICU – medical intensive care unit
Moral injury – the emotionally difficult experience of clinicians who feel they cannot uphold their ethical obligations to put their patients' needs first because the system in which they are working instead prioritizes non-patient care related goals such as increasing revenue
N95 mask/respirator – a specialized mask with a tight seal and enhanced filtration system to better filter airborne particles
Nebulizer – a machine that turns liquid into a mist; often used to deliver medicines into a patient's airway to improve breathing
NIH – National Institutes of Health
NGO – nongovernmental organization
PACU – post-anesthesia care unit; a unit where patients stay only temporarily while recovering from anesthesia
PAPR – powered air purifying respirator; a device consisting of an enclosed hood that goes over a person's head and connects with a battery-operated air purifying system so she does not breathe contaminated air
PCR – polymerase chain reaction; a laboratory technique used to amplify a sample of DNA (and in the case of COVID-19, identify if viral DNA is present in a person when testing for the virus)
PPE – personal protective equipment; includes items such as masks, gowns, and gloves worn by healthcare workers to minimize the likelihood of acquiring an infection from a patient
Prone/proning – lying on one's stomach; patients in respiratory failure are sometimes placed in the prone position to improve their respiratory mechanics
Resident – a physician in training (i.e. has completed medical school but is still learning a specialty and thus cannot practice independently)
RT – respiratory therapist
SARS – severe acute respiratory syndrome; the viral respiratory disease caused by SARS-associated coronavirus 1; this outbreak occurred in Asia

xiv   *Voices from the Front Lines*

in 2003
SARS-CoV-2 – SARS-associated coronavirus 2; the strain of coronavirus that causes COVID-19
TB – tuberculosis
WHO – World Health Organization

List of Images

Cover
Self Portrait: Intubated and Cannulated, Justin Fiala, 2022. Image courtesy of the author.

View from the Emergency Department Social Worker, Kelly Pabilonia
Family visiting hospitalized relative, 2020. Photo courtesy of the author.

A Pandemic Memoir, in Parallax, Robert Duncan
Figure 1. Drs. Reginald Atwater, Wilder Penfield, and Roger Graves (left to right) outside the Peter Bent Brigham Hospital in October 1918. Note the patient beds on the raised outdoor porch. Courtesy of Brigham and Women's Hospital Archives.
Figure 2. Program for Child Health Week in Cattaraugus County, May 1-8, 1932. Note the photograph of Charlotte Penfield Atwater and John B. Atwater. From the collection of Dr. Duncan and family.
Figure 3. Dr. Reginald Atwater and Mrs. Mary Lasker at the 1948 Lasker Awards Ceremony. From the collection of Dr. Duncan and family.
Figure 4. Doctors at the Peter Bent Brigham Hospital in Boston, Massachusetts wearing personal protective equipment, 1918. Pictured are Drs. Robert Curtis, Clifford Walker, and Harold Martin (left to right). Courtesy of Brigham and Women's Hospital Archives.

We are Demons, a Blind Old Woman, a Nurse Who Does Nails, We are Musicians, Tim Lahey
Figure 1. Masks awaiting reuse (top); A View Outside, through masks (bottom). Photos courtesy of the author.
Figure 2. Plague doctor. Drawing. Wellcome Images, London. October 9, 2014. Courtesy of Wikimedia Commons, available under Creative Commons Attribution 4.0 International License at https://commons.wikimedia.org/wiki/File:Plague_doctor_Wellcome_L0025222.jpg

How I Learned about the 1918 Flu and Why it Matters, Anne Hudson Jones
"Gone So Soon," Headstone for Annie Ethel Wylie in Hampton Springs Cemetery, Carthage, Arkansas. Photo by Janice Williams for Find a Grave, used with permission.

On Wearing Masks, Richard M. Ratzan
Figure 1. Disparate Masks (as presented in clockwise order in essay)
a) An ancient Greek tragic mask by Silanion, photo by Giovanni Dall'Orto courtesy of Wikimedia Commons, available under the Creative Commons License at https://commons.wikimedia.org/wiki/File:7302_-_Piraeus_Arch._Museum,_Athens_-_Tragic_mask_-_Photo_by_Giovanni_Dall%27Orto,_Nov_14_2009.jpg
b) Jacques Plante's original ice hockey fiberglass face mask, photo by Horge, courtesy of Wikimedia Commons, available under the Creative Commons Attribution 2.0 Unported License, available at https://commons.wikimedia.org/wiki/File:Plante_Mask.jpg
c) Mort Henderson, aka "The Masked Marvel," donning his trademark full-faced black mask, posing before a fight in 1915. Courtesy of the Library of Congress, available at the Library of Congress, with no restrictions, at https://www.loc.gov/pictures/item/2014700714/
d) Hospital Corpsman 3rd Class Brennan Leary wearing an N95 mask while treating a COVID-19 patient in the intensive care unit of the hospital ship USNS Mercy (T-AH 19). Courtesy of Wikmedia Commons, available under the public domain at https://commons.wikimedia.org/wiki/File:USNS_Mercy_Sailor_Treats_Patient_%2849785699691%29.jpg
e) The mask of a late medieval executioner, courtesy of the Science Museum Group, available under the Creative Commons Attribution 4.0 License, available at https://collection.sciencemuseumgroup.org.uk/objects/co155266/executioners-mask-europe-1501-1700-executioners-mask

Figure 2. Guy Fawkes mask, courtesy of Wikimedia Commons, image by Pierre Selim, available under Creative Commons Attribution-Share Alike 3.0 Unported, available at https://en.wikipedia.org/wiki/Guy_Fawkes_mask#/media/File:Protest_ACTA_2012-02-11_-_Toulouse_-_05_-_Anonymous_guy_with_a_scarf.jpg

Figure 3. Emmett Kelly as "Weary Willie," courtesy of Wikimedia

Commons, available under the public domain at https://commons.wikimedia.org/wiki/File:Emmett_Kelly_1953_(cropped).jpg

Figure 4. The Minnesota Theatre Company 1965 - Caucasian Chalk Circle, image courtesy of Hennepin County Library, under the public domain, available at https://digitalcollections.hclib.org/digital/collection/p17208coll15/id/1004/

Figure 5. Mask of QŌ'LÔC in Boas, Franz. 1897. The Social Organization and the Secret Societies of the Kwakiutl Indians In Report of the U.S. National Museum for 1895. Washington, DC. p. 491. Image courtesy of Internet Archive, under the public domain, available at https://archive.org/details/32882002790031/page/n271/mode/2up

Figure 6. Women in Algeria wearing haiks, courtesy of Wikimedia Commons, under Creative Common, adapted from https://commons.wikimedia.org/wiki/File:HAIK_2015.jpg

Figure 7. Esmarch's chloroform inhaler in Von Esmarch, Frederick. 1888. The Surgeon's Handbook on the Treatment of Wounded in the War. Translated by B. Farquhar Curtis. London: Sampson Low, Marston, Searle, and Rivington Ltd. p. 145. Image courtesy of Internet Archive, under public domain, available at https://archive.org/details/surgeonshandbook00esma/page/144/mode/2up

Figure 8. Civil War soldier, Corporal Andros Guille, a) before and b) after facial reconstruction in Kingsley, Norman W. 1880. A Treatise on Oral Deformities as a Branch of Mechanical Surgery. New York: D. Appleton and Company. p. 349-350. Image courtesy of Internet Archive, under the public domain, available at https://archive.org/details/treatiseonoralde00king/page/350/mode/2up

Figure 9. Francis Derwent Wood with soldier, courtesy of Wikimedia Commons, under the public domain, available at https://commons.wikimedia.org/wiki/File:Captain_Francis_Derwent_Wood_RA_puts_the_finishing_touches_to_a_cosmetic_plate_made_for_a_British_soldier_with_a_serious_facial_wound._Q30456.jpg

Figure 10. Soldier a) before and b) after mask made by Anna Coleman Ladd, courtesy of the Library of Congress, under the public domain, available at https://www.loc.gov/pictures/item/2017666793/ and https://www.loc.gov/pictures/item/201766679t/

Figure 11. Plague doctor, courtesy of Wikimedia Commons, under public domain, available at https://en.wikipedia.org/wiki/Plague_doctor

Figure 12. Clinicians wearing simple masks during pneumonic plague epidemic in Manchuria, 1910-11 and 1920-21 courtesy of ResearchGate, under Creative Commons 4.0, available at https://www.researchgate.net/figure/Wearing-anti-plague-masks-front-and-side-views-Manchurian-Plague-Prevention-Service_fig1_328947930

Figure 13. Public health poster, undated, courtesy of the National Library of Medicine, under the public domain, available at https://collections.nlm.nih.gov/catalog/nlm:nlmuid-101453084-img

Figure 14. Red Cross workers make anti-influenza masks for soldiers, Boston, Massachusetts., courtesy of the National Archives under the public domain, available at https://www.archives.gov/news/topics/flu-pandemic-1918

Figure 15. Seattle policemen wearing masks during 1918 influenza pandemic, under the public domain, courtesy of the National Archives, available at https://www.archives.gov/exhibits/influenza-epidemic/records-list.html

Figure 16. Conflicting media messages and public reception on masks, San Francisco Chronicle, 29 Oct 1918: 9, under the public domain.

Figure 17. Anti-Mask meeting advertisement, San Francisco Chronicle, 25 Jan 1919:4, under public domain.

The Great Matter of Life and Death (or Morning in Kilauea), Craig Blinderman

Mandala covered walls. Photo courtesy of the author.

On Witnessing: Photojournalism and Visualized Trauma, Ryan Christopher Jones

Five photographs from the sacrament of last rites in Boston hospitals, Spring 2020. Photographs courtesy of the author.

To Susan, the consummate clinician and storyteller
and
To Paul Farmer, who understood the front line better than anyone

Introduction

Medicine and the humanities have been intertwined since humans could communicate. Attending to the sick is an essential component of our continued existence, and reflecting upon and documenting that attention (or, at time, inattention) has been a focus of storytelling, art, philosophy, and their related disciplines. As the enormity of the COVID-19 pandemic was just starting to reveal itself in the Spring of 2020, my father proposed we undertake a book project consisting of commissioned essays from frontline hospital providers and those well-versed in the medical humanities to reflect on the experience of the pandemic. I was skeptical to say the least. His vision, and my skepticism, while certainly windows into our overall personalities, are also windows into the eras we trained in and our roles as they currently stood in Spring 2020. Thus, we start with origin stories, followed by a broader introduction to the book in general.

Rich's Tale

At age 12, thanks to my mother, I was now in a new school. Although it was Brooklyn, and 1957, once you entered the doors of Poly Prep, you were in England. There was a headmaster instead of a principal, and you were in the First Form rather than seventh grade. (It was years, thankfully, before I realized how pretentious this all was, but the mystique worked on this impressionable 12-year-old and, in fact, was successful in instilling the concomitant *noblesse oblige*). I had to take two years of Latin, like everyone else, but, unlike everyone else, I loved it. And I continued for another nine years, finishing up as a college Classics major who was only 2 or 3 courses shy of a double major in pre-med, a self-indulgent decision based, mostly, by the intense love I had for languages and literature and the fact that I knew within months I would never again meet such fascinating and learned professors as Jim Notopoulos and Albert Merriman in the Classics department. And I was right.

It was not surprising, therefore, that my interest in medicine has always included the medical humanities, i.e., art and medicine, literature and medicine, ethics and medicine, music and medicine, and history and medicine. My publishing life has been immeasurably enriched by conferences and publications with like-minded colleagues, many of whom were new at first but are now very good friends.

In 2020, I experienced a triple whammy: I had let my Emergency Medicine boards lapse as planned, figuring, at age 74 I did not need to recertify so I could practice until I was 84; my hospital had recently passed a bylaws requirement to be certified in one's primary specialty, which was no longer true for me; and COVID-19 hit with all the force of a freight train. As much I wanted to serve – when else in peace time is an emergency medicine physician needed more than mass casualty or, its equivalent, a pandemic? – I now could not. And yet, not only was I sidelined by my certification lapse but also by both hospital and family strictures about my working the front lines at age 74 in this particular pandemic.

Not devastated but severely disappointed, I turned to whatever service I could, serving on the early telephone lines for COVID-19 testing, prompting a paper about this redefined notion of service (Ratzan 2022).

This book is the culmination of all the above – medical humanities, family (what a joy to work with one's wonderfully intelligent adult daughter!), and new friends – contributors from all walks of the medical service community, describing their paths and, to borrow from one of our family's favorite movies, "The Princess Bride," their perilous journey through the Fireswamp of COVID-19 as seen through their various eyes and pens.

Katie's Tale

I came to medicine "late." As a somewhat surly teenage girl with two physician parents, I had decided I wanted to be "not a doctor." But recognizing my subconscious choice to always land in health-related work-study jobs in college (and that I actually deeply admired my parents and their work), I enrolled in a premedical program at University of Connecticut after graduation. At UConn, I took my first medical anthropology course, and dove headfirst into the world of anthropology, human rights, and global health while concurrently finishing my premedical studies. The possibilities of what I could do with medicine outside the clinical realms seemed suddenly endless to me. I wanted to investigate human rights atrocities as they pertained to health and use those findings to advance health and rights-promoting policy changes. This was the mindset with which I entered medical school.

The next eleven years of medical school, pediatrics residency, and pediatric critical care fellowship were incredible but also full of uncertainty.

I had begun volunteering with the non-profit Physicians for Human Rights while a premed. Throughout medical school, the only thing that was clear to me was my desire to work at the intersection of health and human rights. Given the failed state of our country's asylum system, this seemed like the perfect place to focus my learning and work. But *as a trainee*, I didn't know how to get there. I didn't like primary care, I didn't want to go into infectious disease, and I didn't want to work in the Emergency Department – the three classic places where physicians end up who focus on immigrant health. So I taught myself about our asylum system, learned how to perform forensic physical exams to lend credence to peoples' asylum claims, and worked on policy advocacy projects. And, what almost felt like a side activity, I attended medical school, trained as a pediatrician, and then pursued critical care. Those fields fit my personality, and I loved the physiology and human connection to those who needed care when they, or their loved ones, were truly, truly sick. Functionally, I now have two professional personas – Katie the immigrant rights researcher and advocate, and Katie the pediatric critical care physician. And I liked it that way. Until the pandemic hit.

As routine life came to a halt in late winter 2020, the significance of my clinician persona came squarely into focus. As I note in my essay for this book, I did not know how to feel. I both wanted to be in the thick of the action but was simultaneously nervous about possibly having to treat adult patients in our pediatric ICU. Mostly, I felt confused and ashamed about being nervous. In the end, children needed our care too – for COVID and its related pediatric afflictions, for emergency mental healthcare, and for their "normal sick care." Providing physical and psychological care to the pediatric patients who needed us made me feel less adrift, but I still felt unsettled.

Bioethics, anthropology, journalism, law. Understanding the nuances of the right to health through these fields is what I love to do. Exploring health through the humanities is how I add color to otherwise dry data about the wretched state of affairs of immigration detention in the US. I am fortunate to have trained, and now teach, in an era of medicine where learning pathophysiology and social determinants of health and bioethics and health policy are recognized (well, not everywhere …) as equally important in understanding and treating a patient's illness. It is this persona that struggled early in the pandemic, worried that only my clinician persona with pathophysiology knowledge had anything to offer. But, of course, that was naïve and wrong, for so many reasons. We needed the humanities to witness and make sense of this COVID story. We needed them to help us connect this pandemic to lessons from ones in the past. We needed the humanities to create connections with our patients in the hospital and overall in a world that felt increasingly lonely and scary. And we needed the humanities to elucidate – again – why vaccines, ventilators, masks, and medicine were never going to be sufficient in and of themselves to stem the tide of this pandemic. My father already knew this. I vaguely understood this when I agreed to this project, but only now, four years and 45 essays and poems later, do I get it.

Participating in this book has helped me to understand the many roles and perspectives that occurred and were necessary to help us process this pandemic. I cherish my role as a doctor at the bedside, and I realize now that my fear of taking on a potentially new clinical role in the midst of a crisis was misplaced. My real fear was losing my other persona – that of immigrant health advocate. In putting this latter hat back on, I found light in my personal darkness. I worked with others to improve conditions in detention during the pandemic and assisted in many successful efforts at decarceration, all of which improved the health of people seeking asylum in our country during a time when they needed our help more than ever.

This is a book about relationships. Parents and children. Spouses. Clinicians and patients. Science and fiction. Lessons from pandemics past to actions of pandemic present. Art and healing. The intersections of fear and love and anger and confusion and kindness and so many other emotions. Behind and in front of the camera, or the pen. *Voices from the Front Lines* (*VFL*) is neither comprehensive nor representative of the infinite experiences we have had during these first few years of the COVID-19 pandemic. Rather, it is a slice – a thin sampling – of persons working on the medical front lines and of persons eloquent in the medical humanities. We solicited essays, poems, and art. Our contributors range from colleagues to strangers to others recommended by old friends. Still others were authors whose published works we admired. Certainly, we have missed many unique voices and experiences and vantage points. We suspect and hope that other similar collections will be published, collections that expand even further the voices experiencing this pandemic and that will add to the understanding of it for future generations.

VFL is divided into three sections: Care, Support, and The Humanities. "Care" includes reflective essays and poems by contributors who participated directly in care – broadly defined – at the front lines of the pandemic in the US. We drew mostly from inpatient (hospital) providers. We considered pertinent and frontline all kinds of care – clinical care by nurses, physicians, and respiratory therapists; spiritual care by clergy; supportive care by social workers; and care of the patient's environment by environmental services staff.

In the "Support" section, *VFL* features essays by persons either tasked with, or personally committed to, improving systems of care. These writers organized ever-changing infectious disease policies, found ways to disseminate knowledge locally and globally, and assessed the continually evolving needs of medical trainees. The final section, "The Humanities," includes photographs, poetry, and essays by contributors with professional experience in the medical humanities—historians, anthropologists, journalists, poets, and philosophers to name just a handful. We asked them to consider the ethical, cultural, and historical questions that they reflected upon during the first year or so of the pandemic.

Of course, these distinctions are artificial and blurry. Many of the works would fit well in more than one section. Joe Betancourt's essay is as much about frontline care as it is about thinking creatively about how to provide additional inpatient interpretation services. Rob Duncan writes from his perspective running his hospital's infection prevention program but also as a curious grandson *cum* historian as he dives into his family tree. To aid the reader, there is a glossary at the beginning of the book of commonly used acronyms and terms. Guidelines and terminology, best practices for medical care and transmission prevention, and how we as a global community and as individuals felt, evolved frequently throughout the pandemic. As such, each essay or poem includes the date it was submitted to give the reader a sense of when during the pandemic the contributor was writing. My reference to "pediatric inflammatory multisystem syndrome" (PIMS) was outdated within a month of my writing that essay. PIMS has become MIS-C or multisystem inflammatory syndrome in children, and even MIS-C has become almost non-existent (for now) as the ebbs and flows of different COVID strains and immunities come into play. The feelings and experiences and challenges of March 2020 were not the same as those of September 2020, January 2021 or February 2022.

We invited our contributors to consider some of the thorny issues COVID-19 brought to the fore, issues much less commonly encountered in "ordinary" healthcare times. For instance, the unsettling specter of medical triage, a practice that arose, appropriately, during wartime but was now occurring hourly, in 2020, in ICUs across the country; the extraordinary problems of masks; public policies restricting normally free behavior, like attending indoor religious services; family forbidden to be present at a loved one's death; a death count both here and abroad that approached levels and rates normally only seen during times of war with stories of entire families succumbing over a week; and the change in centuries-old forms of greeting, the handshake yielding to a "fist bump." Whole office buildings and the nation's schools closed down, turning our country into a land of remote, virtual denizens living in the cocoons that came to be called "bubbles," reminding us of Matthew Arnold's haunting poem "To Marguerite: Continued":

> Yes! in the sea of life enisled,
> With echoing straits between us thrown,
> Dotting the shoreless watery wild,
> We mortal millions live *alone*.
> The islands feel the enclasping flow,
> And then their endless bounds they know.
> (Arnold 1852)

And, finally, how did our contributors feel about the ethical distinction between "ordinary" obligations and duties, and supererogatory actions? Or, as it was sometimes expressed by medical professionals – nurses, respiratory therapists, physicians, EMTs – "This is not what I signed up for." Is a physician with a young family of four obligated by medical duty, by her Hippocratic Oath, to care, before vaccines were available, for a desperately sick COVID-19 patient who openly defied mask-wearing and social distancing? Or is that same physician duty-bound to care for a critically ill COVID-19 patient who maliciously spread disinformation about COVID-19 vaccines and refused to get them himself? David Orentlicher and Sandeep Jauhar address some of these issues, but they remain terribly complex. One heaves a huge sigh of understanding, therefore, by the end of her thoughtful essay, when one reads that Emmy Rubin has effectively – and wisely – thrown her hands up in semi-surrender after having tried to wend her way through the labyrinth of ICU-ventilator triage.

Our essayists and poets and writers and artists did not disappoint. From philosophers like Fiona Woollard to spiritual caregivers like Reverend O'Donnell to emergency medicine physicians like Brad Dreifuss and Ken Iserson, they addressed, or tried to address, these issues and more with sagacity, erudition, eloquence and compassion. And with insight. As Justin Fiala writes about his painting, a wonderful piece of art that graces the front and back cover of this book:

> Occiput, eyes, and maxillae: the catharsis was underway, and I knew there was no other direction to follow. I was sure it was me.
>
> In the same way that authors occasionally describe a phenomenon of characters in their novels "writing themselves" I would say that, from that point on, the figure in the portrait similarly began to paint himself into being: heart, lungs, and support devices.

One hundred and twenty years ago, Oscar Wilde, in his almost metaphysical prose, agreed:

> For out of ourselves we can never pass, nor can there be in creation what in the creator was not. Nay, I would say that the more objective a creation appears to be, the more subjective it really is. Shakespeare might have met Rosencrantz and Guildenstern in the white streets of London, or seen the serving-men of rival houses bite their thumbs at each other in the open square; but Hamlet came out of his soul, and Romeo out of his passion (Wilde 1913, 184).

We like to think that this moment of anagnorisis is the explicit realization that despite our many differences, we are all in this together.

References

Arnold, Matthew. 1852. "To Marguerite: Continued." 1852. Accessed 23 Jun 2023. https://www.poetryfoundation.org/poems/43609/to-marguerite-continued

Ratzan, Richard M. 2022. "They Also Serve Who Only Sit and Answer COVID-19 Hotline Telephones." *Journal of Emergency Medicine* 62 (4): 513-515. https://doi.org/10.1016/j.jemermed.2021.11.015

Wilde, Oscar. 1913. *Intentions*. Methuen: London.

Part I: Care

Waiting for the Rubber to Hit the Road: Ethical Frameworks and Clinical Realities During the Covid-19 Pandemic
By Emily Rubin

Originally submitted March 23, 2022

It is early March 2020. I am standing outside room 56 in the medical intensive care unit talking to one of my favorite ICU nurses. It is strangely quiet in the unit. We do not know what is coming. She is optimistic. "We'll all get through it together," she says. "Just like we did with H1N1. Remember that?" she says. "How awful it was?" I was an intern during H1N1, just starting out in medicine. I did remember it, but only snippets. A lot of men in their 30s, previously healthy, then suddenly critically ill with the flu. On machines called ECMO that took the blood out of their bodies, put oxygen into it, put the blood back. I barely understood it at the time.

***

It is the second week of March 2020. I meet a New Yorker reporter named Benjamin Wallace-Wells at a bar across the street from the hospital to talk about the possibility of an impending critical care crisis. We talk in theoretical terms about the kinds of ethical questions that could come up, the difficulty of triage decisions, the fear that the hospital will be overwhelmed, the worry that patients could die alone. I will be starting work in the ICU next week.

***

It is just before Thanksgiving, 2021. I am sitting outside room 76 in the medical intensive care unit talking to the same ICU nurse. We're going down the row of rooms, trying to remember who was in each one during the first COVID-19 surge. We can remember each person's circumstances, but it is hard to remember all the names. I remember a time when there were six patients on ECMO, all of them Hispanic. I remember the details of what happened to each person – room 70 had a catastrophic brain bleed, room 74 had dead bowel and was rushed to the operating room,

room 78's cheeks were so sunken that it was startling every time I walked in the room. They all died. And for the life of me, I can't remember all of their names.

On March 14, 2020, the conversation started in earnest about what we would do if our hospitals were to become overwhelmed with critically ill COVID-19 patients. I had yet to take care of a single patient with COVID-19. It was a Saturday, and I was with a friend who is also a doctor, walking in the woods north of Boston. We were trying to escape for what we knew would be one of the last days of relative calm before a storm whose ferocity we could not predict. I got a phone call asking me to start thinking about a protocol for triaging critical care resources if demand were to exceed supply. The moment it all started is etched in my mind like a snapshot. I can remember the exact stretch of path I was walking when my phone rang. For several months after that, I would think about little else.

As I do in non-pandemic times, during the COVID-19 pandemic I have worn multiple hats. As a pulmonary and critical care doctor, I take care of individual patients, many of whom are desperately ill or have medical conditions that put them at high risk of serious illness. As a medical ethicist, I help navigate complex individual cases that frequently involve the use of a range of life-sustaining treatments, often stepping in to help resolve conflicts between teams and family members of patients who are critically ill about the appropriateness of ongoing aggressive medical treatment. I also help think about the big picture, how to address ethical challenges at a systems level and formulate policies and protocols that can be applied generally across a range of individual patient situations.

The discipline of medical ethics tries to apply guiding principles to the practice of medicine, which involves humanity with all of its messy, flawed characters, emotions, cognitive biases, irrational and inconsistent behaviors. The intersection of the two has always been challenging. Trying to marry something that is fair and defensible in theory with something that will work in reality is hard. The difficulty with textbook medical ethics is that academic approaches are often ill-suited to real world situations. These challenges have never been clearer than they were during the height of a respiratory pandemic. And reconciling my roles as a bedside clinician and a medical ethicist would prove disorienting at times.

It is the third week of March 2020. I arrive in the medical ICU. On rounds with the residents, the one-line descriptions of the patients blur together. "This is a 52-year-old man with a history of hypertension admitted with COVID ARDS, on day five of mechanical ventilation, proned." "This is a 78-year-old man with a history of diabetes and congestive heart failure admitted with COVID ARDS, on day three of mechanical ventilation, proned." How is it possible that all 20 patients in this unit have the same disease that we had barely heard of two months before? Where is everybody else?

We were used to taking care of patients with acute respiratory distress syndrome, but the similarity of all these patients to one another is immediately disquieting. It feels dystopian. The sameness in every room, patients on their stomach in order to help ventilate their lungs, very hard to see their faces. The eerie quiet of an ICU with no family members at the bedside because of restrictions on visitation. Except for the clumsy navigation of personal protective equipment at the beginning, going through all the donning and doffing steps in my head, rounds are unusually fast. We go through all the patients, one by one. But it is very hard to remember their names. Now they stream in, and we make room for them, creating new intensive care units as we go.

As Benjamin Wallace-Wells wrote in the New Yorker article he was working on when I met with him, "[i]n the Mass General ICUs – the best-resourced units in one of the very best-resourced hospitals in the best-resourced country in the history of the world – the general American assumption of infinite possibility reaches something like an apogee" (Wallace-Wells 2020). In line with that assumption, those who wish to receive critical care – who want their lives prolonged with medicines and machines – generally get their wish. That is typically true regardless of how old they are, what is wrong with them, or how long they might be expected to survive once they are admitted to an ICU. The answer to imminent death in a hospitalized patient is often, for better or worse, to transfer a patient to the intensive care unit for life-sustaining treatment. This standard of care was about to be challenged, at least in theory.

Crisis standards of care are defined as "a substantial change in usual healthcare operations and the level of care it is possible to deliver, which is made necessary by a pervasive (e.g., pandemic influenza) or catastrophic (e.g., earthquake, hurricane) disaster" (IOM 2009). The same week I took care of my first COVID-19 patients in the ICU, I started working on the crisis standards of care for our health system. Shortly thereafter, I would join an advisory panel for the Commonwealth of Massachusetts and help to develop the Commonwealth's crisis standard of care guidance for the COVID-19 pandemic.

Crisis standards of care address a broad range of questions related to the provision of healthcare during disaster conditions. The most pressing question in March 2020 was how we would allocate critical, life-saving resources such as ventilators or intensive care unit beds if the system could not create enough capacity to provide them to everyone who needed and wanted them.

When we first started thinking about critical care triage during COVID-19, the scenario we wanted to avoid was the one in which critical care beds filled up quickly on a first-come, first-served basis. The beds would all be full, and then we would have no way of accommodating patients who might arrive for care later but have a better chance of surviving than the patients already receiving critical care. Withdrawing life-sustaining treatment once started is, in many ways, much harder than never starting it in the first place, so freeing up capacity would be very challenging. We feared that, if we didn't find a way to distinguish meaningfully between patients arriving for care up front and save some capacity for those who would come later, "first-come, first-served" would be the default. But holding back capacity – which would require withholding life-saving resources from a patient at death's door in order to save those resources for a theoretically better off patient who would present later – would be very hard.

There is a reason that many states did not have crisis standards of care protocols in place prior to COVID-19. The conversation about how to assign priority for life-saving resources in an emergency is painful and fraught with controversy. No one wants to have this conversation until it is absolutely necessary, at which point it is almost – by definition – too late. The conversation would often be so agonizing that it made me question at times whether the harm of having the conversation in advance was greater than the harm of just dealing with triage the best we could if and when we had to.

From a 10,000-foot view, many agree that the primary goal of a critical care triage protocol should be utilitarian – doing the "greatest good for the greatest number." The devil, as always, is in the details. Does that mean saving the most total lives without considering how long those lives have already lasted, or how much longer they might last once you save them? Does it mean saving the most "life years" by prioritizing those who are likely to have more time left if they survive?

And do other ethical imperatives require us to prioritize certain people who have been historically subject to discrimination and inequity that has resulted in their being more vulnerable to severe illness and death? Do they dictate that we should give some priority to essential workers whose jobs require them to take greater risks than others? Or should assignment of scarce resources be done by random lottery, without regard to prospect for survival or any other individual patient characteristics?

Although crisis standards of care are, by definition, meant to be rooted in public health ethics and focused on how to maximize benefit for populations, it became clear early on that, in a culture of plenty where concern about individual rights is paramount, it would be difficult or impossible to center the discussion of critical care triage on public health ethics alone. In many ways, it was like trying to fit a square peg into a round hole.

Every answer seemed problematic and unfair in some way. It wasn't fair to prioritize certain people based on age, as this would be age discrimination. It wasn't fair to consider underlying life expectancy, as life expectancy is affected by systemic racism and historical inequity. Depending on who you talked to, it was either absolutely imperative or entirely inappropriate to consider whether a person is an essential worker who has no choice but to interact with the public as part of his job.

Many things about critical care triage are true at the same time. We often do not have good information when someone presents critically ill. Even with significant information, we do not have perfect tools to predict short-term prognosis. The tools we do have are prone to bias and are likely to be inaccurate in predicting survival in patients with COVID-19.

Taking into account life expectancy in allocating scarce resources magnifies historical inequity by deprioritizing members of certain groups who carry a high burden of chronic disease as a result of previous inadequate access to care, during a pandemic that disproportionately burdens members of those same groups. Everyone who is 80 years old is not the same physiological age and does not have the same life expectancy. Not prioritizing essential workers for access to critical care resources would feel like a slap in the face to those who get sick on the job. Prioritizing essential workers in a framework would risk, in practice, giving priority only to those we recognized as doctors or nurses and overlooking those whose essential work might not be immediately known, turning social status into a criterion and potentially discounting many have put themselves in harm's way to keep the world turning during the pandemic.

It is May 2020. We are in a conference room gathered around the phone. With the assistance of a Spanish interpreter, we are talking to the husband of our patient, a woman in her 50s who has been on ECMO for over a month with no signs of improvement. We explain to her husband, who got COVID while long-haul truck driving, and gave it to her, that it is time to stop. When we know we can't get a patient better, we do not continue. We encourage him to come and be with her. In halting, broken English, he asks, "What time will you perform the disconnection?"

An ethical framework is only useful if it accounts for clinical reality. There are two truths that seemed to get short shrift in the debate about how to allocate resources fairly. First, any allocation framework has to differentiate meaningfully between patients in order to be useful. Second, any allocation framework has to be tolerable to people who would be relied on to implement it in a crisis. Every basis for distinguishing between patients for access to critical resources can be viewed at some level as unfair, but any framework for allocation of scarce resources that does not differentiate adequately between patients will not work.

At least as applied to the COVID-19 pandemic, most of the allocation frameworks that exist suffer from a similar problem: they would not draw enough lines between patients to be useful if the system were truly overwhelmed. It is so odious to say that we would deprioritize certain people for access to life-saving resources that the frameworks all risk failing to differentiate between people at all. To differentiate, they incorporate the notion of tie-breakers, which fails to account for the reality that most people in need of access to critical care will present sequentially and not simultaneously. This makes the concept of side-by-side comparisons between patients significantly less relevant and useful.

Given this reality, any allocation framework that does not meaningfully distinguish between patients on criteria other than order of presentation will result in the vast majority of resources being allocated on first-come, first-served basis. This is how we allocate ICU beds in ordinary times, which is tolerable because in ordinary times we are largely able to accommodate most everyone whom we think we can help.

When I receive a call from an outside hospital that wants to transfer a 29-year-old previously healthy patient with severe influenza for advanced ventilator management and we do not have a ready ICU bed, I look around the ICUs and see many people receiving critical care who are vanishingly unlikely to recover sufficiently to leave the hospital. This state of affairs is tolerable now only because we can almost always find a way to flex the system to find room somewhere for the 29-year-old. If resources were strictly scarce and the 29-year-old would actually die if we did not have capacity, it would rapidly become intolerable that an older adult with multiple life-limiting medical conditions received the resource because he got there first. That would be even more intolerable if the person who got there first could afford a pulse oximeter to monitor his health, had access to a primary care doctor who would tell him when to seek medical attention, and had someone to bring him to the hospital, whereas the person who got there later couldn't afford the pulse oximeter, had no access to a helping provider to guide her, and had limited access to transportation.

Any allocation system ultimately has to be implemented by human beings with moral intuition and clinical judgment. It would be very hard to tell an 83-year-old with multiple life-limiting medical problems who wished to have all measures taken to extend her life that we did not have enough ventilators to go around, and we were unable to offer her one. It would be unbearable to say the same thing to a previously healthy 40-year-old. If the rules did not allow differentiation between patients who would seem to be different in meaningful ways, there would be outcomes under the framework that were widely viewed as perverse, and the people implementing the system would not be willing to implement it. It would descend into chaos, with people gaming the system to make allocation seem fairer. Saying "we can't help you" when we actually might have been able to is anathema to medical professionals.

If we ever were to get there, the ethical alternative to having a framework that would delineate between patients based on age or other criteria that seem repugnant to many is not that these impossible decisions would not have to be made. It is that they would get made in the shadows, most likely idiosyncratically, to the detriment of all those making the decisions and many of those on the receiving end.

It is April 2020. A young man in his 40s comes into the ICU very sick with a bloodstream infection. He is one of the few whom I can remember from that time who was sick with something other than COVID. He is talking when he gets there. Hours later, he is on the verge of death. The only other thing we can think to do is to take out his sick colon. The trauma surgeon and I lower our masks so the patient's wife can see our faces when we tell her that he will probably die anyway. Hours later, after he returns from the operating room, the afternoon light is streaming in through the window as I hold the iPhone in a plastic bag, the priest on the other end of the line performing last rites.

One of the most controversial issues in the discussions about triage of critical care resources was whether healthcare workers and other "essential workers" should receive priority for critical care resources if they were to become ill. One rationale for giving priority is that people who have put themselves at risk to provide assistance to others during a pandemic should as a matter of fairness receive priority. The other is that returning essential workers to the work force is critical in a public health emergency. Giving priority only to healthcare workers in an ethical framework would be self-serving, and a broad priority for all essential workers could be very complex to operationalize.

How would we define essential worker? How would we know in an emergency who was and wasn't one? We would always recognize the world-renowned physician, but we would risk missing the custodian who has been cleaning the hospital rooms on the night shift, the woman driving the train, the young man at the checkout counter selling us groceries. It was imperative that we not perpetuate the unspoken but prevalent injustice of favoring people based on who they know in the middle of a pandemic that was targeting the most vulnerable among us. But I also could not skirt the human reality that, in an emergency, it was inconceivable that healthcare workers would not prioritize their own, fairness be damned.

It is sometime during COVID. I have lost track of time. It is early evening on a weekend, close to change of shift. A colleague of mine has just been admitted to the ICU for a medical issue unrelated to COVID. He was awake and stable when I saw him in the emergency department shortly before to check in on him. He is coming to the ICU out of an abundance of caution. Sometime later, I hear an overhead page for the ICU to come urgently to one of the rooms in the ICU. With a sinking feeling, I realize it is the room my colleague was assigned to. The nurses tell me that he was fine a minute earlier. Now he is completely unresponsive – eyes open but blank. I am nearly paralyzed by fear - that he is having a stroke, that he is bleeding into his brain. He will be fine. I am shaking all the way home thinking what it would be like it he hadn't been.

***

It is many months into the pandemic. I walk into a patient's room. She is a Cambodian woman in her 70s. She was critically ill for many weeks and has been very delirious since leaving the intensive care unit. She is now awake and oriented for the first time. I ask her how she is doing. "My husband died," she says.

"I know," I say. "I'm so sorry." I do not tell her that I know her husband died because I was there, that I took care of him too. That I talked to her daughters many times late at night when both of their parents were in the ICU. That I was there when his heart stopped. That I called his daughters to tell them that he would die. I was happy to see her alive, but you could have cut the melancholy in that room with a knife.

So, what should be considered relevant in deciding who gets priority for potentially life-saving resources? Very strong voices emerged to argue that the only thing that should be relevant in critical care triage is saving the most lives. That is, the person's probability of surviving the acute illness is the only ethically relevant and fair consideration. Other considerations, including how many years a person might have to live following the acute illness (whether by virtue of age or underlying medical condition) were considered by many to be ethically irrelevant. And still others posited that every life is equally valuable, and trying to distinguish between them based on age, underlying health conditions, role in society, or any other criterion is wrong.

The concept of saving the most lives, while appealing in its simplicity, incorporates an assumption that, at the time we need to make these decisions, we know with any sort of accuracy what a given patient's odds would be of surviving the ICU. It is reassuring, but ultimately illusory, to think that the probability of survival can be known with certainty when a patient presents with critical illness.

It is my first ICU block since COVID began. A previously healthy man in his late 40s, one of the first critically ill patients with COVID-19 at our hospital, is desperately ill. He is on maximum support ECMO, and he cannot be touched without destabilizing him. After many conversations about whether there is anything else to add or change that might make a difference, we know that there is nothing to do but support him, try to avoid catastrophe, wait to see if he can get better. I sit in my office, take a deep breath, and call his wife. She begs me to tell her honestly what I think. I tell her that, if she wants my honest opinion, I think it is more likely than not that he will not survive. I tell her we will do everything we can and that I hope I am wrong. We arrange for her to come visit. He will go on to make a miraculous recovery.

***

It is one year into the pandemic. I am in the respiratory step-down unit, taking care of a man in his 50s who was close to death in the ICU two months before. He is still delirious. He intermittently needs a ventilator and is still on kidney dialysis, but I have a sense that in time he will wake up and recover. In preparation for a meeting with his family, I scan the notes from his time in the ICU. I see records of several family meetings in which his family was told that he would almost certainly die. Almost certainly. Five weeks after I meet him, he walks out of the hospital on his own two feet.

The focus of almost all the thinking about critical care triage was on how to decide who would get access to resources in the first place, with much less attention paid to the idea of stopping critical care interventions once started.

It is a dictum in medical ethics textbooks that withholding and withdrawing life-sustaining treatment are ethically equivalent. But any clinician who has been involved in many of these very difficult decisions – who is familiar with the psychology that surrounds them, and who is well-versed in the logistics of implementing them – can appreciate that these decisions are so different in degree as to be different in kind. Under most circumstances, not offering a life-sustaining treatment in the first place is a much easier clinical decision and act than stopping a life-sustaining treatment once started. For certain family members, consenting to the withdrawal of life-sustaining treatment feels like they are affirmatively causing the death of a loved one, and opposition to stopping treatment once started can be vehement. It is extremely rare that a medical team will take someone off a ventilator without the patient or family's consent when the consequence will almost certainly be imminent death. Although we routinely stop interventions/treatments once started in the ICU, it is often a long process to get there.

Even so, I ultimately came to believe that deciding who would get resources up front during the COVID pandemic would be so challenging and complicated that even the shortest trial of critical care, if wanted by the patient, followed by discontinuation if the patient was felt to have a poor prognosis, might be preferable to denying resources to people in the first place. Because the one situation in which withholding critical care resources is arguably more complex than withdrawing it once started is the one that was most common during COVID – an awake patient who is acutely in respiratory distress.

Ideally, a patient will not be allowed to struggle to breathe. If a patient is in acute respiratory distress, the choice is not between a breathing tube or no breathing tube. It is between a breathing tube and giving medications like morphine to treat air hunger. Making the sudden decision to focus on comfort only in an emergency when a patient is acutely facing his mortality is extremely difficult, particularly with no family present. The benefits of a trial of critical care, no matter how short, can be significant. This allows the patient to be made comfortable, permits time to gather more information about the patient's situation that might inform prognostic estimates, and gives assurance that the patient has been given a chance.

The trade-off of offering more people resources up front is that we would have to be willing to withdraw those resources relatively quickly once started if the prognosis for a patient was poor, even if families objected. This would be a departure from usual care, but in many ways a more humane departure than denying initial access to critical care resources up front to patients in extremis.

It is June 2020. I go down to see a patient in the emergency department. His oxygen saturation is low and dropping. He is breathing 40 times a minute – shallow and jagged. He is delirious and pulling at the oxygen mask on his face. I know only his name and age, nothing about his medical or social history. He either needs an airway and a ventilator or medicine to make him less short of breath. No one would do nothing.

***

It is May 2021. The calls from outside hospitals about ICU transfers come fast and furious. I talk to the doctors in other places, who are taking care of patients who are desperately ill with respiratory failure. In some cases, the doctors themselves sound desperate to transfer the patients to a hospital with more resources and more critical care expertise. Most often, the answer has to be "no". Our ICUs are full to exploding. I try to offer some guidance, sometimes saying that we will keep them on the list in case something opens up. It is hard not to wonder what happens to all these people, whether something could have been different if we had been able to get them here.

Fortunately, push never really came to shove in our hospital. But if it had, would we ever really have been able to implement a system that relied on not helping the person in front of us in order to be able to help those coming later? During the throes of the most difficult discussions about equity in allocation of scarce critical resources, a wise colleague suggested to me that a first-come, first-served system only seems unfair to people who start out expecting the system to be fair. To people who have never expected to be treated fairly, it might seem like the least unfair of all the unfair possibilities. That has stuck with me. What was it Winston Churchill said? "Democracy is the worst form of government – except for all the others that have been tried" (Churchill 1947).

It is sometime during COVID. There is a patient on ECMO with COVID who has no signs of lung recovery and no way out. We have explained that we will need to discontinue the ECMO. I get a call that the patient's son has shown up with a letter from a lawyer saying that we can't stop ECMO without the family's permission and that, if we do, he will accuse us of murder.

One subject that rarely came up in the course of the extensive discussions about triaging critical care resources in the event of scarcity is the reality of how we use intensive care in the United States. The truth is that there are many people we treat in our ICUs who we know from the outset we won't be able to help. We nevertheless use intensive care to stave off death, even if only for a little while. If someone wants to be rescued from impending death, we can often do that by putting in a breathing tube, by infusing potent medicines to keep the blood pressure up, by replacing the kidney function with a dialysis machine. For a host of complicated reasons – including the fact that in this country people are generally ill-prepared for death and the fact that medical professionals are often uncomfortable addressing death head on – we offer these options to many people who will not truly recover from illness. This reality gets lost in the discussions about critical care triage, which at times seem to assume that we are able to get people better regardless of age or condition. The fact that the possibilities are not actually infinite might not provide comfort in a crisis to a patient or family who wants to believe that they are. But in all of these discussions, we should not lose track of the limitations of what we are able to do with medicines and machines.

It has been two years since we started thinking about critical care triage in the era of COVID-19. Much has changed and we have navigated many other complicated decisions, including how to fairly allocate therapies for COVID-19 like monoclonal antibodies and antiviral treatments that are in short supply. Burnout among healthcare professionals has set in with a vengeance. The triage issues now have more to do with a constant level of strain on the system as a whole. The system is backed up at every level, with few skilled nursing or long-term acute care beds available to accommodate patients ready to be discharged from the hospital. Allocating resources during a global pandemic to those who have chosen not to get vaccinated, when rescuing those patients may be at the expense of the optimal care of others, has presented new ethical challenges.

It is January 2021. I brace myself for a conversation with the daughter of a dying, unvaccinated COVID patient. I am prepared to be resentful that she is angry and feels like we haven't done enough. The patient has been critically ill for over a month and is now imminently dying. We cannot get enough oxygen into her lungs. Her daughter is distraught. She says that people have mentioned to her that the only thing that could have prevented this was a vaccine. She begs for more time, begs us not to give up on her mother. I ask her if she feels like people are treating her mother differently because she didn't get vaccinated. She does. "All I have is my word that we have done everything we can to try to save her life," I say. "It must be awful," I say, "to think that something else could be done to save your mother's life and we're not willing to do it." And I mean it. In that moment, my heart goes out to her. And I am relieved that I can still find empathy.

With COVID cases waning, people are turning their attention to how to do better when the next pandemic arrives. We should not stop thinking about how to implement ethical decision-making in a critical care crisis, although it is tempting to give it a rest. For after all of the agonizing, we are left with more questions than answers. In some ways, we will be better prepared the next time around. In others, I imagine we will be right back at square one, looking for answers to questions that have none.

It is early March 2022. I escort a patient into an exam room in the pulmonary clinic. He had a mild case of COVID a few months ago and is here for some nagging post-COVID symptoms. He is better now, which is a relief, and we mostly just chat. He tells me how his mother and cousin both died from COVID. He has risk factors for severe disease. I ask him if he's planning on getting a booster shot. He isn't. "I don't think I need it", he says. "They've been wrong about so much. I think these extra shots are just a way for the drug companies to make more money." He is wearing a funny t-shirt and I laugh and tell him I like it. He looks well and is breathing comfortably. As I listen to him talk, I start to see him in a hospital bed. Initially he's awake and breathing on his own. But then his breathing starts to get harder, more ragged. Now he's unconscious, face down, all tubes and lines, beeping and whirring. I can't see his face or his funny t-shirt anymore.

"I hear you", I say. Then I say a few words about the data and my perspective on booster shots. But my heart isn't in it today. "Think about it," I say.

***

It is mid-March 2022. It has been just over two years since that walk in the woods on the North Shore when everything started. I am attending to patients on the pulmonary consult service. A patient with a very weak immune system was diagnosed with COVID nearly two months ago and he has never cleared the virus. Now he has pneumonia and is not improving. Outside his room, I don my mask, gown, gloves, eye protection. It's second nature to me now. I take a deep breath, steel myself, and walk in. He is tired and demoralized. I sit down on the end of his bed. He asks me if this will get better. "I hope it will," I say. "We'll do everything we can."

References

Churchill, Winston S. 1947. "The Worst Form of Government." *International Churchill Society*. Accessed April 19, 2023. https://winstonchurchill.org/resources/quotes/the-worst-form-of-government/

Institute of Medicine (IOM). 2009. Guidance for Establishing Crisis Standards of Care for Use in Disaster Situations: A Letter Report. Washington, DC, National Academies Press.

Wallace-Wells, Benjamin. 2020. "The Coming Coronavirus Critical-Care Emergency." The New Yorker, March 18, 2020. https://www.newyorker.com/news/news-desk/the-coming-coronavirus-critical-care-emergency

Emily Rubin is an attending physician in pulmonary and critical care medicine at Massachusetts General Hospital (MGH) and an Assistant Professor of Medicine at Harvard Medical School, both in Boston. She serves as co-chair of the MGH clinical ethics committee and is a co-director of the hospital's ethics consult service. During the COVID-19 pandemic, she helped lead the development of crisis standards of care protocols for MGH and the Massachusetts General Brigham health system, played a pivotal role in developing the Commonwealth of Massachusetts COVID-19 crisis standards of care as a member of the Massachusetts Department of Health's Crisis Standards of Care Advisory Committee, and served on the Commonwealth of Massachusetts COVID therapeutics working group that formed policies related to allocation of biologics and drugs to treat COVID-19.

Essential
By Audrey Shafer

Originally published in Spring 2020 as part of the 2020 Arts + Anesthesia Soirée: COVID-19 Highlights, hosted by the Stanford Department of Anesthesiology, Perioperative and Pain Medicine. Reprinted with permission of the author who retains copyright of the essay.

I am an essential worker. I just didn't realize how essential I was, and never would have described myself that way, until the coronavirus pandemic. Millions cannot go to work due to shelter-at-home rules, but I have to: I'm an anesthesiologist. As I pass through the checkpoint to enter the hospital with other essential workers, I am reminded of what my single-parent mother instilled in my sister and me when we were little. While we sat in the dark, unable to pay the electricity bill, she said: "If you don't want to live like this, get an education."

We were never homeless or hungry, but the apartment was also not well maintained, with holes in the plaster, and bars on the back windows after the woman who lived on the floor below us was raped. My mother never complained to the landlord – she taught us "Never ask for help, the world is not here to help you." If I didn't have enough money for a packet of bus tokens, I was not to ask anyone for a handout. At a young age, I stuffed envelopes and babysat to earn money.

On the other hand, I had an unbelievably rich childhood – my mother was a costume designer and I saw *The Misanthrope* and *Endgame* from the wings of the theater during dress rehearsals. I also loved the library. Even though I was afraid of librarians, the library was a safe place to go after school, and safety, besides a livable wage, was another lesson drilled into me. At home, my sister and I played a game with our library books, placing them along the floor and pretending that if you stepped off them, you sank into a watery abyss. But we knew, or at least we believed, the abyss wasn't real.

When my mom said get an education, I listened. I went to an outstanding public high school – a magnet school that drew the brightest kids from all over Philadelphia. I attended college on full financial aid and majored in biochemistry. I planned to get a PhD but during a summer work-study job, I met a post-doc – someone who already had achieved what I was convinced was the pinnacle of education. He told me he didn't have a job the next year. This blew my mind. In that moment, I knew I needed to seek a new direction, something where I could *always* have a job.

Later that year, I had an epiphany while walking outside my dorm at a site rumored to be a film location for *Love* ('means never having to say you're sorry') *Story*. Everyone gets sick, even Ali MacGraw's character. If I became a physician, I'd always have a job. Eureka! Of course, in medical school interviews, I couldn't come clean about my reasons. As much as I loved science, I knew I had chosen this path because I felt I would always be employed.

Yet, at medical school, something changed. Love happened in an unlikely setting. I felt strangely fatigued during my anesthesiology elective, but enjoyed the people and culture of this hidden part of medicine. Delirious and febrile from mononucleosis-induced hepatitis, which I did not initially know I had, I fell deeply in love with the quirky, fulfilling specialty of anesthesiology.

Fast forward through decades of academic anesthesiology practice – and, despite risks to mental health from stress and the myriad ways in which a minor disability could render the anesthesiologist useless, I had (you'd be proud, mom!) a safe and secure job every day of my life. But the job and its safety have changed.

Donning enhanced personal protective equipment, I check the barriers protecting me as an anesthesiologist during and after the airway procedures I will perform - procedures which make the virus even more contagious. I mouth breathe, pant really, in my N95 mask and hood, and, encumbered by impermeable layers and double gloves, move my limbs slowly as if I was in a phony moon landing scenario. I loudly ask the nurse to leave the room; sometimes I have to shout to be heard by the respiratory therapist. I look down at my frightened or too-far-gone-to-be-frightened patient. I'm the last person they will see before I push sedatives and place a plastic tube between their vocal cords. "I'm giving you medicine to make you very sleepy," I say. "Medicine to put in a breathing tube to help you breathe. We will take good care of you." It sounds harsh because I have to speak so loudly.

I understand, retrospectively, that I was an essential worker through HIV/AIDS, SARS, MERS and Ebola. But because of where I live, my limited exposure, and how these diseases are transmitted, I never felt the fear that is my steady companion now.

There is a longstanding analogy involving airline pilots and anesthesiologists, which compares take-off, flight, and landing to stages of an anesthetic. There are benefits to the analogy – it's why simulation and communication training, developed for pilots, is now standard in anesthesiology education. There is a big difference, though: if the plane goes down, the pilot dies too; but if the anesthetic goes awry, only the patient dies.

As another overhead code call to the emergency room blares, and I, on the COVID airway team, grab equipment we pack in wheeled suitcases, respond to texts from team members, and don my N95 and eye protection before hitting the ER – the rest of the equipment will need to be donned and checked outside the patient bay – I realize, almost cellularly, that things are different now. With COVID-19, I could die. Or I could cause my loved ones to die if I bring the virus home. It would be like a slow but inevitable plane crash.

A younger colleague (and now they are all younger) came up to me one pandemic day. He said his heart rate was 130 but he otherwise felt fine. His temperature, heart rhythm, oxygen saturation, and blood pressure were fine. I told him, "It's okay, go home, drink some water and relax. I'll do your case." He went home and his heart rate normalized. It was anxiety, not virus. This level of anxiety would have never happened to him pre-COVID. It's not just the virus that threatens all of us, it's also the fear.

Until now, I hadn't truly thought about the danger of being an essential worker. But my mom equipped me to deal with enormous stress. Taught me I was loved. And maybe, in watching her go it alone for so many years, taught me to live a life different than hers. She taught me to be a lifelong learner, and what I learned from my colleague, to seek help from others, is one of the most valuable lessons of my life. It's okay to be vulnerable, it's okay to tell the teacher selling bus tokens you don't have enough money.

What I learned in the pandemic is this: we are all in this together. We are all needed. None of us is alone in this world. And asking for help, especially if you are an essential worker, is, ultimately, the essential thing to do.

Audrey Shafer, MD, is Professor Emeritus of Anesthesiology, Perioperative and Pain Medicine at Stanford University School of Medicine and the Veterans Affairs Palo Alto Health Care System, both in Palo Alto, California. At Stanford, Dr. Shafer is founder of the Medicine & the Muse Program in the Stanford Center for Biomedical Ethics, founder of the Biomedical

Ethics and Medical Humanities Scholarly Concentration, and co-founder of Pegasus Physician Writers. She completed her undergraduate studies at Harvard University, medical school at Stanford, anesthesiology training at University of Pennsylvania, and research fellowship at Stanford. She is the author of *The Mailbox*, a children's novel on post-traumatic stress disorder in veterans. Her poetry has been published in journals and anthologies.

Frontline Experiences from a Paramedic on the US-Mexico Border
By Angel Taddei

Originally submitted November 1, 2020

I remember hearing rumors about a respiratory virus that was creating havoc in China in January of 2020. It seemed so far away, so distant, happening on the other side of the world. It would surely go away like the Ebola scare of 2014 that ended up with one dead in the United States (CDC 2019a), or the H1N1 pandemic in which the CDC estimated approximately 12,469 deaths in the US (CDC 2019b). With the Ebola outbreak, our department acquired PPE kits consisting of impermeable gowns/coveralls, N-95 respirators, gloves, and boot covers. There was a protocol in place for suspected Ebola cases as well, but there was never a need to implement it. As COVID-19 began to make its way to the United States we began following the CDC guidelines established for firefighters and EMS responders. The protocols were in place to protect us if the virus reached our town, but we were not prepared with extra PPE to handle multiple patients with a highly contagious respiratory disease. The pandemic had crept up on us as a nation, and it was reflected in the nationwide shortage of PPE.

When I first heard about COVID-19 arriving in the US, I asked myself, if and when we would get exposed. Now, I have learned to accept that our new "normal" is daily exposure to this biological enemy. I never imagined that it would end up changing the way we live. The way we respond to calls has changed; the way we interact with patients has changed. The social distancing from our family and loved ones is something that I would have never foreseen happening. As of this day, I have not been able to give my mother a kiss on the cheek for fear of putting my parents at risk. For all I know, I might be carrying the virus without knowing. Fears and thoughts of spreading the virus to our loved ones linger in the backs of our minds as first responders.

This all came to reality when several of the members of our department were infected with COVID-19 in June and July of 2020. The virus had hit us and had added an extra load on a burden that was already heavy. The added stress from sleepless nights due to working extra shifts to provide coverage for those who were now infected and/or in quarantine will in some way or another take a toll. It has not been uncommon for some of us to work 120 to 144 hours per week. Initially, we had few PPE resources as the nation had exhausted its supply and cities had high demands for gowns, masks, respirators, gloves, and necessary medical equipment to protect medical staff and first responders. Most of that equipment was on backorder for several weeks to months. We were fortunate to have our fellow firefighters in Nogales, Sonora, Mexico, who were quick to act when they knew of our lack of PPE and provided each member of the Nogales Fire Department with a washable Tyvek suit to use for suspected COVID-19 patients.

The number of coronavirus cases in our county spiked in June and July, a few months later than in the Northeast. One case that I remember is of a family that all contracted the virus. We got a call for a male patient in his late 40s. He was waiting for EMS arrival outside his residence complaining of shortness of breath and presenting with a dry cough. An elderly person (the patient's father) is about 10 feet away from him sitting on a chair. As the medic crew contacted the patient, one person from the engine crew approached the father. Based on the symptoms which the patient presented, the father was advised to maintain social distancing and self-quarantine since there was a high chance of exposure due to both the son and father living in the same household. The father's response was: "No pasa nada, estaré bien," which translates to "Nothing is going on, I'll be ok." The patient was transported to the hospital, and as the fire engine was leaving the scene, I remember seeing the father walk across the street to talk to his front neighbor, disregarding the fact that he as well might be infected. The following shift, we were back at the same residence for shortness of breath, but this time for the father. The fact that many took this virus as a hoax or an exaggeration was astonishing. It took a couple of weeks of seeing people sick with the virus and hearing of people in the community dying of the virus to take it seriously. A couple of weeks later I met up with the brother of the initial patient (the son). He told me that eventually his brother had lost his battle with COVID-19 and ended up dying of COVID complications after being on a ventilator for several days. He also mentioned that his father, sister, and he himself had also contracted the virus, and were able to recover. The father was right in what he said to us that day, he did end up "ok." Unfortunately, that was not the case for his son.

The pandemic increased our vigilance and our situational awareness. The extra PPE and our method of response made it feel like a scene from a movie. As we arrive on scene, we are usually met with a group of spectators, either watching from their windows or just outside their homes in curiosity, observing as we get off the units with our gowns, masks, respirators, shields, booties, gloves and all the personal protective equipment needed to maintain our safety and minimize the risk of infection. In our small town we had never experienced anything like this.

Ordinarily, our method of response to medical emergency calls consists of an ambulance with a crew of two, and usually an engine with two, three, or four depending on our staffing levels for that day. During the pandemic, on many days we were down to two people on the engine due to short-staffed stations. Our dispatch began a new method for screening callers to determine if it would be a possible COVID case and give us a heads up. For any respiratory distress, altered mental status, cold symptoms, diarrhea, we would respond in full PPE. If possible, we would request dispatch to advise the patient to meet us outside the residence to minimize exposure to personnel. Once on scene, if we needed to enter the home, one member of the medic unit would do a "recon." He would make an entry, assess the scene, and establish patient care. The other medic partner would stay at the entrance and wait with the gurney. The engine crew would also wait outside readily available in case there was assistance needed with loading the patient onto the ambulance or providing support in patient care with critical and unstable patients.

The pandemic has made us more resilient and has prepared us for future threats. Decontamination has become a meticulous ritual that occupies a significant amount of time in our shifts. At the beginning of the shift the units, equipment, and station are decontaminated. After each patient encounter, we would repeat the process. The implementation of multiple daily temperature checks and screenings for any symptoms amongst ourselves has been another method used to mitigate the risks of infection.

The town I work in is right on the international border with Mexico. On March 21, 2020, restrictions were placed into effect for non-essential travel at the ports of entry in Nogales, Arizona. Despite this fact, our crews respond daily to COVID and non-COVID related calls at the Morley, DeConcini, and Mariposa ports of entry. Although the travel restrictions have been in place since March, it has not changed the number of emergency medical calls we respond to at the ports of entry. The department responds to the ports on almost a daily basis; sometimes up to three or four times per shift. It is common to see US citizens living in Mexico cross into the United States to seek medical attention. Weekends or holidays will usually bring us US citizens involved in motor vehicle crashes. The reality is that travel restrictions are in place, but mostly for Mexican Nationals with tourist visas. US residents have not stopped crossing into Mexico for medical or tourism purposes and visiting family or friends. The fact that there has been a high number of COVID-19 cases in the US has not deterred migrants from attempting to cross the border illegally by jumping over the international wall, causing all sorts of injuries from minor sprains and fractures to severe injuries including death from the fall itself, or lacerations and life-altering amputations caused by the concertina wires that are attached to the wall.

This virus knows no international territories or borders, much less respects the boundaries established by man. What it has created though is a significant negative impact in the revenue on which the city of Nogales, Arizona depends. All you need to do is take a drive to the downtown stores and see all those local businesses closed until further notice. Others, I am afraid, will never be able to reopen. The city of Nogales depends heavily on the income generated from sales tax. A drop in the amount of sales tax revenue means a drop in the budget available to fund the fire department, detrimentally affecting the safety of the community. On any given day, you could take a drive to any of the big chain stores we have in town and see Nogales, Sonora (Mexican) plates on many of the vehicles at the parking lots. Now their absence is just a reflection of what is happening to the economy of the town. I do not know how we will be able to manage as a community, if we continue with the travel restrictions, and with the closures of more businesses.

The year 2020 has affected people all over the world, in one way or another. To me, parts of this year have been like a blur, almost with a sense of losing track of time. Most of the year has been consumed by work. Everything else has been placed into pause. Vacations were canceled, sports and concert events postponed until further notice, and gatherings with friends and family almost nonexistent. It makes no difference if it is a weekend or a holiday – all of the days are the same.

Although it has been a very difficult year that brought many deaths and tragedies, it has also united us as first responders and EMS providers, but more importantly, as human beings. I have learned to appreciate the simple things in life, family, friends, and the importance of taking care of one another. Life can be so fragile at times, which reminds us that we cannot afford to take things for granted, that we must live our lives to the fullest without regrets, and be grateful for the things we have, more importantly our loved ones and our health.

References

Centers For Disease Control and Prevention (CDC). 2019a. "2014-2016 Ebola Outbreak in West Africa". *Center for Disease Control and Prevention.* Modified March 8, 2019. https://www.cdc.gov/vhf/ebola/history/2014-2016-outbreak/index.html

—. 2019b. "2009 H1N1 Pandemic (H1N1pdm09 virus)". *Center for Disease Control and Prevention.* Modified June 11, 2019. https://www.cdc.gov/flu/pandemic-resources/2009-h1n1-pandemic.html

Angel Taddei is a Fire Captain/Paramedic at Nogales Fire Department with 18 years of experience providing public services to the community of Nogales, Arizona. He specializes in technical rescue and leads the department's training in that area. He is motivated by the mission of helping others and providing the best to the community and his loved ones.

COVID-19: A Paramedic's View
By Peter Canning

Originally submitted August 14, 2020

I am sixty-one years old and had been a full-time paramedic in Hartford, Connecticut, for over twenty-five years when I got sick at the beginning of last February—a sickness that knocked me down, leaving me prostrate in bed for several days and short of breath on exertion for weeks afterwards. While working three 12-hour shifts a week on the ambulance, for the last ten years I also worked part time as an EMS coordinator at the UConn John Dempsey Hospital in neighboring Farmington. As I recovered from my mystery illness, I read about the COVID-19 disease spreading in China and decided I needed to get myself healthy if I was going to survive it, should it land hard on our shores. The hospital promised me a slight bump in my hours, so I informed my boss at the ambulance I could no longer get up at 4:00 in the morning three days in a row to work 12-14 hour shifts and would need to go part time. I promised to work twenty hours a week as I was not ready to give up the job that I loved and my identity as a street paramedic.

I remember early in March, standing next to Rob Fuller, the physician head of our hospital emergency department, a man with expertise in disaster medicine who had been among the first doctors on the ground after the Thailand tsunami, the Haitian earthquake, and other notable disasters, as we prepared our hospital's COVID response. The virus was in New York City and reports of its virulence were growing by the day. "Two weeks from now," Rob said, half-joking, "this could be a different world. We could be driving to work through the fires and roadblocks, carrying side arms along with our stethoscopes." As the days went by with no sign of COVID in our territory, I felt like a soldier in the old movies where all is eerily quiet and while you look up at the hill line for the sight of the enemy.

The first COVID case that came into the hospital was a patient from Hartford. The patient coughed in the paramedic's face before the paramedic could put her mask on and she was now in tears in the EMS room lamenting her mistake, after learning he had tested positive days earlier. The EMS guidelines at the time were for us to put on a surgical mask only if the patient met the screening criteria—of cough, fever, and recent foreign travel. Ideally the screening should be done at six feet of distance. This patient coughed in her face when he opened the door to her knock.

There was much confusion in the early days about mask wearing. We were told we had a limited supply, and, compounding the matter, while normally we were trained to wear an N95 mask, which filters out all but the smallest virus particles, the CDC, anticipating a shortage of N95 masks, said in cases of shortage the surgical mask was okay instead. That didn't sit right with many of us, but we also understood if we put an N95 on for every possible COVID patient, we would burn through them quickly and run the risk of finding our PPE cupboard bare.

Once the virus hit, it came hard and fast. In my hospital office, right by the ambulance entrance doors, stretchers started coming through with crews gowned in yellow isolation robes. Next door to me was the decontamination room where those needing intubation went. Some days as soon as one patient was wheeled out on a vent, another patient was wheeled in for the next intubation.

When I worked the ambulance, nearly every 911 call I went on, I had to gown up due to the possibility of COVID. I am six foot eight and the gowns didn't fit. I had to tie a second gown around my waist just to get coverage to my knees. The gowns ripped easily and there were gaps between my wrists and gloves. The first time and only time I put on the new one-piece suits that came in, I ripped the leg, arms, and chest like I was the Incredible Hulk.

We were doing a lot of cardiac arrests in March. A woman in her sixties not feeling well for several days, acting funny, drops dead. A man at work fighting a fever collapses on the shipping dock and is found by workers fifteen minutes later. Both patients received CPR, advanced airways, and IV epinephrine, but were presumed dead on scene after the resuscitation efforts proved futile. They never got tested for COVID-19. Other people we found home alone, cold and stiff. None of them was getting counted in the growing numbers. We had a new paramedic precepting—she did five cardiac arrests in her first two weeks, which is more than most preceptees get in two months of training.

At the hospital I informed EMS services when patients their crews brought in turned out to be COVID-positive. These positive patients didn't all meet the guidelines of fever, cough, and foreign travel. One of the most common presentations was low pulse oxygen saturations without dyspnea. I did a call in a town where the first responder told me the patient was COVID negative based on the screening questions. The patient's pulse oxygen saturation was only 88% even though she was talking in full sentences without any effort. I had another patient whose daughter told me she had never left her room. In the five minutes I was there, eight people came in and out of the apartment. Both patients tested positive for COVID.

Dr. Fuller said we should be wearing masks for every patient encounter, and we should be putting a mask on all our patients. This wasn't EMS policy at that date. We were still getting limited rations of face masks with instructions to only use the few N95s we had for procedures like intubations, CPAP, or nebulizers that produce aerosols. I began to feel uneasy when it soon became apparent that paramedics and EMTs were the only people in the EDs not wearing masks. In the early days many crews got sent home for exposures. Then a new guideline came out from a local hospital saying as long as we weren't with a patient for more than 15 minutes without a mask, it shouldn't be considered an exposure. That didn't make much sense and seemed to come from the same school of science as the five second rule when you drop food on the floor and still wish to eat it. The back of an ambulance is a confined space and an unmasked patient hacking up a mist of respiratory droplets is not a safe working condition. I didn't believe COVID only activated itself when the 15-minute buzzer went off.

Soon EMS workers went from being put on home confinement for an unprotected exposure to being required to have an exposure and symptoms to miss work. Just like with the PPE, it seemed the system was geared not for the protection of EMS workers but for the protection of the healthcare system—making certain the system didn't run out of PPE or providers.

I am a swimmer and my normal after work routine has always been to stop at our town's aquatic center and swim sprints in the cool water, washing the dirt of the city off me and setting me in a calm relaxed state of mind when I come home to my family. Then COVID shut the pool down. Every night I came home now my wife had me strip in the laundry room, putting my working clothes right in the washer, cranking on the high heat, then, with my daughters averting their eyes, parading in my underwear right up to the shower.

People asked me if I considered sidelining myself since I was over sixty and technically on the list of those who shouldn't be leaving the house. I never considered it. I am and have been an EMS provider for over thirty years. I've been stuck by needles, splashed with blood and vomit, physically had to wrestle with combative patients, been in ambulance accidents, and caught more than my share of winter bugs. It comes with the territory. I like what I do. The danger doesn't bother me. After a while I learned to detach. It's like things are just moving around you, and you are watching yourself. One day I had a COVID-positive patient from a nursing home who was out of his mind with delirium. He was rolling naked on the floor when we got to the unit. We wrapped him up in a sheet and got him on the stretcher. On the way to the hospital, when I went to grab the radio mic to let the ED know we were ten minutes out, he suddenly grabbed my arm, pulled me down on him, and started spitting on me. It wasn't a malicious act; he was just out of his mind. I had a face shield on, and it caught the full of his spit and even though he ripped my gown I was able to break free and get him restrained.

Our call volume was way down, but that didn't mean we were less busy. There were just fewer ambulances out on the road. It seemed the only ones calling 911 were those with COVID, those who thought they had COVID, and people having psychiatric crises.

A large man stands handcuffed, surrounded by six police officers by the side of the road. Nearby two citizens have their iPhones out recording. The man does not mince his words. "I'm going to kill all of you. I hate cops. I'm going to eat you. You're gonna be in my belly."

It is clear that this man is having a manic episode. He will not shut up. On and on he goes on about the horrible things he's going to do to. "I already took my drugs! Now let me go!"

I end up giving him a shot of Versed to get him to calm down so I can transport him without the handcuffs. Despite the sedative, he never stops his talking.

"You look stressed," he says to me.

"Well, all this COVID stuff has me a bit drained."

"You know where COVID came from?"

"Wuhan, China?'

"No, it came from my right eyeball. I set it loose on the world cause I'm death. D-E-A-T-H."

"Are you planning to summon it back to your eyeball?"

"No, I got a girl staying there right now. My soul sister. I'm getting mine." He punches his fist against his hand several times rapidly.

"Maybe you could make some room in the other eyeball and get that corona back in there somehow."

"You look stressed," he says, again. "You should quit this job. Go buy yourself some weed. Take the load off. You're old."

He ends up four-pointed in the psychiatric wing.

The more I learned about COVID, the more I began to wonder if maybe I hadn't had it back in the beginning of February. When I convinced myself I had already had it, it gave me a bit of false confidence that I was immune. When I thought I hadn't had it, it gave me fear. If the mystery bug had kicked my butt, what would COVID do? Every time I had a little ache and pain or headache or felt tired and fatigued – symptoms of just being sixty – it made me wonder if maybe COVID had found purchase in my lungs. In a few days, I could be lying in bed, in a fever, struggling to breathe, worrying maybe I needed to go to the hospital where they'd put me on a vent, and then I'd be gone from this world. It was a stressful time. I knew two medics who were already on vents and others who were struggling at home.

I've always had vivid dreams and COVID began showing up in them at night. The first time COVID appeared, he came as a little SpongeBob gremlin about the size of a tarantula who just kept coming after me. I would kick him off, and he'd come right back, making a weird beeping sound. I kept kicking him off, and he'd come right back at me like a crazed banshee. The next time he appeared he was a Bengal tiger prowling through my basement, searching methodically for me. I watched silently through a garbage can sized hole in the upstairs floor, trying not to move. Then he sprang up at me on his haunches and I felt his hot breath on my face. The third time COVID was a terrifying dinosaur alien from the future throwing spiked black fireballs at me.

I was getting my temperature taken six and seven times a day, on entering hospitals or nursing homes. I never ran a fever and often the reading was just plain low. On hot days when I was all gowned up with N95 and face shield with the sun beating down, I would have expected myself to test much higher. I dreaded the humidity of summer if I felt this bad in April.

The ambulance company started giving us a shopping bag full of PPE gear now that the supply chain was starting to come through. I carried the bag in with me on every call. Normally I would go in first, scout the scene, and then call down if I needed my partner or any of the first responders. By now we were putting masks on all patients as well as ourselves, but that was not always easy. I entered a room where a hypoglycemic diabetic rolled on the floor wrestling with two family members. He was a dialysis patient and had no easy IV access, so I had to put an IV in his jugular vein. It took four of us to hold him down to give him the dextrose he needed, and he had no mask as he screamed profanities at us. There were also five or six family members crowded in the room shouting at him to behave, none of them masked. I thought of all the COVID in the air trying to get through my defenses.

The nursing homes were the worst in the beginning. Sometimes they wouldn't tell us that a patient had COVID. The nurse was a pool nurse and had never met the patient before and was rifling through papers to get us information. No COVID, she said, but then reading the papers ourselves at the hospital there would be the notation COVID +. This happened more than once. Eventually, we just assumed all the patients had it. One day we went into one venue, and they were now all wearing space suits. And the hallway was bright white and smelled of bleach. For everyone standing at a med cart, there was someone else wiping the door handles and rails down. Finally, it was being taking seriously.

One day when we parked at the nursing home's ambulance entrance around back, I noticed room numbers on the outside windows. Through closed glass was how family members were now visiting their loved ones. Another day, coming through a lobby, I saw on the wall where the home had put up newspaper obituaries under the sign "Gone but Not Forgotten". There were over twenty notices, most freshly posted.

An old man with a stooped back, wearing tan work pants got out of his old Pontiac, and wearing a face mask, walked toward us as we came out of the dialysis center with an old woman on our stretcher. He nodded to us respectfully, and then looked at the woman and said, "Pearl, Pearl, it's your husband, George. I love you, Pearl."

She looked at him and said nothing. Her eyes squinted, trying to recognize him.

"Are you doing okay? I just wanted to say hi and tell you I love. I love you, Pearl. You look pretty today," he said. "I just wanted to say, hi. It's me–George, your husband. I love you, Pearl."

"Hello," she said.

"Are you doing okay? You look nice, Pearl."

"I'm doing okay," she said.

"That's good. That's good."

He nodded to us, and then stepped back as we lifted her into the back of the ambulance.

When we got to the nursing home, he was there again, and had the same conversation with her. I heard from other crews who witnessed the same encounter that took place on the three days a week she went out for dialysis.

In May, the COVID calls slowed, both at the hospital and on the road. The deconning (decontamination) after every call stopped, and the number of notifications I had to send out to services was fewer. Instead of bringing patients into the hospital, EMS crews gowned up to take patients out of the hospital, often to special nursing homes just for COVID patients.

Spring came in full bloom and there was a feeling in the air like maybe this was going to be over soon. The state announced that in June, pools and gyms were going to open again and kids would be allowed to play outdoor sports.

It is a beautiful day. The sky is robin's egg blue. The air smells like fresh cut grass. We cut our sirens on approach and are driving now through a residential neighborhood. Kids are out on their bikes. There are joggers aplenty. Nearly every house has someone out beautifying their yard. Neighbors talk and laugh with one another. Optimism abounds. In just a matter of days, the state will begin phase one of the opening, but in this neighborhood you can already see a future that looks just like the past-- a return to glorious normalcy. The neighbors pause and watch us drive slowly past their homes before returning to their conversations.

Just a few blocks away, a man and his wife sit holding hands on the front steps of the home they have lived in for thirty-five years. Red and yellow tulips line the driveway. There is a basketball hoop above the garage door and an old swing set in the backyard. The man, his eyes wet, looks at the woman with concern. Her hands shake. A man in a bright yellow hazmat suit wearing a gas mask stands over them, checking the woman's pulse saturation. It is 84. The couple tested positive for COVID three days ago, and have been on self-quarantine, but her fever grew worse and she became short of breath, so he walked slowly to the phone in the kitchen and dialed 911.

"I made a mistake," she tells in the back of the ambulance, her hands and voice trembling. "We went to an office party two weeks and no one wore masks."

She looks out the ambulance's back window at the house where she has raised her family. She may be wondering if she will ever see her husband, her family, her home, her neighborhood again. I know that look of fear in her eyes. I have seen it in many patients.

COVID is an especially cruel virus. I think the disease is going to be with us for a long time. I read as much as I can and worry that vaccine projections are optimistic. I get an antibody test and a COVID test and am negative for both. I thought the antibody test finally confirmed I didn't have COVID back in February, but then I read antibodies don't last so it still remains a mystery.

It is July now and we seem to be doing okay in Connecticut. Most of us have been wearing our masks and practicing physical distancing. My daughter has started playing sports again, but the pool and the gyms I belong to remain closed. I have always been a hermit, so I don't mind hanging at home. It is nice having my daughter home with me. I miss the pool and hope it will open soon. I get upset when I see people on TV not wearing masks and talking nonsense about COVID.

Peter Canning, the EMS Coordinator at UConn John Dempsey Hospital, has been a paramedic in the Greater Hartford area since 1995. He is the author of *Killing Season: A Paramedic's Dispatches from the Front Lines of the Opioid Epidemic* (Johns Hopkins Press: April 2021), *Paramedic: On the Front Lines of Medicine* (Ballantine: 1998) and *Rescue 471: A Paramedic's Stories* (Ballantine: 2000), as well as three works of fiction. He writes the popular blog Street Watch: Notes of a Paramedic (www.medicscribe.com). Canning lives in West Hartford, Connecticut with his wife and three daughters.

This Crisis! It's Always Been a Crisis
By Chase Samsel

Originally submitted April 1, 2022

I have been a child psychiatrist for over nine years and currently run the inpatient consultation service at one of the premier children's hospitals in the United States. In the following piece, I recall many snippets of conversations I have participated in surrounding the individual and collective crises that exemplify the state of pediatric mental and behavioral health. Sometimes the interlocutors are parents, sometimes hospital administrators or psychiatric trainees. Sometimes it is me in my more professional voice simply relaying the facts. In italics, however, you will find my personal voice – what I was really thinking, what I wanted to say but couldn't, what it feels like to be a professional and a person and a parent all at once – to be someone who understands but is perhaps not understood. Perhaps exactly like the patients and families I am trying to help.

"This is a crisis! We're overwhelmed! We can't handle this volume! Our beds are being taken up by all these kids who are suicidal—do something! We're got to fix this problem. What solutions do we have to this crisis?"

I know. I feel the urgency. I understand the problem.

More anxious and depressed teens. More distressed parents. "They've been arriving in higher numbers and higher acuity than ever before." And they are still coming. It is a relentless mental health fallout of the pandemic. It is a simultaneous second pandemic. Even worse, it is not abating with receding COVID surges, school re-openings, or life supposedly returning to normal. In fact, it is continuing and often worsens when schools re-open and previously normal routines resume.

This isn't new for me, it's just worse.

"Isn't there something we're just not doing? Can't we just send them to a psychiatric facility? Just discharge them and have them follow-up with psychiatry in the next day or two? This is a crisis!"

> *I hear this every day. Now it's just more often. It's a travesty, and, no, there are no beds. And no, follow-up will take months on a waitlist. That's why they're here.*

Sadly, it has always been a crisis. For the past decade, there have been increasing numbers of suicidal children presenting to emergency rooms and in serious psychiatric distress each and every year all around the United States (CDC 2020, McEnany et al. 2020, Nash et al. 2021). There have never been enough mental health clinicians, and now that there is an acute on chronic crisis, people are paying attention.

> *We've been trying to fix this decades and now people really understand and seem to care?! I wish they had been listening for years!*

The kid who came in depressed in the past is now suicidal. The kid who came in suicidal has now attempted suicide. The kid who attempted suicide in the past now has had a more serious and almost completed attempt.

> *It's not just a numbers problem. It's also an acuity problem. We can't keep doing this, we're losing this battle.*

This is what happens when we do not invest in the mental well-being and care of our children and youth. It is not as simple as one single cause – it's not just school closures; it's not just frightening media images or stories; it's not just disconnectedness and social media usage; it's not just fear of death and getting ill or seeing your loved one dying from COVID.

It's everything. It's being a kid. It's school being more stressful than home. It's not being able to find a therapist. It's not being able to find a therapist who takes your insurance. It's not being able to get off the waitlist to get a therapist. It's having no child psychiatrists in your state.

> *The system is broken and was broken long before this pandemic. Every kid who comes in and waits for weeks for an inpatient psychiatric bed is a failure of the system.*

And now there is a pandemic that our distressed youth have added to their list of stressors. Over 140,000 children have lost a primary caregiver or secondary caregiver during the pandemic (Hillis et al. 2021). Closing schools and having remote learning as problems pale in comparison to these major traumas.

> *Why can't we collectively acknowledge each other's suffering? Why must it be comparative with the most or the worst?*

Yet, kids are more isolated than ever before and yet more connected than ever before. Social media allow for connectedness but are unfiltered, programmed to attract attention with advertisements and algorithms focused on insecurities, impossible ideals, and unsafe viral phenomenon—the perfect challenge and prey for adolescent minds.

> *Fighting with each other, the antagonism, the single-issue focus won't lead us anywhere productive. Will this be yet another outcry that results in no change?*

Parents are even less able to monitor their children's behavior during the pandemic due both to children's increased time on social media and parents' juggling of multiple responsibilities.

> *Full time parent and full time teacher. It's impossible.*

"Doc, you have to help my kid get better!" Distressed parents equal distressed kids. This is not blaming. It's a reality. No one person is an island, and family systems naturally affect one another. Parents' distress around finances, job loss, family, schooling their children, safety, et cet is abundant. Your children know you best, they see it, and it affects them.

> *"Doc, how can you also help me?" they're actually asking.*

Social media and cyber bullying have reached all-time highs. Most parents find it impossible to be proficient and knowledgeable about their kids' technologies—both how those technologies work and how their kids use them. This online bullying is vicious. Parents are aware, but there is no school yard or teacher to stand in the way to prevent this from happening, and it is impossible to truly have a pulse on what is going on. "They keep seeing all this stuff online about … what is that app called again?"

> *Things are moving at warp speed. How are you going to realistically catch up?*

It is not possible for a family to completely filter inappropriate or disturbing online images on social media or curate the news about all the racism, insurrection, and injustice exposed in the past few years. One can only hope to discuss it and help one's child process it.

> *Given the daunting circumstances, how do I help? There's no pill or talk therapy session that'll fix your financial woes, reverse the death of your child's loved one, or prevent*

> *cyberbullying. This is not just a rising tide. It's a crashing tsunami.*

"Can't you just tell them it's going to be alright? They won't listen to me."

> *Is it going to be alright? I'm not going to lie to you or this child.*

"It's just these lockdowns and schools. If they would just re-open..." With schools intermittently closed, isolation is certainly a problem. Loss of routines and consistent socialization have been challenging for many kids. However, some of our patients are grateful for remote teaching. School is important but not a benign place. Many children are less anxious and happier than they've ever been not to feel the same academic pressure and in-person bullying or social isolation they experienced with in-person schooling. Year after year over the past decade there have been more children presenting as suicidal and distressed to emergency rooms on school days than on weekends, holidays, and school breaks (Black 2022).

> *School is not always a sanctuary. Often, it's the opposite.*

The mental health field has always suffered from shortages – shortages of staff, funding, and appreciation of its necessity and importance for a healthy society. Suicide is the second-leading cause of death of children ages 10-14 in our country (CDC and NCHS 2021). Mull on that. More child psychiatric inpatient units close year after year. They cannot afford to stay open unless they are 100% full all the time, and even those that are at capacity have started closing due to low reimbursement.

> *You can tell a lot about how much we value something by the money assigned to it.*

If this was cancer there would be social outcries, big rallies, and fundraising walks. But that stigma rears its ugly head, and that is not what is happening for mental health and hasn't been even before this pandemic. You get brought food and well wishes by your neighbors when your loved one is in the medical hospital but not the psychiatric hospital.

> *If it's too hard to talk about, feels embarrassing, or is shunned, then we still have a long way to go.*

"Oh, finally, a psychiatrist is here. Where have you been?! Do you know how long we were asking for you?!" Child psychiatry is the most needed specialty in all of medicine. All 50 states in the US have been designated as critical shortage areas, and only two states, including the one that I practice in, are considered slightly less critically short than the other 48 (AACAP 2020).

> *I know, I know. I've been talking to 12 other families who felt the same way as you, and this work takes time and consideration. It's not a quick surgical snip and tie. But I'll keep showing up and am trying for you and your family.*

Not only are there not enough of us but folks are leaving. Not leaving the institution or a given practice but leaving the field. Doing something different. Not mental health. It takes a toll, bearing witness to intense emotions, loss of hopes and dreams, bullying by peers and adults, minimization of suffering, structural and individual injustice, abuse and neglect, and helplessness and hopelessness. And feeling devalued and joked about as a profession. "But I need someone to help my kid. I understand now. We have to fix this!"

> *I hope I can keep this up. The conditions and situation is not only hard for the kids but*

> *also the clinicians. This is not sustainable and may get worse instead of better.*

"Well, just pay folks more money! Open more positions! Can't we fix this?!" The workforce shortage is going to take many years to fix. Incentivizing trainee clinicians, exposing them to this work, creating more training programs and positions, and consistently paying a working wage for social workers and psychologists and a competitive physician wage for psychiatrists are just the start. We must reduce stigma associated with seeking mental healthcare and with providing it. We must fix inequities in the system so providers don't burnout and leave the profession and so others are enticed into joining. There are not appropriately trained people just sitting at home on their couch waiting for a mental health position to open up. It's just drawing people away from other similar psychiatric positions, reshuffling the pieces.

> *This crisis has always been a crisis.*

References

American Academy of Child and Adolescent Psychiatry (AACAP). 2020. "Severe Shortage of Child and Adolescent Psychiatrists Illustrated in AACAP Workforce Maps." *AACAP*, https://www.aacap.org/aacap/zLatest_News/Severe_Shortage_Child_Adolescent_Psychiatrists_Illustrated_AACAP_Workforce_Maps.aspx.

Black, Tyler. 2022. "Children's Risk of Suicide Increases on School Days." *Scientific American*, August 22, 2022. https://www.scientificamerican.com/article/childrens-risk-of-suicide-increases-on-school-days/

Center for Disease Control and Prevention (CDC). 2020. "Youth risk behavior survey data summary & trends report: 2009–2019." *CDC*. https://www.cdc.gov/healthyyouth/data/yrbs/pdf/YRBSDataSummaryTrendsReport2019-508.pdf.

CDC and the National Center for Health Statistics (NCHS). 2021. "2020 National Vital Statistics System, Mortality 1999-2020 on CDC WONDER Online Database." Compiled from data provided by the Vital Statistics Cooperative Program. Accessed November 7, 2022. http://wonder.cdc.gov/ucd-icd10.html.

Hillis, Susan D, Alexandra Blenkinsop, Andrés Villaveces, Francis B Annor, Leandris Liburd, Greta M Massetti, Zewditu Demissie, et al. 2021. "COVID-19–Associated Orphanhood and Caregiver Death in the United States." *Pediatrics* 148 (6): e2021053760. https://doi.org/10.1542/peds.2021-053760.

McEnany, Fiona B, Olutosin Ojugbele, Julie R Doherty, Jennifer L McLaren, and JoAnna K Leyenaar. 2020. "Pediatric Mental Health Boarding." *Pediatrics* 146 (4): e20201174. https://doi.org/10.1542/peds.2020-1174.

Nash, Katherine A, Bonnie T Zima, Craig Rothenberg, Jennifer Hoffmann, Claudia Moreno, Marjorie S Rosenthal, and Arjun Venkatesh. 2021. "Prolonged Emergency Department Length of Stay for US Pediatric Mental Health Visits (2005–2015)." *Pediatrics* 147 (5): e2020030692. https://doi.org/10.1542/peds.2020-030692.

Chase Samsel is an Assistant Professor of Psychiatry at Harvard Medical School. He completed Brown University's combined Triple Board residency program in Pediatrics, Adult Psychiatry, and Child Psychiatry and is triple board-certified. He is the Medical Director of the Psychiatry Consultation Service, lead psychiatrist for the Pediatric Transplant Service, and Associate Training Director of the Child and Adolescent Psychiatry Fellowship and Triple Board Residency at Boston Children's Hospital. These positions enable him to work with seriously ill children and their families, further exploring the interface of pediatric and psychiatric care, focusing on mentoring and teaching pediatricians and psychiatrists.

Across a Border, a Pandemic Unfolds
By Nicholas Cuneo and Rebeca Cázares-Adame

Originally submitted April 6, 2022

February 29, 2020: Tijuana, Baja California, Mexico – Nick and Rebeca
Mexico (4 confirmed cases), USA (25 confirmed cases)
(Ritchie et al. 2020)*

¡Alto! Prevenga la propagación del COVID-19
(Stop! Prevent the spread of COVID-19)

We glance at each other, half bemused, as we walk up to the new screening area in front of Tijuana General Hospital. Two young hospital staff members, masked and gloved, greet us inside a newly erected white tent just beyond the gate – one with a quick thermometer check to the forehead, the other with a squeeze from a giant bottle of hand sanitizer. Not a single case of the novel coronavirus has yet been reported in Tijuana, yet here we are, going through the motions. The illusion of preparation is undoubtedly intended to provide reassurance, but the reality of what is to come feels both far-off and inescapable.

Neither of us has been spending much time staying up to date on the news. We're already on the front lines of another public health disaster. The Trump administration's steady assault on the right to asylum, which has given way to the diabolically effective Migrant Protection Protocols (MPP), is forcing asylum-seekers to "remain in Mexico" indefinitely while their cases proceed. Stuck in Tijuana and other border cities, newly arrived migrants are being crowded into informal encampments while they wait for their chance to hop onto the seemingly endless conveyor belt of hearings that govern the new makeshift "border court" system, designed to create the pretense of justice while effectively shutting out asylum applicants from finding a lawyer or being granted protection. Without a reliable source of healthcare for the migrants, grassroots NGOs like the ones we are working for have been struggling to fill in gaps in their care,

---

* Ritchie et al. (2020) serves as the reference for all COVID-19 case statistics cited in this essay.

operating on shoestring budgets, volunteer labor, and donated supplies.

The hospital staff members usher us through. We're there to discuss a small outbreak of new HIV diagnoses among newly arrived pregnant migrant women seeking to establish prenatal care in Tijuana while they are waiting to cross over. We don't know what to make of the signal, but it is unusual enough to merit investigation. We have an appointment with the local epidemiologist to discuss our observations and enroll the women in Mexico's public HIV program, through which they can begin receiving treatment.

March 11, 2020: Boston, Massachusetts, USA – Nick
Mexico (8 confirmed cases), USA (1.1k cases)

The Beth Israel Deaconess Medical Center is eerily quiet. I'm there not to work (I'm actually a resident physician down the street at a different hospital), but rather to accompany my godmother to an elective procedure. "Is it crazy to do this now?" she asks me.

"It may actually be the best time, before they begin cancelling everything," I respond, hoping to provide reassurance. It's been just a few days since I got back home from my global health rotation in Mexico, and I barely recognize the world I've come back to. As we wait in the pre-op area, watching the news on an overhead television, a reporter announces that Harvard University is cancelling in-person instruction for the remainder of the semester.

"Where Harvard goes, others follow," my mother says when I text her about the news. The weight of the current moment begins to set in.

The world is changing. My world is going to change.

March 16, 2020: Tijuana, Baja California, Mexico – Rebeca
Mexico (82 confirmed cases), USA (4.7k cases)

I wake up with a cough and a sinking feeling in my stomach. It's been only a few days since I got back from my conference in San Francisco, and I can no longer ignore that I'm sick. Cough, congestion, cold, thankfully no fever. I call and report my symptoms to the supervisor of our local health department, and he tells me that they are sending out a mobile team to my place as soon as possible, since I just got back from a high-risk area.

The next morning, I see neighbors looking on nervously as several health workers, gowned up in hazmat suits, enter my apartment and collect their specimen. It will be a week before the results come back – negative – but in that time, the first confirmed cases in Tijuana begin to get reported, and I wonder how many people assume I am one of them. Some people are starting to panic, while others are going on as if nothing has changed. One local news outlet carelessly publishes a photo of the outside of the apartment of the first confirmed patient. A local nurse, dressed in scrubs, gets doused with bleach by an onlooker on the way out from her clinic.

Where did all the toilet paper go?

March 20, 2020: Boston, Massachusetts, USA – Nick
Mexico (203 confirmed cases), USA (20.0k cases)

"When the Director determines that the existence of a communicable disease in a foreign country or place creates a serious danger of the introduction of such disease into the United States ... a temporary suspension of such introduction is necessary to protect the public health" (CDC and HHS 2020).

With the stroke of a pen, CDC Director Robert Redfield effectively closes the border between the US and Mexico and ends the right to asylum in our country. It happens quickly and quietly, while people are too afraid and distracted to notice. I almost fit this profile myself – I've just come down with cold symptoms after returning from a weekend ski trip days before. I go into the hospital to get tested, feeling guilty for making use of a limited resource and cavalier for having taken the trip. It's probably nothing, but what if it isn't? New York City is seeing an exponential rise in cases, and Americans are starting to die of the virus. Massachusetts will lock down in three days. It feels almost unpatriotic to challenge the CDC order, but I can't ignore the cruel irony behind its wording. The United States – quickly becoming the world's epicenter for the pandemic – vastly eclipses Mexico in case numbers.

I think of the asylum-seekers for whom I conducted forensic evaluations in Tijuana, documenting the physical and psychological scars from the abuse that caused them to flee their countries of origin. I think of the endless waiting and despair that MPP has already forced upon them. I pen an impassioned editorial and send it off to a number of different outlets. Finally, one accepts. "While COVID-19 has brought about new uncertainty and dangers, our response cannot be to abandon those seeking asylum under the false guise of concern for their health, particularly when the alternative could be their assured death" (Cuneo 2020).

April 9, 2020: Boston, Massachusetts, USA – Nick
Mexico (3.4k confirmed cases), USA (478k cases)

I text Rebeca about a pregnant Haitian migrant woman with HIV in Tijuana whom I have continued to follow from afar via WhatsApp. Unable to speak Spanish and deeply ashamed of her HIV status, she has become increasingly isolated. She tells me that she has been shuttled around all day from hospital to hospital, trying to figure out where she is supposed to go for her planned Caesarean section, which was originally supposed to be at the general hospital before it became the designated COVID hospital. On top of this chaos, she is struggling to find someone to donate blood for her, evidently a pre-requisite for surgery in Mexico given their critically low blood supply nationally. "I don't have anyone here," she writes me, and my heart sinks.

I call an American doctor I know in Tijuana who is miraculously able to arrange for two volunteers to accompany them to donate blood on her behalf, ensuring that she will be good to go for the procedure. I shudder as I consider the number of patients getting left behind who do not have access to this level of individual attention amid the tectonic reconfigurations in healthcare that are occurring everywhere as a response to the pandemic.

My phone goes off – I'm being redeployed to start working in one of the COVID ICUs that my hospital has set up to accommodate the surge of critically ill COVID patients in Boston. I feel a wave of simultaneous adrenaline and relief. My husband – an emergency medicine doctor – has been going into the hospital for weeks now, stripping down to his underwear in our driveway when he returns and running immediately to the shower to decontaminate. At night, he's started to sleep under a weighted blanked – an obvious metaphor, I feel. I've felt discomfited to be sitting comfortably at home while he's been in the throes of battle, barely armed to defend himself. Indeed, only recently has our hospital revised its purportedly "evidence-based" guidance to allow for the routine use of N95 masks with patients under investigation for COVID, conveniently following a donation of over a million respirators by Robert Kraft, the controversial owner of the New England Patriots. While I am of course grateful for the haul, I try to wrap my head around the world I am living in – one in which my husband's safety is dependent on the generosity of a billionaire trying to rehabilitate his public image. In some senses, it seems the perfect solution for the present moment.

The blood supply issues seem not to be isolated to Mexico – with the lockdown, the pool of available donors has dwindled in the United States as well, while the number of critically ill patients has shot up. We are getting increasingly desperate emails from the hospital, hoping that frontline workers can help meet the demand. "Here they won't take my O negative blood because I am married to a man," I text Rebeca, simmering inside at the FDA's blanket ban against sexually active gay men donating blood, even those who have been in monogamous relationships for years, like me.

April 20, 2020: Tijuana, Baja California, Mexico – Rebeca
Mexico (8.7k confirmed cases), USA (794k cases)

"How's it been in the ICU??" I text Nick.

"There are almost 100 COVID patients on vents right now…It's fucked up," he replies. "It is kind of the Wild West – nothing is standardized."

Boston has been hit hard, and I wonder when Tijuana will start seeing a real surge. We've been lucky so far, with very manageable numbers. It's bizarre to see the US floundering like this, to see colleagues who have never really lacked for anything experience resource constraints for the first time. On some level, it makes me feel a little less alone, but I feel immediately guilty for drawing any comfort from the mess. Even before COVID, it wasn't uncommon for doctors or nurses in public hospitals here in Tijuana to purchase their own gloves or masks or even just cotton balls sometimes. But I can't feel too sorry for myself either – scarcity is everyday life for my patients.

I worry about my patients, particularly those who inject drugs, and what will happen to them if they get sick. Our efforts at counseling them on basic COVID prevention measures, like masks, don't seem to be sticking. I can't say I blame them – when we talk about the seriousness of COVID, many reply, "so it's just one more thing I won't be seen for at the hospital." They tell me, "Don't worry about us *doctora*, those of us that use *chiva* (heroin) are immune to this virus, we'll be OK." I tell them I hope that's true but in the meantime here's a mask (which they won't be able to wash and re-use), here's some soap (in case they have access to water once the clinic closes), come for a checkup if you have COVID symptoms (which they all do to some degree on a daily basis because they resemble withdrawal symptoms), stay at home (which they don't have). Nobody on the street is wearing a mask.

The health department is working, slowly, on renovating a space next to our clinic so that it can serve as an isolation center for the most vulnerable when they have symptoms or test positive for the virus – those without a home, those who are actively using. They've asked me to serve as Medical Director when it opens. I feel incredibly anxious but also excited that this is actually happening. I wish more than anything to help create a dignified space for the community I work for, especially for people with substance use disorder.

I get called to check in on a patient of mine close by, whose son is worried because her blood pressure is reportedly spiking. We've just gotten some new PPE, so I decide to break it in. When I get to her house, she is moving slowly and does not look well. I sit her down and take her blood pressure, which is through the roof. "I've been taking my meds," she says defensively, out of breath. "They told me I had the flu last week." I place the pulse oximeter on her finger and look down in disbelief – 64%. As we wait for the ambulance to arrive to take her to the hospital, a crowd gathers around the house. Everyone looks on in shock. Days later, she dies, and her PCR returns positive for SARS-CoV-2.

As I move through the neighborhood now, I notice people have begun wearing masks.

April 22, 2020: Boston, Massachusetts, USA – Nick
Mexico (10.5k confirmed cases), USA (850k cases)

Rather poetically, I'm back on the same floor on which I began my intern year in my hospital's modern cardiovascular tower. Back then, and up until a month ago, it was a cardiac step-down unit. Now it has been converted to a bio-unit, one of five new makeshift COVID ICUs in my hospital. I've come full circle – because of redeployment, I am back to functioning as an intern, presenting on rounds, which seems to be occurring more frequently than necessary, with everyone on the team consumed by a nervous, impatient energy. I begin counting the days to graduation.

It's not an exaggeration to say that in the past two weeks, I've managed more refractory hypoxia than over my five preceding years of residency. I can't help but notice that most of these patients are Black or Brown, and many are coming from immigrant backgrounds – an unusual demographic profile for my rich hospital in a city where healthcare continues to be deeply segregated along racial lines. But unlike Boston's safety net hospitals, mine has been designated as a center for the remdesivir trial, so many patients are being transferred with the hopes that they may qualify for the experimental drug. I try *not* to think of a recent editorial I read in the *Wall Street Journal* by a retired (and tone-deaf) medical school dean who is clearly not on the front lines right now, alleging that medical schools have not adequately prepared my generation of doctors to fight this pandemic because of their recent focus on "social issues in medicine, including … the impacts of disparities in health care on medically underserved populations" (Goldfarb 2020). Screw that.

I'm tasked with trying to convince one patient–a middle-aged woman from Haiti–to agree to being intubated, as she continues to desaturate on her face mask. Normally we would trial her on high-flow oxygen next, but this method of oxygen delivery has been advised against at the hospital level given that it is an "aerosolizing procedure." I patiently explain the risks and benefits of intubation to her, but she remains firm that she does not want this for herself, no matter how I frame the situation. "You can give me the higher dose of oxygen," she repeats, "but my life is in God's hands." I leave her room dejected, convinced that she's written her own death warrant. She will end up proving me wrong and make a full recovery weeks later. "*Si Bondye vle.*" ("God willing").

So much of what we are doing seems to be experimental. Case reports out of Italy have led without question to major shifts in the practice of critical care, despite their anecdotal nature. Patients are being intubated very aggressively. "More and more I think they are realizing that people may be getting put on vents prematurely," I text Rebeca. On the other hand, arbitrary rules and norms that used to limit care seem to have evaporated overnight. Suddenly, our nurses who were previously forbidden by their union to start IVs are placing ultrasound-guided lines. And proning – once considered a quixotic suggestion in only the most extreme cases, given the effort involved by ICU staff – is now accomplished quickly and with nary a hitch or grumble by a dedicated "proning team" composed of orthopedic residents and physical therapists available 24/7.

I am notified through a cavalier message in the electronic medical record that one of my former primary care patients has been found dead at home, presumably due to complications of his alcohol use disorder and not COVID, though it's unclear. I wonder how the lockdown must have affected his drinking and if I could have done anything to stop it. I wonder how many others there are like him. Defeated, I get home and mindlessly browse through my social media in an attempt at distraction. I see that Alicia Keys has released a new music video for a song she has written about the pandemic response, which she has dedicated to frontline workers. I call my husband over and we sit and watch the video together on my phone. Tears soon begin streaming down both our faces.

You're doing a good job, a good job
You're doing a good job

Don't get too down
The world needs you know
Know that you matter
Matter, matter yeah

June 15, 2020: Tijuana, Baja California, Mexico – Rebeca
Mexico (150k confirmed cases), USA (2.11m cases)

The isolation center is now fully operational, and I am serving as Medical Director as planned. Our patients are being referred from different places– outpatient clinics, shelters, the International Organization for Migration's hotel shelter, the public hospital. Some are coming directly from immigration authorities, casualties of the unforgiving Title 42 policy. One patient, a man who had been living in the United States for decades, is brought by Customs and Border Protection directly from a US hospital where he tested positive. It is chilling to witness his despair at the prospect of never reuniting with his family back in the States, and I reflect on the large number of my patients who inject opiates – nearly 70% – who have been deported from the US.

When patients arrive, they are evaluated by a doctor who determines whether they need to be admitted and where to place them. They each get their own room, and many get their own bathroom. Sicker patients and those with mobility issues are assigned rooms on the ground floor, where we can keep a closer eye on them. Patients who inject drugs and are dependent on opioids are started on opioid replacement therapy with methadone. To be able to offer this, the NGO I work for had to fundraise directly to purchase the drug.

We've trained the staff on working with people with substance use disorders or who are unhoused, and they have risen to the challenge. A psychologist has been doing art therapy with the patients, and we have been trying to keep up morale as much as possible. Collectively, we've managed to create a dignified space for all our patients. Virtually everyone is staying to complete their full isolation course. It is encouraging to see what I've always held as a core belief play out in practice – that when you give people the right medical care and treat them nicely and provide them with basic needs like housing and food, they are fully capable of demonstrating that they can care for their health. Even more inspiring is seeing the staff come to that realization from many different starting points. Our resources are low, but everyone is pulling their weight to make sure our patients' needs are met, and we start getting donations (food, clothes, blankets, cleaning supplies) from all over, including staff and very low-income people in the neighborhood. It's a crazy world, but for now I will take comfort in this moment and pride in the effort that went into it.

June 20, 2020: Boston, Massachusetts, USA – Nick
Mexico (175k confirmed cases), USA (2.25m cases)

COVID numbers have come down in Massachusetts and I feel a weight has been lifted. From a peak of nearly 2500 cases/day in late April, we are now down to 220/day in the state – the tail end of a bell curve. After five years of training in Boston, I am gearing up to move down to Baltimore to begin life as an attending. I've had four graduation ceremonies effectively canceled this spring due to the pandemic. I don't allow myself to grieve the dearth of pomp and circumstance when people are dying in droves, our president is a megalomaniacal narcissist, and the country is going through a racial reckoning, but the lack of closure is unsettling. It feels anticlimactic packing up our things and leaving our lives in the city without saying goodbye, so we decide to host a small birthday party outside my parents' house to mark our departure. It's the first time we've seen many of these people in months. As I look around at some of my closest friends all finally together again – smiling, swimming, and sharing a collective moment together after months in isolation – I feel an unusual sense of peace and normalcy.

But I know it's not the same everywhere, and the moment is fleeting. I am starting to hear increasingly desperate messages from my former patients in Tijuana. One's partner has taken to verbally abusing her, threatening to disclose her HIV status to their community and locking her and their baby in a room during the day. "He's humiliating me," she sends. Another, whose asylum court date continues to be pushed back indefinitely, is starting to be harassed and threatened by the cartels, who are trying to get him to sell drugs for them. "Mexico's becoming more dangerous," he writes. I touch base with Rebeca to come up with action plans for each, feeling guilty for placing more of a burden on her at a time when I know she already has her hands full.

References

Centers for Disease Control and Prevention (CDC) and Department of Health and Human Services (HHS). 2020. *Notice of Order Under Sections 362 and 365 of the Public Health Service Act Suspending Introduction of Certain Persons From Countries Where a Communicable Disease Exists*. https://www.federalregister.gov/documents/2020/03/26/2020-06327/notice-of-order-under-sections-362-and-365-of-the-public-health-service-act-suspending-introduction

Cuneo, C. Nicholas. 2020. "The U.S. is abandoning asylum-seekers by pretending to care about their health." *WBUR Cognoscenti*, April 6, 2020. Accessed May 1, 2022. https://www.wbur.org/cognoscenti/2020/04/06/asylum-immigration-covid-19-c-nicholas-cuneo

Goldfarb, Stanley. 2020. "Med School Needs an Overhaul." *Wall Street Journal*, April 13, 2020. Accessed May 1, 2022. https://www.wsj.com/articles/med-school-needs-an-overhaul-11586818394

Ritchie, Hannah, Edouard Mathieu, Lucas Rodés-Guirao, Cameron Appel, Charlie Giattino, Esteban Ortiz-Ospina, Joe Hasell, Bobbie Macdonald, Diana Beltekian and Max Roser. 2020. "Coronavirus Pandemic (COVID-19)." *Our World in Data*. https://ourworldindata.org/coronavirus

C. Nicholas Cuneo, MD, MPH, is an assistant professor of Pediatrics and Medicine at the Johns Hopkins University School of Medicine with a joint appointment at the Johns Hopkins Bloomberg School of Public Health, where he is affiliated with the Center for Public Health and Human Rights and the Center for Humanitarian Health. He is the founding Medical Director of the HEAL Refugee Health and Asylum Collaborative, which provides trauma-informed, affirming care and supportive services to immigrant survivors of torture and trauma, including Baltimore's first comprehensive pro bono forensic evaluation clinic.

Dr. Cázares-Adame is the Director of Cross-Border Initiatives at University of San Diego's Joan B. Kroc Institute for Peace and Justice. In that role, she utilizes a public health lens to examine violence dynamics at the border and works with local partners to generate innovative strategies to reduce cycles of violence and help build a more peaceful and inclusive border region. From 2014 to 2022 she worked at PrevenCasa, a community-based organization that provides free health services to underserved populations in Tijuana. In 2020 she ran a COVID-19 voluntary isolation center that provided housing and medical care for people experiencing homelessness or housing instability.

Coronavirus Disease 2019: Who Has My Back?
By Janet M. Shapiro

Originally submitted October 29, 2020

COVID-19 shook us to the core. What I held onto was the trust I had in my colleagues, the hospital, the physicians, and of course, my family and friends. We depended on our layers of people and institutions to keep us safe and to cope with the needs of the pandemic in the hospital and at home. Trust here means life.

During the pandemic in New York City from March through May 2020, our physicians were always in the hospital. You could count on that. The pandemic left us in the hospital for long days, often tired of breathing through two layers of masks and sweating in plastic gowns. Nurses, physicians, respiratory therapists, housekeepers all went into patient isolation rooms with purpose and courage. It was remarkable that everyone believed in the obligation, no one called in sick or declined performing any task. The physicians were running from patient to patient, situation to situation. We were always asking for opinions. Frustration about lack of effective treatments and uncertainty in what studies to trust were ever-present. So we had to trust ourselves, depend on our clinical judgment, and adjust quickly to new ideas. We attended daily discussions among critical care leaders to share knowledge. But with so much uncertainty about this disease, we had to trust the principles of medicine and trust our training and abilities as intensivists and internists. Intubate patients when they need it, don't jump to intubate otherwise. Be cautious with medications with uncertain benefit and certain risks.

Fear was present but did not overwhelm. Seeing what could happen to patients, now intubated for COVID-19 pneumonia, made me reconsider my feeling of invincibility as a physician. We learned, and then taught, to donn and doff PPE; we had buddies – literally watching our backs.

In a disaster situation, you need to have faith in leaders, faith that there is some order to the system. Our hospital leaders were right with us. Meetings for situational awareness occurred throughout the day. Chief medical and nursing officers walked the floors. The infection prevention and control directed the engineers how to set up critical care units in procedural areas and figured out how to be sure PPE was available for every staff member for every emergency of every patient.

COVID-19 brought out conversations among colleagues that implicitly asked for trust. A few colleagues voiced their advanced directives: if it ever came to it, they did not want tracheostomy and wanted these wishes to be honored. Here was trust in word and promised deed.

Patients and families trusted us. Families left their loved ones in the hospital, perhaps seeing them for the last time, with no physical access to them, trusting that we would tend to their medical and emotional needs: that we would do our best, with no one watching, that their loved ones would live or die with caring people around them. We had to care deeply and work intensely to be worthy of their trust. I remember speaking to numerous patients before intubation and feeling the weight of knowing this may be their last conversation. These patients trusted us to take care of them during this frightening, life-threatening moment. Trusted that we would do our best. We spoke with families on the phone or on video meetings. I felt they needed for the trust to be almost palpable. This was not the trust of usual circumstances.

How did we show we were worthy of this trust? My image is of a Sunday afternoon in March 2020. Patients were being admitted to the ICU, one after another. A team of nurses, RTs, physical therapists, and a critical care fellow gathered outside a room, donned PPE, eager to enter the room of a 30-year-old intubated man who needed to be turned prone. They gathered with energy, courage, and no hesitation. Our actions conveyed our convictions. In our dedication, we earned trust.

During my personal COVID-19 illness, I was blessed by the care provided by physicians, colleagues, and technologists. Others protected me when I returned to work. My hospital had my back – with calls/texts/emails from hospital leadership telling me to take time to recover. My family and friends helped to get me through. I knew that my husband would cook dinner to get me stronger (he cooked steak to give me strength even though I could not taste it), my friends sent food. My siblings would call daily, my college friends would Zoom.

I trust that our community will get through COVID-19. And after all the sickness, death, sorrow and exhaustion of the Spring of 2020, New York City is starting to recover. We offered our experiences to help physicians in other locales who were seeing new cases. We depended on other New Yorkers to honor their duty to the community and maintain proper infection control so that we would emerge from COVID-19. Now we go outside and walk, eat, see people from a distance. We depend on our community to do the right thing so that we all can live.

In this heart-breaking, life-threatening crisis, we need each other to do the honorable, just, brave, caring action. Trust is an active choice that is made moment by moment. Having trust in someone, and being trusted, give peace, comfort, and a feeling of protection. So I gratefully acknowledge so many who have had my back. I do my best to deserve the trust of my patients and the people in my life. And I always remember: trust is a blessing.

Dr. Janet Shapiro, MD, FCCP, is Professor of Medicine at the Icahn School of Medicine at Mount Sinai and Director of the Medical Intensive Care Unit in the Division of Pulmonary, Critical Care and Sleep Medicine at Mount Sinai Morningside Hospital in New York City. She is board-certified in Internal Medicine, Pulmonary Diseases and Critical Care Medicine. Dr. Shapiro has published in the areas of critical care including cardiac care, respiratory failure, end-of-life care, quality improvement, and simulation education. Dr. Shapiro is the co-chair of the Ethics Committee whose work includes consultations, education, and attention to the moral climate of the hospital.

Divergent Roles: Pregnant Mother, ER Physician, and Human
By Elizabeth P. Clayborne

Originally submitted February 20, 2022

I was six months pregnant when the COVID-19 pandemic hit. As a busy young mom and emergency physician working in a hospital just outside of Washington, DC, I already had a full plate. Managing a sixteen-month-old at home, juggling my new academic career, and caring for an underserved and sick patient population while growing my medical device startup had me maxed out. I remember early in 2020 when I first started to hear rumors about the coronavirus, we hardly knew what to expect. Since ER docs are always aware that they are likely the first to encounter patients with a new illness, I wasn't particularly worried. My only angst was that I was pregnant with my second child, and I knew that being pregnant wasn't particularly conducive to being an emergency physician. We often work long and odd hours, spend a lot of time on our feet, and frequently manage a chaotic and stressful environment. I was excited that two of my female physician colleagues were also pregnant, all of us with our second child, and all of us having girls. We were happily planning play dates for maternity leave and had no idea what was on the horizon for each of us and the difficult decisions we would have to make in the coming weeks.

It seemed things changed overnight. All of a sudden there was a flood of sick patients, arriving in respiratory distress with dangerously low oxygen saturations. I remember an increase in the number of CPR-in-progress patients showing up to the ER. These are patients who are actively being resuscitated from the field. I'll never forget a middle-aged man who was briskly rolled in, shirt torn open with the LUCAS device (a motorized CPR machine) thumping on his chest providing compressions. The paramedic who was providing the man breaths through a bag-valve-mask was sweating and wide-eyed. The patient was only 42 years old, and his toes were purple and cold. In his pocket we found his wallet and pictures of young kids. We worked on him for nearly 40 minutes before calling the code. I then had to call his wife and tell her that her husband would never be coming home and that she wouldn't be able to come to the department to see his body because we were too full, and it was too dangerous. It was heartbreaking.

The momentum did not stop. None of us had ever seen anything like it. Ambulances were lined up outside when I walked into work, we were running out of supplies, and it was clear that we didn't have enough PPE. This last problem was especially unnerving for those of us who were pregnant since it became clear that not just the elderly and immunocompromised were becoming very ill. I personally intubated several people in my own age group and the images of lungs ravaged by COVID-19 was sobering on a daily basis. At this point, each of us considered leaving work to protect our babies. There were no official recommendations coming from my obstetrician and several of my family members thought I was crazy to keep working in the ER. But I knew our help was needed.

The community of patients that we serve is largely Black, underserved, and have poor access to care, making the emergency department one of their only options for help. My particular hospital was carrying over 50% of the COVID-positive patient load for the entire system of over 10 hospitals. In fact, the governor had to reopen a hospital that was scheduled to close and bring in state and federal resources to designate it as a COVID treatment venue just to manage the onslaught of patients with COVID-19.

It was around March of 2020 that I started to do some local and national media. It was important to me to represent a knowledgeable and articulate female physician of color who could shed light on issues that I thought were important and not getting enough attention. I did several TV interviews and wrote op-eds describing my experience as a pregnant frontline provider and discussed why my two pregnant colleagues and I had decided to stick it out in the ER as we battled through the first wave. It became obvious to me that those who were at home during shutdown could not imagine the devastation that I was experiencing on a daily basis. I could understand why people struggled with quarantine and isolation; unless you are watching people die and putting breathing tubes in 30- and 40-year-olds, it's difficult to understand how dangerous the coronavirus really is. Fortunately, my colleagues stepped up and as I approached my due date, I stopped doing our highest risk procedures and focused my efforts and background in bioethics to help organize our surge and scarce resource protocols. Several health policy issues that I had always been passionate about were now front and center on the global stage.

Two of these issues were advance care planning and end of life care. It was essential now for people to take the time to consider what would happen if they became acutely ill and to make sure they knew how to utilize various online platforms that can make it easier for physicians like me to know their medical history, family contact information, and what to do if they need immediate interventions. I find that Americans in particular struggle with addressing these topics and will put these discussions off until a crisis is at hand. But a healthcare crisis is the worst time to make sensitive and difficult decisions. Such procrastination often puts pressure on family members to guess what their loved ones would want rather than being able to call upon the patient's previously established goals of care. I found myself with a unique opportunity to speak about this critical issue at a time that resonated with many people experiencing the pandemic.

In a TEDx talk I did in 2020 entitled "How to protect your body and your doctor's soul during COVID-19", I mentioned that I always tell people that "DNR" (traditionally meaning "Do Not Resuscitate") can mean "Die Naturally and with Respect" (Clayborne 2020). For some patients, they would rather have their pain and symptoms controlled and focus on the quality of their life rather than the quantity of days that they are alive. Others wish to be put on life support for a variety of reasons. It is simply essential that patients be given the space and resources to make an informed decision.

Issues surrounding health equity were also coming to a head at this time. I could see firsthand how communities of color with long-standing health disparities were suffering from a lack of resources to battle COVID-19. The population I cared for in Prince George's County, Maryland, was a prime example of these inequities. Even as a Black female physician, I find it hard to advocate for my patients who are suffering from years of chronic comorbidities, from difficulty accessing care, and from a lack of understanding and research that address their specific needs. Data was mounting showing that Blacks and other minorities in particular had disproportionately higher rates of morbidity and mortality associated with COVID-19. It was with these issues weighing heavy on my mind that I finally stopped working and swapped to thinking about the birth of my "corona baby" in May of 2020.

I stopped working when I was 35 weeks pregnant per the recommendation of my obstetrician. I spent two weeks at home with my then 18-month-old, enjoying the cocoon of isolation and remembering that, for our children, life at home with parents and family may be a special treat in a society that is otherwise focused on hustle and bustle without time to savor the small joys of life. My daughter arrived a little early but healthy. I was relieved that I was able to bring a beautiful baby girl into the world after working through the first wave and imagined that all would be back to normal by the time I returned from maternity leave. I also gave birth on the exact day as my sister who was living in Germany at the time. It was interesting to compare the different experiences we had as mothers giving birth in different countries during a global pandemic. She was not in healthcare but like me, she found the process of having a baby in a hospital where so many were sick and dying to be unnerving and isolating. Both of us were grateful that we had successfully delivered our daughters without complications but didn't know what to expect as the pandemic continued to spread throughout the globe.

When I returned to work three months later in September of 2020, the number of COVID patients had decreased, yet we were clearly not done with the pandemic. By the end of the year what seemed to be a miracle arrived: a vaccine had received emergency authorization. I remember being tearful when I got my first shot of the Pfizer vaccine. I was so relieved that I had some layer of protection and that I would worry less about infecting my two small children at home. They didn't understand why I always came home through the garage, stripped off all of my clothes and wouldn't let them touch me until I showered, washing away any traces of COVID along with the stress, anxiety, fatigue, and pessimism that cloaked me at work every day. But the celebration was short-lived as it became obvious that the uptake of the COVID vaccine was a problem and mistrust of the healthcare system and our government dominated the news. Soon, new variants arose—Delta and then Omicron, each time further stressing an already fatigued healthcare workforce and compounding the grand exodus from medicine in which one in five healthcare workers was leaving the profession (Galvin 2021). Who could blame them? We went from being praised as frontline heroes with clap outs and hashtags to defending science and the overwhelming evidence that showed us that vaccinating and masks were essential tools to exit the pandemic successfully.

Even I was burnt out. I shifted focus to my company, NasaClip, which is working to bring a novel treatment device to market that will help people better treat nosebleeds at home. I still worked in the ED regularly, advocated for at-risk communities through my media opportunities, spoke about the importance of advance care planning, and did as much community outreach as I could. It is important to remember that those of us who are now going into the third year of the pandemic continue to put themselves and their families at risk. My entire family got COVID in January of 2022 during the Omicron surge. Thankfully, we all had mild symptoms, but it was worrisome since my young children had not been eligible for a vaccine.

My experience as a woman of color, an emergency physician, and a mother has highlighted different challenges, priorities, and resiliencies that are all a part of the human spirit. I hope that we overcome the COVID pandemic with a more unified front. This experience should have brought us closer together, yet it is disappointing to see the many ways in which society is more divided than ever. We must grow and learn from the immense grief and loss that has occurred across the globe. New diseases and new pandemics will continue to plague us in the future. I hope we rise from the ashes of COVID-19 with the understanding that we are all vulnerable, we are all human, and we are all strongest when we work together and see the humanity in each other.

References

Clayborne, Elizabeth. 2020. "How to protect your body and your doctor's soul during COVID-19." YouTube video, 14:11. TEDx Talks. Oct 27, 2020. https://www.youtube.com/watch?v=e7WjTluDqjE.

Galvin, Gaby. 2021. "Nearly 1 in 5 Health Care Workers Have Quit Their Jobs During the Pandemic." *Morning Consult*, Oct 4, 2021. https://morningconsult.com/2021/10/04/health-care-workers-series-part-2-workforce.

Dr. Clayborne is an emergency medicine physician faculty member at the University of Maryland School of Medicine with an academic focus on ethics, health policy, and innovation/entrepreneurship. Most recently, she developed a novel nosebleed device, NasaClip. Dr. Clayborne has been interviewed on networks such as CNN, MSNBC, CBSN and TEDx discussing COVID-19 and health equity and ethics issues. She looks forward to continuing her career as a practicing emergency medicine physician, innovator and leader in healthcare policy and reform and can be found on Twitter and Instagram @DrElizPC.

The Bedside and Beyond
By Pascale Audain

Originally submitted November 5, 2021

I joined Boston Children's Hospital's BCU in 2015 when our hospital was designated as an Ebola treatment center. The MICU, my home unit, was identified as the location where a suspected or confirmed Ebola patient would be admitted. I jumped at the opportunity to be part of the volunteer unit so I could be as informed and prepared as possible. For five years, we discussed and simulated what it would be like to care for a patient with a highly communicable disease. The BCU functioned in a world of hypotheticals and "maybe's". We were the "just in case" safety net that everyone hoped would never have to be utilized and for a while, that's all it was. That is, until the COVID-19 pandemic established its grip on the globe in late 2019.

At its inception, the BCU was designed as a "just-in-time unit," to literally have its walls constructed within our MICU at a moment's notice and nurses pulled from their home units to provide care for a single patient with a highly infectious pathogen. We were ready for one Ebola patient, but how was a unit that was only ever intended to care for one patient expected to accommodate the eventual influx of pediatric patients affected by this novel coronavirus which was wreaking havoc all over the world? The answer is: we weren't. The powers that be decided to deploy the BCU nurses in an entirely different manner. Our expertise in high-level PPE and willingness to learn and innovate on the fly made us a prime and previously untapped resource. In early March 2020, I was one of the nurses pulled from my home unit to act as a BCU site manager assisting with the COVID-19 response. My duties became less about hands-on patient care and more a focus on education and assistance to other frontline staff across the entire hospital system. Essentially, I was charged with providing staff, in a significantly shorter amount of time, with the skills and information needed to develop a comfort level that took me five years to develop.

Those early days were a blur. Questions were presenting faster than answers, and the answers we did have were subject to change. The fluid nature of the pandemic, particularly in those first few weeks, made the job seem impossible at times. The ever-changing recommendations made it extremely difficult to establish trust with staff who were expected to dive headfirst into these patients' rooms. At times, I encountered staff who were downright hostile towards our educational efforts and offers of assistance. To be honest, I couldn't blame them. We had all entered a scenario where no one had a choice as to whether they wanted to go above and beyond the original expectations of providing safe care to our patients and their families. All of a sudden, by simply going to work and caring for our patients, healthcare providers were putting themselves at greater risk than the "usual" risk of our "normal" work settings. Healthcare providers were being hailed as "heroes" just for showing to up to work. "Hero", a term often associated with those who knowingly and willingly put themselves in harm's way, became less a badge of honor and more an unwelcomed burden. Questions swirled about our own mortality and whether we would be the reason someone we loved could contract the virus. Everyone was scared, stressed, and exhausted.

Personally, I struggled at times. While I had volunteered to be a part of the BCU, the COVID-19 pandemic was completely outside the realm of anything I had ever imagined. During pre-COVID-19 BCU training, PPE was abundant and donning and doffing was a rigorous, but fun exercise. Flash forward to when the BCU became a reality and not just simulation: I was now having to explain to staff why we had to decontaminate and re-use our N95 respirators and provide just-in-time training regarding donning and doffing procedures to an already overwhelmed workforce. Staff would lament over how the respirators were never intended to be multiuse and how unsettled they were by having to re-wear them. I would listen to their concerns and attempt to comfort them with the facts available and how I understood their hesitations and frustrations. But I also felt an intense level of guilt. I consider myself a doer.

In my ICU, I want to be in the action—ready to jump into whatever situation presents itself. As a BCU site manager, I had to stay on the periphery. I had to get everyone who was meant to go into the room ready instead of charging in myself. On an intellectual level, I understood that I was fulfilling a different role and providing an important service to the enterprise, but emotionally it didn't sit right with me that as one of the people who had knowingly volunteered to enter rooms with highly communicable diseases. I wasn't the person actually doing it now. Tensions were high amongst my co-workers and the site manager team, escalating to the point where I had to have a conversation with one of my closest work friends about whether their feelings about my role was negatively impacting our friendship. Thankfully through open dialogue we were able to move past it. But knowing that my co-workers, especially one I consider to be one of my closest friends and one on whom I relied upon so much for emotional solace, resented me for not being at the bedside compounded my guilt even more.

Additionally, I felt an overwhelming sense of conflict when it came to my experience working in a pediatric hospital. I would see how COVID-19 was ravaging adult hospitals all over the daily news and how our adult healthcare counterparts were working in unfathomable conditions, consumed by death, capacity issues, and a strain on resources. While the atmosphere at Boston Children's was intense, it seemed to pale in comparison to the stories I would hear from nurses in adult hospitals. Our pediatric patients were still able to have a member of their family physically by their side, whereas nurses caring for adult patients had to facilitate video and phone calls to connect their patients with their families, even at the end of life. My heart was breaking for them knowing they were having to endure and persevere through impossible situations.

Eventually, staff began to trust the BCU Site Managers as we established our role and reinforced that we supported them in whatever capacity they needed us. We were the constant presence at the beginning of every shift and new admission, checking in to make sure that frontline staff had everything that they needed to care safely for their patients. We also responded to all ICU emergencies and established ourselves as part of the hospital-wide code team to provide supplemental PPE and reinforce safety protocols. Some staff members even expressed an interest in joining the BCU once everything settled down because they saw the utility in of our work.

When I reflect back on my time as a BCU Site Manager, I am proud of what I contributed to Boston Children's COVID-19 response. We were educators, innovators, collaborators, and a source of support throughout the enterprise. The BCU was deactivated at the end of August 2020. Towards the end of our deployment, staff were increasingly more comfortable with safety protocols as well as donning and doffing, which was our ultimate goal. It is still hard to wrap my head around everything that occurred during the height of the pandemic and how we've all had to settle into our "new normal." I am enormously grateful for each and every healthcare provider and support staff member at Boston Children's and in the healthcare community at large. Without having to be asked, we answered the call and did everything within our power to keep our patients and each other safe.

Pascale Audain started her nursing career in 2011 after graduating from Northeastern University. She began as a new graduate nurse in the Medical Intensive Care Unit at Boston Children's Hospital and has worked there ever since. When asked to join the volunteer Biocontainment Unit in 2015, she jumped at the chance to take on a new challenge and expand her knowledge base. Her professional interests also include infection prevention and quality improvement. Pascale earned her Master of Science in Nursing in 2023. She can be found in the kitchen baking or behind her camera when she's not in the hospital.

On the Front Lines, but of What Battle?
By Katherine R. Peeler

Originally submitted April 2020

My pediatric intensive care unit (PICU) is a bizarre place to be right now. We are vastly below our usual census: we have canceled all elective surgeries, most of our chronic patients seem to be staying at home, and our usual spring asthma admissions are nowhere to be found. This is despite being one of the only remaining PICUs in the region as most others, as well as many neonatal intensive care units and general pediatrics wards, have been converted to adult beds.

Even in the face of a slower pace than we are used to, the same heightened fear occurring at hospitals around the country has taken root here – fear for our patients, fear for our own health and that of the families we go home to, and fear that our lives and the jobs we signed up for will never be the same. Additionally, there is the guilt that lurks. "We are on the front lines," we say, followed by the whisper, "but are we?" While a handful of our pediatric patients are critically ill from COVID-19 or the novel inflammatory response (referred to presently as pediatric inflammatory multisystem syndrome, or PIMS, by some), the majority are admitted for other reasons.

Our hospital has transformed in the last few months, putting into place COVID-19-specific guidelines for PPE, testing, and visitor restrictions. We have modified our procedures in attempts to make intubation and resuscitation safer. These steps have felt necessary, timely, and appropriate, but the lingering disquiet that we are frontline imposters remains. While adult hospitals are overrun with a tidal wave of patients, we exist in an uncomfortable emotional limbo—fearing everything that comes with taking care of COVID-19 patients and simultaneously feeling guilty that we are not shouldering our share of the burden in this pandemic.

What if we are compelled to take adult COVID-19 patients because the adult hospitals truly have no more beds? I know I am not the only one who puts on a brave face but is secretly terrified of treating a population I have not routinely cared for since medical school. I cannot reconcile my desire to be in the thick of it with the crippling anxiety that accompanies knowing I may be the responsible attending caring for "previously healthy" adults. What kind of intensive care doctor am I if I cower in the face of this emergency? What if someone dies because I do not know enough adult intensive care? With the ever-looming possibility of becoming, at least in part, an adult ICU, I am beginning to doubt myself. What is my role here, and what does it mean if I privately dread taking it on for fear of failure? Mostly what I feel is shame.

Over the last few weeks, however, these feelings of guilt, shame, and anxiety have slowly dissipated. We have not had to take on adult patients, and it is clear that our pediatric patients and their families need us, especially now. No one wants to bring their children to the hospital in this current environment, fearing they will catch the virus from being here, so emergency room visits are delayed and the patients who eventually show up are incredibly sick. We have seen this in our COVID-19 patients, but also in a rash of COVID-negative children presenting in severe diabetic ketoacidosis, metabolic crisis, or the late stages of other medical conditions.

The "front lines" conjure up images of healthcare workers tending to those wounded from a relentless external foe. What I have found most striking and poignant, though, are the experiences of the patients who were already in our PICU when the pandemic started – the front lines within.

It is common custom in our unit to discharge long-term patients through a parade of bubbles blown by various members of the care team. One little boy was finally ready for discharge after more than a year of intense ups and downs in our unit. "Is blowing bubbles an aerosol-generating procedure?" his nurse quietly asked. Ever quick on her feet, our child life specialist rounded up all the bubble blowing machines in the hospital, and we held the bubble parade in a COVID-compliant fashion. But his mother, whom we had all hugged many times over the last year, could only wave and blow kisses as she left, crying in happiness, with her son.

And there have also been the losses. Several of the children our team has come to know and love over prolonged hospitalizations this past year have died in the midst of the pandemic. One child in particular, Marybeth (a pseudonym), had been in our PICU for almost a year. Celebrating her birthday while hospitalized, she never got well enough for discharge to a rehabilitation center. Rather unexpectedly, she suddenly deteriorated and died. Her family was devastated. We were devastated. Like many of the medically complex children we care for, Marybeth had amassed an enormous team of supporters—primary and specialty care providers, classmates, and community members. But how can a family mourn and celebrate a child who was larger than life when none of those supporters can join them at a funeral or memorial service? Having attended the funerals of many patients, I appreciate that ceremonial closure as well, remembering the life of a child lost in communion with other people in close proximity.

Everyone I have worked with has swallowed the initial fear of the unknown, stepped up to the plate, and done what was needed for our patients—COVID-19 or otherwise. Despite the stress of the added layers of complexity to our everyday routines, we have provided the same high level of medical and psychosocial care to Marybeth and the other children who have passed away in the last several months in our unit. In doing so, we have served as a reassuring constant for our patients and families in an otherwise constantly shifting equation that is the current COVID reality. And where our role ended, these children's communities have often visibly and inspiringly stepped up.

Marybeth's mother recently told me about (and gave me permission to share) the incredible surprise they received from community members they had not seen in over a year or never knew at all. Shortly after Marybeth's death, a family friend suggested they sit outside their house. As they did, a parade of more than 100 cars, police vehicles, fire trucks, and ambulances – all decked with red balloons capturing Marybeth's favorite color – drove by in Marybeth's honor. It was a creative and powerful celebration of life. Her mother also commented on how strange it was to stay inside all day now, not to come to the hospital. We talked for a while because that's all there was to do. When possible and desired by the family, I find connecting with a family after a patient's death invaluable—to acknowledge their ongoing grief and process my own experiences of the loss of a patient. In a time where traditional physical connection cannot exist, this connection feels more pressing than ever.

Like our colleagues who care for adults, we are in fact on the front lines of this pandemic. I see this now, and recognize that, while our numbers may be smaller, our role is not. We are treating sick and critically ill patients suffering from COVID-19, but we are also supporting all of the other children and families living and dying during COVID-19. In a time where uncertainty reigns, we are a dependable presence for all – for the families who know us well and are safely sheltering at home, for those who have never entered a hospital before but worry their child might be the next to fall seriously ill from the virus, and for those who are currently in our unit. Yes, the way we care for our patients has been modified, with extra PPE and bubble machines, but these modifications have not lessened our connection to our patients. Instead, they have demonstrated our unwavering commitment to their care. In embracing this multi-dimensional front line and transforming the foreign into the familiar, I have worked to regain my sense of purpose and professional identify in this pandemic.

Katherine Peeler is a pediatric critical care physician at Boston Children's Hospital and an assistant professor of pediatrics at Harvard Medical School (HMS). She additionally holds faculty appointments in the Department of Global Health and Social Medicine and the Center for Bioethics at HMS. For more than two decades, Dr. Peeler has been a volunteer with Physicians for Human Rights and is a national expert in the health rights of asylum-seekers in the US. At HMS, she runs an immigration lab that explores questions at the intersections of ethics, policy, and human rights. Dr. Peeler lives in Cambridge, Massachusetts with her husband and two children.

The Tempest
By Stacy R. Nigliazzo

Originally submitted March 3, 2022

In the past two weeks, the number of cases of COVID-19 outside China has increased 13-fold, and the number of affected countries has tripled. There are now more than 118,000 cases in 114 countries, and 4,291 people have lost their lives ...

We have therefore made the assessment that COVID-19 can be characterized as a pandemic (WHO 2020).

5920 Days Pre-Pandemic: It watches from the ceiling, from her blue-black skin, from the door of her breathing, oiling the lock with its fingernail. I feel it scratching as the nurses flock over what is left of my mother.

I pray for a cure. Then for her to die, mercifully.

I want to be a nurse.

60 Days Pre-Pandemic: He needs nasal oxygen, then a positive pressure mask. We intubate. Just thirty-two years old, from the airport.

He's never been sick before ...

30 Days Pre-Pandemic: I browse the bookfair. Eat a candy apple on the Riverwalk.

15 Days Pre-Pandemic: They are at risk. We are at risk.

Ten Days Pre-Pandemic: *N-95 masks have always been single use. Why can't we get more?*

Day Zero: We stand together on the bank, slip into the laden arms of the dark water.

Two Days Out: Our first known-positive patient arrives via ambulance on a BiPAP mask - without a viral filter. We intubate, limiting personnel to minimize exposure.

Fuck, my colleague whispers, as we wash our hands, doff our gowns, and place our N-95 masks in paper sacks at the scrub sink. The ICU nurse weeps when I call report.

Our patient dies the next day.

Nine Days Out: All that we wear is the color of spring cornflowers. We spill over like a rain-filled gutter.

15 Days Out: *Do you have the test? I want a test. They won't test me—I've gone to the ER three times. If you won't test me I'll call the local news. I'll put it on Facebook. I will own this hospital.*

20 Days Out: A local engineer uses his 3D printer to create face shields. There are three duckbill N-95 masks hidden under my desk.

45 Days Out: *Assume everyone is positive, every colleague and every patient, regardless of chief complaint. Keep all the doors closed. And don't forget to wash your hands.*

56 Days Out: The Blue Angels fly over Houston to honor healthcare workers. A local business buys us dinner.

The box of gowns I saved for the isolation cart has disappeared.

65 Days Out: *I've been thinking about it and I can't remember if I touched my mask before I washed my hands.*

75 Days Out: We're told to re-use our N-95 masks up to five days, then to return them for re-sterilization, that they can be used, re-used, cleaned, re-used again, and re-cleaned up to seven times.

19,091 Days Pre-Pandemic: She sat with him as he cried for his mother, volunteering as a student when her father, my grandfather, was the on-call surgeon.

She never knew his name, just that they were the same age.

She always wanted to be a nurse until that night.

90 Days Out: She is COVID negative, cardiac arrest on a plane. We got her back post myocardial infarction—stable enough to go downtown on a balloon pump. Her son kisses her forehead as she is belted onto the transport stretcher.

We need this win today ...

105 Days Out: There are 15 gurneys in the main hallway and six outlets in the alcove behind the registration desk. The aisle by the ambulance bay has a curtain and wall-mounted oxygen. Three recliners will fit outside room 32, still in the eyeline of the charge nurse.

125 Days Out: We stop elective surgeries, screen non-urgent cases out of the emergency department. Volunteers are trained to lead Zoom calls for families of the dying since visitors are no longer allowed.

127 Days Out: That woman from the airport with the MI—she's still alive, in cardiogenic shock.

They cut off both of her legs today.

141 Days Out: The pre-op suite is now a 25-bed inpatient overflow unit. PACU is a temporary ICU. Anyone with RN behind his or her name is plucked to work bedside.

175 Days Out: I leave the room, doff my gown and gloves, wash my hands, put on new gloves, doff my cap and face shield, sanitize my face shield, doff my gloves, wash my hands, put on new gloves, doff my N95 mask, place it in a paper sack labeled with my name, doff my gloves, forget to wash my hands. I wash my hands, pull my mask from a paper sack labeled with my name, put it on along with my sanitized face shield, don a clean cap, gown, and gloves, enter the room, leave the room, wash my gloved hands.

197 Days Out: Whispered in the ambulance bay at 5am: *be a light, a living prayer, always your child; courage, composure, kindness. Let no one die in the hallway today, please.*

215 Days Out: I miss my family. Flying. Faces.

230 Days Out: He called 911 for a cough, shortness of breath, cold sweats, fever, and body aches immediately after an international flight.

And he made the call from Wal-Mart.

245 Days Out: *There are too many, and they're all sick.*

260 Days Out: The author of this deeply flawed study is also the editor-in-chief of the journal that published it.

275 Days Out: We paint Jerry's colors on the ceiling of the ambulance bay; light flameless candles, read his name, dress our badges with strips of black tape over our own names.

290 Days Out: *Let's take a sacred pause, please; ten seconds of silence to honor the life of this patient and all the hard work we've done in this room.*

4745 Days Pre-Pandemic
I passed my boards. I burn beside them in starched white.
I am my mother.
I am one of them.

300 Days Out: I play Requiem, Op. 48, Pie Jesu in my pocket. The lyrics are in Latin but I know it's a prayer.

315 Days Out: Over half of our admitted patients are positive - nearly all of them, unvaccinated.

335 Days Out: This is no longer about best practices.

387 Days Out: I tell you *it's ok*. You fall asleep on a bench seat. I replace your keening oxygen tank hourly – in the lobby. Someone else calls your wife with an update. I have worn this mask for six days.

These are not my hands.

This is not my face.

415 Days Out: *What if I accidentally kill someone?*

425 Days Out: In my dream my mother is alive, still ripe with cancer. Her eyes are the color of rain. I take her to my hospital where there is a line spilling into the street.

And watch her die on the sidewalk.

445 Days Out: It never stops.

481 Days Out: *You can't make me wear a mask. This is all a hoax. You're a crisis actor and you murder people for profit. I have a gun at home and I'm going to come back and blow your goddamn head off.*

500 Days Out: Isaiah was ours for 48 days; from nasal oxygen to BiPAP, to ventilator. We held his hands and prayed, all of us at his bedside. Our hearts break …

I'm just so grateful you said his name.

513 Days Out: We are a seven-pointed star; a crown of thorns.

525 Days Out: A refrigerated truck arrives in the bay. For centuries, in the northern states, the winter dead have waited for spring burial because it's too hard to break the frozen ground. They were saved in barns and caves called "dead houses." In 2005 alone, roughly 1000 burials were delayed in the state of New York.

540 Days Out: *An undergraduate professor once told me she almost drowned as a child, in a rip tide when her life vest snapped.*
She stopped struggling.

Then, her father pulled her out.

530 Days Out: 138 patients have died this month – that translates into a 23-minute sacred pause – 23 minutes to honor 138 lives.
Last year, the corresponding total was 113, the year before that, pre-pandemic, was 32.

541 Days Out: Breaths of blood on white sheets. Black terns in their eyes.

565 Days Out: I have stopped struggling. I am waiting for the hand that pulls me out.
And I am still showing up.

References

World Health Organization. 2020. "WHO Director-General's opening remarks at the media briefing on COVID-19." Last modified March 11, 2020. https://www.who.int/director-general/speeches/detail/who-director-general-s-opening-remarks-at-the-media-briefing-on-covid-19---11-march-2020

Stacy R. Nigliazzo is a Houston nurse, an MFA fellow at the University of Houston Creative Writing Program, and the award-winning author of three poetry collections: *Scissored Moon, Sky the Oar,* and *My Borrowed Face* (all published by Press 53). Additionally, she is an instructor at the Humanities Expression and Arts Lab at Baylor College of Medicine.

A Breath of COVID Air: Insights from a Respiratory Therapist
By Deadria Clarke

Originally submitted April 13, 2022

I was among the first respiratory RTs to take care of a COVID-19 positive patient at my hospital. From the start I was apprehensive, mainly due to the unknown nature of this disease. All I knew going into it was that we were changing our practices of how to don our PPE. During those first few weeks, we frequently made adjustments to our standard practices to accommodate the needs of our patients. This meant getting creative with how we treated our patients when we realized that conventional methods were not enough. I joked around with my friends that being an RT during COVID times was just my regular job but on about 50 different types of steroids.

Each day I walked into work in my normal scrubs, then changed into operating room scrubs and changed out of my sneakers into Crocs. I would take off my glasses and put on my contact lenses instead, then proceed to the unit where I put on a PAPR hood on my head, connected the hose, and turned the PAPR unit on. Prior to going into each room, I would don two pairs of gloves as well as an isolation gown. There were several steps to doffing this PPE. When leaving the unit entirely, we would take off our hoods and wipe everything down from our badge to our shoes. After giving a report at the end of the day to our oncoming colleagues, we changed back into the clothing in which we had arrived. The care teams, which consisted of a doctor, RT, and nurses, came up with new ways to minimize exposure as much as possible.

I remember when we were discussing moving patients out of the four-bed BCU to our 24-bed MICU. The BCU was originally designed to care for Ebola patients. We realized quickly, however, that the BCU would not have sufficient space to house the rapidly increasing COVID-19 patient load–especially given their variable and often long lengths of stay–hence the decision to repurpose our MICU into a new COVID unit. The physicians and nurses were passionately discussing the number of staff required to take care of each patient, with the idea that each member would need a break from being in her PPE. Unfortunately, during this debate, they forgot to take into consideration the RTs, so I used this as an opportunity to advocate for my fellow therapists. I mentioned that if we were planning on starting off with 12 patients, we would need a bare minimum of two RTs instead of the single RT who was currently required to take care of our four BCU patients. The therapists would stagger their care so that it would give each therapist an opportunity to take an hour break before she was required to be back on the unit. As we converted more intensive care and intermediate care units to COVID units, we came up with different systems to rotate therapists through the units while allowing them to have enough of a break to recoup.

I worked at two different institutions during the first two years of the pandemic. At my full-time job (at the larger hospital) we had enough PPE, but that still did not prevent me from experiencing compromising situations at both hospitals. During my first full shift working on our main COVID unit at the larger hospitals, the hose became disconnected from my PAPR hood. Suddenly I was not getting filtered air to my hood. I had to hold my breath and exit the patient's room. I grabbed someone to help reconnect the tube to my hood. A few days later, I was performing an extubation–a procedure that requires me to be in the room by myself during a time when they are often coughing. I had the tube in my hand, ready to pull it out of the patient's mouth, when the battery on my PAPR pack died. I once again had to hold my breath, rush out of the room and off the unit. We did not keep extra batteries on the unit, so I rushed into our decontamination room to take my hood off and take a breath.

Even when our individual PPE was working, systems issues arose that compromised safety. During one shift, the negative pressure system shut down for six hours. This meant that we did not have the proper filtration needed to keep the virus contained within the patient rooms. The alarm kept going off. There was a delay in fixing the issue due to the unforeseen challenge of getting the proper PPE to the engineering staff (previously deemed "non-frontline" but now suddenly very much "frontline"). I was floating between two sides of our unit, and one of my patients woke up confused. After the nurse pushed the code button to alert us that she needed help, I rushed from one side of the unit to the other. I threw on the proper PPE and held the patient's breathing tube in place while he was thrashing around. I knew that I was the only thing holding his airway in place. This was very nerve-wracking because this patient was about twice my size. I knew that if his breathing tube came out, he would both be in danger of decompensating from a breathing perspective and we would be at a very high risk of catching COVID with the negative system still broken.

The second smaller hospital that I worked at unfortunately did not have all of the means necessary to keep up with the patient load that we experienced. There were often more COVID patients than negative pressure rooms to put them in, which meant exposing myself to the virus while administering care. Due to a shortage of PPE, I wore the same N95 mask for three months straight. I ended up leaving this hospital because of some of the safety issues that I encountered.

Most healthcare workers do not expect to work in a global pandemic, but the nature of healthcare is one of constant change, and so we adapt. While the general public may have believed that this was what we had signed up for, in fact we did not have a choice whether or not to show up to work. We were thrown into a situation with little (and often conflicting) information, being expected to deliver the same quality of care but without good guidance in how to do so. It was an incredibly uncomfortable situation to be in–personally, professionally, and ethically.

Outside of the hospital, the reception we, as healthcare providers, received from the general public varied widely. I distinctly remember going to Target after a long shift. I often preferred to do my shopping at night because there were fewer people in the store. I ran into a coworker of mine; we exchanged stories of our day since we were in two different units. A lady came up to us and said, "You shouldn't be allowed in this store while wearing that." The "that" she was referring to was our scrubs. Little did she know we had actually changed out of our designated COVID scrubs into our regular scrubs. I was appalled that someone thought that we were just walking around spreading COVID. On the other hand, we had people in the community who were jumping at the opportunity to provide food or snacks for us. I experienced extreme impostor syndrome when people called me a "hero." I didn't feel as if I was doing anything heroic. It wasn't as if I volunteered to take care of these patients. I had no choice but to adapt.

Unlike some of my fellow RTs, I do not have children or a significant other to whom I was coming home each day. It felt isolating at times. One thing I am truly grateful for is my friends and family who stuck by me. All I wanted to do was just take a week off to visit my family; but I knew it would be too risky so instead I called them or chatted with them by video. I leaned heavily on my mental health therapist during this time because I knew that working through this pandemic would have after-effects on my mental health. Sunshine therapy was one of the things my coworkers and I came up with as a form of self-care. When we discussed sunshine therapy pre-pandemic, it generally referred to taking a patient outside to bring them into a different environment. During the pandemic, sunshine therapy meant getting together as a group to take a break from our shifts. We would discuss a time to meet and send out an invitation to everyone who was working. If we were free we would sit outside, take a deep breath, and just enjoy the sun on our faces. This was the time for us to regroup and remember why we were fighting so hard to save every life that we encountered. Most of the time sunshine therapy left us feeling refreshed and ready to finish out the shift. I organized food deliveries for my coworkers, as well as for some of the units that weren't getting the recognition they deserved by taking on the rest of the hospital's load. Self-care was something that I prioritized. Some other forms of this self-care included being out on the water as much as possible when I wasn't working.

It may seem bizarre to say that I am grateful for the pandemic, but in some ways I am. It taught me how to be a more empathetic healthcare professional as well as improved my emotional intelligence. I learned to slow down and relish in the small victories in life. After losing patients or after a particularly stressful day, I would go into an empty patient room, close the door, and just take deep breaths. For every patient whom we were able to liberate from the ventilator we cheered. I held so many hands and had conversations that ordinarily I wouldn't be able to have with patients. In a pre-COVID 19 situation, the workload would often get so busy that I was only able to have short conversations with my patients. Although COVID-19 increased our patient load, we changed how our days flowed, keeping me in patient rooms longer and thus allowing me to have in-depth conversations with my patients. I learned about what each patient did prior to COVID, their hobbies, as well as for whom they were fighting. I sat and told jokes and stories to patients since they couldn't have their family members with them. Although the pandemic is something that I never want to relive, it improved my clinical skills and overall ability to care for my patients in more ways than I could have imagined.

Deadria Clarke is currently in her eleventh year of practicing respiratory therapy. She has experience with neonatology, critical care medicine, as well as emergency medicine.

Healing Wounds, Practicing Compassion
By Matthew S. O'Donnell

Originally submitted January 27, 2021

Ministry in the midst of a pandemic requires patience, persistence, and creativity. Living through a pandemic requires perseverance, acknowledging the unknown, and standing in the gap of all that seems overwhelming. For me, ministry is about serving as an instrument to help reveal the Divine Presence in one's lived experience. As a Roman Catholic priest, I have come to realize the very privileged role I get to have in so many peoples' journeys in life. I stand with people in moments of great joy, immense pain, and everywhere in between. As people began to die from COVID-19, it became clear to religious leaders that an ancient, yet ever new, question, was facing the human family: *Where is God in the midst of such deep suffering?*

The pandemic that began early in 2020 demonstrated to the global community the fragility of human life. A microscopic virus was shutting down cities, wreaking financial havoc for families, filling people with anxieties and fears, and probably most painfully, taking the lives of those we loved. In Chicago, it became a point of real concern for Cardinal Blase Cupich, the Archbishop of Chicago, that the Catholic Church in Greater Chicago had to find a way to minister to those in imminent danger of death from coronavirus. Cardinal Cupich elicited volunteers among the priests to celebrate the Sacrament of the Anointing of the Sick with those who were dying from this strange and scary virus. About twenty priests, myself included, embarked upon this mission of bringing pastoral care to the sick. Beginning in March of 2020 this cadre of "COVID anointers" was sent all throughout Cook and Lake counties in Illinois to pray with those who were sometimes dying painfully from this virus.

In the Roman Catholic religion, there are seven sacraments that help to orient a Catholic's life and spiritual journey. The sacraments in the Catholic Church can be understood as outward signs that help to manifest God's grace and presence in a person's, and in the community's, life. The sacraments of the Church are rituals of celebration that make Jesus Christ's saving action real in one's life. One of the seven sacraments is Anointing of the Sick, which is celebrated with those who are sick, suffering from illness, or are in danger of death. The root of this sacrament comes from the Letter of James in the New Testament:

> Are any among you sick? They should call for the elders of the church and have them pray over them, anointing them with oil in the name of the Lord. The prayer of faith will save the sick, and the Lord will raise them up; and anyone who has committed sins will be forgiven. Therefore, confess your sins to one another, and pray for one another, so that you may be healed. The prayer of the righteous is powerful and effective (James 5:14-16).

This ancient writing animates, and serves as the foundation for, this sacrament. Over the centuries the theology and spirituality of this sacrament have evolved, all of which undergirds the way in which the sacrament is celebrated today.

Each of the seven sacraments is comprised of matter and form—the tangible and the words. In the Anointing of the Sick, that matter is blessed oil and the form is a prayer that is spoken. It is this weaving together of action and spoken word that ushers in the experience of God made present. In the Anointing of the Sick, the priest says: "Through this holy anointing may the Lord in his love and mercy help you with the grace of the Holy Spirit. May the Lord who frees you from sin save you and raise you up." These words are accompanied by the action of the priest making the sign of the cross with the blessed oil on the patient's forehead and hands. Through this prayer and the touch of the minister, God's healing power is unleashed upon the sick person.

It is this ritual that makes the celebration of the sacrament so extraordinary for a patient sick with the coronavirus. The Catholic Church believes that the celebration of this sacrament has the power to heal, to forgive one's sins, and to prepare a person for eternal life. While certain modifications have been made to ensure the safety of the minister celebrating this sacrament, like using a cotton swab to administer the blessed oils on the patient, nevertheless the priest stands near the sick patient to celebrate the ritual, to pray the prayers, and to anoint the patient's body. In doing so, the entirety of the Church is present to the sick person through the ministry of the priest. More powerfully, God is present to the sick person through the celebration of this sacrament.

Roman Catholic priests around the world have put themselves on the front line in order to share the gift of this sacrament for Catholics who are in need of healing. Priests, and many other ministers from various faith traditions, have chosen to be present to those dying from COVID-19 because they understand how important it is for those who are sick to know they are not alone, and for other believers to remember that prayer has the power to change one's situation. In the Roman Catholic tradition priests have risked their own well-being because they believe in the power of this sacrament to bring healing and comfort to those who are suffering from this virus. The coronavirus has left far too many to suffer alone, surrounded only by the heroic healthcare workers caring for them. The celebration of the sacrament of the Anointing of the Sick is a visible sign that in their moment of greatest suffering, those battling this virus are not alone. When the sacraments are celebrated, God shows up and God acts in powerful ways. I truly believe this, and it is because of this conviction that I, and so many other priests like me, will drop everything to rush to be at the bedside of a fellow Catholic believer.

I remember very vividly the first call I received to anoint a patient dying from COVID-19. It was a woman at a hospital not too far from the parish where I serve as pastor. It was one of the very first calls the Archdiocese of Chicago received. I recall speaking on the phone to Justin who was responsible for dispatching us priests to the hospitals. Justin stressed the importance of properly donning and doffing my PPE—a lesson I was both grateful for and one that somehow made everything so much more real. Arriving at the hospital I was met by a gracious and already overworked charge nurse who helped me put on PPE from head to toe. As we passed through the doors and entered the unit the seriousness of the pandemic overwhelmed me. I watched doctors, nurses, and other hospital staff members move from room to room as new patients were brought into the unit. I saw ventilators and IV poles adorning the rooms. I saw the face of the woman I was called to anoint, and in that moment, the reality and weight of where we were – and why – truly hit me.

Since the pandemic began, I have stood in dozens of hospital and nursing home rooms, as well as individual's living rooms to celebrate the sacrament of the Anointing of the Sick. Each time I stand in these ordinary-made-sacred spaces, the pandemic's broad presence becomes acutely narrowed and poignant because before me is the face of someone who is struggling to live. These are husbands and wives, mothers and fathers, sons and daughters, who contracted a virus that threatens their very life. I have spoken to so many family members who almost always lament a similar statement about their loved one: "they were just fine, it's like this came out of nowhere." For some families, in just a matter of days, everything they knew was turned upside down. It is there, in the known being turned upside down, that my ministry to bring the Church and the presence of the Divine becomes real.

In an interview with Pope Francis in 2013, the Holy Father was asked about what the Catholic Church needs today. In part, Pope Francis responded by saying: "The thing the church needs most today is the ability to heal wounds and to warm the hearts of the faithful; it needs nearness, proximity. I see the church as a field hospital after battle. It is useless to ask a seriously injured person if he has high cholesterol and about the level of his blood sugars! You have to heal his wounds. Then we can talk about everything else. Heal the wounds, heal the wounds..." (Spadaro 2013, 32-33). This image of the Church as a field hospital has captured the attention and imagination of many; it certainly has expanded my own notion of what I think the Church should be. To believe that the mission of the Church is to heal wounds is something that has guided me as I have served as a COVID anointer. The wounds of those I celebrate the sacrament with are not always visible. Ventilators, oxygen tubes, IV lines, bandages, and gauze all seem to somehow mask the wounds that lie within a patient's body. A seemingly invisible virus has the potential to cause great wounds in the lives of so many.

As a priest, I have had the opportunity to visit the sick many times. Hospitals and nursing homes are not foreign terrain for Catholic priests. Providing pastoral care to the sick is an essential part of a priest's ministry; however, the many restrictions imposed on visitors to patients in hospitals and healthcare facilities during the pandemic has made it almost impossible to perform this sacred ministry. Those of us engaged in this specialized ministry of anointing those with COVID-19 have been afforded unique access into what so many healthcare workers on the front lines are experiencing. In a word, it is overwhelming. The numbers of those contracting the virus, the amount of specialized care required, and the rising numbers of those dying from the virus have pushed healthcare workers, and priests like me, to a place of feeling overwhelmed and exhausted.

It is an interesting reality to admit that while extensive training may prepare one for their role, the lived experience of what one is trained for is often radically different. This pandemic is an experience unlike anything that any of us have ever lived through. Early on healthcare providers were working diligently to understand how the virus spread. Openness to change and a willingness to pivot became expected practices for all of us. The Christian life is meant to be lived in community, yet the pandemic has left people socially distant from one another. The celebration of the sacraments in the Catholic Church are meant to be signs of hope, yet so many family members were not able to be physically present for the prayers of the Anointing of the Sick. Simply put, the overwhelming effects of the pandemic challenged me to recognize the sacred work I was doing in the midst of a great suffering shared by so many.

My hope has been that this ministry of anointing those afflicted with COVID-19 has helped to begin to heal the wounds of family members. One of the things I value most in life and in my ministry is human connection. As human beings we are social creatures. For the vast majority of people, caring for and tending to the needs of a sick loved one are almost innate. Yet, this particular virus, especially early on when so much was so unknown, forced sick patients to be socially isolated from family. While this may be the right decision in order to stop the spread of this virus, it nevertheless inflicted deep wounds on family members who felt emotionally and physically helpless to care for the one they loved. For a family member to feel the guilt and pain of not being present as a loved one dies is a wound that can have lasting effects; yet, knowing the Church was present through the actions of the priest in the celebration of the sacrament might be a balm for that wound. This gives me hope that my ministry and work in this time is making a difference.

As Pope Francis describes the Church as a field hospital, I have felt that our institutions of healing have been like field hospitals during this pandemic. The sheer volume of need placed upon hospital staff sometimes became too much. My experience of ministry in hospitals over the years has shown me that healthcare is fast paced, always with decisions that have potential to steer between life and death. The world has been engaged in a battle against the coronavirus, and the wounds of this battle are real and felt acutely.

The wounds of this virus were not just felt by patients and families, but they were also felt by the brave and dedicated healthcare workers. I have listened as healthcare workers have expressed their fatigue and the feelings of being overwhelmed with all that they see and experience day after day. I willingly stop to pray with healthcare workers who ask, and I listen as those same brave individuals wrestle with their own faith in the face of so much suffering. I am always inspired when I walk into a unit and see nurses, doctors, respiratory therapists, food service and environmental service employees, and so many others working together to provide the best care for their patients. I have been in units when multiple codes are called in quick succession, forcing staff to run from room to room doing their best to give those individuals more time here on this earth. Unfortunately, such heroic efforts are not always successful. I have looked into the faces of nurses who are tired and the only thing I can say is "Thank you." Such a simple statement, but one that I have genuinely meant and one that I have spoken on behalf of many more than just myself. I hope the presence of priests like myself have been a visible sign that healthcare workers are not alone in this work of healing.

Over these months, I have spoken with so many nurses who have been tasked with the difficult job of informing family members that their loved one has died. At times, such calls have had to happen several times in the course of a single shift. Our healthcare workers have been pushed in ways that could not have been previously imagined. To be confronted with so much death over such a long period of time is going to be a chronic effect of this pandemic. There is something truly sacred and humbling about being with someone when they take their final breath in this life. Healthcare workers around the world have enfleshed what true compassion and genuine concern for one's fellow human being ought to look like. Such compassion and concern personified is a true gift. Woundedness is a mark for anyone in helping professions; how one uses their woundedness for the good of others can be a true act of charity. As human beings we have been together in this race of saving lives and caring for one another. I believe the hurt, grief, feelings of not doing enough, and even the tiredness felt by healthcare workers can allow for deeper connection with one's patients. Accepting that one has done all they could is a first step for healing the wounds of our healthcare workers.

As a priest, I have felt these wounds. I am the type of person who likes to be "all in," giving everything I have to that project or person or endeavor. I decided early on that I was going to do as much as I could to keep ministry going, but what I didn't know was how long the pandemic was going to last! During the pandemic my parish's staff and I worked hard to keep people connected, ensure the doors of our food pantry remained open, and looked for creative ways to minister while we were isolated from one another. I reminded my parishioners that being a Christian and Catholic is not simply about coming to church but being church wherever we find ourselves. Being church is about accepting the mission to move beyond the walls of the church; being church is about bringing the love of God into the world. Knowing that almost everyone I anointed later died is a humbling truth I live with. God allows me to stand with those who are very sick, and for some, my face and the face of their nurse is the last that gazed upon them here on this earth. That reality is a blessing, and something that gives me the energy to keep showing up when I am called. Being physically present to those in imminent danger of death from COVID-19 has made me a more loving priest and has been one of the greatest gifts of my priesthood.

Ministry during this time of pandemic has reminded me that the human spirit is resilient. This ministry of anointing those afflicted with COVID-19 powerfully reminds me of this unique and beautiful opportunity I am afforded to share hope. The reason why I was so willing to volunteer for this specialized ministry during the pandemic was because I truly believed that the sick needed the gift and encouragement of the Church in their moment of suffering. The hope I have seen in the eyes of patients has reminded me of how great this gift of faith is. The thank yous I have heard have reminded me the power of presence, the gift of simply showing up. The joy patients have exuded as we have shared in prayer with one another has inspired me. The peacefulness I have experienced while praying with and for those who are unconscious has reminded me that God can connect people in lasting ways. Ministry is about bringing love and compassion into the lived experiences of our sisters and brothers. Each of us, in our own unique ways, share in this important work.

Returning to that question of suffering, this journey of living through a pandemic teaches all of us that while we may not be able to articulate a clear and concise answer, suffering lets us practice compassion. This may be the greatest witness frontline workers have offered during this pandemic: what compassion in action looks like. Our lives will never be void of sickness and suffering, no matter how much we wish it might be otherwise. Every human person must wrestle with this question of suffering and form their own response to it. As a Roman Catholic priest, my answer is rooted in a deep and ancient belief that God is love and that God never abandons God's people, no matter how overwhelming things may become. As a human being connected to others, my response to suffering is to share compassion. Compassion is the deep concern shown for another person's suffering. Here is how we can all share compassion: be present, spread hope, accept your wounds, and believe that healing is possible. The resiliency of the human spirit comes from receiving the gift of compassion. Show compassion, and together we will heal the lasting wounds from this pandemic.

References

Spadaro, Antonio. 2013. *A Big Heart Open to God: A Conversation with Pope Francis*. New York: HarperCollins.

Fr. Matt O'Donnell is a Roman Catholic priest and serves as the Pastor of St. Moses the Black Parish in Chicago. He is the Chairman of the Archdiocese of Chicago's Presbyteral Council. He is an Adjunct Faculty member in the Doctor of Ministry program at the University of St. Mary of the Lake/Mundelein Seminary in Mundelein, IL.

Are You Listening? COVID-19 Realities and Reflections from an Emergency Medicine Physician
By Bradley A. Dreifuss

Originally submitted May 3, 2022

Four months into the start of the COVID-19 pandemic, when the first surge finally hit Arizona, I wrote a guest essay for the New York Times entitled "I'm a Health Care Worker. You Need to Know How Close We are to Breaking" (Dreifuss 2020). That was June 2020. Now, fully two years later, we are no longer "close to breaking," we are broken.

Despite desperately wanting to share the experiences of my colleagues, my own personal account, and our patient interactions, I find long-form writing to be one of my greatest challenges. This is partially due to emotional exhaustion and partially due to feeling that anything I try to formulate into cogent sentences and paragraphs inevitably winds up sounding either trite or flamboyantly dramatic, thereby undermining the very purpose of trying to capture the sentiment of this pandemic. Most of the time I prefer to catalyze and coordinate, to organize community-centered advocacy programs instead of writing as an observer.

What finally moved me to finish articulating my sentiments for a requested submission for this book was witnessing one of our resident physicians progressing from "close to breaking" to broken. We will come back to her story in due course.

November 10th, 2021

As I pick up and re-read a copy of my June 2020 *New York Times* guest essay, my heart thumps in my chest and my face flushes. More than a full year later, little has changed despite the efforts my colleagues and I have made. We have built advocacy teams, taken risks by speaking out against "the establishment," campaigned for robust and evidence-based COVID-19 public health mitigation measures, and co-founded a nonprofit to support healthcare workers during the initial two years of the pandemic. But the impact feels vanishingly small in the face of the collapse of our healthcare system. Our EDs and ICUs have been crushed; our seasoned nursing staff has largely been decimated by moral injury and burnout. As a result, 60 plus patients frequently languish for hours in our overfilled ED waiting rooms. The actual patient rooms are occupied by already-admitted critically ill patients stuck in the ED with no available hospital beds. Or more likely, there is no nursing staff upstairs available to take them. What I can say is that most of us working on the front lines of our EDs, know all too well how Sisyphus must have felt pushing that boulder uphill.

Christmas Day, 2021

In the month that I have been working on this essay, so much has transpired, including my spending nine nights moonlighting as an ICU attending (to help relieve our Critical Care Intensivists who have been run ragged over the last 20 months) and getting a horrific picture of what it is to run a COVID ICU, with 12 to 13 beds occupied at all times by COVID patients in various stages of illness, imminent death, and (at best) years of recovery in their future.

I offer you a glimpse of what the pandemic looked like during my recent ICU shifts:

- People in their 30s are being made "comfort care only" (i.e., no further curative care is possible so we transition our efforts to making them comfortable at the end of their lives – lives cut short by COVID)
- Our smaller hospital is handcuffed from providing more comprehensive palliative/end of life care due to a lack of a formal Palliative Care service
- An overly-stretched resident, fellow, and attending team (Emergency Medicine physicians are moonlighting to assist in tight staffing of overnight ICU shifts for goodness' sake)
- There is a general lack of well-seasoned nurses required to provide the incredibly complex critical care that patients with severe COVID demand
- New grad nurses with fewer than two years of nursing experience are being "thrown to the wolves" with such high acuity, doing the best they can and still feeling terrible that their best isn't enough, thus leading them to quit nursing all together, leading to an ever-worsening nursing shortage
- Nurses with fewer than five years of clinical experience are forced into working as clinical leads and charge nurses, managing entire ICUs.

It is within these intense experiences that I continue to recount and reflect on the little moments where I was able to bear witness to some of the most touching displays of compassion. Catching staff mindfully brushing a patient's hair in attempts to preserve their dignity as they are flipped back and forth from supine to prone in an effort to improve the oxygenation and ventilation of their COVID-racked lungs.

These patients have endotracheal tubes attached to maxed out ventilators. They have large-bore catheters inserted into their necks for dialysis, bridging their needs as their kidneys fail. They often have a second central IV catheter placed, necessary for the multiple medications needed to maintain a high enough blood pressure for adequate perfusion of their brain, kidneys, and heart. Furthermore, flowing from this already multi-lined patient are urinary catheters helping to measure the kidneys' urine output, arterial lines in the wrist or groin, all to ensure accurate measurement of their blood pressure. And of course, there are the rectal tubes for the diarrhea that comes from the lactulose prescribed to address their liver failure and buildup of ammonia that the damaged liver can no longer handle. Most of these patients are medically sedated and often medically paralyzed to allow their bodies to rest and tolerate the incredibly high ventilator settings.

We discuss the goals of care with stunned families awkwardly, like fine-dining restaurant servers, overloaded with plates, walking barefoot on a floor of glass shards. We dance round as gracefully as possible, all the while hiding the internal pain and suffering of our own moral injury and burnout. Anxious family members wait impatiently—praying for the improbable miracle survival and complete recovery of their loved one.

I watched the faces of these family members embrace radical disbelief as they try to put the pieces of this sudden, unforgiving reality together. I could feel their eyes desperately searching for hope in mine. It was evident that they had never entertained the thought that they might one day have to process hearing the words, "multiple organ failure," in relation to their recently healthy family member. I watched their faces as they were forced to abruptly speculate what their ill family member would have considered a "reasonable" quality of life, or what constitutes a dignified existence. Families struggled to make group decisions, often belabored by complicated family dynamics, coupled with the shock of the brutally harsh realities of what COVID can do to otherwise healthy young and middle-aged adults. Frequently layered within these decisions was guilt around what they could have done to better protect against COVID transmission, and the endless uncertainty of what future lay ahead.

These are huge decisions, based on assumptions about what an ill family member might consider a "worthwhile" quality of life, including potential lifelong dependency on a tracheostomy and a ventilator, and likely, a feeding tube. These patients and families enter these decisions innocently oblivious to what might come next. The very long road may lead toward protracted recovery within skilled nursing facilities, where they may die from the complications of COVID-19 ravaging their organ systems and the body's inability to heal from the relative malnutrition that almost always ensues over a long critical and then chronic illness. Who explains the risks of bedsores? Or the conundrum of how to manage the lethal blood clots resulting directly from COVID and the immobility of critical illness with the concurrent increased risk of gastro-intestinal or intracranial bleeding from the blood thinners we use to prevent or treat the clotting?

What about the mental and emotional damage of acute illness? And the total upending of families' understanding of a patient's personal and professional identities? Or the impacts this illness and these decisions will have on their families, friends, and community? Our community members, patients, their families – they cannot imagine what a severe case of COVID can do, and they sure as hell can't wrap their minds around the cost of care, in the hospital or over the long-term. Consideration for these questions and the insights they lead to don't often occur until it is too late. By then, they or their family member are sick, needing life-saving care in the ED and the ICU.

Almost five months later / May 3, 2022

She was having the ultimate human moment – breaking down in tears of frustration over our hospital's lack of proper staffing and resources, forcing this resident physician to assume responsibility for providing suboptimal care for the critically ill patients I needed to admit from our ED.

This happened on a very busy night shift in our ED, with barely a skeleton crew of four nurses for approximately 20 patients, four of whom were ICU-admitted patients waiting for a bed to open in one of our two hospitals. The 12-bed ICU was already full and had minimal nursing staff.

The second-year internal medicine resident admitting patients to the medical/surgical wards had called me (the ED attending) to inquire why a patient needed to be on her service and not the ICU. While the patient would qualify for a medical step-down bed in pre-COVID times, we were working under federal and state crisis standards of care and the wards were taking sicker patients than usual.

I could sense the tension and anxiety of the distressed, overworked, and under-resourced resident physician, as she expressed her frustration of not having enough nursing and clinical support to care for the patients on the wards. With noble intentions, she called to make suggestions for what was needed for optimal patient care, not realizing she was preaching to the choir. Her voice was quivering with frustration, anger, guilt, and moral injury, simply because she cared so deeply about every patient deserving optimal care for their illness. She was being forced into a situation where she could not provide that optimal level of care. She was trying to shoulder the responsibility for the crisis level of care, but like all of us, she had no agency, and no recourse. We can only do what we can do in these sub-optimal settings of critically ill patients being met with predictable and preventable shortage of workforce and resources.

This resident is committed to a covenant, of one of the several oaths we vow to honor as we provide medical care (e.g., Hippocratic Oath, Oath of Geneva, or a more modern version a medical school class collectively composes). This is a commitment taken to heart by our physician colleagues (History of Medicine Division 2012, Lasagna 1964). These values typically extend to the entire healthcare staff, who largely entered the noble profession of medicine to care for those in need, the sick, and the injured. However, we have been thwarted in our ability to practice medicine up to the standards we know are appropriate or that we would want for our family, friends, and community members.

The healthcare system is crumbling, leaving our residents and medical students stripped of their innocence and passion for the profession as they witness and experience this collapse. The COVID-19 pandemic serves as the catalyst of a rapid implosion of a system that has (de)-volved secondary to perverse corporate priorities over the last 40 years, priorities that place investor, shareholder, and corporate leadership profits above patient and community benefit (Schulte 2022, Berry et al. 2021). Most do not fully consider that the reason our present-day American healthcare system is failing to prioritize patients and communities is that it was never designed to do so. Instead, it was carefully engineered to achieve the outcome of redirecting public and private funds to third party corporations that extract, exploit, and confiscate resources that should be directed to the physician-patient focus of healthcare. We see this in the growth of revenue of pharmacy benefit managers, group purchasing organizations, private equity backed for-profit staffing and revenue-driven hospital systems (Mass 2020).

The resident, teary-eyed, her voice filled with anger, frustration, and sadness, had clearly not felt the psychological safety to speak up prior to this night, to articulate her pain of being foiled in her ability to care for patients. Why is this the case? As a faculty member, I personally struggle to identify ways to increase the psychological safety for our team members to speak up about their concerns, especially in ways that can help generate meaningful change. The struggle comes from the reality that most anyone who is not "towing the line" can be labeled as "not being a team player" and be censured by program or hospital leadership for voicing concerns about sub-optimal clinical staffing and resources. So, yes, naturally, most members of the team withdraw, holding their proverbial tongues and fall in line to prevent potential professional consequences. In the process, they suffer deeply from moral distress and unyielding weariness which often leads to burnout.

There are additional barriers especially for our marginalized residents, e.g., those who are foreign medical graduates who are working on visas that are dependent on their employers' approval and support, as was the case with this empathetic and thoughtful resident. Even faculty, like me, struggle to identify ways to support and empower our residents in ways that can guarantee their psychological and professional safety if they speak up. The hard truth is that they remain at the mercy of our employer's good will, thereby frequently stifled in their ability to advocate for the best interests of their patients and clinical team members.

That is where we faculty must step up and lean in. We must strive to create and support psychological safety in our clinical spaces so that we can nourish a positive learning and clinical care environments.

I stepped out of our physician work room with the resident on the other end of the phone and held space for an empathetic ear. Validating her frustration and acknowledging her moral distress, I made a point of rejecting her apologies for her self-described "unprofessional behavior." I gently offered that there is nothing unprofessional about being human, empathetic in intent, and frustrated by systemic barriers hindering her from trying her level best to provide optimal care in a setting of suboptimal staffing and resources. There is neither room, nor the time, for shaming and blaming. We need compassion, action, and resolution. We must collectively create a healthcare environment that encourages open constructive dialogue such that we can then move onto collective problem-solving to bring about change where it is needed most.

It's been almost 26 months that I have been living the front lines of the COVID-19 pandemic as an attending emergency medicine physician with my faculty colleagues, residents, students and nursing, allied health, and facilities teams. On many levels it's felt like a "dumpster fire." Nay, it's more akin to a recurrent nightmare of watching metaphorical slow-moving burning trains crash into our barely functioning healthcare system, leaving our marginalized communities with the disproportionate burden of death and destruction. Healthcare safety nets and public health infrastructure have been undermined by politicians fighting for illusory control and businesses prioritizing corporate over human interests. Most healthcare workers' energies are spent in survival mode, caring for family, and sometimes self. In the US, one in five healthcare workers have left the field since the pandemic started (Yong 2021, Sinsky et al. 2021).

Sublimation has been the coping mechanism of choice for some of us, doing what we can to highlight and articulate the realities of COVID-19, while illuminating the tragic impact of failing to mitigate the predictable waves of COVID-19 in our local and global communities. We work clinically; we organize family, friends, and community members into community-based non-profit advocacy and service organizations; we conduct research, and we grow our advocacy efforts and skills. Yet, politicization and intentional mis/dis-information often leave us feeling that such advocacy efforts are Sisyphean too.

And yet. We choose to pick ourselves up, dust off our white coats, and move forward. We will continue working with colleagues across professional disciplines to develop tools that empower current teams, trainees, and future frontline healthcare workers to work in supportive environments. We will encourage community members to take an active and informed role in their health and rebuilding of our healthcare systems. We will strive to live up to our professional oaths and personal moral compasses. Time will tell how successful we were.

References

Berry, Leonard, Sunjay Letchuman, Nandini Ramani, and Paul Barach. 2021. "The High Stakes of Outstanding Health Care". *Mayo Clinic Proceedings*. August 16, 2021. https://www.mayoclinicproceedings.org/article/S0025-6196(21)00512-7/fulltext#secsectitle0050

Dreifuss, Bradley. "I'm a Health Care Worker. You Need to Know How Close We are to Breaking". *New York Times*. June 26, 2020. https://www.nytimes.com/2020/06/26/opinion/coronavirus-arizona-hospitals.html

History of Medicine Division, National Library of Medicine, and National Institutes of Health. 2012. "'I Swear by Apollo Physician...': Greek Medicine from the Gods to Galen". *Greek Medicine*. https://www.nlm.nih.gov/hmd/greek/greek_oath.html

Lasagna, Louis. 1964. "The Hippocratic Oath: Modern Version". *PBS*. https://www.pbs.org/wgbh/nova/doctors/oath_modern.html

Mass, Marion. 2020. "Meet the GPOs: Scrubs vs. Suits – the Battle Inside the Nations' Hospitals – Part 2". *Practicing Physicians of America*. May 6, 2020. https://practicingphysician.org/scrubs-vs-suits-the-battle-inside-the-nations-hospitals-part-2/

Schulte, Fred. 2022. "Sick Profit: Investigating Private Equity's Stealthy Takeover of Health Care Across Cities and Specialties". *KFF Health News*. November 14, 2022. https://kffhealthnews.org/news/article/private-equity-takeover-health-care-cities-specialties/

Sinsky, Christine A., Roger L. Brown, Martin J. Stillman, and Mark Linzer. 2021. "COVID-Related Stress and Work Intentions in a Sample of US Health Care Workers". *Mayo Clinic* 5(6): 1165-117. https://doi.org/10.1016/j.mayocpiqo.2021.08.007

Yong, Ed. 2021. "Why Health-Care Workers are Quitting in Droves". *The Atlantic*. November 16, 2021. https://www.theatlantic.com/health/archive/2021/11/the-mass-exodus-of-americas-health-care-workers/620713/

Bradley Dreifuss is a passionate advocate for the well-being of healthcare workers. As an Assistant Professor of Emergency Medicine and Public Health at the University of Arizona, he led a trans-disciplinary effort to develop a new model for community-based pandemic preparedness and support of frontline healthcare workers and their families (HCW HOSTED,

Inc). Dr. Dreifuss has made a wide range of media appearances and has written multiple op-ed articles for media outlets, including The New York Times, where he emphasized the urgent need for COVID-19 mitigation and prioritization of healthcare worker well-being during the COVID-19 pandemic, and beyond.

View from the Emergency Department Social Worker
By Kelly Pabilonia

Originally submitted October 30, 2020

One of the biggest and most difficult jobs I do as a Level I trauma, inner city, Emergency Department social worker is to support families. In March 2020, our Emergency Department stopped visitations for all patients. The COVID-19 Pandemic crisis was a challenge to what we social workers normally provide for support to the patient, families, doctors, and amazing colleagues with whom we serve. When no visitors were allowed at hospitals for the safety of the staff, other patients, and people in the community whom these visitors might infect, we social workers did our best work to create new solutions to provide for everyone and to keep our community together.

Before the pandemic, I would call family into the hospital and support them while our doctors and nurses gave them updates, after they completed x-rays, CT scans, labs or assessments. I would facilitate visitation with patients and loved ones. Sadly, when patients died before COVID, I would facilitate death notifications with doctors and stay by their side while they viewed the body of their loved one, called other family members, and processed the initial shock for often up to two hours. I got to know the patients and families and walked them out of the hospital toward their cars. They often hugged me goodbye and thanked me. It is challenging but rewarding to be a guide to them on their grief journey or such a difficult day. The process of helping families in their journeys provides me with an incredible amount of job satisfaction and reward.

In March of 2020, I remember our first Emergency Department death. The family wasn't allowed in the hospital. I met the family outside and quickly did an assessment to find out who the patient's legally authorized representative was. I then facilitated a death notification outside the entrance of our hospital with the attending physician. The family was in shock and grieving. Security was with me and we shared a look, that was the look was of empathy for this family, support to each other, and shock that this was the "new norm" of how death notifications would happen for a while. None of the family members wore masks. I felt vulnerable talking to them. It was difficult to do what I am used to doing without the usual comforts, e.g., Kleenex, coffee, and a warm place to sit. Some family members stayed too close to me and made me fear for my own COVID exposure; others screamed and could not be contained outside and spread out across the hospital's front lawn: others understood and were able to allow me to support them in this new distant way.

It was hard to establish trust when families couldn't see how hard we had worked to save their loved one's life. They didn't see the mess that a room is post-cardiac arrest code; a visual and physical marker of hard-working staff discarding things on the floor as they feverishly work to save a life. They did not get to see their loved one's body lying in a bed, which helps with denial, a common first grief reaction. It was so much harder to establish rapport with a family member who does not see this and does not believe what I am saying, does not believe that we tried to save their loved one, and now does not believe I am not letting them in the building. It was so hard to tell them – outside on the sidewalk – such private, personal information that their loved one had died, expecting them to go home and process this or stay briefly for me to support them on the sidewalk. I worked so hard to be compassionate and in the moment. Distracted by the fact that I was cold (without a coat on), or I was getting wet (in the rain outside), or bringing COVID back to my families (as they were yelling so close to me without a mask while expressing their grief). Normally I like to sit with families and let them go through the range of emotions from anger, denial, sadness, to acceptance. The experience we have surrounding a death follows us and can work towards a healthy grief process or a dysfunctional, complicated grief process.

With every death notification, I experience my own sadness. That is why it is therapeutic for me to know I helped, which sentiment families usually express to me as I walk them to the exit. In the beginning, I truly missed when families would hug me goodbye after I supported them for hours. The new norm was me finally retreating to the hospital saying my condolences and goodbyes while they stood there not ready to walk away to their cars without seeing their loved ones one more time to say goodbye. Security took on a larger role to support and watch that families eventually made their way back to their cars and didn't block ED entrances.

As time went on and we had more PPE, we were able to facilitate limited viewing or visitation for families. The new challenges involved deciding who could or who could not visit. It was a struggle for every social worker in our department, on every floor, to authorize visitor exceptions. Each area from the trauma ICU to the maternity ward, the oncology floors to the Emergency Department, had distinct considerations to assess prior to allowing anyone to visit. Exceptions were often made for end-of-life patients once we had enough PPE. However, in the beginning if the patients were COVID positive, we still didn't allow end-of-life visits and the patients died without their loved ones by their side. I was often on call and woken up at 3AM by a resident doctor requesting a visitor exception. It was hard to get back to sleep after I made the heart-wrenching decision to enforce the hospital policy, telling the doctor that, "No, the daughter can't see her dying or deceased mother since mom is/was COVID positive."

That sticks with you, the vision of people dying alone. We staff know they were not alone. They were in the busy intensive care units surrounded by many staff and noises, just not with their loved ones, their wife, their daughter, brother or dad. We do not want that for ourselves, we don't want that for our loved ones, and we didn't want this for our patients either.

The difficulty of making this decision was often compounded by the fact that the patient may have been at a skilled nursing facility for the past month and family hadn't been able to visit them there. Then the news was informing us that families were unable to go to funeral homes to see their loved ones for wakes or funerals as well. We had people begging us to let them see their loved ones thinking this would be the only opportunity. "Please, please," they would beg, "I haven't seen my husband in four weeks, please let me hold his hand one more time." The toll it took on staff to make those decisions daily was mentally exhausting.

Policies were for all visitors regardless of where you worked. I found it challenging to tell employees they couldn't visit loved ones during off hours. I was a fierce advocate for employees to be able to visit their loved ones when they were in the hospital since they are familiar with proper PPE use and because they are continually around patients as essential employees when working full time. However, sometimes it was necessary for even hospital employees to be denied the ability to visit their loved ones due to COVID safety policies in place.

Recently a cancer patient shared with me how lonely it was to be a COVID patient. He was on COVID precautions earlier this year since he was positive for the virus. He said his family wasn't allowed to visit and so many auxiliary staff at the hospital didn't visit him either. He felt all alone and the worst part of his hospital stay was cold food. The Food and Nutrition services would leave his food tray outside his room waiting for the next available staff – nurse, doctor or personal care attendant – who needed to enter his room gowned to bring it to him. When he relived how difficult it was to be prevented from seeing his family, not knowing 'how much time longer he had left' and described the experience of being fed cold food, my heart ached for him. No one wants our final days to be like that, no one. But it was the safest way to protect auxiliary staff at the hospital. Every day we make choices weighing how to be both kind and safe.

As time went on, the Social Work Department bought technology to assist with communication with families. I found it rewarding to be able to facilitate communication via video calls for adult children to see their parents. Families appreciated being able to talk to patients and see with their own eyes time how a patient was speaking, looking, or feeling. New challenges were created with the inclusion of technology. As social workers we were now facilitating updates to spouses over the phone rather than in person, and working with the limits of technology to communicate, understand, empathize, and support families remotely. Social workers became the conduit for communication between doctors and nurses and families to provide more detailed updates via phone. We also assisted with doctors talking to legally authorized representatives to get permission for treatments. The past practices of sitting with a family, reading their expressions, and giving them time to express their emotions were now done in a digitally remote mode that challenged our skills to listen and support families. I definitely feel that, during COVID, finding safe and caring ways to support families has been challenging and rewarding.

Families became creative as time went on too. Adjacent is a photo of what I imagine to be two daughters visiting their father. For about a week straight every morning when I came to work I would see them sitting in their own personal chairs, drinking coffee, and talking to their father on the second floor. It was a powerful expression of their love for their father.

New COVID precautions include not only face masks but eye shields too. This has a way of creating a distance between staff and patients and families. Part of my being a good social worker has always been my empathetic listening skills and non-verbal communication. With families being unable to see my smile or my frown, I worry about establishing the same level of rapport with patients. With a covered face and no ability to have a sympathetic smile, I second guess interactions with families and patients. I am conscious of maintaining a six-feet distance, securing my PPE, and monitoring their proper PPE use. Many times, I weigh the effects of my gently asking a son who is grieving the loss of his mother, who pulled his mask down to dry his eyes and blow his nose, to pull the mask back up while I am supporting and counseling him through a death notification. It is hard to make daily choices whether to protect myself or to do what seems like the most empathetic behavior. This instinct, to protect myself, was another challenge during this pandemic.

Early, before meetings were canceled and masks were made mandatory, several of my social worker colleagues and a security guard who works in the Emergency Department tested positive for COVID. We clearly saw that all hospital employees were at risk, not only the direct care staff like doctors, nurses, and respiratory therapists. We were reminded daily of the number of patients who had COVID and given new policies and regulations for all staff in order to protect us, patients, and the greater community. It was hard to keep up with all the new information and changes, and emotionally draining to be on the front lines watching the crisis grow and friends and colleagues get sick from COVID-19.

My family had concerns I would expose them to COVID. We took precautions at home and had a plan to quarantine me if I was exposed or tested positive to protect the rest of my family. I also suffered personally, since friends avoided me. They refused to get together with me to do activities we had done together prior to COVID, like running or hiking. They honestly admitted because of my job I was high risk and therefore they needed to avoid spending time with me. I found having less support from my friends, compounded by the information overload from emails, news updates and policy changes, was overwhelming at times. I learned early on to get outside as much as possible. Every day, sometimes two times per day, I would walk, bike, run, hike and eventually swim and kayak. The fresh air, sunshine and ability to stop thinking about the pandemic, if even for 30 minutes per day, was an invaluable self-care technique.

I have confidence that PPE works, as I have been working full time in the Emergency Department full time for eight months now, and still haven't tested positive for COVID. I hope society continues to use PPE and we develop a safe vaccine for COVID-19 soon. Working through this pandemic as an essential employee has been challenging and overwhelming at times but I feel appreciated and grateful to be still working and helping others during a global crisis. I have learned ways to adjust and still provide needed support to patients and families.

Kelly received a BSW from Eastern Connecticut State University, and her MSW from University of Connecticut. She is also a LCSW. She has been working at Hartford Hospital since 2004. She works full time in the Emergency Department. In this role, she provides support to patients experiencing domestic violence, elder and child abuse/neglect, homelessness, substance abuse, conservatorship, and financial crisis. She provides counseling to individuals and families. She responds to the psychosocial needs of patients and families, including assessment, intervention, treatment planning, and referrals to community agencies. She also assists doctors and patients with end-of-life issues.

Reflections from My Time as a Hotel Doctor – How a Navajo Community Inspired Me During the Pandemic
By Robin Goldman

Originally submitted March 13, 2021 (reflecting on Spring-Fall 2020)

We start each day standing at the trunks of our cars in a motel parking lot along Route 66, on the border of the Navajo Nation. We are here to see patients, many who are Navajo, quarantining or isolating due to COVID-19. Our trunks serve as our supply room. We put on our personal protective equipment and gather the other supplies we need for the day. On windy days, I use a binder clip to pin the bottom of my gown together so it doesn't fly up, potentially dispersing COVID-19 droplets. I learn quickly that many aspects of caring for patients, including our disposable gowns, weren't designed for the outdoors. Most days I am paired with a partner who stays "clean" while I examine patients. She takes notes, pours sanitizer on my hands, grabs various supplies out of a canvas bag, makes calls to coordinate care, and much more. We've adapted, not only to what is needed to care for patients with COVID-19, but also to delivering healthcare outside of hospitals and clinics. We've found a way to care for patients that is more connected with, and more supported by, the community in which they live. It focuses on their needs as human beings and is the reason I keep coming back.

The Navajo have strong kinship structures and typically live with multiple generations of extended family, which has strengthened communities in the face of generations of oppression. It has always brought a smile to my face to hear from my Navajo friends and colleagues about what they learned from living with their grandparents and growing up in the same household as their cousins. But close quarters have served as tinder for a contagious virus. In the midst of the initial outbreak of COVID-19, the Navajo Nation people and government mobilized rapidly to limit the spread of the virus: mandating masks, increasing testing, and limiting movement while delivering food and water to the community. The Navajo Nation is 25,000 square miles – bigger than West Virginia – and many residents live hours away from a healthcare center or clinic. Frequent follow-up is difficult and getting to the emergency room quickly can be challenging.

It became clear early in the pandemic that people needed places away from home where they could safely quarantine or isolate. For some, this separation, while difficult, would decrease the risk of spread to their families. For others, isolating closer to a healthcare facility allowed for their condition to be monitored more closely than was possible at home. To address these needs, local healthcare systems, community organizations, and hotels and motels collaborated on a program known as the hotel-motel program, or "hot-mot" for short. Through the program, patients who needed to isolate or quarantine could stay in rooms in hotels and motels left empty from the decrease in travel. A team of medical assistants, nurses, doctors, community volunteers—and, increasingly over time, generous hotel/motel staff provided monitoring and support. Thanks to a pre-existing relationship between Gallup healthcare providers and a fellowship training program with which I work*, I started coming to Gallup for hot-mot volunteer stints in May 2020, joining the team as one of the physicians seeing patients in their motel rooms.

Once we've put on all our gear from our car-trunk supply rooms, we begin knocking on doors. Before the pandemic, when I sat with my patients, I could show my emotions through facial expressions. Now we've learned other ways to signal that we care. We stand in the doorway, keeping our distance. I hand patients a pulse oximeter, have them walk around their room and ask them to tell me the numbers they see. I listen to patients' lungs selectively, only when I think it's absolutely necessary, in order to decrease my exposure. I struggle to convey my emotions under a face shield, two layers of masks, a hair covering, and a gown. I'm left with slightly muffled words and gestures to convey my thoughts.

Despite these barriers, I feel that I get to know my patients better than I would in a hospital or clinic. It feels easier to center care around their needs. While seeing people in the motel isn't quite the same as seeing them in their homes, I get a deeper glimpse into who they are at the motel than I would have in the hospital. At each visit, one older woman shows me the project she had worked on the day before, some days creating earrings and bracelets, other days crocheting. We chat about her family and her home. She says quarantining is hard. She asks if I can get a bag out of her car that has more beading supplies since she is not allowed to leave her room.

For many patients, art is an important part of their lives. They ask for

---

* UCSF's HEAL Initiative, https://healinitiative.org

pencils and paper and spend their time drawing and show me beautiful drawings the next day. Some of the artwork conveyed something personal, and some of it conveyed the beauty of their people, ancestry, and the world around them. They share how their ability to share or sell their work had disappeared with the pandemic—there were no community events; stores and roadside stands were closed; and tourism was almost non-existent. During this phase of the pandemic, only the few of us who passed by their rooms had the opportunity to see what they had created. In the hospital, I rarely see these glimpses into people's lives. Providing art supplies is not a typical therapeutic intervention, but maybe it should be.

From the very beginning, the hotel and motel staff became an essential part of the medical team, dedicating themselves to the program in a way that far exceeded their job descriptions. Four motels went from serving prepackaged continental breakfasts to providing three meals a day for more than a hundred patients at a time. Motel staff helped patients manage their symptoms, dispensing Tylenol and other over-the-counter medications. They tracked information about patients at the level of detail typical of nurses in the hospital: in the morning they would recount to us which patient got which medication when, what patients called the front desk for during the night, which patients didn't pick up all their meals the day prior. The manager of two of the motels shared with pride each time she made the food options more creative, for example a change from instant ramen to spaghetti bolognese. They approached their new roles with dedication, enthusiastically learning new skills, and repurposing existing ones.

The hotel and motel staff got to know the patients during their time there, much better than we could, which was particularly important in understanding the emotional needs of our patients. One older man had been in the hotel for weeks. Even though he was no longer contagious, he had become debilitated enough that it was hard to find him a safe place to go, as he needed more support than before his illness. The medical team checked on him every few days to see how he was doing and help manage some of his chronic conditions. Most afternoons, he would open his door, pull a chair up to the doorway and chat with the staff. One day, they told me he hadn't been opening his door and had failed to pick up several meals; patterns that I would have missed on my own. After a fair amount of knocking, I convinced him to open the door, revealing a concerning number of uneaten meals. He was so weak from being sick, I tried to explain that eating was an important part of his recovery. He told me that he was tired of being in the motel and would only eat Navajo food. I sensed how lonely and homesick he had become. The next day I picked up some lamb stew and brought it to him, and we chatted while he ate. I heard about his hopes for the future; what he felt his family should do for him now that he was older and required more care; what was unrealistic to expect of them. For all of us, relationships with our loved ones can be complicated and he had had a lot of time in the hotel to reflect and realize the importance of his relationships. We all are seeing effects of isolation from COVID-19 in many different aspects of society. I believe that by having the hotel and program staff spend time and listen to him, the effects of isolation were a little less than they would have been otherwise.

The dedication of the community extends far beyond the hotel staff. Multiple community members have volunteered and continue to volunteer to drive patients to the hospital for tests or other things that we were unable to do at the motels. Others pick up medications and deliver them to the motels. One community organization provides clothes, toiletries, and basic things that patients might need during an unexpected stay. They also staff a 24-hour hotline for people staying at the motels to call if they needed anything. People from the health center checked in on patients and helped with program coordination, in addition to their usual jobs. During a lull in cases, there were fewer patients in the motels and thus fewer people were needed to see patients, which coincided with clinics re-opening. Several medical assistants and nurses told me they missed the motel work, particularly how they were able to support and help patients from their own communities. Before my time with the hotel-motel program, I had never seen different parts of a health center and community come together like this.

In the midst of this pandemic, this program gave me the opportunity to practice a different kind of medicine, one that meets patients where they are and figures out what they really need. For some, that may mean medications or supplemental oxygen; for others that may mean someone to talk to, connections to programs and resources; and for others that may simply mean a place to stay. One patient, who lacked consistent housing, came in for multiple quarantine stays due to repeated risk of COVID-19 exposure. He summed up the value of the program concisely: "I really appreciate what you all are doing. I'm going to stay here until I can get back on my feet."

Helping people get back on their feet, in a broad sense, is what healthcare should be about. We talk a lot about patient-centered care in our healthcare system, and typically that means having a multi-disciplinary team of healthcare workers or encouraging improvements in listening and communication skills, both of which are important. But the hotel-motel program has felt like something beyond a mere improvement in existing systems. It demonstrated to me the power of healthcare provided by a whole community working together. Occasionally a straightforward medical intervention is all that is needed, but more often a patient will need a safe place to stay, a meal, or an extra person stopping by to see how they're doing during a difficult time. In addition to helping decrease the spread of COVID-19 and providing direct care to patients, the hotel-motel program gave us a chance to work in a different way, one that treats patients more as human beings that are part of a community. I've come away from the experience feeling that medicine should always work like this.

Robin Goldman is a physician who is passionate about improving healthcare for marginalized populations. She volunteered in the Navajo Nation during the COVID-19 pandemic and previously worked in Haiti with Zanmi Lasante (Partners in Health). As an associate professor at UCSF, she serves as Director of Evaluation for the HEAL Initiative, which is a health equity program dedicated to training and transforming frontline healthcare workers in underserved areas globally. Currently, she works clinically as an internal medicine hospitalist at the San Francisco VA Medical Center and as a pediatric hospitalist at Washington Hospital in Fremont, California.

Part II: Support

Dispatches from the First COVID Surge: The Creation of the Spanish Language Care Group
By Joseph R. Betancourt

Originally submitted on March 9, 2022

Being at Mass General Hospital (MGH) for twenty years and dedicating my career to health disparities, health equity, and diversity, while also serving as a primary care doctor, was a dream come true for me. Originally from Puerto Rico, the challenges I tackle come from a deeply personal space, informed by lived experiences, passion, and commitment. Helping lead Mass General Brigham's Equity and Community Health COVID Response, however, was the challenge, opportunity, and privilege of a lifetime and I was so fortunate to do it with so many across our system who were equally dedicated to this work. Here is a bit of my, and our, story, and some things that will be both the hardest, and proudest moments of my life.

March 8, 2020

We had been hearing about COVID for months. It was scary, but like so many things in life, there was a general, and absolutely false, sense of security, built on the notion that "we are different, it'll never happen here, it'll never happen to me". Call it hope, one's need to believe for self-preservation, hubris, or our sense of "exceptionalism" – or some combination of all of these – that had taken hold. Despite having been at MGH for 18 years, I was fairly new in my role as Vice President and Chief Equity and Inclusion Officer. For about the last eight months, we had been building a new team, a new set of structures and committees and were just about to host a large retreat of equity leaders across MGH at a local waterfront hotel. This was the culmination of so much work and it was just a week away. The weekend was a typical spring weekend, cold as per usual in Boston, and in my spare moments I became transfixed by social media and dispatches from Italy.

Tweets from doctors across that country were sounding the alarm about COVID, how it was overwhelming them, how it was spreading, and how it was deadly. Photos, testimonials, videos, pleas for help and warnings to the world were flooding in. Finally, it began to seem real to me; it was setting in, that this was real. The one thing I did know is that history has taught us that natural and man-made disasters always disproportionately impact vulnerable populations. Initial research demonstrated that patients with chronic conditions like diabetes or asthma would likely have poorer outcomes if they contracted COVID. Minority populations have long suffered from significant disparities in these and other conditions. Given that my life's work is identifying and addressing disparities, I knew what was coming for the communities for whom I cared deeply. I didn't know exactly how it would play out, but I knew it wouldn't be good.

March 11, 2020

The work week began as usual, but as the week moved on, and it was time for our routine leadership meetings, the decision was made to move it to a larger venue so there could be a greater "distance" between us. The topic of that meeting became, quite simply, "Was it time to begin to make some big changes to our operations, including limiting elective surgery and other non-critical activities both to prepare for the arrival of COVID and to protect our patients and our workforce?" By this time, the first cases of COVID from the Biogen Conference had arrived and been quietly managed at MGH. There was no doubt that COVID was here and that we were starting to mobilize, move fast, and make some hard decisions. As the week went on, we decided to cancel our retreat. This was a difficult decision, but it was clear that we were moving from denial, to acknowledgement, to taking dramatic actions.

March 12, 2020

Going to my office, into which we had just literally moved, now began to seem strange. We were always moving, always in action, and now there was this impending sense of the unknown, but also a need to do something. The CDC had just started to develop documents on COVID in multiple languages on their website. There was also information emerging on other websites. The one thing we knew we could do quickly was to try to help the vulnerable community within our walls—our diverse workforce of essential workers who didn't have access to information via email as we did, and certainly not in their languages. We contacted our colleagues from Nutrition and Food Services, Environmental Services, and Materials Management, offering to speak to their workforce about what we knew about COVID, and how they could protect themselves. I would start by doing this in English and Spanish, but we quickly recruited other doctors who conducted similar sessions for these employees in Haitian Creole and Arabic as well, the predominant languages spoken by these service lines. These sessions would happen in the cafeteria, in the kitchen, in small conference rooms, in the hallways ... anywhere we could gather employees to do it. Employees were concerned, had a lot of questions, and we were off on our journey.

March 16, 2020

I'd been asked to help lead the Mass General Brigham COVID Equity and Community Health effort. I assembled a small but amazing team of colleagues. We met daily, sometimes twice a day, to craft our plans. Our MGH Hospital Incident Command was also meeting daily, led by Ann Prestipino, who was a leader of a caliber I had never seen before—organized, decisive, focused, able to prioritize and manage multiple challenges at warp speed. As we were just getting rolling in the early days, I thought it would be important to create a "multilingual registry," especially since it was clear we would need to do some major redeployment of all staff to meet the impending needs of the pandemic. Our plan was to put out a call to all those in our workforce who could speak another language and who could speak to non-English-speaking patients to meet the needs of our diverse populations. I didn't know quite yet how the need would emerge, and how we would operationalize it. As a native-Spanish speaking primary care doctor myself who cares for a large Spanish-speaking patient population, I had a unique window into the importance of cultural and linguistic competence, and how it would be essential to all of our needs.

March 30, 2020

Over the last two weeks, the COVID inpatient numbers had slowly begun to climb. We had put various workstreams in place and had built equity into everything we were doing. The week prior, I began to receive texts and emails from my colleagues in the MGH Emergency Department sharing that it seemed almost every other patient who had COVID, or had been intubated, was Spanish-speaking. Ditto for the surge floors and the Intensive Care Unit. Since we collect race/ethnicity and language data on all our patients and prepare an Annual Report on Equity in Healthcare Quality as a tool to measure our performance, we quickly moved to quantify these observations.

As we soon discovered, these alarming observations from those on the ground proved to be true. A large and disproportionate number of our COVID inpatients were Latinx and Spanish-speaking, from our surrounding communities like Chelsea, Revere, and East Boston. The same day the official data came in, I decided to do walk rounds on the surge floors to see how we were managing those patients with limited-English proficiency (LEP). MGH has a strong and proud Interpreter Services Department that just a year prior had delivered over 140,000 interpreter visits via live, video, and telephonic interpretation. With COVID however, and the desire to preserve personal protective equipment and keep "non-essential" workers out of the hospital, it became clear that we weren't managing those with LEP well. On the floors I heard people were trying to do their best—using their iPhone apps to interpret and using family members, and even, in some cases using children via FaceTime. This last method was against our ethos and unacceptable in normal times, but the care teams were just trying to do anything they could to manage the crisis in front of them. That night I couldn't sleep. We needed to do something. Our community was being decimated by COVID, and when patients with LEP were admitted, not only did they have to fight COVID, they had to fight to communicate, to understand their caregivers, and to be understood. This was just too much to take amidst all the suffering. Action was needed.

April 4, 2020

I woke up this Saturday morning racking my brain on how we could do a better job caring for our Spanish-speaking COVID patients. By this point, they comprised 40% of our COVID inpatients. I was in the shower thinking, ruminating, and thought that at a minimum I could start rounding with the surge teams so I could help bridge the language gap. As I played with this idea in my head it slowly started to hit me. Since we had put together a multilingual registry, what if we culled the list for native Spanish-speaking physicians to assess their willingness to help? I figured many were sidelined due to COVID since we had shut down many services such as surgery, pediatrics, etc., and they were either being redeployed or had been redeployed already. Why not take advantage of their bilingual capacity as an asset, and redeploy them to assist with Spanish-speaking patients? Somehow we could organize ourselves to provide care across the hospital. It was time to explore quickly what was possible, but undoubtedly this was the day the idea of a "Spanish Language Care Group" – or SLCG – was born.

April 10, 2020

We spent the entire week working on building and operationalizing the SLCG. We started by putting out a call to the native Spanish-speaking doctors from the Multilingual Registry that we had developed, asking if they would be willing to help us care for Spanish-speaking COVID inpatients. An incredible 51 native Spanish-speaking doctors, from 15 clinical disciplines, and representing 15 Latin-American countries, answered the call. The range spanned from a renowned Professor of Surgery, to a junior faculty member in Pediatrics, to an Orthopedic Resident—and everything in-between. They were ready to serve their community in any way possible.

We worked furiously with an incredible team – Elena Olson from our MGH Center for Diversity and Inclusion – who was our backbone and quarterback of our effort, along with Warren Chuang and Steven Knuesel from the Hospital Medicine Group, the key operational masterminds who were the architects of the SLCG. We constructed a work plan that included the need for seven doctors during the day from seven AM to seven PM, four doctors at night from seven PM to seven AM and a doctor in the Emergency Department – amounting to 24/7 coverage – all working shoulder-to-shoulder with the surge teams, covering all floors. On this night we held an introductory Zoom for the group, to explain the process, answer questions, and come together as the SLCG.

To say it was inspiring was an understatement. I have never been prouder in my career to stand with my Spanish-speaking peers, willing to put themselves at risk, with all the unknowns of COVID at the time, to assure that at every bedside of a Spanish-speaking COVID patient there would be a Spanish-speaking doctor with the surge team providing clinical, cultural and linguistic competence for the encounter. Within just six days, we had built the first iteration of the SLCG, and the sign-up Google Doc was almost full with two to three weeks coverage in just a couple of days. All SLCG members were ready, fearless, excited for the challenge, and the full launch was just days away. Never a prouder day in my life.

April 13, 2020

On this day the SLCG evolved from an idea to a reality. The first seven physicians staffed the daytime surge teams, making themselves available, each covering several floors. Demand was limited, as the surge teams weren't fully aware of who we were and what we had to offer. On that first evening, as the day team closed out their shift, and the night shift was coming on, we all gathered in one of the hospital coffee shops to share notes, encourage each other, and commiserate. I remember clearly as I was about to embark on the evening shift sharing text messages with Juan Matute, a Colombian pediatric intensive care physician. Although we had never met, we had a shared common purpose, a shared sense of commitment, and a dedication to each other and to our community. Juan hadn't taken care of adults for years, but he was ready to do all he could to support the surge teams. We texted about who would take the first call, how we could lean on each other if we got busy, and how we would get through the night together. It was truly beautiful and has forged an unforgettable bond between us. Despite the night being quiet, we got through it together. One day and night done. Who knew how many to go, but we were off and running.

April 24, 2020

Two weeks had passed since the launch of the SLCG. The surge teams now knew how to access us, and we had become fully integrated into the clinical care of our Spanish-speaking COVID patients. We were participating in discussions when patients were admitted, when patients were being discharged, when patients were being asked to participate in clinical trials, as patients were being checked on during daily rounds, and in the hardest moments, during serious illness, and end of life conversations. We spoke to families near and far, including all across Latin America, letting them know how their admitted family members were doing, and, in worst cases, letting them know their loved ones were about to die, or had already died.

Surge teams began to depend on us, expect us to be there, and, most importantly, they really understood our contribution and the importance of diversity in healthcare. Our colleagues were literally blown away to see how clinicians who brought clinical, cultural, and linguistic competence to the daily encounters fundamentally improved communication, quality of care, and efficiency and effectiveness of clinical care. Day by day we had earned their trust, respect, and praise. Most importantly, when we walked into a Spanish-speaking patient's room, and through all the masks and PPE they simply heard "Buenos Dias, como se siente hoy?" (Good morning, how are you feeling today?), the look of relief, the sense they would be understood, the feeling that they would understand and be able to communicate, brought invaluable and immeasurable joy to them, and this joy was clear to see. The SLCG had succeeded in its mission to improve quality of team-based care, and provide the most compassionate, caring, and culturally competent patient experience possible.

April 25, 2020

The first surge was just about over. Our COVID inpatient numbers dropped significantly, and the demand for the SLCG was waning. We were slowly downsizing the SLCG, minimizing staff during the day and night, and beginning to retire our group. Over the previous six weeks, we had provided a service to MGH, to Boston Hope – a major field hospital in Boston – and even staffed the telephone lines to help patients get monoclonal antibody infusions if they had COVID and were sick but didn't need to be hospitalized. We filmed over 15 videos in Spanish on all topics COVID that were distributed to the community. We did Facebook videos and interviews, served as trusted messengers, and brought key information to our community in a language they could understand. We shared our model with other hospitals, including Johns Hopkins Hospital, who themselves formed a parallel effort appropriately and beautifully called "Juntos."

The last six weeks had created an incredible win-win-win. Patients loved being cared by Spanish-speaking doctors; the surge teams loved having us by their side; and we absolutely loved being able to come together as a community, to serve our community. Through the crucible of the first surge, the SLCG had forged an incredible bond, built on love for our community, respect for each other, and an incredible sense of commitment and dedication to honor that brought us to where we were in our profession, and in this moment in time and in history. We could all proudly say that when duty called, we answered the call, and hopefully saved some lives, and made many lives better along the way. We were ready to stand down, but also ready to stand up at a moment's notice. In the end, the SLCG remains the single most important, and most special effort I have ever been a part of, and this memory will undoubtedly last a lifetime.

Joseph R. Betancourt, MD, MPH, is the president of the Commonwealth Fund. One of the nation's preeminent leaders in healthcare, equity, quality, and community health, Betancourt formerly served as the senior vice president for Equity and Community Health at Massachusetts General Hospital (MGH) and as Vice President and Chief Equity and Inclusion Officer, where he helped develop and launch the organization's Structural Equity Ten-Point Plan and Mass General Brigham's United Against Racism Initiative. As founder of MGH's Disparities Solutions Center, Betancourt worked to develop the capacity of healthcare organizations to improve quality, address disparities, and achieve equity.

A Pandemic Memoir, in Parallax
By Robert Duncan

Originally submitted March 6, 2022

I first heard of COVID on New Year's Day in 2020 from reports on infectious disease news feeds about a dangerous viral pneumonia erupting in attendees of a live animal market in Wuhan, China. This raised memories of previous pandemics, both SARS transmitted from civet cats, and H1N1 flu spread from chickens in live animal markets and presented an entirely plausible pathway to explain this local outbreak. But within 6 weeks the newly named COVID-19 had traveled around the world, popping up in Italy, and then in a few skiers sharing lodging in the French Alps (Danis et al. 2020). On January 20, 2020, the first person in the United States infected with COVID, a traveler who had visited Wuhan, was recognized in Snohomish, Washington (Holshue et al. 2020). His illness was relatively mild and he soon recovered. But shortly thereafter, despite few known opportunities for exposure to the virus, COVID was wreaking havoc in nearby nursing homes (McMichael et al. 2020). By late February, there were about 30 cases recognized in the Western US. I paid attention to flares of pestilence like this around the world, but usually took comfort that they were at a distance.

Closer to home, the Biogen pharmaceutical company scheduled a scientific conference in late February at a Boston hotel, drawing 300 local and international participants. Somehow, in seminar rooms, over cocktails, or perhaps in a plenary session, one of those 300 was percolating COVID. Whether it had been provoked by one person with a severe infection, a lecture hall with standing room only, or a particularly virulent edition of the virus, a super-spreader event occurred, and SARS-CoV-2 infections tore silently through members of the audience. Within a few days, scores of researchers and executives showed up at local hospitals. Others flew home, carrying the virus to Florida, Tennessee, Texas, California, Australia, and beyond, potent vectors in the vanguard of a barely recognized but mushrooming pandemic. Investigators tracing the phylogenetic fingerprint of viral strains from the Biogen conference later calculated that, within less than a year, attendees and their contacts had generated infections in 29 states, ultimately leading to 245,000 to 300,000 cases of COVID around the United States (Lemieux et al. 2021).

Our hospital admitted its first COVID patient on March 6, 2020. Within a week, we were inundated; by April, we were regularly admitting 40 to 60 patients each day. Many of the patients were desperately ill, quickly filling our ICUs, and as many as six or eight died in a day. We knew a novel coronavirus was the cause but still knew little of its routes of transmission, how to interrupt them, and how best to protect our frontline staff. The first East Coast surge of COVID was upon us and we had precious little to offer for treatment—just oxygen, ventilator support, and steroids. Newly arrived remdesivir, an antiviral drug, offered a glimmer of hope.

As an infectious disease consultant and longstanding hospital epidemiology & infection prevention director, I was mobbed with questions from staff members who were fearful of the daily press of patients jamming the Emergency Department, wards, and ICUs. Hospital leaders wanted to know how to protect our staff while keeping the doors open. Within a week, I was removed entirely from direct patient care for the first time in 35 years to advise the incident command structures activated at our hospital and in our hospital consortium of a dozen members. I had little time to reflect on my disentanglement from patients, as I was suddenly working double time on epidemiology, trying simultaneously to pull useful tidbits from the daily torrent of new information and to dispense sage advice supported by good evidence.

As our COVID cases surged, similar scenes unfolded all over the country and the world. For me, learning about COVID took me back to the medical school experience of "drinking from the fire hose." PDF files replaced the stacks of journal rip-outs and photocopies of yore, all scarred with staple, pen, and highlighter marks. The sheer digital flood of science and discovery to swim through was mind-boggling, if not -numbing. Scientists in Wuhan had already published the complete SARS-CoV-2 viral genome sequence in the first week of January 2020, setting off a tsunami of investigation and the quest for treatments and vaccines. Two years later I have about 2000 COVID-related files in my digital library, ten times the volume from the Ebola scare.

In the evenings, friends and family would call me, apologizing with, "You must be getting thousands of these questions," before asking thousands of questions, often unanswerable. Even though we had a map of its genome, our understanding of this virus early in the pandemic was primitive. Colleagues, friends, kids, and parents were getting infected, and the fear was palpable.

At this same time, my mother was in declining health, increasingly isolated from her six children in an assisted living facility. At 97, she was debilitated and alone, losing eyesight and already quite deaf. She could now barely read and numerous advances in hearing technology had failed to assure reliable phone connections, leaving her with almost no ability or opportunity to communicate. My sisters, during pre-pandemic visits, had sifted through boxes of memorabilia, emerging with troves of family correspondence dating back several generations. These they transcribed, printed in large font for my mother to pore over, and distributed to family. My mother was engrossed and engaged by their content, happy to relive many experiences of her earlier life, and to read about her beloved parents and grandparents. For her children, they provided a window into some untold parts of our family history and lore.

One of those parts involved my grandfather, Dr. Reginald M. Atwater (always known as Rex), a physician and public health professional. Although he had been a central influence on my own professional ambitions, I knew few details about my grandfather's life until well into my career. I had heard tales of his years teaching in China, of the students who came to dinner, and of my pregnant grandmother's transport to the hospital in a sedan chair, dodging machine gun fire in the Tong Wars, to deliver my mother. But I knew almost nothing about the professional life of this family icon. He died when I was two, so I have no direct memory of him at all.

And then I received copies of the letters written by Rex to my grandmother, Charlotte Penfield, during their engagement. In the summer of 1918, Rex was a senior resident at the Peter Bent Brigham Hospital in Boston. How he became a senior, just a couple of months after finishing his fourth year of medical school, is unclear. What the letters did make clear was that he was as busy, fascinated, stretched, and callow as any resident might be. His letters, written almost daily, catalogued his clinical activities, not always with great sensitivity to the personal suffering of his patients. In one letter, he seemed almost gleeful about the exotic nature of the diseases he was seeing, noting "some extremely interesting cases, a number of which have proven rapidly fatal." In early September, he anticipated receiving 100 wounded soldiers from the war in Europe and sounded disappointed when "only 15 were in bed and they went to the City Hospital. Some of the rest went to the Psychopathic Hospital and others elsewhere. None came here" (Reginald M. Atwater, letter to Charlotte Penfield, September 5, 1918).

On September 9, 1918, Rex admitted his head nurse with influenza. He described this somewhat breezily. "There is a very acute variety now about, which is distressing but apparently not dangerous. The Mass. General they say is decimated with it. I trust we will not have it too for aside from the inconvenience, since the nurses are always the most commonly afflicted, I will be swamped. I don't see but that I've got to keep well" (RM Atwater, letter to CP, September 9, 1918).

Three days later, most of his admissions were patients with flu, and Rex speculated that "We are probably in for a real epidemic" (RM Atwater, letter to CP, September 12, 1918). Within a few weeks, he was running an influenza Contagion Ward of 70 to 80 patients, including a medical student a few years younger than him and a fellow resident, both dying. The medical student, a classmate of his from Colorado College and then Harvard Medical School, was admitted with persistent fevers to 106 degrees Fahrenheit for the better part of a week before dying on the 22nd. In a letter of September 30, Rex recalled, "We had, I believe, eight deaths during the day" (RM Atwater, letter to CP, September 30, 1918). He was hopeful that the worst was behind him, noting that with the apparent drop in deaths "the epidemic is perhaps less extensive" (RM Atwater, letter to CP, September 30, 1918). In an early nod to his later career in public health, Rex estimated the mortality rate on his wards as nearly 17%, boasting that this was better than any of the surrounding hospitals (RM Atwater, letter to CP, September 18, 1918). As his chief would later report, this was an underestimate.

In the 1918 Peter Bent Brigham Hospital Annual Report, Physician-in-Chief Dr. Henry Christian summarized admission diagnoses for the year. There were 557 patients admitted with influenza between the onset of the epidemic on September 9 and December 31, the last day of Rex's inpatient ward rotation; 153, or 27.5% of them, died (Pate 2020). One hundred years later, COVID-19 mortality at my hospital, after a century of celebrated medical progress, is in the same ballpark.

It is both disorienting and foundational to experience a universe parallel to my grandfather's, divided by a century of family history and innumerable advances in modern medicine. Just as I waded through the mysteries, fears, and anxieties, searching for answers in a hospital filled with COVID, Rex had been caring for legions of influenza patients. Each of us began with little understanding of how 'our' new disease spread, how to treat it, or whether our masks, gowns, and handwashing would keep it from killing us and our colleagues. With a certain degree of luck, we both survived, he going on to a distinguished career in the emerging discipline of public health.

Not surprisingly, there were also marked contrasts in our experiences. While I was awash in scientific literature in 2020, the literature describing flu in 1918 was relatively scant. It was not until 15 years after the 1918-1919 pandemic that Richard Shope, "identified Influenza A virus as the causative agent," and another dozen years after that before influenza vaccines were introduced (The Rockefeller University). My grandfather and his peers had little or no help from the larger scientific research community.

In 2020, on the other hand, amid the drive for information and knowledge, "pre-prints" of scientific articles appeared before undergoing peer review. Some of it was vital new research, some of it chaff. It became an art form to pick out the high-quality work and then fight off well-meaning guidance founded upon lesser contributions. It didn't help that some national leaders were disparaging expert advice and the value of specialty knowledge. Doubt was inserted into every aspect of COVID guidance. This atmosphere also generated guidance documents from authors assuming the role of content experts, driven by concern, but often lacking a firm basis in fact. Did anyone truly believe that one could catch COVID from farting (Sultan et al 2020)?

Divided by a century, my grandfather and I both were worn down by fatigue. I had been working on COVID, spending hours in committees via now-familiar Zoom meetings, schlepping back and forth to join with our multi-hospital system administration, drafting policy, and giving lectures and information sessions to residents and staff. I was working 70- to 80-hour weeks. The excitement and urgency rewarded the exhaustion. I was tired but felt useful. By June 2021, things were calming down, the pandemic had just about resolved, and I took my first day off in months. After a year and a half of COVID, life was returning to normal, with a promising horizon ... and then alpha appeared.

Suddenly, COVID was rising from the ashes, now with variants. All my tasks resurfaced, now accompanied by a new surge of information, interpretation, nuance, disinformation, and doubt. All the earlier effort and exhaustion seemed wasted, worsened first by alpha and a sequence of anxiety-provoking "variants of interest," but then compounded by a truly threatening delta variant.

The rise in cases once again pushed hospitals and their staffs to breaking points. Many were succumbing to burnout, and I had to watch carefully for the signs in my coworkers. Our workforce was being decimated. Early on, frontline staff in the Emergency Department got infected as patients flowed through the door and spilled into hallways, making it all but impossible to wear masks and face shields first time, every time. Gastroenterologists, cardiologists, and surgeons, unable to see their usual specialized patients, took on unfamiliar and stressful duties, running wards and ICUs designated for COVID patients. Fear of taking infection home led some to spend weeks living apart from their families in hotel rooms. A few of my colleagues peeled off their scrubs in their garages, showered, and only then saw their kids and partners, still afraid of bringing illness home. Another sequestered in the basement, sleeping with the dog.

In the hospital, life on non-COVID wards was generally more relaxed and routine. That is, until a cluster of infection would suddenly appear among patients and staff on the unit. COVID is particularly easy to pass in the first few days of infection, before any symptoms appear, and in those first few days, PCR tests may not detect virus. This "false-negative" result could turn positive within hours and is, of course, a recipe for stealth introduction and circulation of the virus in a perceived safe zone.

It is disconcerting and frightening enough to be infected by a patient you were caring for who had unrecognized, lurking COVID. It's another matter to be the staff member who was infected and passed it, however unwittingly, to other staff, to vulnerable patients already sick with something else, or to family members. Some healthcare staff were infected after sharing just a few minutes for dinner in a break room with trusted coworkers. Others attended a weekend funeral or wedding reception, had kids in daycare, or took a rare chance to relax in a bar or restaurant. Recovery could take weeks or longer. Those left on the wards had that much more added to their plates. Many in healthcare burned out, retired early, or (a remarkable number) left the field entirely and shifted to something less stressful.

I tried to fend off exhaustion. I was no longer on call, but the demands were constant and unending. I scheduled appointments for exercise so I wouldn't skip them and made time for walks with my unusually patient wife. Getting into the woods, away from traffic and noise, and talking about something else counted for a lot.

My grandfather's schedule and duties were different, but he faced the

Figure 1. Drs. Reginald Atwater, Wilder Penfield, and Roger Graves (left to right) outside the Peter Bent Brigham Hospital in October 1918. Note the patient beds on the raised outdoor porch.

same challenges of pandemic-fueled exhaustion. He worked an intense six-month rotation of ward duty, working all days and many nights of the week. Early on in his ward rotation, he described a plan to provide some relief to the residents. He wrote of a policy "... just put in force whereby we each take one day a week in the Out Door [Ambulatory] Department and spend the rest of our time on the wards with flu but every day we will have 2 hours off and every other evening, when we are required to leave the wards regardless of work ... Arrangement is also made for one man to take all the night calls on a night after an easy day" (RM Atwater, letter to CP, September 23, 1918). A distinct departure from the traditions of senior residency, this plan was intended to maintain health, help reduce stress, and fend off flu. Rex spent these off hours playing squash after late rounds, challenging his new and best surgical intern, Wilder Penfield, who shared his fiancée's name and turned out to be a distant cousin (Figure 1).

Reading Rex's letters from the onset of the epidemic in September until the end of his ward rotation in December 1918, it is a remarkable progression in four short months from the brash, rather callous early enthusiasm of "... some extremely interesting cases, a number of which have proven rapidly fatal" (RM Atwater, letter to CP, September 8, 1918) to the exhaustion and sense of inadequacy expressed in his letters of November and December. For example, "The last few days have been so crowded that it took my utmost attention to make my work of even mediocre quality—sometimes I think surely I lack a reasonable capacity for the accomplishment of many things." (RM Atwater, letter to CP, December 8, 1918). By December 21, he was anticipating his first Christmas apart from family and lamenting that, "My Junior left for home tonight. I am absolutely alone now, my lab man being ill and with only a new Junior in prospect for tomorrow ... I am just about worn thin. A new case is no longer a pleasure but only that much more work. I have four new ones hanging over tonight but I simply can't bring myself to work them up" (RM Atwater, letter to CP, December 21, 1918). This was a conscientious man with a prodigious talent for organizing and administering a flood of tasks, feeling defeated by the demands of patient care and leadership washing over him.

Happily, the letters of January 1919 make clear that rather than burning out, Rex made the leap from the inpatient wards to the Out Door [Ambulatory] Department. He enjoyed a respite from the flu pandemic and turned his attentions to planning for a medical mission trip to China, recruiting associates from the colleges of the Northeast, and managing the details of a summer wedding to my grandmother. He was also looking forward to taking a position as the first candidate for a doctorate in public health at Johns Hopkins, beginning October 1, with an annual stipend of $1,800 (RM Atwater, letter to CP, May 7, 1919).

I am a third-generation public health and vaccine advocate. My grandfather spent a decade in the field, focused first on sanitation measures and medical education in China, where he was also called upon at one time "to vaccinate several hundred children against smallpox in a large but old-fashioned public workhouse located in a provincial capital of China" (RM Atwater, letter to CP, 1926). Political unrest ended his tenure in Changsha and he returned with his family to Boston for a short stint as research faculty, living within a mile of my current home. He then moved to a position in upstate New York as a county health commissioner, focusing on the scourges of diphtheria, whooping cough, and cows' milk laden with tuberculosis. There he managed diverse programs, as evidenced by a pamphlet advertising a series of educational health conferences. Topics ranged from maternal health to laboratory services and venereal disease evaluation, health education, and rural health administration. This was

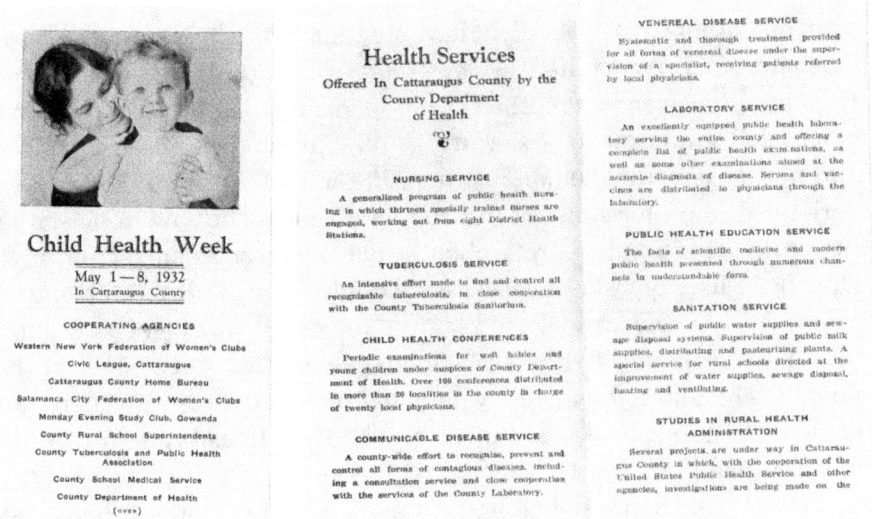

Figure 2. Program for Child Health Week in Cattaraugus County, May 1-8, 1932. Note the photograph of Charlotte Penfield Atwater and John B. Atwater.

also a proving ground for his next career move. The pamphlet (Figure 2), unearthed from my mother's closets, was adorned with a photo of my grandmother looking every part the bedraggled mother, cuddling her two-year-old son, my Uncle John B. Atwater, whose own career would one day parallel his father's.

Uncle John followed his father's path into medicine and public health, with a long career as a municipal and county public health director. I asked him recently about his own experience with the polio epidemic in the 1950s when he was in clinical training. He recalled doing nearly 50 spinal taps during the summer of his internship in an Emergency Room, when he was in the midst of the last significant polio epidemic on the East Coast, seeing at least one pediatric polio suspect every day. He admitted a 13-year-old girl with "rapidly developing paralysis and had to put her in an iron lung" (John B. Atwater, letter to author, February 3, 2022). He followed her progress for the six months she was in the hospital, and they finally weaned her off the machine. Some ten or twelve years later, she walked into his health department office, so changed that he failed to recognize her (JB Atwater, letter to author, February 3, 2022).

My mother played a part in the story as well. She considered going to medical school around the end of World War II, with some urging, I gather, from her father. This push might have stemmed from his experience at the Brigham, where two of the seven members of his service were women from Hopkins. However, my mother chose instead to eschew a professional career, and stay home to raise a large family. Although intensely intelligent and not infrequently demanding herself, she had a certain modesty and perhaps disdain for some of the competitiveness she saw in her father, tinged by occasional regrets about what a career in medicine might have been like. But she revealed few details of her father's role and his prominence in the specialized realm of preventive medicine and public health. Even though I knew little about the details of his career at that point, his history influenced my path and provided direction when I was applying to public health and medical schools—choices that brought my mother great pleasure.

A few years ago, Uncle John sent me a box of his father's books and papers. Included in the box was the winged statue perched on stone that I'd remembered seeing in my grandmother's room when I was a boy. I now knew it was a Lasker Award, bestowed on Rex only months after he died in 1957. Rex met the Laskers in the 1940s in his role as the first Executive Secretary of the American Public Health Association, his next and final move after Cattaraugus County. Albert Lasker had channeled a successful career in advertising into philanthropy supporting medical and public health endeavors. I asked my mother about it a few years ago, who said, "Oh, yes. Dad helped Mrs. Lasker design the award. He refused it himself while he was alive" (Figure 3). I had heard nothing of this before, from my mother or grandmother, learning most of the history from internet searches. It still surprises me that such recognition, and other honors, didn't make it to the dinner table conversations of my youth. But I have found myself reluctant to talk of it as well to my own friends and colleagues—quite a contrast with the man whose letters to his fiancée were filled with accounts of his successes, large and small, including a catalog of those he'd beaten at squash that day.

Contrary to popular opinion, pandemics and novel infectious diseases are expected, regular parts of the infectious disease and epidemiology worlds—the CDC publishes an entire journal of *Emerging Infectious Diseases*. HIV, Lyme disease, and Methicillin-Resistant *Staphylococcus aureus* (MRSA) all first made the scene during my training in public health, internal medicine, and infectious disease, each with profound effects on my trajectory.

Figure 3. Dr. Reginald Atwater and Mrs. Mary Lasker at the 1948 Lasker Awards Ceremony.

In the early 1980s, while I was studying various species of arthropods in public health school and the diseases they carry, my entomology professor became the first in the country to be treated with an antibiotic directed at the Lyme disease he had acquired a few miles up the river while collecting deer ticks. A decade later, Lyme disease had moved well beyond an isolated cul-de-sac in Old Lyme, Connecticut, and occupied wide swaths of both New England and my attention. Another epidemic, another vector.

MRSA was also a new phenomenon, causing outbreaks in a small handful of large US hospitals. I cut my epidemiology teeth studying the first 85 cases of MRSA infection at Yale New Haven Hospital. This provided the subject of my master's thesis and my introduction to clinical medicine, the concept of resistance, and the magic and fragile power of antibiotics. Well after medical school, an oncologist buddy, churning through a procession of clinical chemotherapy trials, once asked me how I could keep 40+ cephalosporins straight. "They work," I said, with a hint of hubris.

HIV and the AIDS epidemic unfolded from an obscure affliction of gay men to reveal a dark and protean mix of the most challenging, awful, fascinating clinical conundrums a career in medicine could offer. When this pandemic arrived, patient care was hazardous. Drawing blood, tapping a pleural effusion, drawing blood gases on a dyspneic patient – a medical student's menu of 'scut' work – each was a chance for a needle stick to join the infected. A head nurse in a nearby hospital had done just that, contracting HIV and Hepatitis C in one such accident, and died within a year after a precipitous course. Discussing the risks of a career in medicine, my medical school dean told how a segment of his own class had died from tuberculosis they had encountered on the wards.

As a resident and fellow, I became proficient at diagnosing and treating *Pneumocystis* pneumonia, Kaposi Sarcoma, cryptococcal meningitis, and the other obscure opportunistic infections revealed by HIV, only to have them relapse or become chronic. As a fellow, I treated a shy and diminutive nurse with AIDS for a couple of years. She had been infected by her husband, her first and only sexual partner, and was a pariah to her family. During our tenure she had it all—*Pneumocystis* pneumonia, *Candida* esophagitis, recurrent pneumococcal pneumonia. Most challenging was a stripe of shingles extending down her left arm, causing lancinating pain. This was barely palliated by narcotics and became chronic and resistant to acyclovir, only to be superseded by cytomegalovirus (CMV) retinitis, causing blindness.

Wasting syndromes and death were commonplace. In contrast, in some cases of sepsis or gangrene, an infectious disease consult offered heroic rescue. Heroic rescues were now accompanied by heroic failure, and we debated whether surgery or intensive care for AIDS patients was appropriate or even ethical. While the reward of an unexpected cure became more familiar, so did the concepts of futility and patients' personal choices favoring comfort, palliation, and hospice care.

Happily, the inevitability of death from HIV succumbed to investigation, science, and time. Today, at its 40th anniversary, HIV has been relegated to a chronic and relatively benign condition, kept at bay with one pill a day. In their narration of the careers of doctors sculpted by the AIDS era, Drs. Bayer, Oppenheimer, and Parisi suggest that "Those who came to medicine after 1996 cannot fathom how bleak it was" (Bayer et al. 2021). The same authors now speak of careers bookended by historic pandemics and, with the advances in HIV care, finding themselves consigned to "becoming primary care doctors dealing with colonoscopies, blood-pressure management, diabetes care, and prostate cancer screening."

Today, two years after the first few cases of COVID appeared, a handful of oral and IV treatments can reduce hospitalization and death from COVID by 85-100%. Enormously effective and safe vaccines have been widely available for over a year, although largely limited to the wealthier parts of the world and rejected by far too many here in the United States.

Reflecting on the challenges facing my grandfather a hundred years ago and those I encountered, I am struck by the parallels. Neither of us knew much about the pathogen we were facing. Both hospitals shut down normal operations, designating special wards to care for the onslaught— Contagion Wards then, COVID Wards now. We were soon overwhelmed by the number of severely ill patients, with little to offer in treatment. We both hoped that preventive measures would protect us and each noted, with some satisfaction, that they "worked admirably." As my grandfather wrote, "So far we have not had a case develop among attendants on the contagious wards, all of whom are masked and gowned (Figure 4), while nurses on the other services have been catching it freely. We are taking unusual care to prevent contacts. It is my first real epidemic and I have learned very much" (RM Atwater, letter to CP, September 22, 1918).

Of course, we were both proven wrong, with coworkers becoming ill

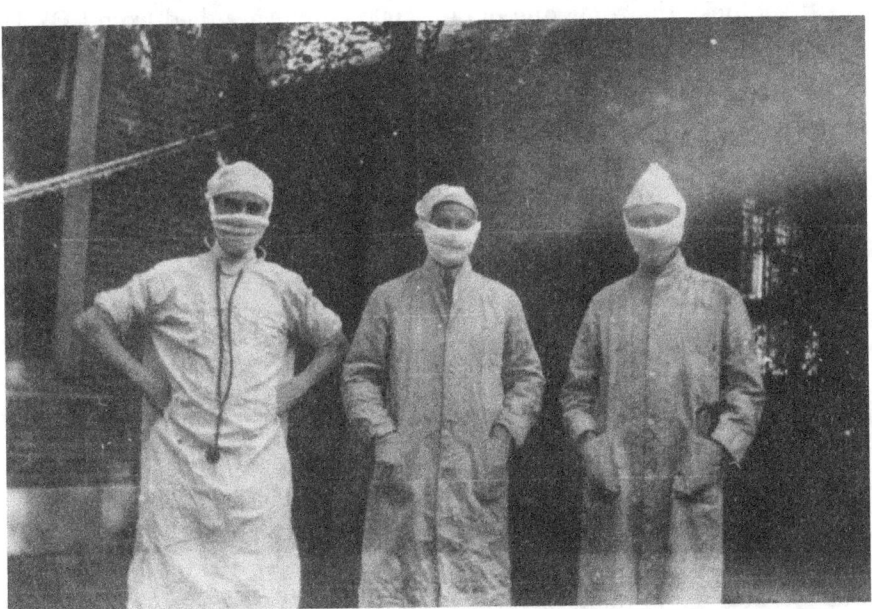

Figure 4. Doctors at the Peter Bent Brigham Hospital in Boston, Massachusetts wearing personal protective equipment, 1918. Pictured are Drs. Robert Curtis, Clifford Walker, and Harold Martin (left to right).

as the epidemic wore on, some of them deathly ill. Within our hospital, we detected a small number of COVID clusters among patients and staff, invariably occurring on so-called COVID-free units. As in 1918, nurses and their assistants were infected most readily. A negative PCR on admission evidently provided enough re-assurance for staff to relax their caution, even if only slightly. Observing staff practices, we noted decrements in hand hygiene and PPE used on non-COVID wards. The degree of precaution followed both the ebb and flow of COVID cases in the hospital and in the community, dropping when a ward was no longer designated for COVID patient care or local infections had waned. In a distinctly modern departure, we were able to apply whole genome sequencing to augment our epidemiologic investigations, never before available to us. We could now demonstrate genetically identical samples of virus shared among patients and staff and distinguish independent strains originating at home or in the community. In addition, we could deduce the direction of transmission—patient to staff, staff to staff, and staff to patient. To our clear advantage, private rooms spared patients from directly infecting each other. Genome sequencing also pinpointed the staff breakroom – a place to share a quick bite with trusted friends – as a spoke for transmission.

I feel lucky that only one of our 8,000 employees died from COVID. Sadly, it was a colleague and friend upon whose expertise I had relied for 15 or 20 years, a brilliant man who understood parasites and loved classic jazz. My role change, early in the pandemic, buffering me from most of the deaths and the emotions they entailed. My practice partners and other colleagues watched hundreds of patients die—elderly couples shortly after celebrating an anniversary with family, patients suffering with major chronic illnesses too afraid to leave home to get vaccinated, and a number of otherwise young and healthy men and women who refused to believe they could be dying of a hoax.

I wonder how much my colleagues will tell of their experiences in coming years, or whether they will leave the war stories untold. My grandfather's letters, despite bursting with the religious fervor of a medical missionary, recorded few of his feelings about the death surrounding him. As my uncle noted recently to me, "What little he talked about that time is consistent with what we learned from his letters. It obviously was physically and mentally pretty tough" (JB Atwater, letter to author, February 3, 2022).

It is fortuitous and a remarkable coincidence that letters should have appeared relating my grandfather's personal experience with the H1N1 flu pandemic of 1918, just as I was encountering the pandemic of the next century. Of all the pandemics I have encountered, none compares so closely as the influenza of 1918 and the COVID-19 we face today. Each illness exploded out of nowhere, involved all corners of the world, infected all sorts of healthcare personnel, and had profound effects on the social and economic welfare of the globe. And in contrast to most other pandemics, these were inescapable. Seeing these pandemics from viewpoints a century apart offers a humbling perspective on how limited our resources are to manage or contain a novel infection, and the toll those limits take on society and the physicians and staff who are charged with managing it.

The history contained within those letters provided more than a narrative of my grandfather's life during the flu pandemic and the parallels to my own experience with COVID. It was a surprise for me to learn – from his own words – how he navigated the uncertainty, fear, and exhaustion. It generated for me a personal connection with a grandfather I never knew – a feeling of being in his shoes – communicated across a century.

References

Atwater, Reginald M. 1926. "The Progress of Public Health in China." *The Scientific Monthly* 1926:117-22.

Bayer, Ronald, Gerald M Oppenheimer, and Valentina Parisi. 2021. "Marking the 40th Anniversary of the AIDS Epidemic—American Physicians Look Back." *New England Journal of Medicine* 385 (14): 1251–53. https://doi.org/10.1056/NEJMp2106933.

Danis, Kostas, Olivier Epaulard, Thomas Bénet, Alexandre Gaymard, Séphora Campoy, Elisabeth Bothelo-Nevers, Maude Bouscambert-Duchamp, et al. 2020. "Cluster of Coronavirus Disease 2019 (Covid-19) in the French Alps, 2020." *Clinical Infectious Diseases: An Official Publication of the Infectious Diseases Society of America* 71 (April). https://doi.org/10.1093/cid/ciaa424.

Holshue, Michelle L, Chas DeBolt, Scott Lindquist, Kathy H Lofy, John Wiesman, Hollianne Bruce, Christopher Spitters, et al. 2020. "First Case of 2019 Novel Coronavirus in the United States." *New England Journal of Medicine* 382 (10): 929–36. https://doi.org/10.1056/NEJMoa2001191.

Lemieux, Jacob E, Katherine J Siddle, Bennett M Shaw, Christine Loreth, Stephen F Schaffner, Adrianne Gladden-Young, Gordon Adams, et al. 2021. "Phylogenetic Analysis of SARS-CoV-2 in Boston Highlights the Impact of Superspreading Events." *Science* 371 (6529): eabe3261. https://doi.org/10.1126/science.abe3261.

McMichael, Temet M, Shauna Clark, Sargis Pogosjans, Meagan Kay, James Lewis, Atar Baer, Vance Kawakami et al. 2020. "Covid-19 in a Long-Term Care Facility - King County, Washington, February 27-March 9, 2020" *Morbidity and Mortality Weekly Report* 69 (12): 339-42. https://www.cdc.gov/mmwr/volumes/69/wr/mm6912e1.htm

Pate, Catherine. 2020. "How One Hospital Handled the 1918 Influenza Epidemic." Accessed April 2, 2020. https://cms.www.countway.harvard.edu/wp/?p=16432.

Sultan, Shahnaz, Joseph K Lim, Osama Altayar, Perica Davitkov, Joseph D Feuerstein, Shazia M Siddique, Yngve Falck-Ytter, and Hashem B El-Serag. 2020. "AGA Rapid Recommendations for Gastrointestinal Procedures During the COVID-19 Pandemic." *Gastroenterology* 159 (2): 739-758.e4. https://doi.org/10.1053/j.gastro.2020.03.072.

The Rockefeller University. n.d. "Richard E. Shope 1957 Albert Lasker Award." Accessed March 17, 2022. https://www.rockefeller.edu/our-scientists/richard-e-shope/2332-albert-lasker-award/

Robert A. Duncan, MD, MPH, was Hospital Epidemiologist and Director of Infection Prevention and Control at Lahey Hospital & Medical Center in Burlington, MA and Associate Professor of Medicine at Tufts Medical School. He received a BA from Wesleyan University, MPH (Infectious Disease Epidemiology) from Yale University, and MD from the University of Connecticut, followed by residency training at New England Deaconess Hospital, and Infectious Diseases fellowship at Boston City Hospital and Boston University. He was Senior Staff Physician in Infectious Diseases at Lahey Hospital & Medical Center since 1993, Hospital Epidemiologist since 1999, and retired from practice in 2023.

COVID-19 from the Environmental Services Perspective
By James E. Odom, Jr.

Originally submitted March 4, 2022

When COVID-19 first hit the country, the environmental services workers viewed it as just another virus we would have to deal with for cleaning and disinfecting. It is just the world we have been accustomed to, which is keeping the hospital clean daily. However, after I saw the effects it was having on patients, our colleagues, families, friends, and the surrounding communities, my perspective changed immediately. This virus was much different than anything I had ever encountered in my career, and for my staff it incited a real fear, the likes of which I had never seen before.

Ebola also had caused fear originally but once it was understood that it was unlikely to become a pandemic, those fears subsided quickly. COVID-19 was a different animal because it was easily transmitted, and you could see the physical and mental effects it was having not only on patients but also on family members and friends. As the leader of my environmental services department, I support my staff in any way I can. Sometimes that means providing emotional support, which is what I found myself doing more than ever during the pandemic. Staff working on these units were mentally and physically tired.

I remember rounding one day and finding a staff member who said she was struggling with the number of patients who were dying and it was starting to affect her own well-being, because she felt there was little she could do about it. I acknowledged her feelings and reassured her that every time she is cleaning a room, she is making the environment safe for her colleagues and patients. I told her that even if she cannot see the benefits immediately, she was having more of an impact on their health than she realized. I also found some staff who had broken down and were crying, feeling as though they were not making a difference and could not keep up with the numerous additional cleaning requests on top of their normal responsibilities. There simply wasn't enough time or resources to take care of them all. I increased my rounding to these areas to make sure my staff felt supported but also to monitor them for any physical or mental concerns. And sometimes I would move them to a different unit so they could take a mental break and recharge.

When the pandemic first started, the biggest challenge was understanding how COVID-19 could be killed from a cleaning perspective with the current cleaning methods we use daily. Or did we have to alter them? The next challenge was to educate my staff immediately and consistently on how we would perform our roles. Complicating all these challenges was the constant change in guidance from the CDC on what PPE needed to be worn when going into a COVID-positive room or area. Ensuring that staff had the proper PPE and that it was being worn properly required my management team and me to round continually to check in with our teams to ensure they had everything they needed for equipment but more importantly our support. And while the majority of my staff comprehend English, some do not. Their multilingual colleagues became excellent resources, communicating with them in their native language, so they felt comfortable performing their roles. I also made sure they were getting the most important parts of the information they needed to help ease their fears.

Once the staff felt comfortable – which took several months due to the ever-changing nature of the virus – it eventually just became a part of our everyday lives and most of the staff were no longer as worried as they had been when the pandemic first started. But this was not universally true. I did have a few employees who refused to go into rooms, and some even resigned because they feared being around COVID-19 patients. The way I dealt with it was being completely transparent that even with proper PPE and training anyone of us could still contact the virus and it may not necessarily be from the hospital since it was in the community as well. But having proper PPE and following the CDC cleaning guidance, as well as guidance from our own infection prevention team and me, meant that they were better prepared and protected and lessened their chance of getting the virus.

Luckily for me I had great support in my workplace from the senior team and other colleagues. Consequently, I never really became stressed personally, but I did worry about my staff because they were really the ones who had to deal with most of the cleaning requests. Their biggest worry was not knowing if they were potentially taking the virus home with them and possibly infecting their loved ones. Early on it was difficult because the only thing we had to rely on was symptoms since testing was hard to come by. We would put staff on paid leave for 14 days, and then test them for clearance to return to work. Having adequate staff became a challenge as our staff started getting sick. Those positions weren't easily replaced.

Most of us probably did more hands-on work than normal to help support our teams which was actually very rewarding. As more testing resources became available, I have to say that I was very proud that my organization put in place a testing program that, if the staff felt they had any symptoms, they could be tested quickly to ease their fears.

I can say that COVID validated what I already knew about my team – they were committed to showing up and providing services, so that the patients and their colleagues had a clean environment to heal in and work. The consistency with which they have to perform their jobs on a daily basis takes dedication, compassion, and resiliency. Although cleaning is their role, we should not overlook how our colleagues deliver these services daily. I know I could not be prouder to have the privilege to lead such an amazing group of individuals.

James "J.J." Odom Jr. has spent his entire professional career over 30 years in the environmental services field first as floor technician and working up to a director's role where he has resided for over 25 years. He loves what he does for a career because it gives him the ability to impact peoples' lives daily.

Health Professionalism, Trainees, and Moral Imperative
By Margaret Rea and Michael S. Wilkes

Originally submitted April 10, 2022

Physicians, nurses, and other health professionals possess expert knowledge, unique skills, and a moral imperative that together encompass their "professionalism" and thus sets them apart from the general public. In ordinary times, but particularly in times of social stress, healthcare teams are confronted with moral and ethical questions that are otherwise ignored. What does it mean to be professional? At what point in training does one take on professional obligations? In what ways should a trainee's safety be weighed against the critical well-being of others? Do unique experiences such as pandemics offer invaluable training opportunities that are not superfluous or unnecessary, but are a core element of training to be a professional? What follows is our attempt to explore these questions.

The basis of the term "professional" is an implicit societal contract. Health professionals gain substantial benefits from society including status, respect, autonomy in practice, self-regulation, and substantial remuneration. These benefits come with an obligation to be competent, altruistic, and moral, and to provide healthcare for individuals and society. Because people without medical training cannot provide complex medical services, the public must rely on professional healthcare workers – and trainees* – in an infectious disease emergency (or other medical emergencies). There are professional obligations that mandate provision of care and prevent the abandonment of those in medical need.

For generations in the past, health professionals around the world have had to contend with a certain degree of personal risk associated with caring for the ill. With the advent of modern antibiotics, antifungals, and anti-parasitic drugs this risk was largely forgotten or ignored—except perhaps in times of war or conflict. A potent recent reminder arrived during the mid-1980s when AIDS emerged as a new fatal infectious disease. Initially, the infectious agent was unknown, and the methods of spread

---

* By "trainee" we refer to health science students (e.g., medicine, nursing, dentistry, psychology etc.) and to those in postgraduate training programs (e.g., residents and fellows).

were unclear. There was no shortage of hypotheses as to the disease's cause—some based on emerging science, and some based on popular lore and religious doctrine. Doctors, nurses, lab technicians and trainees found themselves in the cross hairs with a social responsibility to care for those with the illness, but with an occupational risk of contracting the fatal disease themselves. Technicians, clerks, and food delivery staff often avoided, to an extreme, all patient contact—no matter how superficial. Food trays sat outside of patient's rooms, technicians refused to transport infected people for services within the hospital and hospital rooms were not provided with custodial services. While physicians, nurses and medical trainees theoretically had no choice but to provide care to both the infected person's body and mind, many unfortunately did not live up to their professional and ethical duties, sometimes changing careers or simply providing sub-standard care to patients with AIDS.

Balancing Competing Needs

During the AIDS epidemic physicians and nurses (and their related trainees) were on the front line and thus regularly reminded of their professional obligations and their duty to place themselves at risk. For centuries, physicians have taken an oath at the completion of medical school. The oath reminds them that they enter into medicine not because it is a safe or lucrative profession, but because it is a commitment to care for others in their times of need even when that caring involves personal risk. It is during epidemics and wars when health professionals are most challenged to confront those opposing facets of the profession that are duty and risk. Of course, perceived risk is greatest when uncertainty is high, and prevention is in its formative or unknown stages.

But memories are short, and by and large there is a new generation now on the front lines caring for patients during the COVID-19 pandemic. Health providers and society at large were asked to abide by new, unfamiliar rules. Such social obligations changed our lives including masking, quarantining, social distancing, adapting to school closures, and suddenly relying on remote communication for work, education, and basic social connection. As was the case in the AIDS epidemic, health providers and trainees were again asked to step up and care for those who were infected and/or contagious, while also personally navigating the societal restrictions the pandemic imposed.

Clinicians were placed in situations where they were forced to work with limited resources (medications, ventilators, hospital beds, et cet.), pitting one person's needs against another's —often with little (or conflicting) professional, institutional, or societal guidance. And again, at least initially, the extent of contagion and method of spread were uncertain. Science could offer only limited evidence but a plethora of educated guesses. In parallel, the public and health professionals were initially bombarded with myths, theories, and half-baked ideas which sometime came from people claiming medical expertise. Even high-ranking public leaders sometimes demanded that medical professionals provide "treatments" that the scientific community claimed were futile and lacked even an element of common sense (e.g., use of bleach or antiparasitic agents).

Workplaces pushed health providers to their limits by requiring exceptionally long work hours in part due to patient overflow and in part due to worker shortages because of infection. Those who were on the front lines of the pandemic were worked to the bone with little rest and little emotional support. Early in the pandemic, keeping up the work pace became a Herculean task. Additionally, educators and clinical training program administrators were forced to try to balance patient care needs, the well-being of their trainees, and trainees' commitment to keeping family and friends safe and supported. After working long shifts, often caring for critically sick people, trainees had to make difficult choices whether to go home and rest and see loved ones or stay in a hospital on call room or nearby hotel to protect family from disease.

The Obligation of "Trainees"

Each health professional trainee carries the personal burden of deciding the extent of her obligation and commitment. For the COVID pandemic, trainees on the front lines included students enrolled in health degree programs (nursing, medicine, pharmacy, etc.), and postgraduate trainees (interns, residents, fellows). For some students, the fact that they were paying tuition and not yet fully qualified or licensed provided a justification for insisting on being excused from duty. For other trainees who had responsibilities at home such as caring for small children or elderly parents or relatives, this provided an opportunity to ask to be excused from patient care. Discussions at nursing stations, in clinic coffee rooms, in seminars over Zoom, and in the C suite of health science schools and hospitals focused on whether health professional students deserved full protection (i.e. remaining at home) versus full clinical learning opportunities. Core to these debates was the question of trainee-patient contact: should trainees avoid contact with all COVID-infected or potentially infected persons, or should carrying for sick people during a pandemic be a vital part of their education? They were, after all, not excused from caring for any other group of patients.

Some health science students made the case that as tuition-paying students they were not yet health professionals and had no moral obligation to care for others. Some postgraduate trainees (interns, residents, and fellows) tried to make a similar case arguing that, while they had taken the Hippocratic oath, such moral obligations did not apply while they were still in training. They, or their families, argued that all trainees should be excused from all risky training until they had graduated and were independent practitioners. Certainly, other trainees – students and residents – felt a strong sense of commitment to their capacity to offer service and asked only for complete modern PPE.

Faculty and students with a military background, or those who trained decades earlier, harkened back to prior epidemics like AIDS, MERS, TB, and the flu outbreak of the early 1900s to suggest the importance of all trainees learning approaches to managing disease outbreaks that challenge our knowledge, our ethics, our finances, and our allocation of limited resources. Those who lived through the early stages of the AIDS epidemic or Ebola argued that the experiences obtained were a vital part of their training—acquiring the experience of what it means to be a healthcare professional in the most trying of times. They reasoned that COVID-19 will not be the last such infectious disease pandemic and thus the skills and experience obtained now will be vital in the future.

These conflicts – inter- and intrapersonal – led to health providers being swamped with a plethora of emotions that often changed by the minute - fear, anxiety, guilt, remorse, and even regret for having entered the health professions that could put family and friends at risk. These feelings often turned to blame and anger at those sick people who voluntarily engaged in risky behaviors or failed to take precautions such that they then placed health providers at risk. Conflicting emotions often ensued – a duty to treat those in need, but anger and blame for patients' failures to take personal responsibility.

Moving from Responsibility to Action

Anger toward patients then turned toward the hospitals, health science schools, and community clinics that trainees felt had failed them in their obligations to minimize risk of contagion. In the trainees' minds, such organizations were not communicating accurate, honest, and frequent updates about policies, procedures and evolving scientific knowledge about COVID-19. They were not providing trainees adequate protection from infection or educating them sufficiently in infection control. Trainees were not provided with the necessary training that would allow them to work outside their areas of competence (for instance when psychiatry resident physicians were suddenly asked to work in intensive care units). There was no, or inadequate, psychological support to deal with escalating emotions and worry. There were few resources to allow for family care (e.g., childcare) and communication around safe lodging was often unclear and not specific. There was no overtime pay, and questions remained about sickness benefits and what the impact of absence due to illness would be on their training requirements.

While these emotions and questions swirled around in the minds of health professional trainees, societal reactions to the COVID pandemic were hardly static. There were discussions of healthcare disparities, unequal access to emerging new resources like vaccinations and early-intervention medications, and political resistance from conservatives and libertarians and the Southern part of the nation who even questioned the very existence of the pandemic. Health trainees and practitioners who were of Asian ancestry were often blamed by patients and the public for what came to be known in some circles as "the Chinese virus." All of this led to additional angst, anger, and confusion.

The COVID-19 pandemic progressed in phases, each with certain unknowns and each requiring different professional obligations. Unlike those entering law enforcement, fire protection, or the military, where danger is a recognized part of the occupation, most current medical trainees entered the health sciences without giving any consideration to their personal risk. Most were born after the crisis of the AIDS epidemic and were unaware of any prevalent serious infectious diseases for which no treatments existed. Of course, there are some but most younger trainees working in developed countries are ignorant of them.

The COVID-19 pandemic fell on a period of increased stress within the health profession. Prior to the COVID-19 outbreak, medical educators were already concerned about a high prevalence of stress, anxiety, and burnout among health professions trainees (students and residents). Burnout rates across the medical education continuum range from 30-60% (Erschens et al. 2019; IsHak et al. 2009). In the years prior to COVID-19 (prior to 2020) reports mapped the ways and extent to which stress and burnout progressed from the pre-clinical years onward through residency and fellowship (Dyrbye et al. 2014). Higher rates of burnout and stress predicted poorer mastery of clinical tasks, more frequent medical errors, lower sense of responsibility to society, lower patient satisfaction, less frequent use of evidence-based practice, cynicism over patients, and poorer personal physical health (Fahrenkopf et al. 2008).

COVID-19 then brought new stressors to all health science trainees (pre- and postgraduate) which included a lack of social connectedness with their peers and their anticipated professions, revised course structures and call schedules, new online requirements, social isolation, and reduced student-patient and student-faculty interactions which created barriers to learning manual skills. In many cases trainees were unprepared to address these new challenges and unable or unwilling to ask for help or admit to fallibility. This "go it alone" strategy is dangerous in times of high stress resulting from overwork, new work responsibilities, and personal risk.

Not surprisingly, trainees reacted to these new stressors in diverse ways. Perhaps based on prior life experiences, on personality, or on fortitude, trainees exhibited various degrees of resilience. Research has focused on whether resilience is a teachable modifiable skill given its stress-protective effect (Kunzler et al. 2020). While resilience can be defined differently, we consider resilience to be a set of attributes that allows us to "bounce back" and adapt in the presence of adversity. There are many proposed components of resilience, including self-compassion, adaptive coping, self-efficacy, and mindfulness, all of which have a protective effect against burnout, anxiety, and depression. Research, even early in the pandemic, has identified strategies for building or augmenting resilience in healthcare workers such as seeking positive professional relationships, encouraging personal reflection, and achieving life balance (Pietrzak et al 2020) But these interventions have not been studied for long term outcomes.

In the recent past, health science faculty, residents and community healthcare providers have used a combination of these strategies in an attempt to combat stress from daily workplace challenges, such as high patient volume, low autonomy, and limited support from those who are more senior. But, it is unclear if those who experienced high intensity burnout from COVID-19 can ever regain their original vigor and commitment. It may be that most will, but some may now realize that the obligations of being a health professional are not what they signed on for.

In Table 1 we have broken down the pandemic into four stages (i.e., the stages that we noticed in our interactions with trainees at the time of this writing in the spring/summer of 2022). In each phase there were personal, professional, training, and societal concerns that trainees and practitioners needed to consider—often with little preparation or support.

COVID-19 has profoundly disrupted health sciences education at all levels. It has raised, or re-raised, important ethical issues that directly involve trainees. It has disrupted important social support networks and the structured learning environment that normally bolster health science student well-being. During the first part of the pandemic the work climate changed dramatically. There were no longer in-person case conferences, grand rounds, walking rounds in the hospital, small group "Doctoring" classes, in-person didactic sessions, or informal meetings in the hospital cafeteria where the seating was roped off. COVID set the stage for new approaches to health sciences education that are more individualized, self-directed, and technology-focused. What remains to be seen is whether the cumulative stressors from this pandemic have enduring effects. Just as we talk about patients affected by "long COVID" impacts, will healthcare have a "long COVID" impact on professionals' approach to work? Will the risk of mental health deterioration increase as time moves forward? Will people leave the health professions altogether? Will the relationship between providers and patients become permanently altered as a result of provider resentment, patients' evolving expectations, or the increasing use of telemedicine?

There remain important unanswered questions about resilience: can it be taught and if so, can it be boosted with social inoculations of support and gratitude? The pandemic also challenged many students' and trainees' understanding of their professional identity. For many, they had to wrestle with internal conflicts about showing up despite the risk and fear which further impacted their well-being. Over the short and long term our health sciences institutions including schools, hospitals, and clinics need to focus on provider well-being including short-term academic outcomes, long-term mental health outcomes, work-life balance, and overall provider satisfaction. Of paramount importance are patient outcomes but these are intimately tied to the wellness and commitment of those delivering their care. Perhaps the most important steps we can all take are small, simple, and frequent expressions of gratitude for our trainees' willingness to work and learn in the face of harm. As outlined by Shanafelt and colleagues (Shanafelt, Ripp, and Trockel 2020), what the profession needed during the initial stages of the pandemic, and what it needs moving forward, is attention to five pleas – hear me, protect me, prepare me, support me, and care for me – which, incidentally, are the same pleas we hear from our patients.

References

Dyrbye, Liselotte N, Colin P West, Daniel Satele, Sonja Boone, Litjen Tan, Jeff Sloan, and Tait D Shanafelt. 2014. "Burnout Among U.S. Medical Students, Residents, and Early Career Physicians Relative to the General U.S. Population." *Academic Medicine* 89 (3). https://journals.lww.com/academicmedicine/Fulltext/2014/03000/Burnout_Among_U_S__Medical_Students,_Residents,.25.aspx.

Erschens, Rebecca, Katharina Eva Keifenheim, Anne Herrmann-Werner, Teresa Loda, Juliane Schwille-Kiuntke, Till Johannes Bugaj, Christoph Nikendei, Daniel Huhn, Stephan Zipfel, and Florian Junne. 2019. "Professional Burnout among Medical Students: Systematic Literature Review and Meta-Analysis." *Medical Teacher* 41 (2): 172–83. https://doi.org/10.1080/0142159X.2018.1457213.

Fahrenkopf, Amy M, Theodore C Sectish, Laura K Barger, Paul J Sharek, Daniel Lewin, Vincent W Chiang, Sarah Edwards, Bernhard L Wiedermann, and Christopher P Landrigan. 2008. "Rates of Medication Errors among Depressed and Burnt out Residents: Prospective Cohort Study." *BMJ* 336 (7642): 488 LP – 491. https://doi.org/10.1136/bmj.39469.763218.BE.

IsHak, Waguih W, Sara Lederer, Carla Mandili, Rose Nikravesh, Laurie Seligman, Monisha Vasa, Dotun Ogunyemi, and Carol Bernstein. 2009. "Burnout During Residency Training: A Literature Review." *Journal of Graduate Medical Education* 1 (December): 236–42. https://doi.org/10.4300/JGME-D-09-00054.1.

Kunzler, A M, I Helmreich, A Chmitorz, J König, H Binder, M Wessa, and K Lieb. 2020. "Psychological Interventions to Foster Resilience in Healthcare Professionals." *Cochrane Database of Systematic Reviews*,

	Personal concerns	Professional Concerns
Phase 1: initial outbreak - early 2020 through summer 2020	<ul><li>I know I need to care for patients, but I worry I will get sick or die.</li><li>What if I get my family sick?</li><li>What if I get the others sick?</li><li>I am lonely and isolated and want to connect with my fellow trainees, but we can't connect.</li><li>I made a mistake going into healthcare.</li><li>What happens if I get sick? Do I get sick time off?</li><li>Will they give me a place to stay if I am exposed or infected so my family can be safe?</li><li>How do I get to work when I rely on public transportation?</li><li>Do I get more money for working extra shifts?</li></ul>	<ul><li>Is leadership communicating openly and honestly with us?</li><li>Is this institution protecting me and looking after my best interest?</li><li>Will my program/institution care for me if I get sick?</li><li>Is PPE adequate and available?</li><li>How do I work when I need to help provide childcare?</li><li>It feels exciting to have such an important role at this time in healthcare.</li><li>My specialty is really not engaged in caring for COVID patients. I feel useless and embarrassed.</li><li>Does this place even appreciate me?</li><li>I face huge moral distress when asked to ration services.</li><li>It is painful to keep families away from their dying relatives and I can't change the policy.</li></ul>
Phase 2: late summer 2020-early fall 2021	<ul><li>I feel relief that the epidemic is almost over.</li><li>I feel guilty for having limited time with family.</li><li>My family is sick and needs me and I can't be there.</li><li>I'd like to get access to mental health services, but they are overwhelmed.</li><li>What if I need time away?</li><li>How can I afford new expenses as my family needs financial help?</li></ul>	<ul><li>Will I get vaccines early?</li><li>Are leaders addressing our slipping morale?</li><li>My specialty is still really not engaged in caring for COVID patients. I feel useless and embarrassed.</li><li>What if I am redeployed to a new service and I am not qualified?</li></ul>
Phase 3: early fall 2021 – January 2022 (Omicron)	<ul><li>I am angry that we are not back to interacting as trainees and we are getting each other sick.</li><li>I am angry that the reason we are in a surge is because patients will not get vaccinated.</li></ul>	<ul><li>How do I cope with my anger and stay professional?</li><li>Everyone's morale is low.</li></ul>
Phase 4: moving forward	<ul><li>I need to address my burnout after two years of disruption personally and professionally.</li><li>How has this experience impacted my view of medicine both good and bad?</li><li>Have I been inspired by what healthcare has done these two years or perhaps my priorities have shifted and I want more from life - family, friends, fun?</li></ul>	<ul><li>I am watching many leave healthcare.</li><li>I am coming to terms with demoralized colleagues.</li></ul>

Training/Education Concerns	Response to Societal Reactions
• Because of COVID restrictions I am not getting the education/clinical experience I need and want. • Can I learn the material virtually as well as I would learn it in-person?	• Am I really a hero? • Can heroes be scared and not want the hero job? • This pandemic is disproportionately affecting people of color. I am part of the problem.
• What if I am not ready to advance to the next year of training? • What if I am not ready to graduate? • There are no research opportunities. • Will this delay in standard training affect my ability to get a good job or fellowship? • Will I come across well in virtual interviews? • Will I be able to finish my training on time?	• Am I really a hero? • Can heroes be scared and not want the hero job? • This pandemic is disproportionately affecting people of color. I am part of the problem.
• I worry that I am falling behind in my skills because of a solitary focus on COVID. • I feel disconnected from my mentors and fellow trainees.	• The public is no longer seeing my sacrifice.
• I am reconnecting with my educational mission.	• I am no longer the hero, but rather the vaccine enforcer.

no. 7. https://doi.org/10.1002/14651858.CD012527.pub2.

Pietrzak, Robert, Jordyn Feingold, Adriana Feder, Dennis Charney, Lauren Peccoralo, Steven Southwick, and Jonathan Ripp. 2020. "Psychological Resilience in Frontline Health Care Workers During the Acute Phase of the COVID-19 Pandemic in New York City." *The Journal of Clinical Psychiatry* 82 (December). https://doi.org/10.4088/JCP.20l13749.

Shanafelt, Tait, Jonathan Ripp, and Mickey Trockel. 2020. "Understanding and Addressing Sources of Anxiety Among Health Care Professionals During the COVID-19 Pandemic." *JAMA* 323 (21): 2133–34. https://doi.org/10.1001/jama.2020.5893.

Margaret Rea, PhD, is a clinical psychologist, clinical professor in Emergency Medicine and is the Director of Student and Resident Wellness at the UC Davis School of Medicine, the Betty Irene Moore School of Nursing, and Office of Graduate Medical Education, UC Davis Health. She is responsible for overseeing wellness programs and services for medical students, nursing students, residents, and fellows. She is engaged in developing and providing mental health services and wellness prevention programs for students, trainees and faculty providing her with in-depth experience into the many personal and system factors that impact clinician and physician well-being.

Dr. Michael Wilkes is a senior leader in medical education, a past medical school dean with a broad background in health, medicine, education, and public health. He is also an award-winning teacher and medical journalist having worked for National Public Radio, and leading newspapers, television stations, and magazines. He has lived and worked all around the world – USA, UK, Africa, and Asia and understands the immense value of global experiences, the importance of cultural humility, and the value of genuine collaboration and team work. Michael practices clinically as an adolescent physician. He is an accomplished and well-funded researcher often studying clinical practice and learning behaviors.

Adaptation, Compromise, and Resilience: COVID in a Pediatric Intensive Care Unit
By Michael SD Agus

Originally submitted March 15, 2022

Building a plane while flying it. Turning a cruising aircraft carrier on a dime. Never letting a crisis go to waste. Staying nimble in these unprecedented times. These were some of the swirling expressions that colleagues employed to capture the tumult of the COVID-19 pandemic as it unfolded in our hospital in late winter and spring of 2020.

At Boston Children's Hospital (BCH), the seeds of our response to the pandemic were sown back in the fall of 2014 when, together with our hospital epidemiologist, he and I were privileged to be founding co-medical directors of our new BCU and to have a role in shaping our institutional response to Ebola virus disease. The turbulent three-month sprint of near daily meetings with our activated Hospital Incident Command System (HICS) brought to life a BCU replete with a 30-member nursing team as well as ICU and infectious disease doctors. We launched the team into existence as Ebola threatened to appear at our doorstep seemingly any day. After the initial activation, we moved into a seven-year quiescent phase, training quarterly, improving our donning and doffing protocols, developing audio and video communication systems for in and out of the room, and always maintaining camaraderie.

When we received word in January 2020 that a new virus had emerged in Wuhan, China, we activated HICS once again and the BCU leadership was included considering the unlikely eventuality that the virus would require a specialized response here at BCH. While I thought the expertise of our team had grown to become truly outstanding, I did not expect to be useful to the hospital at large, and not in this scenario. As we learned more about the situation in Wuhan, however, it became clear that specialized PPE was going to be required to care for these patients, and that the average healthcare worker was quite nervous about how to don and doff PPE carefully and methodically. The BCU team, on the other hand, had developed a primary expertise in donning and doffing PPE while providing critical care. By the end of February, we had deployed the BCU nurses in a new and innovative role to fan out throughout the hospital as PPE coaches, mentors, and implementers of new institutional Infection

Prevention and Control measures. They were well received.

As our preparations ramped up, news headlines became more frantic, but life continued fundamentally unchanged into March 2020. For me, that all changed during an extraordinary conversation with two Italian physicians in Bergamo, Italy, early in the morning on Friday, March 13, 2020. A colleague had been conducting a regular podcast focused on pediatric cardiac critical care but pivoted to address the emerging pandemic with two intensivists at the epicenter of the Italian infections. I was invited to participate given my roles as intensivist on our BCH COVID-19 leadership team and with the BCU. The conversation, a videoconference call, was simultaneously heartbreaking and terrifying. Our Italian colleagues had gone from a normal society to one completely overrun by illness, overwhelmed resources, and extraordinary rates of mortality in a matter of two weeks. They were exhausted, afraid, and with very little idea how they and their overwhelmed hospital would fare. A story that stuck with me as an indicator of the utter mayhem that had struck their region was that, in halting vehicle traffic and enforcing mandatory stay-at-home orders, the police had also inadvertently shut down all hospital deliveries of medical supplies. By the end of that day in Boston, all schools in the region had been shuttered, and Americans were beginning to process the pervading sense of impending doom.

As the subsequent week proceeded, traffic thinned as businesses serially went into hibernation. Those who were able began to convert to working online from home. Two of my teenage sons had just returned home from a large 15,000-person conference in Washington, DC, when we learned that two of the attendees had been diagnosed with COVID-19. Upon learning of the connection, one of the boys was sent home from college as a precaution. While it did not seem fair for him to be excluded, we figured a few days home would not change much. Of course, a few days turned into six months. Our third son was on spring break playing ultimate frisbee in North Carolina as a senior in college. His college extended his break by a week and he made the most of it. When he finally returned to campus, classes had been canceled. He stayed in his apartment for two more weeks, but when he developed a sore throat and body aches, we instructed him to rent a moving truck immediately and drive the six hours home. Upon his safe arrival, I moved out to a nearby hotel while he settled into quarantine in his room. After a couple of days in the hotel, I opted to move home into our basement keeping a safe distance for a full week until it became clear his illness was not COVID-19. The tumult in our home quickly returned to relative calm as we began to come to terms with the fact that we had reconstituted our family for the first time in many months, and that we were safe.

In addition to my day job, which required my being on site every day for COVID-19 leadership meetings, trainings for innumerable clinical teams, simulations, protocol discussions, and research oversight, I soon became a consultant to several other organizations aware of the need for expert consultation around their operations. I provided varying degrees of consultation to 13 Boston-area Jewish day schools, a synagogue, a private university, a graduate school, a camp, a funeral society, and numerous families who needed guidance in navigating the perils of the pandemic. I found myself interviewed on local and national news and giving webinars to community groups. At the same time, my brother David, a Los Angeles oncologist, doctor to the stars, multiple book author, and all-around superstar, was a regular contributor on CBS News. A fan's comment under one of his postings read, "I love Dr. Agus. I just don't understand how he does so much and still has the time to work in both Boston and LA." Although neither of us traveled much, we both shared our hectic lives with one another frequently. I would describe my conversations with hospital leaders; he would regale me with his conversations with world leaders. We both had our roles to play.

As the pandemic wore on, one theme that came to dominate my thinking and my conversations with everyone from hospital colleagues to school leaders was compromise. As much as we hated to admit it, we had to strike the right balance between safety and action. The companion of absolute safety is paralysis, and the associate of efficient action is reasonable risk. We experienced it all - from the early debate outside an operating room with a surgeon who didn't think he could perform a long operation with his usual expertise if he had to wear the uncomfortable N95 respirator, to the senior outpatient doc who would not enter the room of an asymptomatic patient without full PPE. ICU nurses struggled mightily with the moral weight of delaying a resuscitation by moments while they donned PPE to protect themselves before engaging in the aerosol-generating, contagion-spreading procedure of CPR, especially when it entailed endotracheal intubation.

In one of the most heart-wrenching developments of the pandemic, school leaders and government leaders initially agreed that the safest approach to containing spread was to close the schools. But as time wore on, the psychic trauma of being cut off from friends, peers, and community began to manifest plainly in the astonishing number of depressed, anxious, and suicidal teens who were being admitted to the hospital. What had already been affirmed to be a public mental health crisis spiraled to an unprecedented magnitude due, in large part, to adults' interest in being safe from COVID-19. As teachers' unions became more entrenched in their fears for the health of the staff, children were suffering at home in increasing numbers due to the virus, but not with cough or fever.

2021 eventually arrived to zero fanfare at midnight on the 31st and saw the return of most kids to school over the course of Spring 2021. The summer brought with it a sense of quasi-normalcy that included many seeing their elder parents and relatives for the first time in many months. But everyone seemed to know that we hadn't quite made it back yet.

Fall of 2021 followed, and thanks to COVID-19 vaccines and an increasing percentage of vaccinees in our area, a relatively stable de-escalating pattern emerged: staff at the hospital and people in the community sorted out how to be outside safely, enjoy one another from a slight distance, travel successfully, see family and generally reconnect. But with the fall came stories of an emerging wave of disease associated with a variant. Having a sense that another version of societal shutdown was imminent, I plowed ahead with our division's plans for an all-out holiday party in mid-December, right before the Omicron variant surged in Boston.

An ICU holiday party is a unique phenomenon: doctors, nurses, respiratory therapists, administrative staff—all of us who are up together for countless nights at the bedside of a child undergoing an incredibly sad, stressful, and occasionally triumphant saga and who share an intense bond of serious and important partnership at work. But set up some live music and an open bar, and a different sort of partying solidarity erupts into all out joy and even raucous celebration.

In order to pull this off, our entire administrative team meticulously planned the evening, with every party-goer having to present their negative antigen test at the door for admission (all of whom were also already vaccinated). And all of the event staff, whom we could not legally require to test, wore masks. Except the singer and her sound guy! They had not fit into any category. After chatting with them mask-free for a few minutes, it dawned on me that they were unmasked without testing. I asked them if I could test them, and they obliged. And the sound guy was positive. I asked him to mask and leave, and he promptly did so. No other guests had yet arrived, so I was the only one who was exposed. And seven days later I tested positive. Although a very mild illness, I lost my taste and smell for approximately 30 hours and was scared during that time that it would last much longer.

I received a lot of sympathy during my illness, especially as people were grateful and relieved that there was not an outbreak from the party. But as my illness was wrapping up, Omicron hit Boston hard. Hospital staff were out of work in unprecedented numbers. And children were being admitted to the hospital with COVID in numbers five to eight times higher than at any prior moment in the pandemic. But while society's fears were roiling, clinical care was being delivered calmly. Staff had figured out the donning and the doffing. The BCU team did not need to be re-activated. We got through the surge, staff returned to work, and we just kept at it.

As I write this, with the first hints of spring 2022 beginning to emerge in Boston, the Omicron wave is in our rear-view mirror. There are reports of new surges in the United Kingdom and China, and the re-emergence of COVID is being spotted in Ukraine and the surrounding countries as people focus on feeding and housing refugees from the Russian onslaught rather than masking and COVID testing. But life in Boston is slowly bubbling to the surface. The great majority of people walk outside without masks; restaurants are starting to bustle; supermarkets no longer require masks, but most people can't seem to take them off quite yet. However, it's clear that the process has begun to unravel. We breathe more deeply, more calmly, and realize that we have friends and colleagues at work whose mouths and chins we have literally only ever imagined. I can't help but stare when a facial profile is so different than what I had imagined.

My continued interactions with heads of schools, camps, and other organizations confirm the oft-suspected fears that this generation of children and adolescents has sustained extraordinary emotional and academic losses. Depressingly common are the reports that the 12-year-olds who go to camp act more like 10- or 11-year-olds developmentally. They don't have the skills to interact fluidly. They are mean, insecure, apprehensive, and fragile. They text better than they speak. They don't know how to express an interest in someone as a friend or as more than that. It's hard to be optimistic that society will not sustain irretrievable losses due to the developmental deprivation which they have experienced.

In the hospital, staff are leaving their units or the entire field in exceptional numbers. Physicians, so deeply trained in their fields, seem to be persevering in their roles in general, although the elder ones are exiting in greater numbers than they have in decades. The common driver to this increased and disruptive flux seems to be a recalibration of priorities. In losing connection to family and friends over the course of the pandemic, the primal value and satisfaction in their professional lives seems to have been profoundly diminished, as well.

For my part, I have clung to the live, face-to-face community we have been so privileged to maintain in the hospital throughout the entire period. While I enjoy the occasional morning at home on Zoom with easy access to another espresso or a sunny deck, the camaraderie and unity of purpose that characterize the work we are privileged to do remains deeply fulfilling. I can only hope that the rest of my professional community feels the same way, and channels that energy into the restorative work that we all need to continue to do in order to recover a fraction of what we have lost. It is, in fact, possible that these pandemic lessons, well-learned, will make us smarter, stronger, more resilient, and more effective. When we eventually tell our tales to the next generation who knows nothing of these events other than our stories, I hope that is the ending we are able to report.

Dr. Agus is the Division Chief of Medical Critical Care within the Department of Pediatrics at Boston Children's Hospital where he is the Founding Medical Director of the Medical Intensive Care Unit and the Intermediate Care Unit. He is trained and board certified both as a pediatric endocrinologist and pediatric intensivist and holds the Constantine Anast MD Professorship of Pediatrics at Harvard Medical School. He co-founded the Biocontainment Unit in 2014 which was activated in a novel fashion to help guide the institution through the COVID Pandemic. He is a clinical trialist focusing on endocrine homeostasis in critically ill children.

The Transformational Effect of the Pandemic on Medical Knowledge Exchange: From Webinar-to-Bedside
By Jeffrey Burns

Originally submitted October 30, 2020

The COVID-19 pandemic is a global tragedy in every dimension, with relatively few examples of effective international collaboration necessary to meet the challenge. The Pediatric Intensive Care-COVID-19 International Collaborative is one example of effective collaboration where physician and research experts from over 100 of the largest children's hospitals across six continents, as well as senior representatives from the WHO, US and European Union (EU) Centers for Disease Control and Prevention, NIH, and senior editors from the leading medical journals, are meeting in real time to exchange knowledge on the impact of COVID-19 leading to critical illness in children. What government or NGO organizes and hosts this international collaboration vital to the health of children—the WHO, the CDC, the NIH, the European Commission? None of them. As improbable as it may seem, it is organized and hosted from the laptop on which I write this article, and broadcast on the first Saturday evening of the month from my home outside of Boston.

How did this come about? Entirely by serendipity. Early in the pandemic, March 14, 2020, I was exchanging emails with my counterparts at several of the largest children's hospitals in North America seeking real time and reliable information on the impact of COVID-19 leading to critical illness in children. We quickly realized that serial emails were inefficient, and I agreed to host a Zoom meeting that evening, inviting colleagues from North America and Europe through a long-standing international collaboration and knowledge sharing website I co-direct: OPENPediatrics.org. Five hours later, the impromptu call had rapidly expanded to include experts in pediatric critical illness from approximately 40 children's hospitals across the world exchanging real time information on the effect of the pandemic on children.

This webinar instantly, even if unexpectedly, filled a gap in knowledge exchange for pediatric specialists across the world, exposing the need for more immediate and externally valid and reliable information on the impact of SARS-CoV-2 on children. Up to this time in the pandemic, despite the attempts by medical journals to accelerate the peer-review process, and despite the increased reliance on preprint servers for insights into the emerging literature in this domain, pediatric critical care physicians across the world were desperate for more instantaneous and trustworthy information on how to care for these children. The first webinar on March 14th was deemed to be such a success that we went to a twice a week format, and by the second webinar the audience had rapidly mushroomed to colleagues from all of the largest children's hospitals across six continents.

As with the webinar itself, the chat function of the webinar platform serendipitously filled yet another vital gap in our understanding of the impact of this virus on children. On the second webinar, March 18, 2020, the audience spontaneously started using the chat function to create the only instantaneous, worldwide point-prevalence survey on the prevalence of children critically ill from COVID-19. The chat astonishingly started streaming what amounted to a live report of how many critically ill children were hospitalized in the pediatric ICU from across the world. Improvising as needed, after this webinar we well understood that the recorded chat was both a significant source repository of validated information on the world-wide spread of the virus in children and simultaneously a potential violation of their right to privacy protection. Thus, the third webinar on March 21, 2020, became an 'invitation-only, academic conference' where each participant had to register her hospital or academic credentials to join the conference. Nonetheless, word soon spread through the medical community that this international webinar was the only real-time, accurate, and worldwide source for this information. By the fourth webinar, senior representatives from the WHO, the US and European CDC, the NIH, the European Commission asked to join the webinar in part to specifically monitor the prevalence of critical illness in children from COVID-19, as directly reported from the physicians caring for them in pediatric ICUs across the world.

Each episode of the webinar also featured direct reports from each epicenter on the impact of the SARS-CoV-2 virus on children, providing yet another means of instantaneously transferring reliable information at a rate that could not be matched by the peer-reviewed, medical literature publication cycle. We were hearing directly from our colleagues caring for critically ill children with COVID-19, first from Wuhan, then Italy, next Spain, then Paris, London and finally New York. Our Chinese colleagues were the first to alert us that, compared to the illness in adults, in the relatively few children in Wuhan who became critically ill, they were frequently presenting with atypical symptoms and detectable levels of SARS-CoV-2 in their blood. Thus, from one live webinar, colleagues from over 100 pediatric hospitals across six continents were simultaneously alerted to look for these subtle signs and symptoms. The early insights provided by our Chinese colleagues from Wuhan were soon confirmed by colleagues who reported a similar experience from each of the epicenters. Compared to the experience of adults with COVID-19, children became critically ill from the virus far less frequently, with much better outcomes, but often with a different constellation of signs and symptoms.

The webinar also provided an efficient platform for the global dissemination of information on a previously unrecognized phenomenon—the multisystem inflammatory syndrome. In mid to late April 2020, in the chat function of the webinar, a few colleagues from pediatric hospitals across Western Europe reported the hospitalization of a few children with a new constellation of signs and symptoms not entirely consistent with COVID-19, but with some overlapping features, leading to multisystem inflammation and critical illness similar to toxic shock syndrome and Kawasaki disease. Most noted that this unexplained illness appeared approximately two to four weeks after an apparent infection with COVID-19. Our colleagues from Great Britain asked if we could devote the entire next webinar to a discussion of the emerging research data on children presenting with this multisystem inflammation and critical illness.

Thus it was that this Pediatric Intensive Care-COVID-19 International Collaborative webinar, begun spontaneously only six weeks prior, and organized from a home in greater Boston, became, on May 2, 2020, the gathering place of an international panel of clinicians and researchers in pediatric intensive care, pediatric cardiology, pediatric rheumatology, pediatric infectious disease, and Kawasaki disease—nearly 2,000 colleagues from across the world, as well as representatives from the WHO, NIH, CDC and European Commission, and editors of the leading medical journals, gathering virtually from across the world to discuss this new and emerging illness in children.

Over the next 70 minutes we analyzed the emerging evidence via Zoom in front of colleagues, researchers, and public health officials from six continents. More than a graduate level seminar, this was live analysis and hypothesis generation made possible by real-time, unpublished data (these data were published several weeks later in the *Journal of the*

American Medical Association) (Shekerdemian et al. 2020) and made necessary by a pandemic that will not wait for the traditional medical journal peer-review process.

Our panel concluded that the rise in hospitalizations in children with unexplained fever, first across Western Europe, then across the Eastern seaboard of the US in April 2020, was most likely due to a post-viral mechanism, and called for the international pediatric medical community to adopt the case definition recently put forth by the Royal College of Paediatrics and Child Health (2020) in order to promote immediate awareness and begin world-wide research collaboration. By mid-May 2020 the WHO, US and EU CDC had written world-wide alerts to pediatricians on the signs and symptoms of the newly named Multisystem Inflammatory Disorder in Children (MIS-C) (CDC 2020).

Was it a breakdown of public health organizations or the medical literature peer review process that required my colleagues and me to create this international collaborative webinar to share real-time and reliable knowledge on COVID-19 leading to critical illness in children? In my view, it was not. The astonishing pace of this pandemic did, however, expose an evident gap in the traditional mechanisms for rapid knowledge exchange amongst physicians that demands a venue for more real-time, unfiltered, and global collaboration. Is the webinar format destined to be a disruptive innovation in the field of medicine? Only time will tell. However, in nearly 30 years of caring for critically ill children, I have seen countless times that nothing leads to collaboration more readily and effectively than a willingness to share knowledge on the care of a critically ill child. Our world may not agree on even basic issues like food and water rights, but we do agree on collaboration in the care of critically ill children everywhere, and it is actually happening in the midst of the enormous human suffering caused by this pandemic.

References

Centers for Disease Control and Prevention (CDC). 2020. *Emergency preparedness and response: Multisystem inflammatory syndrome in children (MIS-C) associated with coronavirus disease 2019 (COVID-19).* https://emergency.cdc.gov/han/2020/han00432.asp.

Royal College of Paediatrics and Child Health. 2020. *Guidance – Paediatric multisystem inflammatory syndrome temporally associated with COVID-19.* https://www.rcpch.ac.uk/resources/guidance-paediatric-multisystem-inflammatory-syndrome-temporally-associated-covid-19.

Shekerdemian, Lara S, Nabihah R Mahmood, Katie K Wolfe, Becky J Riggs, Catherine E Ross, Christine A McKiernan, Sabrina M Heidemann, et al. 2020. "Characteristics and outcomes of children with coronavirus disease 2019 (COVID-19) infection admitted to US and Canadian pediatric intensive care units." *JAMA Pediatrics* 174 (9): 868–73. https://doi.org/10.1001/jamapediatrics.2020.1948.

Dr. Burns is Chief and Shapiro Chair of Critical Care Medicine at Boston Children's Hospital and Professor of Anesthesia at Harvard Medical School.

We are Demons, a Blind Old Woman, a Nurse Who Does Nails, We are Musicians
By Tim Lahey

Originally submitted October 31, 2020

Every inch of the walls of the back room of the COVID-19 floor was festooned with reusable plastic face shields. Even the windows were covered.

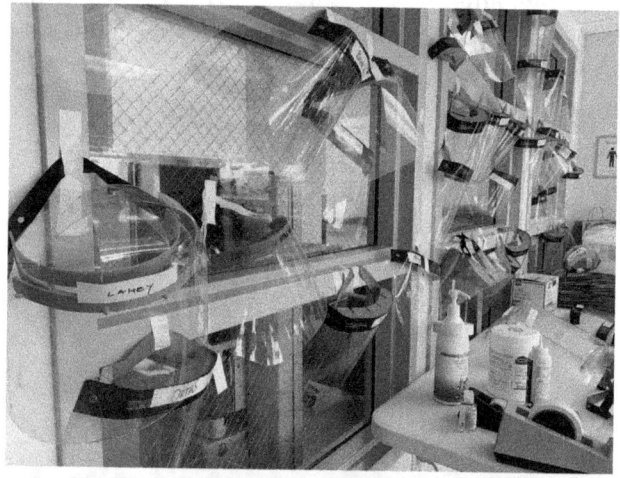

Figure 1. Masks awaiting reuse (top); A view outside through masks (bottom)

There was a sameness to the face shields, one after another, each labelled with the previous wearer's name. The array reminded me of ritual masks I had seen hanging in museums. Sri Lankan *sanni* masks, for instance, allow wearers to personify demons including Deva Sanniya, the demon of epidemics (Bailey and De Silva 2006). Did we, the masked entrants into the hot rooms of our patients' dyspnea, come to personify COVID-19 itself?

Without doubt we became progressively less and less personally identifiable as we donned PPE. We covered our clothes with a gown, our faces with a mask and face shield, and our skin with gloves. Patients too were changed, by a mask if they were lucky and by a plastic tube in their trachea if they were not.

Healthcare workers certainly have become demons to some people. And, as the story unfolds, I have learned more about who we really are.

One rainy day, I retrieved my face shield from the wall on the COVID floor and saw that there were still droplets of rain on the hospital windows.

Droplets. The little lip and tongue percussion of the word once conjured the sound of a forest after a storm, the wind shaking soft drops off the leaves and onto wet duff. Now droplets and aerosols conjure danger. Church choirs and horn players send plumes of killing air twenty feet from where they made their music (Hamner et al. 2020, Plautz 2020). Blowing out birthday candles can extinguish lives (City News Service 2020).

"I never had much sympathy for the plague doctor," wrote Dr. Mark Earnest. The image of a physician from the Middle Ages wearing a beaked mask "represented the triumph of fear and superstition over the more noble impulses I hoped would drive me in a time of crisis." Earnest found new sympathy for his physician forebearers when he walked for the first time into the room of a patient with COVID-19 in full PPE (Earnest 2020).

The physical environment of hospital rooms felt newly foreign as well. Before we knew our PPE would keep us safe, the familiar act of knocking on a door and walking into a COVID-19 patient's room felt more like walking through an airlock and onto the surface of the moon.

Beyond changing us and the spaces where we work, the year 2020 asked us to make innumerable public and private calculations about protection from COVID-19. About sufficiency of protection and sterility.

The word "sterile" derives from the Latin *sterilis* or "barren," "unproductive," "unfruitful," and even "unrequited." Conversations that take place in full PPE certainly can feel barren and unproductive. Meant to pertain to microbes, these unmeant meanings contaminate our efforts

Figure 2. Plague Doctor

to connect.

Across town from the hospital, at a nursing home decimated by a COVID-19 outbreak, a palliative care doctor was putting on PPE. He was part of a team sent to the nursing home to help beleaguered staff, minister to dying residents, and to build outbreak containment measures that would make the nursing home safe again.

He remembered his first day in the nursing home. "The staff looked like zombies," he said. "Their faces were so blank," he guessed from the trauma of watching so many of their longstanding patients die gasping for air. I imagined them wearing masks that closely resembled their own faces—but were not.

The nursing home staff called their patients "Guests." In time the palliative care doctor helped the Guests who did want hospitalization to die without gasping. A seasoned clinician, the palliative care leader said he was acutely aware of how much harder it was to relieve suffering when the right medicines weren't on site and the nursing home staff were willing to help but operating well outside their usual clinical skills.

One ordinary day in the stretch of weeks he would eventually call some of the most meaningful of his career, the palliative care leader was preparing to examine an elderly woman who was blind. Trying to connect, to "see" him, she reached out to touch him before he finished donning his PPE. He remembered her dry hand touching his shoulder and moving up to his face. He froze, wondering if he should back away until fully covered or let her touch him. He chose contamination and did not get sick.

This was one of the first moments in which I saw clinicians make profound human connections despite their fear, their patients' sickness and the many layers of PPE between them.

Outside that same nursing home, early in the pandemic, one nurse arrived for work with her raincoat folded on the passenger seat of her car. Rain was forecast but now the sun was out. The nurse stepped out of her car, closed its door, and started to walk into work. Then the nurse reopened the car door and pulled her raincoat out. She had remembered that the nursing home had gloves and surgical masks but too few goggles and N95's. To feel safer, she put on a raincoat and walked in.

It was a quiet act of courage I would not have known had someone else not noted the disconnect between her clothing and the current weather.

As the nursing home effort to save lives and alleviate suffering continued, I met with the palliative care group to debrief. At first, we talked about logistics. Could the hospital's pharmacy supply packets of end-of-life opioids for use at the nursing home where hospice care was not typically provided? How long would it take the National Guard to build a hut outside the nursing home where clinicians could wash their hands and don PPE without getting drenched by rain or snow?

Many healthcare systems faced similar and even larger challenges providing high quality care. Early in the epidemic, health systems struggled to address the palliative needs of their patients. Symptom control suffered; in-home hospice care delivery was complicated by visitation restrictions and family quarantine; PPE shortages made clinician engagement perilous; and many patients died separated from the people they love. Now that we have confronted those realities and health systems have grown more accustomed to managing COVID-19, planning to address such end-of-life needs more effectively is critical. For instance, Colorado clinicians developed a three-tiered plan to ensure that patient end-of-life care improved despite the epidemic, including widespread advance care planning drives, development of alternate care sites where patients can still receive high quality end-of-life care, and expansion of the palliative care consultation infrastructure (Abbott, Johnson, and Wynia 2020).

Through all of these efforts, which naturally focus on the logistics of healthcare delivery, our teams fought to stay connected to patients. One palliative care nurse painted the nails of an elderly woman in the nursing home while wearing full PPE. The mundane was made exotic, she felt personal danger, and yet still she found a way to take her time to be kind to an old lady.

After the hustle of those and other logistics abated, and the Guests who were going to die had died, the usual rhythms of the nursing home resumed. That was when conversations with the palliative care team went deeper. Nurses talked about guilt they felt for the care they provided to Guests before the right medications and other infrastructure needs were there. They wondered if they should have refused or helped as best they could. Physicians talked about heart-wrenching goodbyes they saw patients say to families on the other side of the nursing home's windows. Families miming love to each other, crying, unheard.

One image stuck with me. After the palliative care team arranged for families to say their farewells to dying loved ones by video, one family held a small concert for their dying patriarch, a former musician. The nurses held an iPad for him so he could hear his family making music and saying they loved him. The image struck me as worthy of a richly shadowed Baroque painting by Caravaggio or Ribera. The gowned nurses with worried brows. Their masks. The exhausted smile of the dying man lit up by the iPad screen. All of them attuned to the indomitable music of human connection.

Despite the ever-present threat of the virus, the ubiquitous masks, the growing social isolation, and the simultaneous fear and numbness of the pandemic's epidemiology, we have also grown accustomed to witnessing these daily acts of heroism and kindness.

Those moments are a balm to me, and a reminder. "This is who we are," I think, as I get up to do it all again another day. "This is who we are."

References

Abbott, Jean, Daniel Johnson, and Matthew Wynia. "Ensuring Adequate Palliative and Hospice Care During COVID-19 Surges." *JAMA*, 324(14), 1393–1394. September 21, 2020. https://doi.org/10.1001/jama.2020.16843JAMA

Bailey, Mark S. and Janaka de Silva. 2006. "Sri Lankan sanni masks: an ancient classification of disease". *BMJ* 333(7582):1327-8. 10.1136/bmj.39055.445417.BE

City News Service of NBC4 Pasadena. 2020. "Large Birthday Party Sparked COVID-19 Outbreak, Pasadena Officials Say". *NBC Los Angeles*, May 9, 2020. https://www.nbclosangeles.com/news/coronavirus/large-birthday-party-sparked-covid-19-outbreak-pasadena-officials-say/2359797/

Earnest, Mark. 2020. "On becoming a plague doctor." *New England Journal of Medicine* 383 (10): e64. https://doi.org/10.1056/NEJMp2011418

Hamner, Lea, Polly Dubbel, Ian Capron, Andry Ross, Amber Jordan, Jaxon Lee, Joanne Lynn, Amelia Ball, et al. 2020. "High SARS-CoV-2 Attack Rate Following Exposure at a Choir Practice — Skagit County, Washington, March 2020". *MMWR* 69(19):606-610. http://dx.doi.org/10.15585/mmwr.mm6919e6external icon

Plautz, Jason. 2020. "Is it safe to strike up the band in a time of coronavirus?" *Science Direct*, July 17, 2020. https://www.sciencemag.org/news/2020/07/it-safe-strike-band-time-coronavirus

Tim Lahey is an infectious diseases physician, educator, and ethicist. His scholarship has focused on HIV and tuberculosis immunology, medical education, and clinical ethics. He has written about challenging moments in clinical care for *The New York Times, Washington Post, Atlantic*, and beyond.

Anomalous: Respiratory Care Delivered During, and Redefined By, COVID-19
By Eric Jones

Submitted on April 14, 2022

The effects of this pandemic will be felt for many years in the healthcare community, even after operations return to normal.

I have always thoroughly enjoyed my role as an RT on the multidisciplinary healthcare team. The ability to help patients transition from being critically ill on a mechanical ventilator in the ICU to being downgraded to floors receiving nebulizers assisting with breathing, to helping rehab and strengthening lungs, speaks to the diverse role that I get to play throughout the hospital stay.

In addition to being a charge therapist, I am also a member of a specialized BCU, organized even before the COVID-19 pandemic. There we train to deal with highly infectious diseases such as Ebola, SARS, smallpox, and anything else that may emerge to threaten population health. When I first learned of a respiratory illness occurring in Wuhan, China, it was too distant for me to be concerned about.

In March 2020, we welcomed our first critical COVID-19 patient into the BCU, with a few more following shortly afterwards. In this controlled environment where I spent a decent amount of time, I felt a little apprehensive but was confident in the training that I had received. My wife and family were already worried about me going into work with this virus after the WHO officially declared it a pandemic. As the month progressed, it was clear that this one unit would not be enough, so the hospital began the process of transforming units throughout the hospital into 'Biounits' to care for the incoming COVID patients.

The process was well-planned but still a level of anxiety for all involved existed. As time passed, increasing numbers of patients began rolling in. More and more Biounits needed to be created as existing ones were filled. Many of the patients within our hospital were sick enough that they required high flow nasal cannula (HFNC) or intubation with proning techniques or inhaled nitric oxide, among other therapies. Though we were very lucky at my institution to have planned early on for the pandemic and had stockpiled ventilators and PPE, the respiratory department became stressed quickly as there was not enough staff on hand to deal with the patient workload. To help with this, nurse anesthetists and medical residents were brought on to help ease daily assignments. Physical therapists helped with checking and documenting on all patients on oxygen and head turns for the many proned patients we had in our units. Though we were very grateful for the assistance, stress still existed as we had to train those brought on to assist us while still handling our daily duties. Even with the added help, there was still a need for RTs to work mandatory overtime so that patients would get the care that they desperately needed.

Along with everyone, I felt the toll of spending the majority of my 12-hour shift in a PAPR hood or N95 mask. On many shifts I ran from room to room providing nonstop care with limited bathroom breaks and water because my patients needed me. Working in the ICU, I am used to dealing with the sickest patients, even as they make the transition to end-of-life. Unfortunately, working in this pandemic was emotionally gut-wrenching at times as patients expressed loneliness from being isolated and fear as they were told that they needed a breathing tube in order to survive this disease process. Worse still was that family members were not allowed to be present to support their loved ones. Zoom meetings were set up to provide some contact, though it was not the same as holding your loved one's hand and providing comfort. At the height of the pandemic, as deaths mounted throughout the country and at my hospital, I felt taxed to the point that I needed to detach myself somewhat from work in order not to become immersed in the mentally and emotionally exhaustive work that my colleagues and I were doing.

I remember at one point in the beginning of the pandemic when I had a patient who was maxed out on support with HFNC and talks began with him about having to be intubated. Even on the high amount of oxygen support that he required, his disposition was still quite cheerful, and he expressed gratitude for the work that all the staff were doing. He was very witty and funny, often causing the staff to joke along with him and keeping spirits high. Unfortunately, his oxygenation status continued to worsen, and non-invasive support was no longer an option. He agreed to intubation and was given a few short minutes to call his wife to tell her that he wouldn't be able to talk to her for a while. "I love you babe. I'll talk to you when I get on the other side of this," he said. The phone call ended, and he was placed on mechanical ventilation and proned. This situation – wherein some patients were not fortunate enough to see or speak to loved ones again – seemed to recur over and over throughout the pandemic.

Throughout the whole ordeal, I was always concerned that caring for these patients may also put my very own family at risk. Although it may be possible for some to minimize exposure to droplets and aerosols, most of what I do as a respiratory therapist requires exposure. I am normally right by the airway of patients giving nebulizer treatments, encouraging them to cough up secretions, involved in aerosol-generating procedures like intubation, extubation, and non-invasive therapies like HFNC and BiPAP. We would hear accounts of nurses and doctors who acquired the virus and passed away, which caused more concern for the RTs. Even with that anxiety, I couldn't let fear get in the way of caring for my patients. I would go into work wearing separate scrubs and then at the end of my shift I would be sure to strip these off, wash up, and put on another pair of scrubs before coming home. In the very beginning, because of the newness of this virus I even separated myself from my family and stayed in my basement for a short period of time. This certainly placed a stress on my family, and they were constantly concerned for me every time I headed into work.

One thing that I can take away from working in this pandemic is the camaraderie built among everyone who went through it. Given the extreme circumstances, we all had to lean on each other for support which brought us closer together. Though some have transitioned from healthcare after experiencing burnout or even continue working with a level of post-traumatic stress disorder, I can honestly say that I have been lucky to have the level of support within my family and at my institution that has allowed me to keep going. The historical gravity of this experience is not lost upon me. I hope we are able to learn from the lessons of this pandemic for future pandemics, both in caring for our patients and ourselves.

Eric Jones is a respiratory therapist currently working at Johns Hopkins. With a passion of caring for patients, he has 17 years of experience working within the healthcare setting. He has experience working in inpatient critical care, outpatient, trauma, and is also a member of the National Disaster Medical Service. He is currently working to obtain his MBA at Johns Hopkins Carey Business School. Eric is married with two wonderful kids. His passions include traveling, reading, learning, writing short stories, and watching movies.

Tripping the Pandemic
By David Hellerstein

Originally submitted January 14, 2022

Whether it descended on us mortals through the influence of the heavenly bodies or was sent down by God in His righteous anger to chastise us because of our wickedness, it had begun some years before in the East, where it deprived countless beings of their lives before it headed to the West, spreading ever greater misery as it moved relentlessly from place to place. Against it all human wisdom and foresight were useless.
—Boccaccio, *The Decameron* (2013)

March 8, 2020

Saturday night we're at the theatre seeing *Girl from the North Country*, a musical of patched-together Dylan songs. Behind us someone keeps coughing: A large man in a down vest who speaks in a thick accent, German, I think, and can't catch his breath. At intermission I grab the usher.

"Listen!" I point at him. "I'm a doctor, you have to get him out of here!"

She leads me to the house manager.

"We can't make him leave," the manager says. She offers us seats only three rows from the stage.

I keep haranguing her: "Don't you know what is happening? It's spreading here from Europe! It's coming! It's coming! Why do you let him stay? You'll be shut down in a week!"

March 16, 2020

Now it is here: Our first pandemic. No doubt thanks to my witches' curse Broadway has gone dark. And my wife has fallen ill: fever, fatigue, cough, COVID-like enough to freak us out, but there's nowhere to get tested. Myself, for a few days there's been a strange aching rawness in my throat. We definitely caught it at the theatre.

We are locked down at home, hoping to recover. Above all we are avoiding the emergency room only two blocks away. We cough, we struggle to breathe, we pray.

In the park last weekend before we fell ill, we masked up and ventured out for a walk. Down the hill in a sunny field near the baseball diamond a woman lay among daffodils, blond hair tied back, her black purse fallen to the side. She was well dressed and motionless. Nearby stood two men, one punching numbers into his iPhone. I hadn't seen death on the street since the crack epidemic in the early 1990's, a disheveled man on the steps of the Metropolitan Museum as I pushed my daughter in a stroller early one Sunday morning, undoubtedly an overdose.

Today, the woman lay there, mostly ignored by people rushing by. Could she have come here, ready to sit in the park on a beautiful Spring afternoon, then died of COVID? Seems unimaginable, but who knows?

Eventually we moved on. When would EMS arrive? We kept looking back as we walked uptown past the turtle pond and climbed the stairs toward home, and there was no sound of a siren. We couldn't even tell if the two men were still there.

March 24, 2020

We are not going to die. We can breathe, our coughs are gradually resolving. The pulse oximeter from CVS reports oxygen saturations above 97%. But the world is burning.

Like everyone else we are searching online, buying toilet paper and paper towels, hunting for masks and gloves and Purell, checking up on relatives and friends. Beyond that, I am worried about my patients. Patients from my practice and from my studies. Trying to figure out how to keep them safe, even from a distance.

I am a research psychiatrist in New York City, US pandemic central. My specialty is clinical trials. This past year, I've been doing research on psilocybin in major depression; we are one of 25 sites in a major international study. After being classified as Schedule 1, drugs with no medical uses, for over 40 years, psychedelic drugs are making a huge comeback, and the FDA has fast-tracked our study.

Already we have dosed a dozen people with severe 'treatment-resistant' depression. To enroll, they need to have failed to respond to several antidepressant drugs. We phone-screened hundreds of people; we bring in likely candidates for evaluations, for labs and physical exams. To participate, they need to taper off antidepressants, then wait several weeks for psilocybin dosing.

Psychedelic treatment is not for the faint-hearted, hardly the same as college kids doing shrooms at a rave. Beside the challenges of managing patients who have come off ineffective medications before psilocybin treatment, there's the delicate art of managing them after dosing, when brain networks are entropic, chaotic, forging new connections, and emotions run high. Post-dosing weeks can be hair-raising.

As COVID approached we began shutting down our site, turning away the hordes. For patients already dosed, we must figure how to follow them since the clinics are closing and we can no longer see them in person. Huge barriers arise from mundane issues: how to reach them and our scattered staff, how to use a virtual private network (VPN) to access hospital charts when the Internet has slowed to a crawl.

A bigger problem: patients already in the pipeline, awaiting dosing. What to do? Can we dose them amidst rising COVID? Will we infect them, will they infect us? Versus their risk of suicide, off all meds for weeks, desperately awaiting transformation.

Last Thursday, we dosed one patient. And tomorrow, the second one. We will see them in person for a post-dosing visit or two, then they plan to flee the City, heading for faraway states.

April 11, 2020

Gradually we have settled into a new routine.

On the doorknob of my study hang various masks, airing out, ready to be re-used. A vat of chlorine wipes snagged off nearly-empty shelves at CVS sits on the kitchen counter. Outdoors, we dodge passersby and curse at lunging joggers. We wake at three AM seeking online grocery delivery slots, or just because.

We set up for work at home, my wife and I on the couch and dining room table, Zooming and FaceTiming and emailing. After sundown we wander around the deserted university. The usually buzzing restaurants are dark, a few passing takeout bags through barricaded doorways, others piled with dusty tables and chairs with flapping paper signs promising new hours. Our building looms with ghosts. Of two dozen apartments maybe four are occupied, everyone else having fled to the countryside, to cabins and cottages and overpriced Airbnbs on dark lakes.

The deserted streets echo, thanks to the vastly amplified ambulances – *why ramp the sirens up when no one is on the streets?* – and all-too-frequent patrol cars sirening through darkness. Not to mention helicopters hovering like angry dragonflies when something bad happens below, something you won't find in the Times but that may pop up in a *Daily News* feed. Even groceries are complicated, as we shun the markets on Broadway, and no Fresh Direct or Instacart deliveries are available. We rarely leave home, and when we do, we double-mask, we hold folded paper towels to avoid touching naked doorknobs. We pay our once-a-week housekeeper to stay home.

Meanwhile no one goes to the hospital except essential workers. I'm not essential, it turns out; neither are most of my fellow psychiatrists. But the psychiatry *residents* – recently awarded their MDs – are called in. Two of my residents are drafted to work the COVID ICU, despite not having set foot on medical units since internship. They tell of emergency room horrors, of gasping women on gurneys in hallways, of shortages of PPE and dialysis fluids, of jury-rigged ventilation systems blowing air into stairwells, of heroic exhausted nurses and clerks, and how they are supervised by doctors who have never worked in ICUs.

But back to psilocybin. *At a time like this, why even think of research?* But I do.

We have a dozen vials of this Schedule 1 drug at the Research Pharmacy ready for study participants, but now gradually approaching their expiration dates. Of course, there are no new participants since we had to shut down recruitment. Will we ever start again? How ridiculous to obsess about this, to spend endless hours trying to figure how to get my patients tripping safely through the pandemic.

Why bother doing research when the world is shut down and a vaccine is likely years away?

But why bother doing anything?

This is what we asked nearly twenty years ago, when New York City was the epicenter of a different pandemic, after the towers fell and we watched columns of charcoal smoke fill the air. Back then we swore to start again too. The thing is, it is hard to imagine the virus disappearing anytime soon, so if we want to ever do this research, this is what we need to live with; we must find a way to dose safely in a coronal tsunami.

First thing every morning, at seven AM or even earlier, I open the New York Times iPhone app to check the City's body count. Then I walk our elderly dog along the dark margin of the park, take the elevator home to coffee and a bagel, fire up my MacBook, and ride the VPN into the hospital network, trying to get the study going again.

April 22, 2020

And then there is my private practice. Like many medical academics, I supplement my salary by treating a small number of private patients. In my case, I have been seeing them in an office a few miles downtown. Once the pandemic hit, I switched to 'telepsychiatry'—to phone and Zoom and FaceTime. I still go to my office, though, driving or bicycling for miles on deserted streets, partly because that's where their charts are, but more for a change of scene.

Most of them are struggling. Their shows are canceled, their stores shuttered, their partners and college-aged kids stranded overseas. Homebound, they worry, they pace, they battle helplessness and despair. The patient who works in a nursing home tells me about her sick coworkers, about how they assume 100% of their residents are infected, how staff wear black garbage bags over scrubs, how against all the rules they re-use N95 masks. Some get infected, and struggle to survive. With everyone virtual, I can pace around too in my office, I can lie on my own therapy couch, feet up, for sessions, no worries about breathing shared air, about who touches what. I don't even take checks anymore, just credit cards. It's all virtual, except the suffering.

Strangely, some patients tell me that they feel *better* than usual in lockdown, that they've been prepping for catastrophe all their lives, and for the first time feel validated, vindicated: their horrific fears having materialized, cannot be denied.

Tonight, while driving home, my sister the obstetrician calls from Boston. COVID-positive women are delivering babies into her hands; inadequate PPE is being issued to nurses and clerks; they are canceling surgeries for women with uterine cancer. Our risks in psychiatry are less visible, I tell her, it's just from hearing all the woe, uncertainty piled upon uncertainty, furloughs, closed offices, vanishing savings. All day, isolated people, locked in their homes, call and email and text, their uncertainties multiplied by 25- and 50-minute increments. That takes a toll.

Uptown, I park below scaffolding of the building whose renovation has been halted suddenly. So many, many parking spaces. Today, a trove of N95 masks has arrived, twenty of them, sent by a student in Hong Kong. I set the box on a chair, except one mask which I hang with several others on the door. I have quite a collection: the hand-made cloth mask from a tailor shop in the West 80s; the one a lady at the Bronx Fairway mercifully handed out to me a few weeks ago; the oversized blue surgical paper mask from when I went to the Psychiatric Institute earlier this week; and pocketed extras from the security desk. I add my new 3M N95 mask, which may even not be counterfeit, but is illegal to wear at the hospital.

April 29, 2020

Two white refrigerated trucks are parked at the hospital a block from home, one pulled into the loading dock, another flush to the curb, an improvised plastic canopy over raw framed two by fours so they can load bodies without getting their PPE wet.

The worst is at seven PM every day when the hushed silence is shattered by sirens and horns and bells and wailings of all sorts and banging of pots and blasting of *New York New York!* And ragged cheers, but you don't hear it as single sounds, instead as a massive agglomeration of the earth's distress as you are peeling cucumbers or dicing carrots for yet another tossed salad and only gradually do you realize that another day has passed, and it's cheering for the essential workers, not a general alarm. Though perhaps it is such an alarm, since otherwise it would be a quiet hour, everyone arriving at home after work. Instead, we are already at home, having tried to work, now trying to relax, and the only certain thing is that we will be here for a whole lot longer.

On the streets, like fallen flowers everywhere, there are blue masks, some with strewn long white ties like the legs of crushed arachnids, others with neater ear loops, and fallen blossoms or leaves, and purple and flesh-colored gloves like hands that have fallen off their owners. There is the dance on the sidewalk as we walk our daily 10,000 steps, wearing our own homemade bandanna masks or purloined hospital masks, trying to maintain six-foot distances, often veering out into the empty street. People pull their dogs away from yours, and the dogs have gotten the message, barely straining at the leash, rarely even growling.

At night, we schedule Zoom cocktail hours with Steve and Evie, with Caryn and Stephen, with Susan and John, but we already have Zoom fatigue, and jokes about refilling wine glasses through the computer screen fall flat.

On Broadway, uptown, near the subway station, the crowds are thicker, and the panhandlers, mostly Black men in their sixties or prematurely aged to appear in their sixties, sit in front of West Side Market, pitching to a hurried street. At the bookstore they will bring some chosen pre-ordered volumes out and place them on a metal chair but only if you stand six feet back. Takeout places are largely closed but we did get pizza once from a place that shortly afterward shut down and lukewarm burgers and "concretes" (i.e., milkshakes) from the local Shake Shack which remains open.

Inside the apartment, I have a ritual of putting on gloves and using hospital-grade chlorine wipes to clean all knobs, handles, switches. Which to fear more, touching or breathing? They are now saying touch brings little risk, but my strangely reassuring ritual persists. Everything is left with white streaks and smears.

Each day is more of the same. In the morning—or before dawn if I can't sleep—I check the *Times* statistics, almost reassured by seeing that only 400 died in the City yesterday, compared to over 800 at the peak. There's no clear road back. Rumors of effective treatments are based on one doctor's experiences, one hospital, one politician.

May 13, 2020

We are all virologists these days, public health experts, lay epidemiologists. One of my research assistants (RAs), a pre-med who is getting a master's degree in epidemiology, shares scuttlebutt from experts at the School of Public Health. *How does COVID really spread indoors? How far away is safe? Airborne but how airborne? How often to scrub our hands?* My skin cracks from over-washing: his expert opinion is that touching surfaces isn't a major risk with COVID, that it only protects from other viruses so you won't catch so many colds.

Every Wednesday, I log into the department's town hall meeting to find out when (*if!*) we will be able to go back to work at the hospital. The latest update: looks like my studies will be Phase 3 at best, more likely Phase 4, which could be late this summer, maybe early Fall. Or maybe Phase 5, as far away as 2021. Depending on so many things, including a possible second COVID-19 wave.

For such fantasized future dosing sessions, we struggle to imagine how we will ever start again.

If you read Timothy Leary's papers from the 1960s – the Harvard PhD psychologist turned counter-culture guru who started out as a solid researcher – you apprehend that psychedelic drug-dosing requires the following: an optimal 'set,' or mindset, psychological preparation for the trip; and optimal 'setting,' or place, the location and dosing room and its reassuring ambience. Otherwise, there is a risk of bad trips, and, with depressed people, horrendous outcomes.

In the now distant pre-COVID days, we had pretty much optimized our set and setting. We outfitted a room on a quiet hospital corridor with a comfortable bed, beautiful pictures, and stylish easy chairs. Our patients prepared by watching videos, meeting weekly with study therapists, and on dosing day they would wear comfortable clothes, donning noise-canceling headsets which streamed a soothing playlist, and comfortable eyeshades. At the appropriate moment, I would come into the room, and shake five identical white psilocybin capsules into their hand. They would lift a glass of water and wash the capsules down, then lie back, covered with warm blankets. Two therapists would accompany them the next eight hours, guiding the psychedelic trip, as they sank into hallucinatory states, and gradually reemerged into consensual reality. Our dosing rituals were well-honed, our therapists invariably kind and professional, sitting silently in the twilit room until the patient asked to talk, or merely keeping watch.

Now, thanks to the mutant Coronavirus, everything is askew. Nothing can be taken for granted. Even breathing common air can bring danger. The biggest problem: our therapists must stay in the room, during the whole psychedelic session, eight or nine hours with a tripping patient.

Is there any way to restart psychedelic treatments?

Our staff meetings get heated, we generate endless new ideas: *Maybe with the appropriate PPE. But what sort of PPE should they wear? Should the patients wear masks (even gloves?) along with the eyeshade and headphones that they normally wear? Would wearing masks, and seeing therapists with masks, reassure our patients, or freak them out? What kind of ventilation is needed, what about the risk of aerosolized breath? Would a HEPA air purifier suffice? Should the therapists perhaps be stationed outside the room? No, no way; the patient would feel abandoned. Maybe we could move our treatments to a larger room, with more ventilation?*

I study Institute floorplans, seeking a large room on a quiet corridor, where we could move a hospital bed. Classrooms, conference rooms, libraries? Or, if windows could be opened in the current room, would there be a way to install window exhaust fans, a low-tech negative pressure setting where droplets and aerosols would have no time to linger? But how to make sure that the aerosols won't pass from the patient onto the therapists, or the reverse?

And: *What about testing, couldn't we test the staff and patients and make sure they are all negative? Wouldn't it help to measure temperature pre-dosing, to use a pulse oximeter? What about rapid COVID testing? Plus, masks, gloves, scrubs, frequent handwashing, smearing Purell or chlorine solution on every live surface? There's got to be a way to mitigate risk.*

It's not up to us, though. Our institutional review board, our IRB, must be satisfied.

One Sunday morning I reach Ned, our IRB director, at his country home in Connecticut, and we hash out possible solutions. The study sponsor also has to approve, but first we need the IRB's okay.

"What if we treated our patients in a tent?" I ask. "Outdoors? We could put up a safari tent in our patient park—which is fenced in—and have our patients and therapists basically outdoors, where the risk of viral spread would be essentially zilch."

Ned laughs. "That's not going to happen!"

There's got to be a way.

June 6, 2020

Suddenly, a new era of protest explodes. I had thought it would be more directly related to the economy tanking, to unemployment, boredom, not Black Lives Matter, but of course this makes sense in view of rising desperation resulting from the clear and horrifying differential outcomes for Black and Brown persons infected with COVID. Our few remaining neighbors put BLM signs in their windows in solidarity, perhaps also hoping to be spared rocks and bricks. We again feel urges to flee, to join the exodus of neighbors, friends, other doctors from the hospital. One research colleague drives to Vermont, then heads further north until penned in by the Canadian border. My friend Pat, who practices near Grand Central, is hunkered down in Westchester, hesitant even to pick up patient charts from his Midtown office.

What's our escape plan? Our kids tell us that we are old folks at high risk.

Today, June whenever that is, 2020

We have been told to start making plans for return to work, as deaths are dropping, fewer than 500 in the US yesterday—only 500, amazing, down from over 2000 per day in April, but 500 more dead.

Today at our Zoom staff meeting, my youngest RA—the one who Zooms from her childhood bedroom, a shelf with stuffed animals over her frilly bedspread—tells us that she has had COVID symptoms for the past week, with a fever of 99-point-something, shortness of breath, a nonstop metallic smell. She mutes Zoom so we don't hear her coughing.

July 11, 2020

Storms, storms, lightning, ennui. Dead ends.

I pore through Institute blueprints seeking a larger room. I am told that therapists must sit or stand outside the dosing room, that there is a policy stating that is safer. I ask for a copy of the policy but nobody seems to have it. We look into a revolutionary next-day testing method done at a local university lab. The lab starts to make plans with us, then stops returning our calls. The desk in my home office gets covered with yellow Post Its, documenting remote follow-up visits for our far-flung psilocybin patients.

I have grown a COVID beard, like everyone else. My hair has grown long and scraggly. Finally, our barber shears arrive and are used to cut the hair of the dog and then me. My wife refuses tonsorial offers and resorts to elaborate barrettes and pins rather than face inexpert shears.

August 4, 2020

The study sponsor has approved using clear face masks for our psilocybin study. At the Institute, the Engineering department will test the various rooms we have earmarked to determine which has the best ventilation. So, we now have a path toward restarting.

A relief since before now I couldn't see any way forward.

Today taking a walk before lunch, I am caught in a thunderstorm, rushing back uptown to our apartment, drenched.

September something, 2020

Centuries ago, when the Black Death was approaching the noble city of Florence, as Giovanni Boccaccio wrote in the Introduction to *The Decameron* (his collection of short stories about the 14th century bubonic plague), citizens responded with fear, denial, courage, with wild debauchery, clutching sweet flowers before their noses to purify the air, deserting their own families and abandoning their homes. Even funeral rites were abandoned. The city filled with corpses and "when all the graves were full, enormous trenches were dug in the cemeteries of the churches, into which the new arrivals were put by the hundreds ..." (Boccaccio, 2013, 12).

Every night I read one of the hundred *Decameron* stories, told by the seven young Florentine women, Pampinea and Fiammetta, by Filomena and Emilia, and Lauretta and Neifile and Eliassa, and by three young men, Panfilo, Filostrato, Dioneo. Having escaped from the city of the dead, they hide in the countryside and tell nightly stories of love and friendship and betrayal and magnanimity.

I am more than halfway through the *Decameron*; our lockdown stretches endlessly.

October 9, 2020

A monumental week.
In the world, crazed leaders everywhere, flies land on rotting meat, our President roars about California watering fishes in the ocean as the cause for drought and threatens to arrest his rivals.
The White House is a super spread node.

Election Day, November 3, 2020

Is this end of the nightmare or start of a new one?
We walk to a large university hall downhill near the projects to vote. Despite warnings of crowding, it is nearly deserted, eerily quiet. We vote, are given a sticker to put on our jackets, a colorful ballpoint pen. Eyeglasses fog above our masks as we walk home.
On TV at night we watch Trump supporters in pickup trucks as they are smashing, smoking, leering, brandishing, swaggering.
There is an Austrian terrorist following upon a French decapitator.
I try to calm myself, listening to Jenny Lewis's album on Pandora. *Acid Tongue*: pretty bird, pretty bird go west to the setting sun.

November 18, 2020

I have been daring to go up to the Institute again. Mostly in recent weeks I have been biking so I can avoid the subways and the headache of the jammed parking garage. Somehow the cactus in my hospital office, which I have had for over twenty years, has survived.

Amazingly, our psilocybin study has been approved to restart, so we will soon be scheduling in-person visits. I have been trying to get the staff to do their parts. Not surprisingly, everyone is afraid. Afraid of coming back onsite, even more afraid of the thought of sitting with a patient for an 8-hour dosing session. Despite two weeks of pre-dosing isolation, despite questionnaires and temperature checks. Even though the patient and both therapists will get rapid COVID tests the day before dosing, and we won't proceed unless everything is negative.

After looking at every large conference room, meeting room, and classroom at the Institute, we discover that our old dosing room is the safest place in the Institute. Located in a unit designed for human studies, it was already designed with optimized airflow with complete air turnover every 8 minutes. Plus it has positive pressure, which means that air quickly leaves the room, exiting into the hallway. The HVAC system has two levels of HEPA filters, and is adjusted to provide 100% fresh air, no recirculation. So even our small 10x12 foot room is safe.

Engineering department airflow tests confirm all this.

But our therapists are still nervous. It's safe as it can possibly be, but still we worry. At times I wonder: which of Boccaccio's types of fools are we?

Heading home early, I bike through Riverside Park before 4:30PM sunset.

November 23, 2020

Today I drive to the Institute. The parking garage is crowded, having been opened to all hospital staff to keep them off public transport, so I park on the sidewalk. Illegal but the NYC parking inspector somehow doesn't issue tickets.

My goal today is to get study psilocybin that has expired out of the pharmacy vault and order a new supply. My research coordinator, Peter, has filled out the forms. He shows me where to sign, then we walk together to the research pharmacy, to meet Robert, the head pharmacist.

As a Schedule 1 drug, illegal in nearly every country, a drug categorized as having no legitimate medical uses, psilocybin must be stored securely. It took a year to get all the approvals for this drug, with visits from the Drug

Enforcement Administration, the FDA, and the New York State Bureau of Narcotics Enforcement. It is kept inside a locked safe bolted to the wall of an alarmed vault inside a locked pharmacy. The lockbox has two keys, one for me and one for the pharmacy director. Our security, I tell everyone, it's like *Ocean's 11*—we have everything but the lasers and the acrobats in black leotards.

Today, Robert lets me into the vault, and I climb a stepladder up to the lockbox, which already has his key in the lock. I turn my key, and remove the seven remaining bottles, and hand them to Peter.

"Good to go," Robert says.

Our daughter, a primary school teacher, is recovering from COVID, with some fatigue and headaches but the oximeter shows 97% and she sounds good. No one knows how she got it; none of her kids or co-teachers are sick.

December 15, 2020

Our first in-person visit in nine months. Our RA leads me to the patient, a masked woman who sits in the deserted waiting room. I motion her to follow me to my office. We have short-circuited the evaluation process: before coming in, a psychologist Zoomed the diagnostic interview and got her to fill out intake forms online. Now we just confirm her history, draw blood, get an EKG, and do a physical exam. The familiar process restarts, reassuring as all rituals are, but both the RA and I need to check the study manuals to remind ourselves how to submit data to the sponsor.

While I'm finishing my writeup the pharmacy calls. "Doctor, did you order something?"

Down at the research pharmacy I encounter a heavily taped box the size of a Whirlpool washing machine. I cut the tape and lift a smaller box out of the huge box, and a yet smaller boxes inside that, finally arriving at a heavily taped Styrofoam cooler with a thermometer inside and a dozen white bottles, each containing five identical capsules. Having forgotten my lockbox key, I need to go back to my office to search for it in the back of a drawer.

Then I climb the stepladder inside the vault, the pharmacist and I each turn our lockbox keys, and I put the new psilocybin safely inside.

January 3, 2021

On a quiet Sunday morning, I drive to the deserted Institute and take the luminescent walkway over Riverside Drive and enter a nearly deserted New York Presbyterian Hospital building and get my first vaccine dose in the auditorium. Our hospital system has already given out 16,000 doses to its many employees. Afterward, I need to sit for fifteen minutes before I am released by the nurse. Three weeks from now, I'll come back for my second dose.

January 28, 2021

Turns out we are at the absolute peak of this wave of COVID in the US. Yesterday, there were 4401 deaths, a weekly average of 3302 per day. There are over 280,000 new cases per day, 136,000 people hospitalized, including 28,522 in ICUs. Regardless, we are restarting our dosing ritual. Everyone has been COVID-tested, everyone has answered the health questionnaire, everyone is afebrile. We are good to go. We have done what we can do. I retrieve today's drug supply from the pharmacy and walk down the block-long hallway to the Biological Studies Unit to meet the patient and therapists in the dosing room.

Our RA has dimmed the overhead hallway lights and put the wooden sign in the hallway: *Study in Progress*, it reads. Electric candles in the corridor light the way to the bathroom.

The air in the hallway seems chilled, as if rushed in from outdoors, and the chilled feeling continues as I enter the dimmed room. The therapists have pulled on their clear masks with plastic visors. I can see their lips, their distorted facial expressions. I don't know, somehow plain opaque masks would be more reassuring, but the sponsor wants these. Everything is set, the playlist is streaming. The patient is wearing workout clothes, has her eyeshades and noise-damping headphones in hand, and a facemask pulled tight. I'm wearing my N95 mask, now legal in the hospital. It's eerie, how covered up we are, our very apprehension so difficult to discern.

I unseal the white bottle and shake the five identical capsules into the patient's hand.

She takes her mask off, lifts her hand to her mouth, and washes them down with water from a plastic cup.

"Hope it goes well," I say. "I'll be checking in periodically with your therapists."

She pulls her mask back on. "Thanks."

Back in my office, there is no shortage of mundane things to do, most notably typing notes from my yellow Post Its, my many months of notes from remote visits when I was unable to use VPN to access the electronic charting system. After a few hours, I'm almost caught up, too tired to finish. It's weird, sitting here, to think about our activities of a year ago, dinners out, plays, meeting friends and kids—it's all unimaginable at this point. I used to swim three or four times a week at a pool in the basement of the medical student dorm. It's nine months since I've been there. I wonder if they're ever going to reopen.

Outside, the West Side Highway is nearly deserted, and the Hudson River has the gray opaqueness of icy water, and no boat traffic.

I text Elizabeth, the lead therapist: "How's it going?"

"Fine, she's having a great experience."

At the end of the day, I go back to the room. The patient is calm, a bit washed out, ready to go home.

So, back to the pre-pandemic routine: per protocol, I need to ask about adverse events, the effects of treatment, check vital signs. She'll come in tomorrow for a several-hour debriefing visit, and have more visits over the coming weeks, many conducted remotely. It's almost like this corner of life is normal again.

Of course, I'll be checking everyone's COVID status. Not just the patient's but the therapist's too, and the RA's. We've mitigated what risk we can, we have been given a green light, we have implemented procedures and gotten required approvals. But we have lost a type of innocence, of confidence, not only in the process of doing research but in the informality of daily human contact.

June 30, 2021

Our last dosing today, number 27. We dosed thirteen subjects before COVID and somehow have done fourteen more since January, and so far, no one has gotten infected. For what it's worth, our site is one of the top two recruiting sites for the study's 25 sites.

I guess our Engineering Department was right about airflow. Our testing procedures have been effective. Or both. Regardless, we have established a bubble of relative safety. A system that, fingers crossed, may work. Not eliminating risk but mitigating it, managing it, which is what doctors have always done. And which may be how life is in the COVID era.

I almost wrote post-COVID era, but that is impossible to imagine, with new variants emerging every few months.

Now we have new RAs to hire. Two of them are leaving, one for a PhD in clinical psychology, one finally getting into medical school. I always say I want to hire people who aim for further education because they are so smart, so motivated. But then they leave us, and we need to replace them. That's a normal thing. And normal, I've concluded, is good. We are planning more psilocybin studies. That's also the normal thing to do.

References

Boccaccio, Giovanni. 2013. *The Decameron*. Translated by Wayne A. Rebhorn. New York; London: WW Norton & Company.

David J. Hellerstein, MD, is a Professor of Clinical Psychiatry at Columbia University. He is a research psychiatrist and Director of the Depression Evaluation Service (DES) at the New York State Psychiatric Institute. In recent years he has been conducting studies of psychedelic drugs for psychiatric disorders. Dr. Hellerstein has published over 150 scientific articles and book chapters. His literary writing has received wide recognition, including six books, and nonfiction and fiction in numerous magazines. His 2023 book *The Couch, the Clinic, and the Scanner: Stories from Three Revolutionary Eras of the Mind* is published by Columbia University Press.

Hunkpati at Harvard: Stories of an Indigenous Medical Student During the COVID-19 Pandemic
By Victor A. Lopez-Carmen (Waokiya Mani)

Originally submitted February 23, 2022

Seven Generations

I write this chapter as a son of two Indigenous Nations. I am a member of the Crow Creek Sioux Tribe (known traditionally as the Hunkpati Dakota) on my father's side and am Yaqui on my mother's. When I was a young boy growing up amidst both my Nations, I was taught a Dakota value passed down from our ancestors, crystalizing a sacred responsibility to be caretakers of future generations. It teaches us to honor the generations around us by making decisions that will benefit those seven generations in the future and honor the legacies of generations that came before us. My people integrate this value into our daily lives through a phrase: "Mitakuye Oyasin", which in Dakota or Lakota means "all my relations." Mitakuye Oyasin is said at the end of our prayers and reminds us to respect past, present, and future relations because we are all related. These relations extend beyond just our human relatives. We strive to understand how we relate to the rest of creation – the plants, the animals, the winds, the water, and the cosmos. This way of thinking brings our ancestors, the unborn, and all life on earth into perspective and informs how we carry ourselves.

The excerpt below is from the book "The Vanishing Race: The Last Great Indian Council," during a council meeting between many of the Chiefs of the Oceti Sakowin (referred to in the English language as the Great Sioux Nation) and leaders from other plains Tribes:

> *Bear Ghost, Chief of the Yankton Sioux, with great calmness and deliberation said: 'I am glad that I am here to shake the hand in peace with all the chiefs of the various tribes assembled. It is a great day for me, a great day for us all. I rejoice that a record is to be made of this council that it may live for future generations …* (Dixon 1913, 195).

Chief Bear Ghost is my great grandfather by direct lineal descent. The quotation documents my ancestor participating in a council of Chiefs, where major decisions were made, rejoicing because a record of the council would "live for future generations." Even in the highest political councils, my ancestors were thinking of future generations, thinking of us, thinking of me.

As an Indigenous youth, the seventh-generation value is very real to me. I grew up with hardship. My parents worked hard and fostered a loving family, but we lived paycheck to paycheck. My middle school offered easy access to drugs and gang life, and I had a complex time navigating the pressures of staying off the streets in Tucson, Arizona. Many of my best friends from that time of life ended up in jail or prison. What kept me strong, and true to my path, was intergenerational resilience. It was the stories my parents and elders told me about my ancestors. It was being on my traditional territory, walking the same land as my ancestors. It was the ceremonies, passed down thousands of years. But it was also the hard things, the things caused by colonization. It was hearing my Dakota grandmother, a fierce woman with wrinkles at the corners of her eyes, tell me she was sad because our ancient language was at risk of dying. It was watching my relatives struggle with alcoholism, suicide, and drug addictions. It was governments and corporations threatening my friends and family members and criminalizing my mentors. And lastly, it was the stories of my peoples' struggles which gave me strength.

The following is a story told to me by my Yaqui elders. In 1533, a Yaqui warrior drew a line in the sand, and proclaimed to the Spanish invaders: *"Up to this line, and as far as the eye can see in these three directions, is Yaqui land. No invaders will be allowed to enter."* For 500 years, we Yaquis have battled three separate colonial governments (the Spanish, Mexican, and US), lived through brutal wars, massacres, deportation, slave labor, and a policy of extermination and genocide. My Yaqui great grandmother survived by hiding herself and her little brother behind a rock while the Mexican army slaughtered her village. If one of those soldiers had found her, I wouldn't be here. It is a miracle that I am here. Now, I have a responsibility to help make things better for future Yaquis. Indigenous youth around the world live with these realities. Beauty and trauma mature us, and give us the privilege to live our lives for others, past, present, and future. Because of these teachings, the two questions I ask myself when I feel like giving up are: "How am I living up to the dreams of my ancestors?" and "How will future generations know that I loved them?"

During the COVID-19 pandemic, I had to ask and re-ask these questions many times. I am an Indigenous medical student and an elected United Nations (UN) representative for Indigenous youth, with responsibilities to both of my Tribes, family, studies, and Indigenous young people all over the world. Figuring out how to support my loved ones and do what I could to help Indigenous Peoples was especially difficult given Indigenous Peoples are often invisible, left behind, and underrepresented in medicine. However, I knew that given my unique position as an Indigenous medical student at a preeminent school with vast institutional resources, I had to do something. Thankfully, I had the skills and experience to organize responses to the pandemic and its impacts on Indigenous communities.

Since freshman year of college, I have worked within the Indigenous policy space across the UN. In 2019, I was elected Co-Chair of the UN Global Indigenous Youth Caucus, tasked to represent Indigenous youth interests at various UN fora, which meant working with UN agencies and lobbying UN member states. In this work, I have had the great honor of working with Indigenous Peoples from over 60 countries. In that time, I have witnessed common intergenerational virtues reflected in Indigenous nations: our extended family systems, decision-making through consensus, division of labor that respects all genders, communal education, restorative justice, sharing of wealth, collective responsibility, and respect for all life. During the pandemic, I saw that these values would be needed in order for our communities to stay protected from the virus. Yet, I knew the task would not be easy as centuries of colonization and oppression of Indigenous Peoples have led to structural and physiologic consequences that have placed them at greater risk for severe disease from the virus.

Oakland

It was February 2020, and almost midnight, when my medical school sent its students an email that we would have to leave campus. I had to decide where to go, and quickly.

I thought of going to South Dakota, where one of my Chiefs invited me to a thunder welcoming ceremony, or Arizona, where a healing ceremony was taking place for a family member. A few days earlier, I had been in two of Boston's major healthcare centers and had recently been with patients. Cases of COVID-19 had already popped up in the city. I couldn't risk bringing the virus to my two Indigenous Nations. I finally decided to go to Oakland, California, to live with my older brother, sister-in-law, and their child (my nephew and godson).

My older brother's place in Oakland sat at the bottom of a large steep hill. The day I arrived, he asked me to go on a run, and up the long hill we went. I lagged behind, but decided that I would run up it every day until I could do the entire thing. The second day, I could only muster 20 meters at a time. Slowly, I could run longer and longer, and eventually, I could do the entire thing without stopping. I would do these runs in between online classes. I listened to wellness and mental health podcasts on my walks down the other side of the hill. While most of my time was spent studying, I also practiced archery and boxing.

Yet, this transition was not without challenges. At one point, my responsibilities taking care of my baby nephew conflicted with live Zoom classes. Afraid to miss the materials, I requested recordings, but was unsuccessful. I was not doing well on my exams. Eventually, the Crow Creek Sioux Tribal Council successfully intervened on my behalf, writing to the medical school about the cultural importance of Indigenous kinship and responsibility of helping my family by taking care of my nephew, and still being able to learn via recorded lectures. After failing all three prior exams due to not having access to lectures, I passed the final exam with an above average score.

I hadn't been struggling to understand the material. I just needed access to it, and a little understanding of my situation to succeed. The Crow Creek Sioux Tribal Council's successful intervention for recorded lectures also ended up helping other students in my class, who were dispersed in different time zones around the country (and some around the globe), trying to balance maintaining their medical studies while caring for family members during the pandemic. I was relieved that the Crow Creek Sioux Tribe was able to help my school recognize the value of adapting their rules during unprecedented times. This helped me focus on the pressing concerns the pandemic was presenting to my communities and Indigenous Peoples globally.

Language is Life

Indigenous Peoples make up around 5% of the world population but represent the vast majority (>4,000) of the spoken languages on Earth (Amnesty n.d.). Each language is specific to the ecosystem and land that a particular Indigenous Nation has lived on since time immemorial. In the global medical community, the vital connection between Indigenous languages, planetary health, and Indigenous community health is underappreciated. Loss of an Indigenous language is not only detrimental to the health of Indigenous Peoples from that Indigenous nation, but to the ecosystem in which they have developed the language for thousands of years. It is also detrimental to everyone else on the planet due to the protective nature of knowledge stored in Indigenous languages with respect to biodiversity and climate change intensification. This recognition is further magnified by Indigenous Peoples currently hosting and living with eighty percent of the world's biodiversity (Gafner-Rojas 2020).

As Indigenous Peoples lose their languages, they begin to lose the cultural practices and traditional knowledge that has allowed them to maintain this extensive biodiversity. Loss of this biodiversity has direct health impacts on them and the entire world, via propagation of climate change and loss of healthy traditional food systems, such as salmon networks or sustenance hunting. Loss of traditional food systems and the replacement of traditional diets with cheap alternatives due to increased Indigenous poverty can lead to higher rates of cardiovascular disease. Thus, Indigenous languages are a connection between traditional ecological knowledge, biodiversity, planetary protection, and Indigenous community health that the global medical community has long overlooked, especially during the COVID-19 pandemic.

Slowly, but surely, Indigenous Nations across the country like mine began to feel the pandemic's disproportionate impact on our communities. Then, we, as Indigenous Peoples, started losing our most precious resource, our elders. All of our teachings and knowledge are verbally transmitted. With every sentence, our elders share pieces of knowledge worth more than gold. Losing elders was incredibly scary. It meant potentially losing our cultures and languages. For my Tribe, and all other Dakota and Lakota Tribes in the Oceti Sakowin, our language was already at high risk of extinction. In response to this crisis, the Oceti Sakowin Tribes designated all language speakers as "essential workers" and gave them first access to vaccination. Given the very real risk of losing our language and cultural history, the Crow Creek Sioux Tribe asked me to take time away from medical school during the pandemic to focus on cultural responsibilities like continuing to learn our language. In support of this mission, Peter Langkeek, Chairman of the Crow Creek Sioux Tribe, authored an official tribal letter to my medical school in which he wrote (shortened for brevity):

"This is Peter Langkeek, Chairman of the great Hunkpati Dakota Nation, also known as the Crow Creek Sioux Tribe. I am writing to formally notify you on behalf of our Tribe, that Waokiya Mani/Victor A. Lopez-Carmen

will be taking one-year of spiritual and religious leave from February 2022-February 2023 to learn our language and participate in sacred ceremonies ... The Dakota, Nakota and Lakota languages are of utmost importance to the health of our people. Every two weeks, an Indigenous language dies. During the COVID-19 pandemic, the Oceti Sakowin, also known as the Great Sioux Nation, has lost many elders and language keepers. Our language is at extreme risk. Our language is a fundamental aspect of our mental, physical, and spiritual health ... The possibilities of a future Dakota medical doctor who speaks our language to improve healthcare is also immense and cannot be overemphasized. Lastly, our languages are also protected and recognized as an integral aspect of our spirituality in the UN Declaration on the Rights of Indigenous Peoples, endorsed by the United States."

Harvard Medical School (HMS) honored the importance of my learning my language as my right as an Indigenous person, my Tribal government's right to take measures to improve their intergenerational well-being of its citizens, and a public health measure that would benefit me, my community, and the planet. It felt like a momentous and progressive step for academia in moving toward understanding the rights of Indigenous Peoples, including Native students, around language and health.

During the pandemic, I also began to hear stories from Indigenous communities who had no access to COVID-19 information in their languages. In these communities, Indigenous languages are still the dominant means of communication. So, through no fault of their own, they could not understand COVID-19 information in major world languages. Unfortunately, due to the lack of Indigenous representation in the health professions, reliable COVID-19 information in Indigenous languages was sparse and difficult to create. Indigenous Peoples who still primarily spoke their mother tongues were being left behind in the global public health response.

Recognizing this, I convened a group of HMS classmates and faculty, Indigenous youth leaders, and interested members of the public to work with Indigenous communities across the world and advise them on their COVID-19 public health responses. We raised thousands of dollars for Indigenous communities and organized a webinar series with the United Nations to shine light on the impact of COVID-19 on global Indigenous communities. We also began to create COVID-19 information in Indigenous languages, in partnership with community translators,

Indigenous physicians, and a team of over 30 medical students. We called the initiative "Translations for our Nations."

Over the course of two months, we translated basic, reliable, and culturally aware COVID-19 information into 40 Indigenous languages from over 20 countries globally. This initiative was profiled in the Boston Globe, Global News Canada, Nature, Corriere De La Sera, and other major news networks, helping shape how health professionals considered the role of Indigenous languages in COVID-19 literacy. During the initiative, I was often asked why Indigenous languages were being left behind in the pandemic response. Time and time again, I stressed that the lack of reliable information in Indigenous languages is a symptom of the lack of information about Indigenous Peoples who speak those languages in healthcare. To bridge this systemic gap, and others, we need more Indigenous Peoples in medicine globally. Moreover, we need the field of healthcare to invest in our innovative solutions, many of which are based on thousands of years of intergenerational knowledge passed down through the generations, even linguistic knowledge.

Going forward, the field of healthcare must actively recognize the importance of Indigenous languages to Indigenous health, and planetary health. As I try to do my part and honor the letter the Crow Creek Sioux Tribe wrote so I could learn my language, I envision a day where my great grandchildren can walk into a health clinic and speak to a Dakota doctor in our language. That Dakota doctor might pray for them in our language, treat them with the best that modern medicine has to offer in culturally sensitive ways, prescribe them traditional foods like buffalo, and give them a patient summary in our language before they go home and speak Dakota to their family and friends. I pray that the documentation of my experiences as an Indigenous medical student will help Western medicine better support Indigenous Peoples towards the manifestation of this vision. I rejoice that a record of my time as a Dakota and Yaqui medical student during the COVID-19 pandemic will live on for future generations.

References

Amnesty International. n.d. "Indigenous Peoples." Amnesty International. Accessed March 27, 2023. https://www.amnesty.org/en/what-we-do/indigenous-peoples/

Dixon, Joseph K. and Rodman Wanamaker. 1913. *The Vanishing Race: The Last Great Indian Council, a Record in Picture and Story of the Last*

Great Indian Council, Participated in by Eminent Indian Chiefs from Nearly Every Indian Reservation in the United States, Together with the Story of Their Lives as Told by Themselves-Their Speeches and Folklore Tales-Their Solemn Farewell and the Indian's Story of the Custer Fight. Garden City, NJ: Doubleday Page & Co.

Gafner-Rojas, Claudia. 2020. "Indigenous Languages as Contributors to the Preservation of Biodiversity and Their Presence in International Environmental Law." *Journal of International Wildlife Law & Policy* 23 (1): 44–61. doi: 10.1080/13880292.2020. 1768693.

Victor Lopez-Carmen is a Dakota and Yaqui student at Harvard Medical School and the first documented Indigenous person on the Forbes 30 under 30 list in healthcare. Prior to medical school, he clerked for the Subcommittee for Indigenous Peoples in the US House of Representatives, completed his Master of Public Health on a Fulbright Scholarship, and served as Co-Chair of the UN Global Indigenous Youth Caucus. His writing and work focus on Indigenous global health, minority recruitment in medicine, climate health-justice, and health equity. Mr. Lopez-Carmen serves as a research project Advisory Board Member at Ariadne Labs, a member of the City of Boston's COVID-19 Health Inequities Task Force, and a member of the White House Health Inequities Roundtable Leaders Group. He has written for Teen Vogue, Forbes Magazine, the Boston Globe, and Harvard Health Publishing.

Part III: The Humanities

Reflections on "Self Portrait: Intubated and Cannulated"
By Justin Fiala

Originally submitted April 26, 2022

A self-portrait can be many things to an artist. The painting that graces the cover of this book is no exception. It is at once a psychological exploration, social commentary, and catharsis of pent-up trauma. Entitled "Self Portrait: Intubated and Cannulated" the piece explores the boundaries of human existence and the ways in which modern medicine shapes the precipice at existence's end.

I was working as a physician in the medical ICU of a large, academic referral center in Chicago from the earliest days of the coronavirus pandemic, and I felt the despair and distress of those first weeks and months deeply. Twelve-day stretches of 12 hour shifts alternated with whole weeks of isolation created a pernicious state of emotional whiplash that left me reeling. Amid the turmoil, oil painting seemed to be one of the few activities that could get me out of the toxic headspace I'd otherwise been inhabiting, and it quickly became a form of meditation and self-care. I'd listen to whole operas ("Nixon in China" was on heavy rotation) while obsessing over various details of the painting, spending entire days at a time in front of the canvas.

Perhaps unsurprisingly, the painting started out as an abstract piece made up of intersecting planes of color, each meticulously layered on top of one another and applied to its given spot on the canvas based solely on inspiration. In aggregate, the planes formed a visual stream-of-consciousness, the specific subject of which was never really the focus of the endeavor. Painting was therapy, and therapy was the point. So, I let the lines, curves, and shadows take their ultimate form more or less spontaneously. A bold arc in dioxazine purple, so dark it appears black at first glance, sweeping in from the edge of the canvas seemed to cradle the forms that followed: curves in opaque layers of Hooker green and French aquamarine that amalgamated into spheres, and a dramatic near-right angle cutting through the colors that preceded it with an arrogant, deep phthalo green. Occiput, eyes, and maxillae: the catharsis was underway, and I knew there was no other direction to follow. I was sure it was me.

In the same way that authors occasionally describe a phenomenon of characters in their novels "writing themselves" I would say that, from that point on, the figure in the portrait similarly began to paint himself into being: heart, lungs, and support devices.

As the figure's mouth took shape, several lines coalesced to form an endotracheal (breathing) tube that went through the mouth and into the throat. Several more lines near the nose became a nasogastric (feeding) tube that passed down below the chest into the abdomen. Then, at the neck, just north of where the clavicle announces the start of the thorax, a thick line developed and started charting its path southward. The line cut its course down the internal jugular vein as it dove into the chest cavity. It continued snaking its way down to the heart and pushed its way into the right atrium before passing into the right ventricle and making a hairpin turn to come to rest in the trunk of the pulmonary artery. It was unmistakable: this last line was an ECMO catheter.

For the uninitiated, ECMO is a form of advanced life support which uses large cannulas (tubes approximately the size of a garden hose) to bypass the failing lungs and/or heart to keep a person alive while awaiting recovery or organ transplant. For brevity's sake, perhaps it is best described by the adage: "capable of miracles when it works, and a nightmare when it goes wrong." And the longer a patient is supported on ECMO, the more likely things are to go wrong.

Pair that unfortunate truth of the ICU with the fact that sometimes, despite all our best efforts as healers, neither recovery nor transplantation is possible, and those who have been maintained on ECMO to that point become captives in the ultimate purgatory, physically tethered at the heart to an increasingly fleeting existence.

The figure in the painting embodies this idea of autonomy lost. Figuratively shackled and physically bound by his various tubes he appears trapped. Amidst splashes of loud colors falling in nondescript forms, he is disoriented and occupies a rarefied existence somewhere between life and death, a universe unto itself in an ICU room.

In its physical form, the painting is a respectable 3' x 5', with the silhouette of the figure appearing around the same size as the average person. Though not overtly intentional, the near-to-life size of the being in the painting creates a certain gravitas when viewing the painting in person. His stark silhouette and lifeless eyes form an imposing reminder of the cruelty of critical illness and all that it robs from the ones we care for. It is also a reminder that there but for the grace of God go any one, or all, of us.

Justin Fiala, MD, is an assistant professor dually appointed at the Feinberg School of Medicine at Northwestern University and the Shirley Ryan Ability Lab in Chicago, IL. He completed his residency training in Internal Medicine, including an additional year as chief medical resident at the Mayo Clinic in Rochester, MN, and went on to complete fellowships in Pulmonary and Critical Care and Sleep Medicine at Northwestern. His clinical interests include diseases of ventilatory control and chronic respiratory failure. He is also passionate about health equity and spends his free time providing pro-bono sleep-related evaluation and treatment for uninsured patients across Chicago.

Corona Radiata
By Fady Joudah

Originally published in the Los Angeles Review of Books on March 23, 2020. Reprinted with permission of the author who retains copyright of the poem.

The rats are invisible.
The bats are beautiful.
Here's the livestock and fish market,
and there's the institute for the biologic.
We're ravenous. Our hunger travels
in fueled suitcases packed with desires.
The virus is real,
gave up its passport,
stops for no officer
save immunology's guards
in epidemiology's tribe.

For decades, millions die every year:
from TB, poverty and malnutrition, attrition,
pneumonia, diarrhea, millions the count
of Spain's, England's, or Italy's population
annually wiped off the earth,
untouchables outside history,
and though their geography be
diverse, it's short of total.

The pandemic is real. If hospitals are overwhelmed,
the virus will add to the otherwise
preventable deaths and lawsuits.
Diabetes, heart disease, kidney failure,
our bread and butter,
colonoscopies, too,
and organ transplants
may be placed on hold:
people, there is no human system
for this sort of pandemonium

and there won't be
unless echo is one.

But if so many die
in a single season,
what will happen to life insurance
firms? If one percent
of Americans die in one swoop,
what will become of grief?
What if rent and mortgages,
utility bills, phone and car payments,
student and small business loans
are waived for a month,
pardoned? What if CEOs
give up their salaries
for 8 weeks so that the faucet
drips the tub full
with buoyancy for all?

The virus is indebted to no one.
Distances close in on us.
The curve and the herd and this
much death on our soil.
Antibiotics, globulins, gloves, masks,
and numerator to denominator
as yin to yang, if we're lucky,
when the virus returns
it will be wearing less imperial clothes.

Every 2 minutes a child dies of malaria.
Infomercial, how many minutes in a year?
Malaria lyses more than the blood of children
and their mothers. Extreme measures
against the virus should be taken.

This pandemic, one sorrow,
one love, this pandemic hangs
on a strand of the helical tongue.
This pandemic brings me back to eros.

And to hysteria's translation
in the mind. Pleasure evolved
out of life inside life
wanting no more than life itself.

Then things got sweet,
complicated. Evolution
has some capitalist features
yet isn't capitalist, and we know
what else evolution isn't,
we've been unimaginative of late,
since we've run out of land
but not out of real estate:

the virus teases us
with the bliss to come
after detention is served.
To hold the estranged.
To touch strangers.
An ecstasy worth waiting for.

And our detention is the earth's respite
from our jets and flues
and wireless energy.
A little rest, not for long.
So, extreme measures, why not?

Have you been displaced by war,
scattered by wind, tattered by abundance?
In the last fourteen days,
have you experienced the endemic flare up
like a bad knee, immobilizer bad,
a migraine in the dark?
Extreme measures,
healthcare a human right,
and infrastructure, infrastructure, people,
culling of militaries, monopolies,
but who'll go first?

20 million Iraqis ravaged for generations.
20 million Syrians and 20 million Yemenis.
And the curable after excision
with clear margins. The virus doesn't speak,
doesn't want to be written,
doesn't give voice to the voiceless
or pay low wages
to the lowly. And the looting,
always the looting. This kind of talk
is part of the problem not the solution.
Still as a friend said: amidst all this
uncertainty and concern
the camellia in my garden
is glorious and serene
in the knowledge of Spring.

Far and near
the virus becomes our alibi
to obey more in sickness and in wealth.
Far and near the virus awakens
in us a responsibility
to others who will not die
our deaths, nor we theirs,
though we might, but must direct
our urgency to the elderly, our ancestors
who are and aren't our ancestors.
And to the compromised.
The virus won't spare the poor
or the young or anyone
with architecture primed for ruin.

This August the quarantine on small joys
should lift. Fifteen years ago this August,
I came back from Darfur
to Hurricane Katrina: it was mostly
Anderson Cooper on TV.
In Gaza the virus breaches
the siege as document of science
and will not exit. Israel offers

to track the virus on cellphones
of the infected, a treasure trove.

Does economy lament? Is it an individual
or a corporation? Can it repent?
Can capital grow catatonic
or speak Chinese?
What is avarice with God or without?
Let's not say the virus is blaming the patient.
Lacking objectivity these words
don't dismiss progress, the sample size,
who'll analyze the data,
or who'll get the bailout?

Without people there's no power over the people.
How much for a mosquito net?
Three a year per person
if the swamp isn't drained
and heaven's mouth isn't shut?
During the carving of the Panama Canal.
During penicillin fungating
in shrapnelled limbs.
During smallpox and sex.
What if a pandemic kills
far fewer than other non-pandemic ailments?

The panic's in the pan,
and vaccines are real.
An organism lives to reproduce
its servant, master, and host.
We're all equally small.
And after survival,
which shall not be pyrrhic
if measures are enforced,
surveillance will multiply,
careers will be made,
grants will be granted,
a depression aborted, attenuated,
and a call to papers:

spend a penny, save a dime,
invest a nickel, make a quarter.

The birth rate exceeds the mortal wound.
Our overlords will return us to our dreams of
forgetting.
And our lords,
who aren't in heaven,
give us this day
and lead us not
but deliver us
and the pulverized,
if they're still warm,
if light enough for the breeze.

Fady Joudah is the author of five poetry collections and several volumes of translation.

How I Learned About the 1918 Flu and Why It Matters
By Anne Hudson Jones

Originally submitted March 6, 2022

I learned about the 1918 flu in 1987, when Galveston Arts sponsored a Horton Foote Film Festival. At the time, I did not recognize Foote's name despite my having seen and admired *To Kill a Mockingbird*, for which he had received an Oscar in 1962 for Best Adapted Screenplay, and *Tender Mercies*, for which he had received another Oscar, in 1983, for Best Original Screenplay (Hopwood, n.d.; Rapp 2020a). The only screening I attended during the festival was of his 1985 film *1918*, and only because after the screening Foote gave the annual Elizabeth and Chauncey Leake Memorial Lecture, sponsored by the Institute for the Medical Humanities, of which I was a faculty member. From its title, I expected the film to be about World War I, and it is an important backdrop in the film. The focal subject, however, is the influenza pandemic that ran through the small fictional town of Harrison, Texas, leaving grief-stricken survivors to mourn lost family members and friends amidst the townspeople's patriotic fervor for waging and winning the war. The poignant yet powerful closing scene of a mother visiting her young daughter's grave while celebratory music can be heard in the background and wind blows away the flowers on the grave is emblematic and has stayed with me over the years.

I was captivated by Foote's film and could not understand how I had not known about such a devastating pandemic before. It seemed impossible that I had not learned about it in my American history courses in high school and college. I still had the large stack of books from my two-semester university honors course in American history, and I went back through them to see if I really had just forgotten what I had read about the pandemic, but I found nothing. I did not know then about the military censorship of news about the pandemic or how long its effects would last (Little 2020).

My maternal grandmother, born in 1900, was still alive in 1987, and I was able to ask her about the 1918 flu. Like Foote, who grew up in the small Texas town of Wharton, model for the fictional Harrison in his film (Rapp 2020b), my grandmother grew up in a small Southern town that she always referred to as Tulip Ridge, Arkansas. When I asked her about the 1918 flu, she immediately began to recount her still vivid memories of its coming through the town, sickening so many, and killing her beloved thirteen-year-old sister. Although she had mentioned her sister's death several times over the years, she had not told me about the pandemic. When I asked her why she had not told me about something so important, she had no ready answer and seemed surprised that I wanted to know about it. For her, as for so many others in the country, the larger context of the war no doubt played a role in her silence, but so did personal events. By the time I was of an age to have received what she might have told me, she had married, had three children, lost her father, her husband, and her mother. Her oldest child, my mother, had lost her husband too. The events of the country at large had run through her family's life, from World War I and the 1918 flu, through the Great Depression, and then World War II. By the time I was born, the 1918 flu was a long way back, and the polio epidemic had replaced it in family fears for their children's health and survival. I remember those summers of no swimming in the town pool and forced naps in the afternoons to try to protect against the disease.

Along the way, however, I suddenly became extremely ill one morning at school, not from polio but from what I have since learned was the 1957-58 Asian flu. Because my mother was at work, my grandmother came to get me from school that morning, took me to her house, and cared for me there during the next week or so while I was the sickest I can ever remember being. Only after I learned in 1987 that her sister had died of the 1918 flu did I realize that caring for me must have reawakened my grandmother's memories of her sister's illness and death and heightened her concerns for me. I also wondered how she could have cared for me all those days without having caught the virulent Asian flu herself. Not until 2009 and the outbreak of the so-called swine flu, which was the same A virus, subtype H1N1 as the 1918 flu, did I do a bit more research and learn that the 1957-58 Asian flu was an A virus, but subtype H2N2. The 1918 virus my grandmother had survived forty years earlier probably would not have given her any immunity to the 1957-58 Asian flu from which I had suffered so severely.

Coming as it did just the year before COVID-19, the centennial of the 1918 flu brought renewed scholarly attention and several new histories of the pandemic, as well as Elizabeth Outka's fascinating book *Viral Modernism: The Influenza Pandemic and Interwar Literature* (2019). Several sessions at this year's Modern Language Association conference featured the centennial of modernism, said to have begun in 1922 because both James Joyce's *Ulysses* and T. S. Eliot's *The Waste Land* were published that year (Jackson 2017). It was a strange convergence: celebrating the stylistic effects of the 1918 pandemic in literature and the arts as part of the 1922 birth of modernism at a January 2022 conference that had to be converted, last minute, from in-person only to almost completely virtual because of Covid's Omicron surge.

Called "the seminal novel about the 1918 flu" (Agresta 2020), Katherine Anne Porter's short novel *Pale Horse, Pale Rider* (1939) incorporates many elements of modernist style, even as its title is a well-known biblical allusion to the fourth horseman of the Apocalypse in the Book of Revelation, who brings Death to all the world. Porter's work itself is so well known now that it is not surprising that one of the new histories of the 1918 pandemic appears to echo its title, *Pale Rider: The Spanish Flu of 1918 and How It Changed the World* (Spinney 2017). The modernist style of *Pale Horse, Pale Rider* is very different from the simpler and consistently more realist style of Foote's *1918*. Porter fictionalizes her own experience of the flu, using stream of consciousness and dream sequences to convey the effects of the delirium that accompanied her many days of extremely high fever. The backdrop of war is even stronger in her work than in Foote's film, reported realistically at first but then transposed by delirium into nightmares in which her protagonist, Miranda, believes the German doctor treating her is a wartime torturer. As did Porter, Miranda survives but, like Porter, she must recover from not only her physical illness but also her profound grief over the death of her fiancé, a young army officer who, like so many others, died of the flu rather than the war.

After initially hesitating to add Porter's novel to an interdisciplinary graduate course on plagues and epidemic because of the challenging demands its modernist style makes on readers, I was pleasantly surprised when many of the students found it the most memorable work we read that term. Yet, truth be told, I do not think that if I had read Porter's *Pale Horse, Pale Rider* before I saw Foote's *1918*, I would have found my ignorance of the pandemic so startling or the need to talk with my grandmother about her experience of it so urgent. I still struggle to understand and articulate why, but I think my emotional engagement was enhanced by the relatively simpler style of Foote's telling, as well as by the similarity between the film's closing scene and a photograph of my grandmother's sister's grave, Annie Ethel Wylie, "gone so soon," this young girl for whom my mother, Ethel, and I were named, a generation apart.

Foote was only two years old in 1918 so could not have had such intense personal memories of the pandemic as did Porter, who was twenty-eight at the time of her illness. It was two decades later before Porter published her novel about the pandemic, and almost seven decades before Foote's film was released. Why did it take them so long to deal with such a powerful and compelling subject? And what might we learn from the time lapse between events and their representations that might be important to our understanding now of all that is currently being written and published about the COVID-19 pandemic as it continues to unfurl?

Viet Thang Nguyen, author of the 2016 Pulitzer Prize-winning novel *The Sympathizer* (2015), about the Vietnam War, attempted an answer to the question often posed to him: Why did it take you so long to write your novel? The personal question is contextualized in the larger question of why after decades of relative silence about what had happened in Vietnam, there were significant works being written and published about that war. In his answer, Nguyen talked about the Vietnamese custom of dual burial. The body is buried first in a field far away from the family home. Years later the survivors must dig the body up, and if the timing has been right, only the bones remain. The survivors must wash and then rebury the bones, this time close to the living (Nguyen 2017). Nguyen offers this as a metaphor to explain why it took him so long to write *The Sympathizer*. The experiences of those who lived through the 1918 flu in the midst of World War I may be similar to his—that is, the enormity of the events and their influence on the world were too great to be conveyed until decades later, when time had provided both distance and a fuller perspective.

How much difference does a century make in the ways that care is provided and stories are told? A quick look at the coverage of the 1918 pandemic gathered many years later by the CDC puts the differences between then and now in stark historical perspective (CDC 2022). The lack of treatments in 1918 is matched by the paucity of first-person accounts by survivors, either patients or healthcare professionals. The CDC began gathering survivors' stories for the 90th anniversary of the 1918 flu, but even now there are few compared to the many that are becoming available from the COVID-19 pandemic. The scientific and technological developments of the past century are obvious not only in the advanced medical care and quick development of effective vaccines, but also in the first-person accounts emerging to record what it has been like these past two years and counting. We are perhaps still too immersed in this pandemic to appreciate the value these first-person accounts will have in the future. If we do not gather and preserve them now, the opportunity and potential value with be lost. The plight of the novelists, however, is somewhat different, and even they, according to report, wonder whether anyone will want to read their works about COVID-19 once the pandemic is finally over (Alter 2022). Even if the general public prefers forgetting to remembering, that will not diminish the value of first-person accounts of patients and families and those who have been on the front lines of emergency response, medicine, nursing, respiratory therapy, and public health during these years of crisis. We have much to learn.

Acknowledgments

I thank my cousin Sandra Coyle Korth for telling me about the journal that our grandmother and her sister jointly kept, Jeannette writing on one side of each page, Annie writing on the other. After Annie's death, our grandmother filled the remaining pages by writing Annie's name over and over again.

References

Agresta, Michael. 2020. "The Seminal Novel about the 1918 Flu Pandemic Was Written by a Texan." *Texas Monthly*, June 24, 2020. https://www.texasmonthly.com/arts-entertainment/1918-flu-pandemic-novel-coronavirus/

Alter, Alexandra. 2022. "The Problem with the Pandemic Plot." *New York Times*, February 20, 2022. https://www.nytimes.com/2022/02/20/books/pandemic-fiction.html

Centers for Disease Control. 2020. "1918 Pandemic (H1N1 virus)". Centers for Disease Control and Prevention. Last modified March 20, 2020. https://www.cdc.gov/flu/pandemic-resources/1918-pandemic-h1n1.html. Archived on September 1, 2023 and searchable at archive.cdc.gov.

Foote, Horton, writer. 1985. *1918*. Produced by Ross Milloy and Lillian Foote. Cinecom International, 2004. 1 hr., 34 min. DVD.

Hopwood, Jon C. n.d. "Horton Foote: IMDb Mini Biography." https://www.imdb.com/name/nm0285210/bio?ref_=nm_ov_bio_sm

Jackson, Kevin. 2017. *Constellation of Genius: 1922: Modernism Year One*. Reprint ed. New York: Farrar, Straus, and Giroux.

Little, Becky. 2020. "As the 1918 Flu Emerged, Cover-Up and Denial Helped It Spread." *History*, May 26, 2020. https://www.history.com/news/1918-pandemic-spanish-flu-censorship

Nguyen, Viet Thanh. 2015. *The Sympathizer*. New York: Grove Press.

Nguyen, Viet Thanh. 2017. "Inprint Viet Thanh Nguyen Reading." Interview by William Broyles. *Inprint Margarett Root Brown Reading Series*, Rice University, November 13, 2017. https://inprinthouston.org/event/inprint-viet-thanh-nguyen-reading/

Outka, Elizabeth. 2019. *Viral Modernism: The Influenza Pandemic and Interwar Literature*. New York: Columbia University Press.

Porter, Katherine Anne. 1939. *Pale Horse, Pale Rider*. In *Pale Horse, Pale Rider: Three Short Novels*. New York: Modern Library.

Rapp, Anne. 2020a. "*Horton Foote: The Greatest Playwright You've Never Heard Of.*" December 1, 2020. Factual America. Podcast. https://www.alamopictures.co.uk/podcast/horton-foote-anne-rapp/

Rapp, Anne. dir. 2020b. *Horton Foote: The Road to Home*. Directed by Anne Rapp. https://www.hortonfootefilm.com/

Spinney, Laura. 2017. *Pale Rider: The Spanish Flu of 1918 and How It Changed the World*. New York: PublicAffairs.

At the time of this submission, Anne Hudson Jones, PhD, was the Hobby Family Professor in Medical Humanities in the Institute for Bioethics and Health Humanities of the University of Texas Medical Branch at Galveston (UTMB). A founding editor of *Literature and Medicine* and its editor-in-chief for a decade, she has published two books – *Images of Nurses: Perspectives from History, Art, and Literature* (Penn Press) and *Ethical Issues in Biomedical Publication* (JHUP) – and many journal articles. Her work has been recognized with awards from UTMB's Academy of Master Teachers, the University of Texas Board of Regents, the American Medical Writers Association, the American Osler Society, and the American College of Physicians.

Quarantine Dreams, Other People's Lawns, and Bulldog
By Peter Pereira

Originally submitted January 10, 2021

Quarantine Dreams

Healthcare workers who had a high-risk exposure should be restricted from work and remain quarantined with active monitoring for COVID-19 symptoms for 14 days after the date of last exposure. If at any time the worker develops fever or symptoms, they should undergo medical evaluation and COVID-19 testing, if indicated.
—CDC guidelines November 19, 2020

There is a long line of strangers in my kitchen,
waiting patiently at the refrigerator door.

I say, but this is my house, my refrigerator!
They all turn and stare, mouths covered, eyes wide.

An old woman with an oxygen tank is shuffling down the middle of
    the street.
I call her a taxi, and everybody piles in.

Cher's giving a concert. She's singing *If I could turn back time* …
But someone in the front row keeps coughing.

On the 12th day of Christmas my true love gave to me.
That one verse, spinning around in my head.

I'm swimming underwater, no mask, no snorkel,
my mouth blowing an endless stream of bubbles.

I'm standing on the peak of a debris field,
trying to open a tin can with a pocket knife.

In the morning, when I wash my hands,
I feel thankful I can still smell the soap.

Other People's Lawns

Martinez Landscaping was just a glorified way
to say the father and son mowed other people's lawns.
Until one day the father got sick: fever, cough,
a vice-like headache so bad the ER doctor

said testing him would make no difference.
He went home and quarantined with his family
bringing meals outside the bedroom door, until gasping
fingers blue he insisted on walking himself to the ambulance.

He called that night from the hospital to say he was dying.
The family was permitted to say goodbye, dressed in moon suits
and gloves, one person at a time. Five days later the son, just as sick,
fell blue face first into the ambulance door, was pronounced dead on
    arrival.

Father and son buried together in the same grave.
Soon there will be nothing over them but grass.

Bulldog

Throughout the weeks of protest and quarantine
our Black neighbor walks his old white bulldog
every evening after dinner. He follows close behind
as the dog waddles its arthritic hips, wheezes, coughs,
then stops to catch its breath before sniffing the grass.
Seventeen, he tells us. Ancient in human years,
a relic, half blind, half deaf. His master
trailing behind, empty leash wound up in his hand.

Peter Pereira is a family physician in Seattle, Washington. His books include *Saying the World* and *What's Written on the Body*, both from Copper Canyon Press, and the chapbook *The Lost Twin* from Grey Spider Press. His poems have also appeared in *Poetry, Prairie Schooner, The Virginia Quarterly Review* and other magazines, and have been featured on BBC Radio and The Writer's Almanac.

On Wearing Masks
By Richard M. Ratzan

Originally submitted February 20, 2023

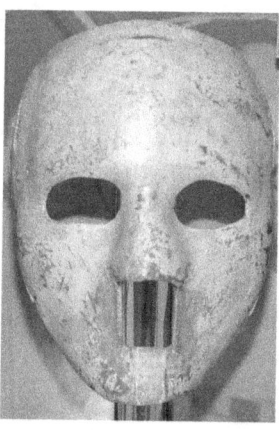

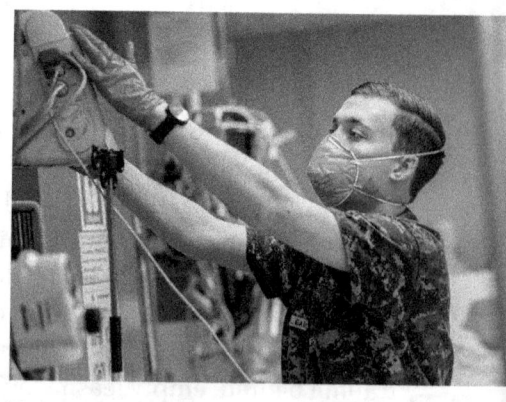

Figure 1: Disparate Masks (clockwise from top left): An ancient Greek tragic mask by Silanion; Jacques Plante's original ice hockey fiberglass face mask; Mort Henderson, aka "The Masked Marvel," donning his trademark full-faced black mask, posing before a fight in 1915; Hospital Corpsman 3rd Class Brennan Leary wearing an N95 mask while treating a COVID-19 patient in the intensive care unit of the hospital ship USNS Mercy (T-AH 19); The mask of a late medieval executioner.

These disparate characters are seemingly unrelated: a famous ice hockey goalie who pioneered the face mask in the National Hockey League; a late medieval mask worn by an executioner; a 20th century wrestler inaugurating the professional wrestler's mask for entertainment; and a modern-day hero caring for COVID-19 patients during the COVID-19 pandemic. Not pictured (for copyright reasons) is the dynamic duo of Batman and Robin, perhaps the icons of masked heroes. One denominator, however, is common to all of these characters – the use of masks. And yet how different the functions of their masks – from masks for entertainment to physical protection against large (hockey pucks) and microscopic (COVID-19) foes to a device to instill terror.

They also demonstrate the *sine qua non* for understanding masks: the necessary inclusion of context in interpreting the role of that particular mask at that particular time. Thus, we would be hard pressed to know whether that is Plantes's goalie mask or a prop from the movie "Friday the 13th," which adopted a Detroit Red Wings hockey mask for the film (Tyler 2019). Is this Guy Fawkes mask (Figure 2) part of the November celebration in England or the announcement of a cyber-terrorism attack?

Figure 2. Guy Fawkes mask.

The COVID-19 pandemic has prompted a new look at masks - all masks. In this essay I shall be looking at the role of masks in human culture broadly—from ritual to theater to medical uses before and during the COVID-19 pandemic. A prudent first step is a working definition, especially since mine – one of several I shall be discussing – differs from most others' definitions.

Virtually all scholars who define masks have done so in a manner that speaks to identity, As Efrat Tseëlon writes, "[the] mask provides a means for both delineating self from others and interrogating the other within the self" (Tseëlon 2001, xv). Donald Pollock, an anthropologist, proposes that "we treat the objects conventionally called 'masks' as only one of a variety of semiotic systems that are related through their conventional use in disguising, transforming or displaying identity" (Pollock 1995, 581).

My first definition for "mask" emphasizes the importance of the context in which the mask is being used. I concur with Sieber that:

> the presentation of an isolated mask in a museum constitutes a gross misrepresentation, not only of the social values inherent in the complex comprised of mask, costume, dance, music and other related traits, but of the esthetic component of the mask in its original context (Sieber 1962, 9).

Although I shall offer several variations on the definition of a mask in this essay in order to highlight different aspects of masks, I shall initially define a mask as

> Anything that may, when utilized, affect part or all of one's facial appearance and/or identity whether actually utilized (usually meaning "worn") or not and whether that was its intended function or not.

This definition may strike some as unwieldy, but I wish to emphasize that using the words "obscure" or "conceal" or "hide" or "shield" in any definition of a mask only defines one function of some masks since the same mask that conceals the identity of Anakin Skywalker affirms that of Darth Vader. As Heyl comments, "One should keep in mind that masks both obscure their wearers and attract attention at the same time" (Heyl 2001, 114). The mask of Anthony Hopkins in his brilliant portrayal of

Richard Nixon in the film "Nixon" – an actor's turning his own face into the mask of another – is not the physical mask one sees on an intensivist in the ICU caring for a patient with COVID-19. One might say that masks focus the eye of the beholder on several truths at once, as I shall elaborate more fully below.

The word "utilized" in my initial definition underscores the fact that a mask need not be a material object that is actually "worn" on the face. For example, some scholars, with whom I agree, would define an assumed voice or a pseudonym or a literary pose as a mask. Or even a heavily painted or cosmetically altered face, like that of Emmett Kelly, whose persona, "Weary Willie", wears a mask of grease paint (Figure 3) (Wikipedia 2002).

Figure 3. Emmett Kelly as "Weary Willie"

Indeed it is not a co-incidence that the words "persona" and "mask" are frequent bed fellows in the same sentence, for the etymology of "persona" is the Latin word for "mask." The Greeks and later the Italians have also contributed to our vocabulary for masks. As Wiles notes:

> ... when fifth-century Greeks spoke of masks, they had only the *prosōpon* [πρόσωπον], the regular term for "face". This in turn is derived from the preposition pros ("before") joined to *ōps*, a noun related to words for seeing and the eye. 'Before the gaze ...' yet the gaze in question might equally belong to me the seer or you the seen (2007, 1).

It now becomes clear how the Latin *persona* becomes our word "personality", and the Greek word becomes the basis for "prosopagnosia," also known as "face blindness," or an inability to recognize the faces of people you "should" know. The etymology of "mask" is less certain. The Oxford English Dictionary (OED) favors "masca" a post-classical Latin word for "evil spirit," also crediting Italian "maschera" and "mascara," and French "masque," the last of which, of course, yields "masquerade." However, the OED and Sedivy both mention a possible Arabic source (*mas<u>k</u>ara*; *mashara*) variations of "fool, teasing, joke, joker" (OED 2023; Sediyy 2021).

Whether it is a joker like a clown colleague of Emmett Kelly, a wrestling match, or Brecht's play "The Caucasian Chalk Circle" (Figure 4), the mask is a non-negotiable fact with which the perceiver must engage and mediate. Using her attention, her imagination, her intelligence and her willingness – or not – her mind will entertain imaginary alternatives to what her eyes are telling her is just a mask, and will, more often than not, perceive emotions on an immobile mask. As Ralph Lee, a Manhattan-based prolific creator of masks and puppets described this process:

> There is something mysterious about masks...and the core of that mystery is that an inanimate object takes on a life. You really want the masks to be able to breathe. The mask has a fixed expression, but if it's manipulated properly you would swear that you can see the expression change (Gussow 1998).

Figure 4. The Minnesota Theatre Company 1965 - Caucasian Chalk Circle

Masks are not signposts with strictly interpretable, unmistakable directions. They are two-way mirrors reflecting emotions of the beings on each side of the mask. However, as so many have observed, the mask one wears when one wishes to be incognito is often the mask of one's "true self." Fielding, in his poem "Masquerade," observed:

Known prudes there, libertines we find
Who masque the face, t'unmasque the mind (1751, 9).

Discussing masquerade, Tseëlon notes that the

paradox of the masquerade appears to be that it presents truth in the shape of deception. Like a neurotic symptom it reveals in the process of concealing (2001, 5).

Behavior that was otherwise proscribed was condoned, at least temporarily and contextually, during the masquerades of 18th Century England. Masquerade was a space wherein people could enjoy fleeting liberty from social and sexual and psychological constraints (Castle 1986) Whereas masquerade has quite a Bakhtinian and Rabelaisian aspect to its air of revelry, carnival, and devil-may-care fun, masks in quotidian, work-a-day personal and business life play more subtle and implicit roles in individuals' behaviors. For, as sociologists Robert Ezra Park (1950), and later Erving Goffman (1959), so eloquently pointed out, we all wear masks in the way we present ourselves in social interactions:

It is probably no mere historical accident that the word person, in its first meaning, is a mask. It is rather a recognition of the fact that everyone is always and everywhere, more or less consciously, playing a role ... It is in these roles that we know each other; it is in these roles that we know ourselves.

In a sense, and in so far as this mask represents the conception we have formed of ourselves – the role we are striving to live up to – this mask is our truer self, the self we would like to be. In the end, our conception of our role becomes second nature and an integral part of our personality. We come into the world as individuals, achieve character, and become persons (Park 1950, 249-50).

The range of role-masks that women have used is particularly important. From make-up to dress to body movement to behavior to voice—women have often disguised their natural selves. Without such "masks," women have worried they would otherwise be diminished or disregarded by men (Riviere 1986). This tension between apparent and real, masked and unmasked identities in both men and women in daily life suggests a dynamic oscillation between selves, a force multiplier, as it were, of identity.

Another reasonable definition of a mask, then, is that it is a device that multiplies the relationships of the identities of the user to the perceiver and vice versa by a minimum of a power of two. The person perceiving the masked individual, knowing it is a mask, must negotiate a pair of identities. The masked user understands who she is, unmasked, but, in wondering which of her pair of identities the perceiving is "seeing," may hope it is her "true self," a sentiment Wilde so characteristically captures in two of his many inimitable aphorisms:

> A mask tells us more than a face ... Man is least himself when he talks in his own person. Give him a mask, and he will tell you the truth (1913, 62 and 185).

This alternation between one's masked self and one's unmasked (private) self characterizes not only superheroes who routinely transition from one self to the other, but also real life villains, e.g., Nazi doctors who engaged in unconscionable behavior during the day in prison camps only to go home and play lovingly with their own children, in a process that Robert Jay Lifton described as "splitting" (Grodin and Annas 2007; Lifton 1986). Furthermore, it suggests the phenomenon of doppelgängers.

The concept of a doppelgänger – that is, a person with an uncanny resemblance – physical or psychological or both – to someone – is an old one, dating back to its first use by Jean Paul Richter (Keppler 1972; Rogers 1970). Doppelgängers represent a fertile way to understand the relationship of the masked to the unmasked self, what Aristotle calls man's "dual or composite being" (Aristotle 1934, 535). The notion of doubles or doppelgängers appeals to our inclination to see the twofold in human nature. Although Plank is writing about doppelgängers, he could just as well be describing masks:

... the profound sense of the double lies here - that the double allows the self to escape the perimeters of the self and to become the other while maintaining its self-identity (1981, 170).

The various selves of a mask and the protean forms masks can take highlight the question, "To what purpose?" "Why and how do masks increase the user's selves?" And "how does the perceiver interpret these simultaneous selves?" It is to these questions we now turn.

To understand the various functions of masks, it is useful to begin with a very influential 1938 essay by sociologist and anthropologist Marcel Mauss, in which he posited the mask as the starting point of mankind's slow evolution from highly defined roles to a person with an individual personality (Mauss 1968; Carrithers, Colins, and Luke 1985). Citing anthropological evidence from civilizations as diverse as the Kwakiutl of the Pacific Northwest and ancient Roman society, Mauss postulated that the mask was an important early identification of one's role in the community. It was only with the passage of centuries and the influence of Christianity that the notion of an individual possessing a unique personhood took hold. Intimately aligned with the notion of one playing the role dictated by that particular societally and culturally defined mask is the concept of performance.

Whether one endorses Mauss's theory or not, it is easy to understand how an early ancient Greek drama playwright might have utilized masks as a means to convey extra-textual meaning to the audience. Likewise, masks are a natural medium to enhance not just theater but the theater we call ritual performance. Although it is difficult to differentiate ritual performance from drama as performance, Schechner has proposed one definition for doing so:

> The basic opposition is between efficacy and entertainment, not between ritual and theatre. Whether one calls a specific performance ritual or theatre depends on the degree to which performance tends toward efficacy or entertainment (1976, 207).

From Greek drama to Kwakiutl ritual (Boas 1897) (Figure 5) to modern day plays staged by Yeats and Brecht, masks have played a prominent role in both the efficacy and, at times, the entertainment of performance.

Figure 5. Mask of QŌ'LÔC

Masks have also been used outside performance both to conceal an identity and, simultaneously, to reveal the unmasked's alter ego identity. Strictly concealing one's identity is not always the primary goal of a mask, however, as burqas illustrate. Islamic women's use of burqas, or, as in Figure 6, haiks, arose not from a wish to conceal their identities. Rather, the burqa probably originated as an attempt to maintain a woman's modesty and chastity by thwarting onlooking men's temptations (Ruby 2006; Siraj 2011).

Figure 6. Women in Algeria wearing haiks

The functions masks serve when not strictly utilized for the purposes of regulating identity most often involve the promotion of health. Even before physicians and nurses began using masks as a barrier to microbes, inventive providers used mask-like apparatuses to apply medicines like anesthetics. One of the earliest masks created for administering anesthesia was Esmarch's mask (Figure 7). Johann Friedrich August von Esmarch was an enterprising and incredibly inventive 19th Century Prussian surgeon (Ball 1995; Von Esmarch 1888).

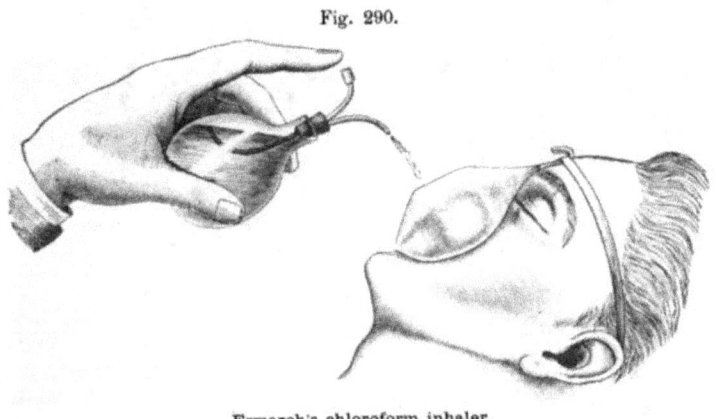

Figure 7. Esmarch's chloroform inhaler

A revolutionary and sophisticated mask-making enterprise to improve health was the attempted reconstruction of faces mutilated by disease or, more commonly, weapons of war. The 19th century US oral surgeon Norman W. Kingsley helped reconstruct faces ravaged by syphilis and Civil War injuries like that of Corporal Andros Guille (Figure 8) whose face had been mutilated at the battle of Mission Ridge outside Chattanooga, Tennessee (Kingsley 1880; Ring 1991). As Kingsley explains, "In September 1864, I constructed the artificial appliance ... in the following manner: I first took an impression of the upper part of the mouth, extending it up as far as possible in front, and from this I secured a model upon which I formed a structure to take the place of the destroyed hard parts and to act as a base for the teeth" (Kingsley 1880, 349-50). Kingsley then made a model of the remainder of the face upon which he built a plaster "appliance" from which he carved the forms of the nose and lip, using "spectacles" to secure some of the component parts. This was not plastic or reconstructive surgery. It was art.

Figure 8. Civil War soldier, Corporal Andros Guille, a) before and b) after facial reconstruction

Similarly, in World War I, two artists, like Kingsley, became makers of masks to allow injured men and women, especially soldiers, to return to a life without disfigurement. Two sculptors, British Francis Derwent Wood (1871–1926) (Figure 9) and American Anna Coleman Ladd (1878–1939), created copper masks coated with silver to restore the mutilated faces of British and French World War I (WWI) soldiers, respectively. Their creative restorations speak for themselves (Figure 10) (Wood 1917; Romm and Zacher 1982; Meier 2016).

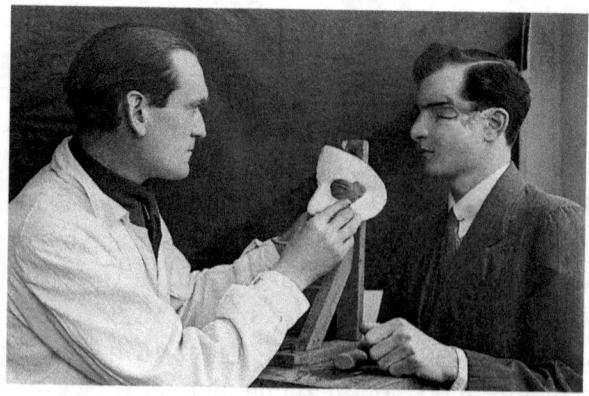

Figure 9. Francis Derwent Wood with soldier

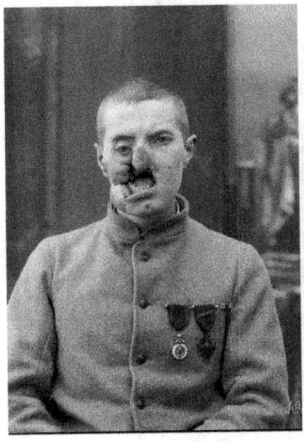 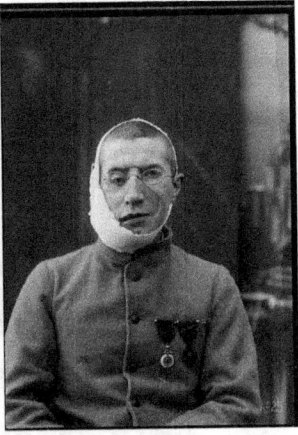

Figure 10. Soldier a) before and b) after mask made by Anna Coleman Ladd

Harold Gillies was an innovative plastic surgeon who attempted to replace the mutilated remains of WWI soldiers' faces with a reconstructed mask of tissue from their arms. Of course, the reader will appreciate the irony of creating a surgical mask based on the soldier's original facies, i.e., a surgical mask that restores, not alters or conceals, the "true identity" behind the mutilating mask of a war injury. In addition to being a mask-maker clinician, he likely also wore a surgical mask in the operating room (Fitzharris 2022; "All Things Considered" Podcast 2007). The elegant research of Adams et al. shows the slow acceptance of modern operating room attire over the early 20th Century (2016). The history of the use of gloves and masks to lessen the transmission of microbes, however, began centuries before, with medieval plague. One of the most fanciful outfits is an oft-reproduced image (Figure 11), the historicity of which some modern-day historians refute (Ruisinger 2020).

The scientific use of masks to protect against contagion begins in the late 19th Century, in large part owing to the efforts of Pasteur (1822 - 1895), Lister (1827 - 1912) and Koch (1843 - 1910) in proving that transmissible agents were a major source of man's illness (Matuschek 2020). This growing awareness of the utility of masks in retarding, if not preventing, air-borne transmission was gaining momentum. Wu Lien-Teh, a Malaysian born, English educated and trained physician of remarkable talents and courage, used the simple mask to battle the pneumonic plague in Manchuria in 1910-1911, masks that can be seen on his colleagues in Figure 12 (Teh, Han, and Pollitzer 1923; Liu et al. 2015; Michaeleas et al. 2022).

Figure 11. Plague doctor

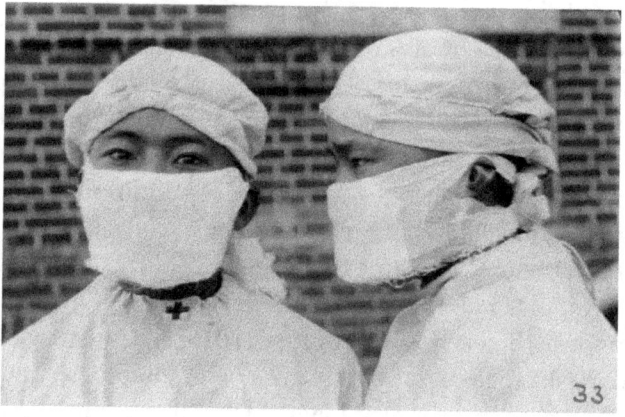

Figure 12. Clinicians wearing simple masks during pneumonic plague epidemic in Manchuria, 1910-11 and 1920-21

Concomitant with WWI was the 1918 influenza pandemic. It raged throughout the world and only ended when it ran out of uninfected, immunologically vulnerable humans. There were no medicines or vaccines to combat it. Sanitation and masks were all felt to be useful by most but not all medical and epidemiological personnel (Arnold 2018; Crosby 2003; Kolata 1999). As this poster indicates, there was an intense public health effort, as today, to educate the country's citizens how best to avoid influenza (Figure 13).

The Pandemic and the Humanities 229

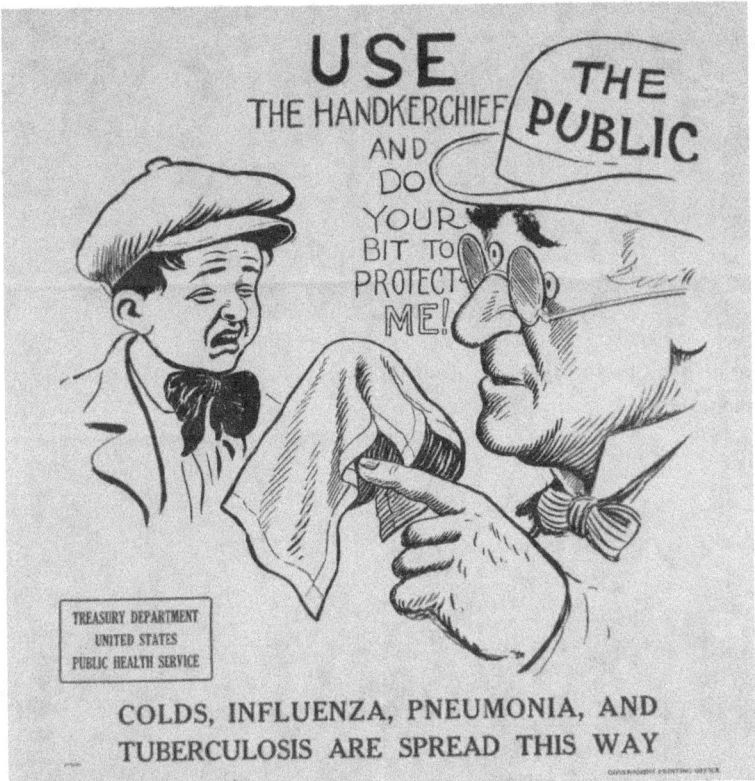

Figure 13. Public health poster, undated

A related ditty was particularly widely promulgated:

Obey the laws
Wear the gauze
Protect your jaws
From septic paws (PBS, n.d.)

Despite the believers and non-believers, many wore masks a century ago. The Red Cross was influential in helping make and disseminate them (Figure 14). Many public events like indoor church services were banned, but essential workers like police and soldiers and street cleaners had to serve, but with masks (Figure 15).

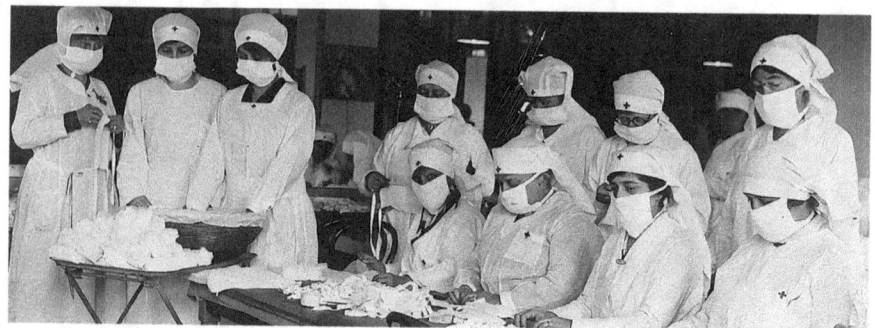

Figure 14. Red Cross workers make anti-influenza masks for soldiers, Boston, Massachusetts

Figure 15. Seattle policemen wearing masks during 1918 influenza pandemic

When COVID-19 landed in the US a century later, Americans, who had no tradition of wearing masks for any reason related to health, responded to the mandates in a complex fashion. This reaction was due, in part, to equal parts fear, denial, and mixed messages from governmental and medical authorities as well as the media, especially internet sources with quite varying motivations. The CDC, for example, waffled early in the pandemic about wearing masks, initially issuing a statement in March 2020 (on a webpage now only retrievable via web archives) that facemasks may have been in short supply and should be saved for providers (Netburn

2021, Jignan 2020). Worse, the US Surgeon General, Jerome Adams, tweeted a frustrated plea to the American public not to exhaust the supply of masks providers needed, which was understandable, but then added that they did not work (Cramer and Sheikh 2020). A statement by the WHO to the same effect a month later also led to confusion (Sample 2020). The conflicting messages and reception were eerily similar to the frenzied public health scene a century earlier as this page from the October 29, 1918, San Francisco Chronicle demonstrates (Figure 16).

Figure 16. Conflicting media messages and public reception on masks in October 1918 *San Francisco Chronicle*

Once it became clear that the US was not going to be spared the full wrath of COVID-19, initial official recommendations fluctuated regarding masks, social distancing, travel and hand washing, all leading, unfortunately, to confusion, which contributed to any undercurrent of mistrust and a willingness to believe in conspiracy theories (Wilson 2020; Falkenback and Greer 2021). This confusion also contributed to what can only be called a national adult oppositional-defiant disorder that manifested itself in many diverse ways and not just towards suggestions or mandates to wear masks or put masks on children. Even once public health evidence and guidance became more clear and consistent, the damage of mixed messaging and resultant conspiracy theories had been done: individuals refused to observe suggested behavior emanating from the CDC and the White House, gathering in large groups from motorcycle rallies to indoor church services. Well publicized episodes of rage against all things mask occurred (Abad-Santos 2020).

Factors associated with the refusal to wear masks were multifactorial. The following factors correlated with differing levels of mask-wearing: gender, place of residence, educational level, work or living environment, marital status, flu symptoms, e-health literacy, and whether living with people in home quarantine (Zhang et al. 2022); political beliefs, specifically whether the participants in the study favored politicians Donald Trump or Joseph Biden (Young et al. 2022); gender and age (with women and seniors more likely to wear masks) (Hitch et al. 2022); and, in present and former college students, greater compliance correlated with being non-white and female (Gette et al. 2021).

Religious beliefs sometimes were cited as a reason to violate local mandates, e.g., the Haredim in New York, who trusted their own intuition more than medical authorities (a failure of that group and its leaders in this author's opinion, not the "US public health system") (Carmody et al. 2021).

The science behind advocating for masks in an effort to avert COVID-19 far surpassed that validating their use in Manchuria's plague or the 1918 influenza pandemic. Yet many early COVID-19 studies only gave masks and mask-wearing a half-hearted endorsement with the ubiquitous use of the word "suggest," (Czypionka et al. 2021; Dismore et al. 2021), a lukewarm endorsement not lost on those already faint of heart about masks. Nor were scientific ambivalence and public distrust in masks new. Indeed, during the 1918 influenza pandemic, there were organizations committed to fighting the recommendations and mandates of mask-wearing in the US, as this advertisement in the same SF Chronicle, but now three months later, illustrates (Figure 17).

Figure 17. Anti-Mask meeting advertisement in January 1919 *San Francisco Chronicle*

As Brian Dolan points out in a wonderfully microscopic analysis of the local players and movements at the time, the risk of coming down with influenza – a deadly disease in each of the two waves that were felt to be due, in part, to antigenic shifts – seemed the least salient of factors motivating well-known participants on both sides of the debate over masks (2020). Most citizens in the current pandemic, however, wore masks when initially advised and a significant number of people continue to wear masks today when in large groups, e.g., a supermarket or theater. A century ago during the influenza pandemic, and, still today, advocates of masks state they are, in part, simply following the precautionary principle, a public policy stance growing out of concern for the environment (Lopez 2020). As described by the European Environment Agency, the precautionary principle is characterized by "a general rule of public policy action to be used in situations of potentially serious or irreversible threats to health or the environment, where there is a need to act to reduce potential hazards *before* [original emphasis] there is strong proof of harm, taking into account the likely costs and benefits of action and inaction" (Harremoës et al. 2001, 13).

It is interesting that such anti-mask sentiment during epidemics reveals (unmasks, as it were) an underlying human antipathy towards some masks, at least towards those face coverings that they believe to have no beneficial purpose or, worse, suggest a mysterious, uncertain, threatening or malevolent one. Such antipathy has generated a number of anti-mask laws in this country and Europe going back almost 200 years (Wikipedia 2013). What the populace is not only willing to encounter in the theater but enjoy on Halloween is not so welcome when in an unaccustomed or potentially threatening manner on the street or in one's back yard (Ku Klux Klan V. Kerik 2004; Winet 2012).

Masks, even when worn as a precaution, are not without their complications, both for medical providers and lay people. The difficulties can be divided into psychological/cognitive and physical. Perhaps one of the biggest psychological complaints was the inability to see another's face and the difficulty in "reading" that other's reactions to what you were saying. Instead of a friendly face, every face we encountered wore a mask. We had become a globe of bandits. Numerous studies have documented the reduced perception of emotions during interactions when at least one of the parties is wearing a mask. This impairment seems amplified in adult subjects with and without autism (Tso, Chui, and Hsiao 2022; Tsantani et al. 2022; Maiorana et al. 2022). The ingenious use of photographs of the provider's face, especially when smiling, improved provider-patient relationships (Wiesmann et al. 2021). (Of course, the irony of using a photograph of the unmasked face to unmask the COVID-19 mask will not be lost on the reader of this essay).

Face masks also proved a significant barrier to understanding speech for both the normal hearing and hearing-impaired, whether the latter was a patient or provider (Sonnichsen et al. 2022; Homans and Vroegop 2022; Crume 2021). Poon and Jenstad suggested transparent face masks and heightened awareness of this impediment and attention to policy to alleviate it when the patient was hearing-impaired (2022). Face masks can also prove troublesome for patients with Alzheimer's disease (Gil and Arroyo-Anlló 2021).

Physical ailments caused by mask-wearing are less common but include corneal abrasions (Ramani et al. 2022; Tang and Chong 2021), dermatitides such as acne and aggravation of eczema, (Teo 2021; Damiani 2021) and migraines (Yuksel 2022). However, in one study face mask use ameliorated allergic rhinitis symptoms (Mengi 2022). Multiple studies documented no significant effects on oxygenation or cardiopulmonary status (Nwosu et al. 2021; Sanri et al. 2022; Wojtasz 2022), including children in a post-operative suite (Dost et al. 2022).

Although many assert that what distinguishes man from other animals is – fill in the blank – differences in intelligence, reason, empathy, etc., I would posit that imagination must be added to the list. High on the list. For, what other animal can you see forging a mask out of the product of her imagination, to symbolize the inner spirit of a remembered ancestor, or a character in a story or play she had made up, to show other hominids her vision, made the more believable with a mask? Much as I find orangutans and apes and bonobos infinitely fascinating, not even the non-human primates have been observed to fashion papier mâché or wooden masks to portray the imagined mythological chimp god they wished to honor in a dance.

It is not a co-incidence that the Latin *imago* (Latin for "image", "imitation", "copy") and *imagines* (the ancient Roman funerary death-likenesses relatives would parade after death), are all cognate with our word imagination (Flower 1996). Not long after the first human realized she had a face, it seems, she felt the need to fashion a mask from her imagination to free her self from that physical face and let it loose into the realms of make believe. That, it seems to me, to take Mauss one step farther, is the birth of *Homo imaginins*.

Why has mankind – across the globe, across the centuries – made masks? The answer to why humans make or appreciate masks, or see in them what chimps and artificial intelligence robots do not, cannot be found in psychology experiments any more than the "answer" to creativity or imagination is to be found in MRIs. Why humans make and wear and enjoy seeing masks in a creative setting is why we tell stories. And enjoy listening to them.

Masks are a human invention. Distinctly human. They have served to amplify, disguise, create and negate identity. Not many human inventions have as many conflicting purposes, sometimes simultaneously. Masks in their various forms have appeared on stage, in comic books, in the office, in novels, in convenience store and bank robberies, in movies and now in the clinic. When we consider the last venue, it is striking that masks have entered yet another new phase of human use and interaction—masks mandated for the least romantic or dramatic of reasons, as a barrier to germs. They now enjoy a purely secondary function—compared to the primary one of conveying inner emotions and thoughts and eliciting them in others who perceive the mask. Medical masks, especially during COVID-19 time when they are ubiquitous in the general populace and not limited to medical personnel in medical venues, are like snow tires, or doorbells, or directional signals on the car. They are mundane, unimaginative, purely functional tools that do not distinguish any one user from another, much as doorbells and directional signals are, for the most part, tediously alike and interchangeable.

Medical masks are a different genus and species than the masks of the theater or one's make-up or the mask of a Batman or Robin that can inspire a welcome sense of adventure. The last are endowed with a sense of witnessing an other-than-native-born-self and, as Elizabeth Tonkin articulates, they can change us. They can do all these since there is, as she notes, an inherent power in masks:

> The observer of Masks is by no means passive, but a participator caught up in a drama through which he or she is sometimes actually changed ... The Mask takes meanings on itself and appears charged with Power because it is the focus of concentrated symbolism, whose associated meanings and emotions reverberate off one another. And when as in some initiation ceremonies, the context is already frightening, the

protagonists' lack of ordinary personality – of the human face which human action ought to have - makes the initiands more frightened still. A terrorist in a stocking mask evokes the same fear – in both cases there is much more happening than the mere avoidance of identification which is so often made explanatory. (Tonkin 1979, 246).

Contrary to most of the masks we have considered so far, COVID-19 masks, particularly when publicly mandated, are neither welcomed nor eagerly worn. It is as though we are aware, at perhaps not so conscious a level, that they are, as Tonkin hypothesizes, changing us. All of us. They are not Halloween masks. They are not ritual masks of a funerary dance. They are not intended, in Schechner's terms, to provide entertainment. Their intended purpose is wholly efficacy. They are masks that individuals have been instructed to wear against their will, to wear for a non-ritual use, a mask publicly obliterating their identities in a way they never wished or planned, and indefinitely. It is a mask of someone else's power.

A legitimate question might be: whose power? That of the virus or the human mandating the mask's use? It is no wonder that so many people have objected to a device that altered their identities in a manner beyond their control, essentially equating their identities with those of everyone else, homogenizing all COVID-19 mask-wearing identities into one single, indistinguishable mass identity – the antithesis of the individual's masked identity we have been discussing. As Heyl observed about 18th century England when many people voluntarily wore masks in public as an everyday matter, these masks have turned our streets and grocery stores and malls into a public theater with all citizens as actors (Heyl 2001). We are unwilling actors in a tragedy called COVID with no idea who the players of the *dramatis personae* are. When the masked identity patient is facing another masked identity provider in the emergency department or the clinic, many patients – Tonkin's frightened "initiands" – find themselves asking, "Who was that masked provider?"

In a sense, we have entered the realm of medical mask-hood I find of most interest. The provider wearing an N95 mask to treat a patient with COVID or suspected COVID has become not just a "hero" by today's long overdue recognition, like a fireman or first responder, but a superhero like The Lone Ranger. Although superheroes and the culture surrounding them are nothing if not controversial with many critics ascribing racist, misogynistic and elitist origins to the genesis of, and fascination with, superheroes, my premise that a masked COVID-19-fighting provider with PPE is a superhero only involves the traditional definition of a superhero: a person with either super powers or doing superhuman deeds based on strength, agility or intelligence; usually wearing an unique and identifying costume that frequently includes a mask; fighting the good fight against evil, evil often being perpetrated by super-villains; often but not always using or displaying devices that are also uniquely hers, like Wonder Woman's Lasso of Truth or The Lone Ranger's silver bullets; and often doing her superhero deeds with a concealed identity less than fully disclosed to the recipients of her benevolence (Packer 2009; Chambliss, Svitavsky, and Donaldson 2013).

Seen in this light, the COVID-19-fighting, mask-wearing provider is a superhero with distinctive garb (not just the blue scrubs one sees worn everywhere these days) using special powers of intelligence and unique implements like MRI machines and antibiotics and ultrasound - implements not available to the lay person much less the villain - and fighting for "Truth, Justice and the American Way." And doing all these good works as an unidentified benevolent hero. Wearing a mask. Or two.

For, when a provider wears a mask, we can appreciate, from the work of Park and Goffman and other cultural critics like Riviere, that she is wearing a physical mask over her provider mask, the latter the same type of role mask an office worker wears to work, or an actor, unmasked, wears on the stage, or a minister wears in the pulpit. The physical N95 mask, atop the provider mask, unmasks, as it were, the question many patients ask themselves, highlighting, by virtue of the now visible mask, the quandary behind every provider-patient interaction: Who is treating me, Nurse X or the Jane Doe who is my Nurse X during this encounter? Does it make a difference? It does if Jane Doe is fighting, despite her desire to be professionally neutral, a personal antipathy to abortion and you are an abortion patient. Who is that self behind both masks?

Psychiatrist Sharon Packer discusses the two identities of superheroes —self and superhero self. She astutely applies the Jungian concept of a shadow, or secret, self versus the persona, or masked self (Packer 2009). Given the necessarily evident nature of these two selves of superheroes, Packer rightly raises the confusing directionality of this pair of selves:

> Superhero stories cause a conundrum when it comes to *personae* and *shadows*. [original emphases throughout this paragraph] Which is the

shadow and which is the *persona*? The iconic superhero is recognizable to everyone—and so the signature costume could constitute the *persona*. On the other hand, the superhero is hidden inside a civilian self, or a secret identity, and so the secret identity that the superhero presents to the outside world may also be called the *persona* (Packer 2009, 134).

In a sense, given the context of a medical encounter, what Edmund Pellegrino called "the fact of illness," the N95 mask on that provider has left the world of purely quotidian efficacious use and now enjoined ritual, which, while it is not entertainment, is itself a therapeutic efficacy (Pellegrino 1987). We can only hope that whichever doppelgänger self the patient is seeing, that self *qua* provider remembers that, for the worried patient, she is wearing the enabling mask of a superhero.

References

Abad-Santos, Alex. 2020. "The face mask meltdowns at Trader Joe's, explained." *Vox* July 9, 2020. Accessed February 4, 2023. https://www.vox.com/the-goods/21318663/face-mask-karen-meltdowns-videos-trader-joes

Adams, Lu Wang, Carol A Aschenbrenner, Timothy T Houle, and Raymond C Roy. 2016. "Uncovering the history of operating room attire through photographs." *Anesthesiology* 124 (1): 19-24. https://doi.org/10.1097/ALN.0000000000000932

All Things Considered. 2007. "Artists' Masks Hid Wounds of World War I Soldiers." *NPR*. Accessed Feb 17, 2023. https://www.npr.org/2007/02/24/7556326/artists-masks-hid-wounds-of-world-war-i-soldiers

Aristotle. 1934. *The Nicomachean Ethics*. Translated by H. Rackham. Cambridge, MA: Harvard University Press; London: William Heinemann Ltd., 535.

Arnold, Catharine. 2018. *Pandemic 1918: Eyewitness Accounts from the Greatest Medical Holocaust in Modern History*. First US edition. New York, N.Y.: St. Martin's Press.

Ball, Christine. 1995. "Esmarch's mask." *Anaesthesia and Intensive Care* 23 (3): 273. https://doi.org/10.1177/0310057X9502300301

Boas, F. 1897. "The Social Organization and the Secret Societies of the Kwakiutl Indians." In *Report of the U.S. National Museum for 1895*,

311–738. Washington, DC.

Carmody, Ellie R., Devon Zander, Elizabeth J. Klein, Mark J. Mulligan, and Arthur L. Caplan. 2021. "Knowledge and Attitudes Toward Covid-19 and Vaccines Among a New York Haredi-Orthodox Jewish Community." *Journal of Community Health* 46 (6): 1161–69. https://doi.org/10.1007/s10900-021-00995-0.

Carrithers, S Michael, Steven Collins, and Steven Lukes. 1985. *The Category of the Person: Anthropology, Philosophy, History.* Cambridge [Cambridgeshire]; New York: Cambridge University Press.

Castle, Terry. 1986. *Masquerade and Civilization: The Carnivalesque in Eighteenth-Century English Culture and Fiction.* Stanford, Calif.: Stanford University Press.

CDC. 2020. "Prevent Getting Sick." Accessed February 6, 2023. http://web.archive.org/web/20200314163759/https://www.cdc.gov/coronavirus/2019-ncov/prepare/prevention.html

Chambliss, Julian C., William L. Svitavsky, and Thomas C. Donaldson. 2013. *Ages of Heroes, Eras of Men: Superheroes and the American Experience.* Newcastle upon Tyne: Cambridge Scholars Publishing.

"Constitutional Law. Free Speech. Second Circuit Upholds New York's Anti-Mask Statute Against Challenge by Klan-Related Group. Church of the American Knights of the Ku Klux Klan V. Kerik, 356 F.3d 197 (2d Cir. 2004)." 2004. *Harvard Law Review* 117 (8): 2777–84. https://doi.org/10.2307/4093417

Cramer, Maria and Knvul Sheikh. 2020. "How the Coronavirus Created a U.S. Mask Shortage." *New York Times*, February 29, 2020. Accessed February 6, 2023. https://www.nytimes.com/2020/02/29/health/coronavirus-n95-face-masks.html

Crosby, Alfred W. 2003. *America's Forgotten Pandemic: The Influenza of 1918.* Second edition. Cambridge: Cambridge University Press.

Crume, Bonnie. 2021. "The Silence Behind the Mask: My Journey as a Deaf Pediatric Resident Amid a Pandemic." *Acad Pediatrics* 21(1):1-2. doi: 10.1016/j.acap.2020.10.002.

Czypionka, Thomas, Trisha Greenhalgh, Dirk Bassler, and Manuel B Bryant. 2021. "Masks and Face Coverings for the Lay Public: A Narrative Update." *Annals of Internal Medicine* 174 (4): 511–20. https://doi.org/10.7326/M20-6625.

Damiani, Giovanni, Laura C. Gironi, Ayman Grada, Khalaf Kridin, Renata Finelli, Alessandra Buja, Nicola L. Bragazzi, Paolo D. M. Pigatto, and Paola Savoia. 2021. "COVID-19 Related Masks Increase Severity of

Both Acne (maskne) and Rosacea (mask Rosacea): Multi-center, Real-life, Telemedical, and Observational Prospective Study." *Dermatologic Therapy* 34 (2): e14848–n/a. https://doi.org/10.1111/dth.14848.

Dinsmore, Jessica, Susan Brands, Steven Perry, Michael Lopez, Yutong Dong, Daniel Palasz, and Jennifer Tucker. 2021. "Efficacy of Various Facial Protective Equipment for Infection Control in a Healthcare Setting." *The Western Journal of Emergency Medicine* 22 (5): 1045–50. https://doi.org/10.5811/westjem.2021.3.50516.

Dolan, Brian. 2020. "Unmasking History: Who Was Behind the Anti-Mask League Protests During the 1918 Influenza Epidemic in San Francisco?" *Perspectives in Medical Humanities* 5 (19). https://doi.org/10.34947/M7QP4M.

Dost, Burhan, Özgür Kömürcü, Sezgin Bilgin, Hilal Dökmeci, Özlem Terzi, and Sibel Barış 2022. "Investigating the Effects of Protective Face Masks on the Respiratory Parameters of Children in the Postanesthesia Care Unit During the COVID-19 Pandemic." *Journal of Perianesthesia Nursing* 37 (1): 94–99. https://doi.org/10.1016/j.jopan.2021.02.004.

Falkenbach, Michelle, and Scott L. Greer. 2021. "Denial and Distraction: How the Populist Radical Right Responds to COVID-19 Comment on "A Scoping Review of PRR Parties' Influence on Welfare Policy and Its Implication for Population Health in Europe." *International Journal of Health Policy and Management* 10 (9): 578–80. https://doi.org/10.34172/ijhpm.2020.141.

Fielding, Henry. 1751. "The Masquerade." In *The Miscellaneous Works of the Late Dr. Arbuthnot: The Second Edition with Additions* (A Supplement to the Miscellaneous Works Etc.), edited by John Arbuthnot, 9. Gale ECCO.

Fitzharris, Lindsey. 2022. *The Facemaker: A Visionary Surgeon's Battle to Mend the Disfigured Soldiers of World War I*. New York: Farrar, Straus & Giroux.

Flower, Harriet I. 1996. *Ancestor Masks and Aristocratic Power in Roman Culture*. Oxford: New York: Clarendon Press; Oxford University Press.

Gette, Jordan A., Angela K. Stevens, Andrew K. Littlefield, Kerri L. Hayes, Helene R. White, and Kristina M. Jackson. 2021. "Individual and COVID-19-Specific Indicators of Compliance with Mask Use and Social Distancing: The Importance of Norms, Perceived Effectiveness, and State Response." *International Journal of Environmental*

Research and Public Health 18 (16): 8715. https://doi.org/10.3390/ijerph18168715.

Gil, Roger, and Eva M. Arroyo-Anllo. 2021. "Alzheimer's Disease and Face Masks in Times of COVID-19." *Journal of Alzheimer's Disease* 79 (1): 9–14. https://doi.org/10.3233/JAD-201233.

Gussow, Mel. 1998. "Fleeting Beasts, Collected in a Fantasy Heaven." *The New York Times*. Accessed May 18, 2023. https://www.nytimes.com/1998/03/13/movies/fleeting-beasts-collected-in-a-fantasy-heaven.html.

Grodin, Michael, and George Annas. 2007. "Physicians and Torture: Lessons from the Nazi Doctors." *International Review of the Red Cross* 89, no. 867: 635-654. https://doi.org/10.1017/S1816383107001208

Harremoës, Poul, David Gee, Malcolm MacGarvin, Andy Stirling, Jane Keys, Brian Wynne, and Sofia Vaz. 2001. EEA. *Late Lessons from Early Warnings: The Precautionary Principle 1896–2000*. European Environmental Agency.

Heyl, Christoph. 2001. "The metamorphosis of the mask in seventeenth- and eighteenth-century London." *Masquerade and identities: essays on gender, sexuality, and marginality*. London; New York: Routledge; 114.

Hitch, Lisa, Marie A. Sillice, Hanish Kodali, Katarzyna E Wyka, Javier Otero Peña, and Terry TK Huang. 2022. "Factors Associated with Mask Use in New York City Neighborhood Parks During the COVID-19 Pandemic: A Field Audit Study." *Journal of Infection and Public Health* 15 (4): 460–65. https://doi.org/10.1016/j.jiph.2022.02.006.

Homans, Nienke C., and Jantien L. Vroegop. 2022. "The Impact of Face Masks on the Communication of Adults with Hearing Loss During COVID-19 in a Clinical Setting." *International Journal of Audiology* 61 (5): 365–70. https://doi.org/10.1080/14992027.2021.1952490.

Jingnan, Huo. 2020. "Why Are There So Many Different Guidelines for Face Masks for The Public?" *NPR*, April 10, 2020. Accessed February 5, 2023. https://www.npr.org/sections/goatsandsoda/2020/04/10/829890635/why-there-so-many-different-guidelines-for-face-masks-for-the-public

Keppler, Carl F. 1972. *The Literature of the Second Self*. Tucson: Univ Arizona Press.

Kingsley, Norman W. 1880. *A Treatise on Oral Deformities as a Branch of Mechanical Surgery*. New York: D. Appleton and Company.

Kolata, Gina Bari. 1999. *Flu: The Story of the Great Influenza Pandemic of 1918 and the Search for the Virus That Caused It.* 1st edition. New York: Farrar, Straus and Giroux.

Lifton, Robert J. 1986. *The Nazi Doctors: Medical Killing and the Psychology of Genocide.* New York, NY: Basic Books.

Liu, He, Mingli Jiao, Siqi Zhao, Kai Xing, Ye Li, Ning Ning, Libo Liang, Qunhong Wu, and Yanhua Hao. 2015. "Controlling Ebola: what we can learn from China's 1911 battle against the pneumonic plague in Manchuria." *International Journal of Infectious Diseases* 33: 222-226.

Lopez, German. 2020. "The evidence on masks and Covid-19: What you need to know." *Vox*, July 15, 2020. Accessed February 5, 2023. https://www.vox.com/future-perfect/21299527/masks-coronavirus-covid-19-studies-research-evidence

Maiorana, Natale, Michelangelo Dini, Barbara Poletti, Sofia Tagini, Maria Rita Reitano, Gabriella Pravettoni, Alberto Priori, and Roberta Ferrucci. 2022. "The Effect of Surgical Masks on the Featural and Configural Processing of Emotions." *International Journal of Environmental Research and Public Health* 19 (4): 2420. https://doi.org/10.3390/ijerph19042420.

Mauss, Marcel. 1968. "Une catégorie de l'esprit humain: la notion de personne celle de 'moi'." In *Sociologie et anthropologie*, edited by Paris: Puf, 333-362.

Matuschek, Christiane, Friedrich Moll, Heiner Fangerau, Johannes C Fischer, Kurt Zänker, Martijn van Griensven, Marion Schneider, et al. 2020. "The History and Value of Face Masks." *European Journal of Medical Research* 25 (1): 23. https://doi.org/10.1186/s40001-020-00423-4.

Meier, Allison. 2016. "The Sculptor Who Made Masks for Soldiers Disfigured in World War I." Accessed Feb 17, 2023. https://hyperallergic.com/314255/the-sculptor-who-made-masks-for-soldiers-disfigured-in-world-war-i/.

Mengi, Erdem, Cüneyt Orhan Kara, Uğur Alptürk, and Bülent Topuz. 2022. "The Effect of Face Mask Usage on the Allergic Rhinitis Symptoms in Patients with Pollen Allergy During the Covid-19 Pandemic." *American Journal of Otolaryngology* 43 (1): 103206–103206. https://doi.org/10.1016/j.amjoto.2021.103206.

Michaleas, Spyros N, Konstantinos Laios, Marianna Karamanou, Nikolaos V Sipsas, and Georges Androutsos. 2022. "The Manchurian Pandemic of Pneumonic Plague (1910-1911)." *Le Infezioni in Medicina*

30 (3): 464–68. https://doi.org/10.53854/liim-3003-17.

Netburn, Deborah. 2021. "A timeline of the CDC's mask guidance during the COVID-19 pandemic." *Los Angeles Times*. Accessed February 6, 2023. https://www.latimes.com/science/story/2021-07-27/timeline-cdc-mask-guidance-during-COVID-19-pandemic

Nwosu, Arinze Duke George, Edmund Ndudi Ossai, Okechukwu Onwuasoigwe, and Francis Ahaotu. 2021. "Oxygen Saturation and Perceived Discomfort with Face Mask Types, in the Era of COVID-19: a Hospital-Based Cross-Sectional Study." *The Pan African Medical Journal* 39: 203–203. https://doi.org/10.11604/pamj.2021.39.203.28266.

Oxford English Dictionary (OED) Online. 2023. "mask, n.3." *OED* Online. Oxford University Press. https://www-oed-com.ezp-prod1.hul.harvard.edu/view/Entry/114608?rskey=8sE6cD&result=3

Packer, Sharon. 2009. *Superheroes and Superegos : Analyzing the Minds Behind the Masks*. Santa Barbara: Praeger.

Park, Robert Ezra. 1950. *Race and Culture*. Glencoe, IL: The Free Press.

PBS. n.d. "The Great Influenza: The San Francisco Story." *American Experience*. Accessed May 3, 2023. https://www.pbs.org/wgbh/americanexperience/features/influenza-san-francisco/

Pellegrino, Edmund D. 1987. "Toward a Reconstruction of Medical Morality." *Journal of Medical Humanities and Bioethics* 8 (1): 7-18.

Plank, William G. 1981. "Différance: Hypostatization of the Dialectic Synthesis." In *Fearful Symmetry: Doubles and Doubling in Literature and Film: Papers from the Fifth Annual Florida State University Conference on Literature and Film*, edited by Eugene Joseph Crook, 163-171. University Presses of Florida.

Pollock, Donald. 1995. "Masks and the Semiotics of Identity." *Journal of the Royal Anthropological Institute*. 581-597.

Poon, Brenda T., and Lorienne M. Jenstad. 2022. "Communication with Face Masks During the COVID-19 Pandemic for Adults with Hearing Loss." *Cognitive Research: Principles and Implications* 7 (1): 24–24. https://doi.org/10.1186/s41235-022-00376-8.

Ramani, Soumya, Aynala Anusha, Divya Sundaresh, and Sathyendranath Shetty. 2022. "Collateral Damage: Corneal Injury Due to Mask Use During the COVID-19 Pandemic - A Case Series." *Indian Journal of Ophthalmology* 70 (1): 306–7. https://doi.org/10.4103/ijo.IJO_1861_21.

Ring, Malvin E. 1991. "The history of maxillofacial prosthetics." *Plastic and reconstructive surgery* 87 (1): 174-184.

Riviere, Joan. 1986. "Womanliness as Masquerade." In *Formations of Fantasy*, edited by Victor Burgin, James Donald, and Cora Kaplan, 35-44. London: Methuen.

Rogers, S. Robert. 1970. *A Psychoanalytic Study of the Double in Literature*. Detroit, MI: Wayne State Univ Press.

Romm, Sharon, and Judith Zacher. 1982. "Anna Coleman Ladd: maker of masks for the facially mutilated." *Plastic and Reconstructive Surgery* 70 (1): 104-111.

Ruby, Tabassum F. 2006. "Listening to the voices of hijab." *Women's Studies International Forum* 29 (1): 54–66. https://doi.org/10.1016/j.wsif.2005.10.006.

Ruisinger, Marion Maria. 2020. "Die Pestarztmaske im Deutschen Medizinhistorischen Museum Ingolstadt." *NTM Zeitschrift für Geschichte der Wissenschaften, Technik und Medizin* 28 (2): 235-252.

Sample, Ian. 2020. "Face masks cannot stop healthy people getting COVID-19, says WHO." *The Guardian* April 7, 2020. Accessed February 8, 2023. https://www.theguardian.com/world/2020/apr/07/face-masks-cannot-stop-healthy-people-getting-COVID-19-says-who

Sanri, Erkman, Sinan Karacabey, Emir Unal, Emre Kudu, Murat Cetin, Cigdem Ozpolat, and Arzu Denizbasi. 2022. "The Cardiopulmonary Effects of Medical Masks and Filtering Facepiece Respirators on Healthy Health Care Workers in the Emergency Department: A Prospective Cohort Study." *The Journal of Emergency Medicine* 62 (5): 600–606. https://doi.org/10.1016/j.jemermed.2021.11.021.

Schechner, Richard. 1976. "From Ritual to Theatre and Back." In *Ritual, Play, and Performance: Readings in the Social Sciences/Theater*, edited by Richard Schechner and Mady Schuman, The Seabury Press: New York.

Sedivy, Roland. 2021. "Beethoven's Death Mask and a Short History of Face Masks." *Wiener Medizinische Wochenschrift* 171(15): 391–96. https://doi.org/10.1007/s10354-021-00875-1.

Sieber, Roy. 1962. "Masks as Agents of Social Control." *African Studies Bulletin* 5 (2): 8–13. https://doi.org/10.2307/523143.

Siraj, Asifa. 2011. "Meanings of modesty and the hijab amongst Muslim women in Glasgow, Scotland." *Gender, Place & Culture* 18 (6): 716-731. https://doi.org/10.1080/0966369X.2011.617907.

Sonnichsen, Rasmus, Gerard Llorach To, Sabine Hochmuth, Volker Hohmann, and Andreas Radeloff. 2022. "How Face Masks Interfere

With Speech Understanding of Normal-Hearing Individuals: Vision Makes the Difference." *Otology & Neurotology* 43 (3): 282–88. https://doi.org/10.1097/MAO.0000000000003458.

Tang, Yi Fan, and Elaine WT Chong. 2021. "Face Mask–Associated Recurrent Corneal Erosion Syndrome and Corneal Infection." *Eye & Contact Lens* 47 (10): 573-574.

Teh, Wu Lien, Chun Wing Han, and Robert Pollitzer. 1923. "Plague in Manchuria. I. Observations Made During and after the Second Manchurian Plague Epidemic of 1920–21. II. The Rôle of the Tarabagan in the Epidemiology of Plague." *The Journal of Hygiene* 21 (3): 307–58. https://doi.org/10.1017/S0022172400031521.

Teo, Wan-Lin. 2021. "The "Maskne" Microbiome – Pathophysiology and Therapeutics." *International Journal of Dermatology* 60 (7): 799–809. https://doi.org/10.1111/ijd.15425.

Tonkin, Elizabeth. 1979. "Masks and Powers." *Man* (London) 14 (2): 237–48. https://doi.org/10.2307/2801565.

Tsantani, Maria, Vita Podgajecka, Katie L H Gray, and Richard Cook. 2022. "How Does the Presence of a Surgical Face Mask Impair the Perceived Intensity of Facial Emotions?" *PloS One* 17 (1): e0262344-e0262344. https://doi.org/10.1371/journal.pone.0262344.

Tseëlon, Efrat, ed. 2001. *Masquerade and identities: essays on gender, sexuality, and marginality*. London; New York: Routledge.

Tso, Ricky V., Celine O. Chui, and Janet H. Hsiao. 2022. "How Does Face Mask in COVID-19 Pandemic Disrupt Face Learning and Recognition in Adults with Autism Spectrum Disorder?" *Cognitive Research: Principles and Implications* 7 (1): 64–64. https://doi.org/10.1186/s41235-022-00407-4.

Tyler, Adrienne. 2019. "Friday the 13th: How Jason Got His Hockey Mask (In Both Versions)." *ScreenRant*, September 12, 2019. Accessed October 3, 2022. https://screenrant.com/friday-13th-movie-jason-hockey-mask-origin-explained/

Von Esmarch, Frederich. 1888. *The Surgeon's Handbook on the Treatment of Wounded in the War*. Translated by B. Farquhar Curtis. London: Sampson Low, Marston, Searle, and Rivington Ltd.

Wiesmann, Martin, Christiane Franz, Thorsten Sichtermann, Jan Minkenberg, Nathalie Mathern, Andrea Stockero, Elene Iordanishvili, et al. 2021. "Seeing Faces, When Faces Can't Be Seen: Wearing Portrait Photos Has a Positive Effect on How Patients Perceive Medical Staff When Face Masks Have to Be Worn." *PloS One* 16 (5):

e0251445–e0251445. https://doi.org/10.1371/journal.pone.0251445.

Wikipedia. 2002. "Emmett Kelly." Wikimedia Foundation. Last modified June 5, 2023. https://en.wikipedia.org/wiki/Emmett_Kelly

Wikipedia. 2013. "Anti-mask law." Wikimedia Foundation. Accessed February 8, 2023. https://en.wikipedia.org/wiki/Anti-mask_law

Wilde, Oscar. 1913. Intentions. 9th ed. London: Methuen & Co.

Wiles, David. 2007. *Mask and Performance in Greek Tragedy: From Ancient Festival to Modern Experimentation.* Cambridge: Cambridge University Press.

Wilson, Jason. 2020. "Rightwing Christian preachers in US 'have links to virus hoax.'" *The Guardian* April 4, 2020. Accessed February 4, 2023. https://www.theguardian.com/us-news/2020/apr/04/america-rightwing-christian-preachers-virus-hoax

Winet, Evan Darwin. 2012. "Face-Veil Bans and Anti-Mask Laws: State Interests and the Right to Cover the Face." *Hastings International and Comparative Law Review* 35 (1): 217.

Wojtasz, Izabela, Szczepan Cofta, Pawel Czudaj, Krystyna Jaracz, and Radoslaw Kazmierski. 2022. "Effect of Face Masks on Blood Saturation, Heart Rate, and Well-Being Indicators in Health Care Providers Working in Specialized COVID-19 Center." *International Journal of Environmental Research and Public Health* 19 (3): 1397. https://doi.org/10.3390/ijerph19031397.

Wood, Francis Derwent. 1917. "Masks for facial wounds." *The Lancet* 189 (4895): 949-951.

Young, Dannagal G., Huma Rasheed, Amy Bleakley, and Jessica B. Langbaum. 2022. "The Politics of Mask-Wearing: Political Preferences, Reactance, and Conflict Aversion During COVID." *Social Science & Medicine* (1982) 298: 114836–114836. https://doi.org/10.1016/j.socscimed.2022.114836.

Yuksel, Hatice, Safiye Gul Kenar, Gorkem Tutal Gursoy, and Hesna Bektas. 2022. "The Impacts of Masks and Disinfectants on Migraine Patients in the COVID-19 Pandemic." *Journal of Clinical Neuroscience* 97: 87–92. https://doi.org/10.1016/j.jocn.2022.01.006.

Zhang, Wei, Shu-Fan Chen, Kun-Kun Li, Huan Liu, Hai-Chen Shen, and Xian-Cui Zhang. 2022. "Mask-Wearing Behavior During COVID-19 in China and Its Correlation with e-Health Literacy." *Frontiers in Public Health* 10: 930653–930653. https://doi.org/10.3389/fpubh.2022.930653

Richard M. Ratzan is a retired internist and emergency medicine physician with a long standing interest in the medical humanities, especially medical ethics, literature and medicine, and the history of medicine.

Whispers
By Amalie Flynn

Originally submitted December 31, 2020

1.
We have not left this house. Ours
For *how many months* or how it
Is close. Closer to a year than not.

2.
I go out at night walk streets pitch
With black. Houses that float on
Oil. This darkness or how I cannot
Sleep because when I do I dream of
Skin on arms I cannot touch. A tooth.
My son's back molar sticky spot that
Was scheduled to be drilled last spring.
The crown and neck. The root of it or
How close this all is. To bone.

3.
I remember when my brother drove me
Past it. Years later the landfill. Where
They put the wrists and tendon. Hips
Or femur. Smooth half shell of skull.
Parts of bodies from 9/11 that they
Could not identify or how.

4.
The morning when planes hit and I
Watched the people jump out of the
Twin Tower and fall from the sky like
Dolls I thought *how*. How when they
Counted them up. All of the missing.
It felt like a hole. How it always feels.
Still feels like a hole.

5.
2,977 died that day. So *many* I whisper.

6.
How you can measure the depth of what
Happened that day in hearts. Livers and
Spleens spines and vertebrae. 5,954 tibias
The amount of ribs. But this. How this.
This is more.

7.
Today there are 220,000 dead.
Today there are 280,000 dead.
Today there are 300,000 dead.
Today there are 335,000 dead.
Today there are. Dead.
Dead Americans.

8.
How many more will die. Hospitals that
Fill like lungs. The pink froth projectile.
Or when the breaths are gone. Face down
And on a gurney. How they flip them. Flip
Them on their stomachs to try. Try to awaken
Lungs filled with cloud.

9.
And I think *gowns are just tissue paper*. Or
The tissue of exposed skin. Slope of a back
And buttocks. The angle of a neck. Crown of
Head or how hair will gather. Stomachs that
Stretch. A chin and throat and tube or how.
How they die alone.

10.
My husband said. Before he went to war.
Listen to me.

11.
Or again when he came home. How what
Scared him was not dying. Not dying but
Living. Getting captured by enemy forces
And *having to live like that*.
How it feels to be alive but almost. Almost
Dead.

12.
Right now. A woman is dying. Dying from
The virus. A doctor holds out the speaker
On a phone. Holds it next to her ear. And
On the other end a son. How he recites
The prayer *for your death* or numbers.
The numbers on her arm. And now.
Now *to die* and *to die like this*.

13.
Letters of the prayer are feathers or
Words like a wing. Ligaments of her
Dying jaw. Cartilage and a digastric
Muscle. Her horn. Greater horn of a
Hyoid bone. And her son in a speaker
Whispering *the sun*.

14.
How *the sun will not harm you by day*.
Not the. This moon. Not this moon. Not
The moon at night.

Amalie Flynn is a poet and author of *September Eleventh* (2021), *Wife and War: The Memoir* (2013) and the poetry blogs: Pattern of Consumption, September Eleventh, Wife and War, The Sustainability of Us, and Border of Heartbreak. Her writing has appeared in *American Book Review, Beyond their Limits of Longing, The New York Times, Time,* Huffington Post and has received mention from *The New York Times* and CNN. Flynn has a BA in English/Studio Arts, MFA in Creative Writing, PhD in Humanities, and serves as poetry editor for *The Wrath-Bearing Tree*.

The Virus and the Border: Reflections on the Experiences of Emergency Responders in Southern Arizona
By Ieva Jusionyte

Originally submitted November 8, 2020

On March 21, 2020, citing the need to prevent the spread of COVID-19, the Department of Homeland Security closed the border between the United States and Mexico to all non-essential travel. Not only did this measure fail to stop the circulation of coronavirus, but it had harmful social effects in border towns, such as the sister cities of Nogales, Arizona and Nogales, Sonora. Disregard for local reality of entanglement and interdependence and disruption of cross-border ties that bind these towns together exacerbated the toll of the pandemic on binational communities and frontline emergency workers who serve them, putting the health and life of residents on both sides at risk.

The rationale for limiting entry into the US was questionable. By the end of March, the US already had over 160,000 cases (CDC 2020) while Mexico only registered a hundred, initially among people who had recently traveled to the US (Linthicum 2020). Although the order was bilateral, it primarily applied to northbound and not southbound traffic, ignoring the direction in which the virus was spreading. Customs and Border Protection (CBP) officers at the ports of entry rigorously questioned Mexican citizens about the purpose of their trip to Arizona, making it more difficult for them to visit family members or go shopping in local stores, while Americans could breeze through the border without having to prove to Mexican officials that their travel to Sonora was essential. The very definition of "essential" was vague. Students attending school in the US were exempt, as were farmworkers and truck drivers "engaged in lawful cross-border trade," and individuals seeking medical treatment in the US (US Department of Homeland Security 2020a). The order also did not restrict the movement of emergency responders and public health officials. Federal authorities recognized that "critical services such as food, fuel, healthcare and life-saving medicines must reach people on both sides of the border every day" (US Department of Homeland Security 2020b). Much of the international traffic in the region consists of just such critical services that were allowed to continue. Extended multiple times, the order had so many lacunae and was so unevenly enforced that it is not surprising it had little effect in stopping the spread of the virus across the US-Mexico border.

Despite the border being officially shut, health officials in northern Mexican states, watching COVID-19 cases in the US rise, were increasingly worried. Public hospitals that routinely experience shortages of personnel and equipment, from gloves to heart monitors, were not prepared to handle the pandemic. In several cities around Mexico, doctors and nurses walked out to protest government inaction (Mexican President Andrés Manuel López Obrador, like US President Donald J. Trump, downplayed the seriousness of the disease), demanding training and supplies (Cervantes 2020). By the end of May, more than 11,000 healthcare workers had contracted the disease, accounting for one in every five COVID-19 cases in Mexico (Kitroeff and Villegas 2020). Disappointed by government inaction, residents of border towns tried taking matters into their own hands. In Nogales, Sonora, protestors blocked several southbound lanes, demanding stricter screening of vehicles entering Mexico from the US (Clark 2020). Local authorities had a different idea. Instead of asking travelers about the purpose of their visit, they installed several "sanitation tunnels," asking everyone coming from Arizona to walk through an inflatable plastic tent where they were sprayed with a disinfectant. The measure was a symbolic reversal of what US health authorities used to do to Mexicans crossing into the US for work: subjecting them to taking gasoline baths and spraying them with toxic chemicals (Romo 2005, Cockburn 2007). Although less harmful than the Zyklon B applied to Mexican laborers a century ago, the medical rationale of the quick application of a disinfectant agent used for cleaning surfaces in food preparation as a measure of prevention of COVID-19, which primarily spreads through respiratory droplets, was questionable. Even Hugo Lopez-Gatell, Mexico's Health Secretary, called the sanitation tunnels in northern towns a waste of money (Blust 2020).

What the order to close the border missed was that in binational towns such as Nogales, Arizona, and Nogales, Sonora, the social life and public health of communities on both sides are intertwined. Decisions made in one country affect the residents on both sides. For example, when President Trump began promoting hydroxychloroquine as an allegedly effective drug against COVID-19, American citizens who believed him drove south of the border to stock up, wiping out pharmacy shelves and leaving long-time patients with lupus and arthritis in Mexico without access to medication (Olivares and Corchado 2020).

Other forms of entanglement are more complex. US-owned assembly plants in northern Mexico, known as maquiladoras, employ thousands of workers to produce goods for the US market, from doorknobs to industrial motors. They also manufacture medical supplies. During the pandemic some factories switched their operations to focus on making masks, gloves and other protective equipment and medical supplies that US emergency responders and hospitals urgently needed. However, as indoor spaces with large number of employees, maquiladoras soon became hotspots for the spread of the virus. While most of the medical supplies and equipment they manufactured were exported to the US to help American healthcare workers on the front lines of the pandemic, it fell on understaffed and underequipped Mexican hospitals to attend to factory employees who got sick and died from the disease (Cengiz 2020). This situation underscores that in Nogales, Ciudad Juárez, and other border towns public health is a binational matter. Just as with economic and environmental concerns, policies that fail to approach southern US and northern Mexico as one transborder region are limited and can be detrimental (Vélez-Ibañez and Heyman 2017).

Emergency responders in Arizona's border towns also work in a binational social space, where their commitments to the safety and health of residents extend across the line (Jusionyte 2018). These American cities have mutual aid agreements with fire departments, civil protection offices and public health authorities in northern Mexico. Under the auspices of federal agendas, such as the Environmental Protection Agency's Border 2012 and later Border 2020 programs, and through mutual aid agreements at the municipal level, they share knowledge and equipment and regularly train together, practicing joint response to hypothetical disasters. These staged emergency exercises have included fires, floods and hazardous materials incidents, some involving biological agents – viruses and bacteria – which require shuttling patients across the border to hospitals in either Mexico or in the US, depending on which country's resources are overwhelmed according to the scenario.

These drills prepare emergency responders to handle more frequent and less dramatic situations that regularly require binational cooperation: transporting critical patients from Mexico to trauma and burn centers in the US; sending donated gear and personal protective equipment from the US to the Red Cross medics and volunteer firefighters in Mexico; dispatching joint Mexican and American rescue teams to search for people carried away by the flooded washes that pass through tunnels underneath the border; working together to extinguish wildland fires that spread from one country to another depending on the direction of the wind. Trying to disentangle the two communities according to the jurisdictional boundary that marks where the US ends and Mexico begins conflicts with the operational logic of this region's binational emergency response.

The decision to partially close the border further intensified the deleterious effects of tactical infrastructure that the US government had been deploying to the region in the name of national security. As the National Science Foundation-funded ethnographic research study I conducted with emergency responders from 2015 to 2017 has shown, the metal bollard fence, now with coils of razor wire, that separates Nogales, Arizona from Nogales, Sonora, has been acting as a "mechanism of injury" (MOI) resulting in predictable patterns of trauma (Jusionyte 2018a, 2018b). Individuals who attempt to scale the barrier, currently extending over twenty feet, routinely experience ankle and tib-fib fractures as well as spinal cord and head injuries.

The pandemic not only didn't stop this practice of extralegal corporal punishment of unauthorized border crossers, but, with the border shut and no recourse to entering the US legally available to them, likely forced more people to take the risk of getting wounded or killed, whether they attempt to climb over the wall or take the perilous trip through the desert. There has been a sharp rise in the number of remains of unauthorized migrants found in southern Arizona in 2020. Gregory Hess, chief medical examiner for Pima County, described it as an "alarming reverse to what was a downward trend" since 2010 (Carranza 2020). By early November, his office had documented the recovery of 181 human remains. Although most are skeletal remains with cause of death unknown, the medical examiner's office has documented thirty-nine cases of probable hyperthermia due to exposure, eight deaths from blunt force injuries, and one from gunshot wounds (Pima County Office of the Medical Examiner and Humane Borders, Inc). The numbers of border crossers who have been wounded – whether the fire department extricated them from the concertina wire added to the fence or the Border Patrol picked them up, severely dehydrated, in the desert – are not made public. It is likely that they, too, are on the rise.

In March 2020, when the government announced it was postponing court hearings, over 60,000 asylum-seekers had been waiting in northern

Mexican towns to make their case in front of the US immigration judge under a recent policy that is misleadingly called Migrant Protection Protocols. Rather than offering protection, it forces asylum-seekers to live for weeks or months in precarious conditions, seeking refuge in makeshift camps and shelters, vulnerable to extortion, kidnapping, and other forms of criminal predation, with little to no access to work, healthcare, or justice. The pandemic became an excuse to lengthen the already drawn-out line of those waiting in limbo. Based on the 1944 Public Health Service Act, which allows the Surgeon General to suspend "the introduction of persons or goods" into the US on public health grounds, the CDC authorized CBP to do "summary expulsions of noncitizens" at land borders, a rule that violates the Refugee Act of 1980 and primarily affects asylum-seekers (Guttentag 2020). Under this rule, border enforcement agents do not need to check whether the noncitizen is ill or is contagious before immediately sending him back to Mexico. This policy pushed even more people to wait indefinitely on the other side of the border.

To make matters worse, the spread of COVID-19 had an impact on the work of migrant shelters and humanitarian aid organizations that routinely provide food, clothing, basic medical aid, and legal counseling to asylum-seekers stranded in Mexico under the Migrant Protection Protocols and Remain in Mexico programs. Some of the most active volunteers who work in soup kitchens and provide other humanitarian services to migrants in Nogales, Sonora, as well as in Tijuana, Ciudad Juárez, Matamoros, and other northern Mexican towns are elderly US citizens, who have been discouraged from traveling across the border due to the double risk of getting infected themselves and of bringing the virus from the US to migrant shelters and camps in Mexico. Voluntary humanitarian aid work also did not count as "essential travel," which added to the hesitation of those involved in this type of aid to cross the border. Pausing these basic services has made the situation of asylum-seekers waiting in Mexico even worse. Stranded indefinitely in a country that did not have adequate resources to care for them even before the pandemic began, people fleeing violence or poverty – often both – become so desperate as to risk their lives by trying to cross the border through dangerous, remote desert trails (what the Border Patrol designated as "hostile terrain") or by attempting to climb over the wall (which CBP calls "tactical infrastructure").

The border may look like the outer limit of their response area, the termination of the jurisdiction in which paramedics in southern Arizona provide care to the sick and injured, but this interpretation is misleading. It does not mark the end of their professional responsibility. Nor does it act as a safety barrier to protect against the spread of infectious disease. Rather, the US-Mexico border has been a risk vector, a conduit of the virus which moves along the routes, both legal and illegal, that people take. Paramedics and EMTs in Nogales are the first to attend to unauthorized border crossers wounded during the crossing, but they also routinely go to ports of entry for patients, usually American citizens, who are returning from Mexico to get treatment in US hospitals. They are the ones providing care to contractors who are building the border wall – the project that was not only not stopped during the pandemic that prompted schools, libraries, restaurants, and other businesses to close but instead accelerated – and who filled up hotels and motels in southern Arizona, raising fears among the elderly in smaller rural communities that the influx of workers from all over the country increased their risk of exposure (Romero 2020). Many local residents, the patients whom emergency responders care for on a daily basis, live in multigenerational households that transcend the international border as family members go back and forth to work, study, visit relatives, shop, run errands. The porous border is the lifeline for the community. These entanglements make attempts to restrict movement in the name of public health untenable. The public whose health is at stake is not circumscribed by the border but extends across it.

The closure of the border did not protect frontline workers from the virus. By the middle of June, eleven Nogales firefighters and paramedics – more than a quarter of the department – were off duty either because they tested positive for COVID-19 or were isolating while waiting for the results (Lara 2020). As weeks, then months passed, uncertainty from fear of exposure and overtime shifts that added up to 60 hour workweeks had worn them down. In his essay in this book, Paramedic Angel Taddei writes about losing the track of time and feeling that much of the year had been like a blur. First responders work in the occupational field defined by high levels of stress. EMTs and paramedics are trained and become used to handling critical situations, where people's lives are at stake. They have mechanisms to cope with difficult experiences and exhaustion on the job. This prolonged state of emergency, with no end in sight, has become the new normal. But what made it even worse were the effects of the pandemic on their families and their community. Unlike with other emergencies they respond to during their shifts – vehicle accidents, heart attacks, carbon monoxide poisoning, etc. – their homes are not insulated; they are not beyond the reach of the virus: their parents, spouses, children are at risk. Knowing that they can inadvertently expose their family members adds another layer of stress, which is further compounded by the disruptions of the daily lives of their loved ones: children can't go to school; parents can't visit relatives; spouses furloughed; family businesses no longer viable with the border shut and Mexican customers gone.

The border, even when reinforced with steel and cement and called "a big, beautiful wall," does not stop drugs, guns, or people from coming across; it only forces them to hide to evade detection. Not surprisingly, the closed border did not stop the virus. Travel restrictions between the US and Mexico gave a false sense of safety to residents of binational towns, where everyday life is never circumscribed by national jurisdictions. The measure, ineffective in curbing the spread of COVID-19, hurt the community whose social and economic wellbeing depends on routine cross-border movement. Emergency responders who live and work in Nogales experienced the psychological toll of the pandemic during extended shifts on duty and through the effects that COVID-19 and the government's response to it – primarily the decision to close the border – had on their families. If there is a lesson to be learnt, it is that federal policies oblivious to regional dynamics and realities on the ground can have a negative rather than a positive impact on public health. Communities with strong binational ties, such as Nogales, Arizona, and Nogales, Sonora, would have done better addressing the threat of the disease on the local level through joint planning and cooperation between public health authorities on both sides of the US-Mexico border.

References

Blust, Kendall. 2020. "'Sanitation Tunnels' At The Border May Do More Harm Than Good In Fighting COVID-19". *KJZZ Fronteras Desk*. May 28, 2020. https://fronterasdesk.org/content/1586470/sanitation-tunnels-border-may-do-more-harm-good-fighting-covid-19

Carranza, Rafael. 2020. "2020 on track to be among deadliest for migrants at the Arizona-Mexico border." *Arizona Republic*. October 28, 2020.

Cengiz, Yar. 2020. "Deaths Prompt Questions About COVID-19 Safety in Mexico Factories." *The Wall Street Journal*. Eastern Edition. June 10, 2020.

Centers for Disease Control and Prevention. 2020. "Total Number of

COVID-19 Cases, by Date Reported. January 22 to April 27, 2020". CDC. April 27, 2020. https://www.cdc.gov/coronavirus/2019-ncov/cases-updates/previouscases.html #anchor_1598477381.
- Cervantes, Rodrigo. 2020. "Public Health Care in Mexico Faces High Risks as The Pandemic Spreads." *KJZZ Fronteras Desk*. April 9, 2020. https://fronterasdesk.org/content/1522196/public-health-care-mexico-faces-high-risks-pandemic-spreads
- Clark, Jonathan. 2020. "Protesters in Mexico block vehicle lanes at port, demand stricter border controls against COVID-19." Nogales International. March 25, 2020. https://www.nogalesinternational.com/news/coronavirus/protesters-in-mexico-block-vehicle-lanes-at-port-demand-stricter-border-controls-against-covid-19/article_a48716fe-6ef0-11ea-a2a4-dbb856260f0e.html
- Cockburn, Alex. 2007. "Zyklon B on the US Border." *The Nation* 285(2):9.
- Guttentag, Lucas. 2020. "Coronavirus Border Expulsions: CDC's Assault on Asylum Seekers and Unaccompanied Minors." *Just Security*. April 13, 2020.
- Jusionyte, Ieva. 2018a. *Threshold: Emergency Responders on the US-Mexico Border*. Vol. 41 of California Series in Public Anthropology. Oakland: University of California Press.
- —. 2018b. "Called to 'Ankle Alley': Migrant Injuries and Emergency Medical Services on the US-Mexico Border." *American Anthropologist*. 120(1):89-101.
- Kitroeff, Natalie and Paulina Villegas. 2020. "'It's Not the Virus': Mexico's Broken Hospitals Become Killers, Too." *The New York Times*. May 8, 2020. https://www.nytimes.com/2020/05/28/world/americas/virus-mexico-doctors.html
- Lara, Genesis. 2020. "Virus Hits Nogales Fire Department." *Nogales International*. June 26, 2020.
- Linthicum, Kate. 2020. "Some of Mexico's wealthiest residents went to Colorado to ski. They brought home coronavirus". *Los Angeles Times*. March 20, 2020.
- Olivares, Valeria and Alfredo Corchado. 2020. "Border tows see run on drug touted by Trump but unproven as coronavirus cure." *Dallas Morning News*. March 23, 2020.
- Pima County Office of the Medical Examiner and Humane Borders, Inc. n.d. "Arizona OpenGIS Initiative for Deceased Migrants." Humane Borders. Accessed November 3, 2020. https://humaneborders.info/app/map.asp

Romero, Simon. 2020. "Border Wall Work in Arizona Speeds Up, Igniting Contagion Fears." *The New York Times*. March 31, 2020.

Romo, David Dorado. 2005. *Ringside Seat to a Revolution: An Underground Cultural History of El Paso and Juárez, 1893-1923*. 1st ed. El Paso: Cinco Puntos Press.

US Department of Homeland Security. 2020a. *Notification of Temporary Travel Restrictions Applicable to Land Ports of Entry and Ferries Service Between the United States and Mexico*. FR Doc. 2022-01403. Federal Register. March 24, 2020.

—. 2020b. *Joint Statement on US-Mexico Joint Initiative to Combat the COVID-19 Pandemic*. US Department of Homeland Security. March 20, 2020.

Vélez-Ibañez, Carlos G. and Josiah Heyman. 2017. *The US-Mexico Transborder Region: Cultural Dynamics and Historical Interactions*. Tucson: University of Arizona Press.

Dr. Ieva Jusionyte is the Watson Family University Associate Professor of International Security and Anthropology at Brown University. She a legal-medical anthropologist and the author of the award-winning ethnographic book *Threshold: Emergency Responders on the US-Mexico Border* (University of California Press, 2018). Her research has been supported by the National Science Foundation, the Wenner Gren Foundation, and the Rockefeller Foundation's Bellagio Center, and she has held fellowships from Fulbright and the Harvard Radcliffe Institute. She has trained and volunteered as an emergency medical technician, paramedic, and wildland firefighter in Florida, Arizona, and Massachusetts.

In a Pandemic, Do Doctors Still Have a Duty to Treat?
By Sandeep Jauhar

Originally published in the New York Times on April 2, 2020. Reprinted with permission of the author who retains copyright of the essay.

It is a question being asked in hospitals across the country: What is the duty to treat in a viral pandemic, particularly one in which health workers are getting infected and there is a dearth of personal protective equipment?

The question could be glibly dismissed. Medicine is a humanitarian profession, the argument would go. Healthcare workers have a duty to care for the sick. By freely entering into the profession, we have implicitly agreed to accept the risks.

Medical societies have generally been supportive of this idealistic viewpoint. The ethics manual of the American College of Physicians, for example, states that "the ethical imperative for physicians to provide care" overrides "the risk to the treating physician, even during epidemics." The American Medical Association asserts that "individual physicians have an obligation to provide urgent medical care during disasters," emphasizing that this duty persists "even in the face of greater than usual risks to physicians' own safety, health, or life."

However, this argument seems to minimize the quandary my colleagues are facing as they try to balance their obligations as professionals with their duties as husbands, wives, parents, and children. The risk to personal health from the coronavirus is alarming enough, but the risk of infecting our families because of exposure on the job is for some unacceptable. With the rates of infection among health workers so high – nearly 14 percent of confirmed cases in Spain, for example – the risk of transmission to our loved ones is not insignificant. How do we balance our professional and personal obligations?

Limitations on professional duties are nothing new. Firefighters, for example, have a duty to rescue people from a burning building, but not when it is on the verge of collapse and certainly not without proper equipment. Can similar considerations be applied to healthcare workers?

The duty to treat during an epidemic is something of a modern idea. For most of human history, physicians often ran away in the face of widespread contagion. During the Antonine Plague of A.D. 165 to 180, none other than the venerable Galen, one of history's most famous physicians, fled Rome. Such behavior was so common that in 1382, Venice passed a law forbidding doctors from taking flight in times of plague. The practice continued, however. During a yellow fever epidemic in Philadelphia in 1793, many distinguished physicians fled the city.

The American Medical Association addressed the issue in 1847 in its first Code of Medical Ethics. "When pestilence prevails," the code reads, it is the duty of physicians "to face the danger, and to continue their labors for the alleviation of suffering, even at the jeopardy of their own lives." This rule was fortified in 1912, and yet during the 20th century, physicians adhered to it with varying degrees of fidelity. In the early days of the AIDS epidemic, for example, doctors often refused to treat HIV-infected patients.

In 1986, the American College of Physicians and the Infectious Diseases Society of America were moved to issue a joint declaration that healthcare workers must provide care to their patients, "even at the risk of contracting a patient's disease." Even so, health workers abandoned patients during an Ebola epidemic in the Democratic Republic of Congo in 1995. And in a SARS outbreak in Toronto in 2003, in which nearly half the infected were health professionals, many healthcare workers refused to show up at their jobs.

Judging from history, doctors and nurses might well rebel during this coronavirus pandemic if a shortage of face masks and other protective equipment persists. This would of course be a disaster. People are in urgent need of care. Without uniform adherence to professional obligations, the healthcare system – and society itself – could fall apart.

I don't think it will happen. I believe healthcare workers will continue to make the sacrifices necessary to treat patients. However, it would be a mistake for people to assume that our professional obligations are unconditional. An unconditional obligation would absolve society of its own responsibilities. And there are many.

For instance, healthcare workers should not be forced to incur additional risk because people don't want to practice social distancing (vacationers flocking to Florida beaches during spring break come to mind). We shouldn't have to pay for shortsighted government policies that have already eviscerated our public health infrastructure and may soon lead to the premature relaxation of social distancing rules. And of course, we need proper masks.

Social order relies on reciprocity. Imposing outsize burdens on one group without sacrifice from others is unfair. Doctors and nurses and other healthcare workers may be heroes in this pandemic, but we will not be martyrs.

Sandeep Jauhar is the bestselling author of several acclaimed books on medical topics: *Intern, Doctored, and Heart: A History*, which was named a best book of 2018 by The Mail on Sunday, Science Friday, and the Los Angeles Public Library, and was a PBS NewsHour/New York Times book club pick; it was also a finalist for the 2019 Wellcome Book Prize. His latest book, *My Father's Brain*, was published in April 2023. A practicing physician, Jauhar writes regularly for the opinion section of The New York Times. His TED Talk on the emotional heart was one of the ten most-watched TED Talks of 2019.

COVID-19 and the Physician's Duty to Treat
By David Orentlicher

Originally submitted January 4, 2021

Principles of medical ethics have long prescribed a strong duty for physicians to treat patients during pandemics. According to the American Medical Association's (AMA's) inaugural Code of Medical Ethics in 1847, for example, physicians were expected to continue their provision of care to patients "when pestilence prevails ... even at the jeopardy of their own lives" (Committee on a Code of Medical Ethics, 105).

Should we think of this obligation as an absolute one, or should there be exceptions, as for example, when the risk becomes too great? According to the current AMA Code (most recently updated in 2016), "Physicians also have an obligation to evaluate the risks of providing care to individual patients versus the need to be available to provide care in the future" (Council on Ethical and Judicial Affairs, 127). Having physicians disabled or deceased because of illness may compromise patient access to healthcare. Accordingly, when the risk to physician health becomes sufficiently high, we should abrogate the duty to provide care. For example, it would not make sense to expect physicians to treat patients who cannot be saved but would readily transmit a deadly infection to their care providers (Sokol 2006, 1238-41).

While some pathogens could pose such a risk, COVID-19 has not been so dangerous. At the time of this writing, the mortality rate for people infected with the coronavirus appeared to be less than one percent for persons younger than age 60, even before the availability of immunization and anti-viral medication (COVID-19 Forecasting Team 2022, 1475). The health risks from COVID-19 do not therefore justify a general exception to the duty to treat.

But should there be limited exceptions to the duty to treat patients with COVID-19? Suppose a patient has acted irresponsibly by not taking recommended – or even required – precautions that impose little burden on the patient, such as becoming vaccinated or wearing a face mask when around other people. Or suppose the physician's healthcare institution does not provide enough N95 masks or other personal protective equipment for the institution's healthcare providers? What about physicians whose own risk is well above the average, as with a 70-year old male physician with a history of heart disease? Or should it matter that physicians might spread their infections to family members?

The irresponsible patient

While patients have considerable freedom to engage in conduct harmful to their own health, say by smoking or skydiving, they have no right to put the health of other people at risk. Thus, a majority of states ban smoking in public places (American Lung Association 2022).

When patients require hospitalization for COVID-19 because they remain unvaccinated or they attended a large indoor event where attendees were crowded and without face masks in violation of public health regulations, the patients unnecessarily increase the risk of infection to hospital staff. It seems unfair to the healthcare providers to require them to provide treatment, just as it is unfair to non-smokers to assume the risks of being exposed to someone else's smoking.

With the availability of immunization and antiviral medication, the risks to healthcare providers have been greatly diminished. But even before the development of vaccines and drugs for COVID-19, denial of treatment could not be justified. While measures should be taken to prevent and sanction irresponsible behavior, those measures cannot include the withholding of healthcare. The medical system is not the appropriate institution for meting out punishments for personal misconduct (Cohen and Benjamin 1991, 1299-301). Health care providers are not trained to judge the moral culpability of their patients, and trying to do so risks compromise of the fundamental duty of healthcare providers to promote the well-being of their patients. This is especially the case given the difficulty in drawing lines between reasonable and unreasonable behavior, as when people have to balance health risks with economic needs, religious beliefs, or the desire to be with loved ones (Baruch 2020).

In addition, we have to worry that providers will exercise their discretion not to treat in biased ways. Providers might be more likely to refuse care for lower income patients or for Black or Hispanic patients just as physicians have been found more likely to report drug use by their pregnant patients when the patients were poor or minorities (Chasnoff, Landress, and Barrett 1990). The risk of bias would be exacerbated by the uncertainty as to whether a particular patient acted irresponsibly, for good reason, or from being misinformed. Finally, and very importantly, denying care would put other members of the public at greater risk of infection.

What if not every patient can be treated, as during a surge in infections that overwhelms a hospital's capacity to provide intensive care? Some have argued that we should give priority to the more responsible patients, such as the vaccinated patient over the voluntarily unvaccinated patient (Iserson 2022). However, just as physicians should not deny treatment based on patient responsibility, they should not assign priority for treatment based on patient responsibility (Wilker 2021). The concerns about physicians judging moral culpability apply in both contexts. That said, it often will be the case that personal responsibility will legitimately affect priority for treatments that are in short supply. In allocating scarce health resources, patient prognosis can be a relevant consideration, and an unvaccinated patient may be much less likely to benefit from treatment than a vaccinated patient (Wilker 2021).

The irresponsible institution

The failure of hospitals or governments to provide adequate protective equipment for healthcare providers and other personnel has been one of the great failings of the COVID-19 pandemic. It is not fair to ask healthcare workers to assume risks to their health unless we do all we can to reduce the risks. Healthcare workers should have access to gowns, gloves, and other necessary personal protective equipment. They also may need access to separate living quarters to protect their families from exposure (Weiss 2020).

Government also has failed in many states or countries by not implementing effective health measures. Far more people have become infected in the United States and other countries for lack of sufficient requirements for vaccination, wearing of masks, or physical distancing, and too many elected officials have encouraged behaviors that exacerbate the risks of COVID-19 transmission (Goldmacher 2021; Rosza 2022). Health care workers have been overwhelmed by surges in COVID-19 cases, leading to rising rates of depression and burnout (Wu 2020; Nuti 2021).

These failings are serious and inexcusable. That said, a failure of healthcare facilities and the government to meet their duties to healthcare workers should not excuse the duty of healthcare providers to their patients. Left untreated, the patients would be the innocent victims in this setting. It would be wrong to penalize sick patients for the misconduct of others.

Rather than relaxing the duty of healthcare providers to their patients, we need to identify ways to ensure that healthcare facilities and governments meet their duties to healthcare workers. This includes better stockpiling of protective equipment for future pandemics and better coordination of public and private responses to a pandemic by the federal government.

The healthcare provider at elevated risk

As discussed, the risk to most healthcare providers from COVID-19 has been quite low. But not for all providers. Should there be an exception for providers at elevated risk of serious consequences of an infection?

A limited exception makes sense. Why require somebody with a risk of death from infection of more than ten percent to provide services that could be provided by someone with a risk of less than one percent? As a general matter, society should take special precautions to protect individuals at greater risk for infection, such as residents of long-term care facilities. Health care providers at elevated risk of infection should not lose their protection because of their professional role. While they may choose to assume the elevated risk of infection, and it would be laudable for them to do so, they should not be forced to assume the risk.

While there is room for exceptions for providers at elevated risk, it is important to limit the extent of the exceptions. Duties to provide care for those in need are more difficult to meet when the burden falls on a smaller number of providers. By way of analogy, all healthcare providers can afford to commit some of their time to unreimbursed care for the poor, but few providers could afford to commit most of their time that way. Similarly, it is much more feasible for any one healthcare provider to assume the risks of serving patients during a pandemic when all providers are sharing the risks. Universal participation minimizes the magnitude of the risk per provider. By contrast, permitting providers to opt out of their duty to treat and thereby increase the risks to colleagues would encourage more providers to opt out, increasing the risks even further and leading even more providers to opt out. Exceptions to the duty to treat can trigger a self-reinforcing cycle of provider withdrawal that ultimately would defeat the duty.

Most likely, it would be safe to excuse providers at high risk from the duty to treat patients with serious communicable microbes like COVID-19. Many providers continue to work despite their elevated risk, and others have come out of retirement to help. As a result, with a limited exception to a duty to treat, it is likely that the number refraining from providing care would be small enough that the risk to their colleagues would remain low.

One also might ask whether the duty to treat should apply differently to providers living alone or with one housemate than to providers living in larger households, especially in households that include older family members. From a perspective of minimizing overall infections and deaths, differential treatment seems to make sense. But even before the development of a COVID vaccine, there were other ways to protect family members besides having the provider refrain from seeing COVID-19 patients, including through physical distancing and wearing of masks.

One also might ask about relaxing the duty to treat for the physician who is a single parent of young children and whose children would suffer if their parent died from COVID-19. For most physicians with young children, the risk of death from COVID-19 will be quite low. Accordingly, an exception for physicians at elevated risk should provide adequate protection for the parents of young children.

Conclusion

We have seen too many breakdowns in the response to COVID-19. Earlier, more aggressive efforts at containment would have saved many patients and healthcare workers from harm. And while there are difficult trade-offs that have to be made during a serious pandemic, the societal response to COVID-19 suffered from the failure to maximize the benefit from simple public health measures, such as the wearing of face masks and physical distancing.

Going forward with COVID-19 or other pandemics, it is clear that we can do a much better job of limiting the risks to healthcare workers. But outside of limited exceptions for providers at particularly high risk, the risks of COVID-19 do not justify a relaxation of the duty of providers to care for their patients.

References

American Lung Association. 2022. "Smokefree Air Laws." *Policy & Advocacy*. Last updated November 17, 2022. https://www.lung.org/

policy-advocacy/tobacco/smokefree-environments/smokefree-air-laws

Baruch, Jay. 2020. "As a Doctor in the COVID-19 Era, I've Learned that Judging Patients' Decisions Comes Easier than It Should". STAT. December 31, 2020. https://www.statnews.com/2020/12/31/judging-patients-covid-19-decisions-comes-easier-than-it-should/

Chasnoff, Ira J, Harvey J Landress, and Mark E Barrett. 1990. "The Prevalence of Illicit-Drug or Alcohol Use during Pregnancy and Discrepancies in Mandatory Reporting in Pinellas County, Florida." *New England Journal of Medicine* 322 (17): 1202–6. https://doi.org/10.1056/NEJM199004263221706.

Cohen, Carl, and Martin Benjamin. 1991. "Alcoholics and Liver Transplantation." *JAMA* 265 (10): 1299–1301. https://doi.org/10.1001/jama.1991.03460100101033.

Committee on a Code of Medical Ethics. 1847. *Code of Medical Ethics of the American Medical Asoociation: Originally Adopted at the Adjourned Meeting of the National Medical Convention in Philadelphia.* Chicago: American Medical Association: 105.

Council on Ethical and Judicial Affairs. 2017. *Code of Medical Ethics of the American Medical Asoociation.* Chicago: American Medical Association: 127.

COVID-19 Forecasting Team. 2022. "Variation in the COVID-19 infection-fataility ratio by age, time, and geography during the pre-vaccine era: a systematic analysis." *The Lancet* 399(10334): 1469–88. https://doi.org/10.1016/S0140-6736(21)02867-1.

Goldmacher, Shane. 2021. "G.O.P. Goveners Fight Mandates as the Party's COVID Politics Harden." *New York Times*, August 31, 2021.

Iserson, Kenneth V. 2022. "Ethics, Personal Responsibility and the Pandemic: A New Triage Paradigm." *Journal of Emergency Medicine* 62(4), 508-512. https://doi.org/10.1016/j.jemermed.2021.11.019

Nuti, Sudhakar. 2021. "I worry that burnout can't be reversed and has fundamentally changed me as a doctor and a person." *STAT*, November 5, 2021.

Rosza, Lori. 2022. "Florida's top health official says healthy children should not get coronavirus vaccine." *Washington Post*, March 7, 2022.

Sokol, Daniel K. 2006. "Virulent epidemics and scope of healthcare workers' duty of care." *Emerging infectious diseases* 12(18) 238-41. doi:10.3201/eid1208.060360

Weiss, Bari. 2020. "Doctors Are Writing their Wills." *New York Times*, March 29, 2020.
Wikler, Daniel. 2021. "When medical care must be rationed, should vaccination status count?" *Washington Post*, August 23, 2021.
Wu, Katherine. 2020. "Covid Combat Fatigue: 'I Would Come Home with Tears in my Eyes.'" *New York Times*, November 25, 2020.

David Orentlicher is the Judge Jack and Lulu Lehman Professor at the UNLV William S. Boyd School of Law, where he specializes in health law and constitutional law. He also serves as a Democrat in the Nevada legislature. Previously, David directed the division of medical ethics at the American Medical Association. He is the author of *Matters of Life and Death*, co-author of *Health Care Law and Ethics*, and co-editor of *The Oxford Handbook of Comparative Health Law*. David has published widely on issues in bioethics and law, and his scholarship has been cited by the US Supreme Court.

Doing vs Allowing Harm and The Freedom Objection to Mask-Mandates and Other Anti-COVID-19 Regulations
By Fiona Woollard

Originally submitted December 15, 2020

We are in the middle of a global pandemic of the deadly virus, COVID-19. A man stands in front of a police officer. The police officer is wearing a mask. He stands impassive as the man, unmasked, shouts, his open mouth less than a foot away from the officer's face. The word that the man is screaming is "Freedom." He is protesting measures designed to stop the spread of COVID-19, such as requirements to wear masks, practice social distancing, quarantines and lockdowns. Like many similar protestors, he sees these measures as a violation of his freedom, particularly when enforced by government mandate. In this essay, I explore the complaint that such regulations violate individual freedom. I call this 'the Freedom Objection.' Libertarianism is the philosophical position which places the greatest emphasis on freedom from government coercion.[1] I argue that even the most determined Libertarians rightly recognize that respecting someone's freedom does not mean permitting them to do whatever they want. Instead, Libertarianism insists that the only legitimate reason to coerce someone is to prevent them from harming others. The Freedom Objection must depend on the claim that these regulations go beyond the design of protecting targeted individuals from harming others and in fact are no different from other non-harm restrictions of freedom. This may be because its proponents think of wearing a mask or staying home as saving others and failing to do so as merely allowing harm to others. I argue that failing to wear a mask, practice social distancing or respect quarantines and lockdowns, is doing harm – or more accurately imposing a risk of harm – to others. The Freedom Objection does not work.

Versions of the Freedom Objection with Basic Mistakes

Some versions of the Freedom Objection depend on basic mistakes.

---

1. For classic defences of Libertarianism, see, for example, Nozick (1974) and Narveson (1988).

Some people see regulations designed to slow the spread of COVID-19 as *paternalistic* restrictions of freedom. Paternalistic restrictions of freedom limit what someone is able to do *for that person's own good*. If you say that it is your decision whether to risk getting COVID-19, that government regulations treat you like a child by taking this decision out of your hands, then you are objecting to these regulations as paternalistic restrictions of your freedom. There's a lot to be said about whether and when paternalistic restrictions on freedom are justified. Most people seem to be happy to accept at least some paternalistic restrictions on behavior – for example, regulations governing the sale and distribution of food products. But that is a side issue because COVID-19 regulations are not primarily paternalistic. The main point of requiring you to wear a mask in the grocery store is not to protect you from getting COVID-19. It is to protect others from getting COVID-19 *from you*. The most important effect of wearing a mask is that it stops droplets from the mask-wearer's breath from reaching others. If the mask-wearer has COVID-19, the mask stops the mask wearer from infecting others (Howard et al. 2021).

Others seem to see these regulations as a violation of freedom simply because they restrict what individuals are able to do. This is a very strange position. Your freedom is not violated just because you cannot do whatever you want. You are not permitted to drive your car over a pedestrian, to set fire to your neighbor's house, or to burn toxic materials creating a poisonous gas cloud. Laws which forbid such behavior are not violations of your freedom, but legitimate limits on your freedom. As the saying goes, "Your freedom to swing your arm ends where my nose begins."[2] We should distinguish between *violations* of freedom – where your freedom is illegitimately encroached upon – and legitimate *limits* to your freedom.

The Freedom Objection is an obvious failure if it is an objection that regulations to prevent the spread of COVID-19 are paternalistic or an objection that any kind of restriction on one's behavior is a violation of freedom. To assess the most plausible argument in favor of the Freedom Objection, we need to think a little bit more about when those for whom freedom is of paramount importance should permit government coercion. Should they see the anti-COVID-19 regulations as violations of freedom or as legitimate limits on freedom?

---

2. The origins of this epigram are unclear. For an interesting discussion, see Quote Investigator 2011.

Libertarianism, the Harm Principle and the Doing/Allowing Distinction

Libertarianism is the philosophical position which places most emphasis on freedom and the limits that freedom sets on government coercion of individuals. The classic statement at the heart of Libertarianism is John Stuart Mill's Harm Principle, which states:

> [T]he only purpose for which power can be rightfully exercised over any member of a civilized community, against his will, is to prevent harm to others. His own good, either physical or moral, is not a sufficient warrant (1977, p. 223).

The Harm Principle clearly identifies one situation in which coercing an individual can be permissible: preventing that individual from doing harm to others. Therefore, consistent Libertarians who object to anti-COVID-19 regulations as violations of freedom must think that we are not in that situation. They must believe that anti-COVID-19 regulations are not properly understood as legitimate attempts to prevent harm to others. The most obvious reason for this would be that they think of wearing a mask or staying home as saving others and failing to do so as merely allowing, as opposed to doing, harm to others.

Helen Frowe argues that both political rhetoric and discussion from philosophers about lockdowns wrongly frame staying home as a way of saving lives – and encourages us to think wrongly about how to assess whether a lockdown is justified. Lockdowns require justification because they have costs: people lose out on pleasurable activities and time spent with family and friends; they may lose their jobs; their mental health may suffer. Bashshar Haydar and Alec Walen (2020) argue that to work out if lock downs are justified, we must consider the costs that we can be required to bear to in order to save the lives of others. Frowe responds that Haydar and Walen's approach is mistaken:

> I do not save your life if I do not infect you with COVID-19. Rather, I refrain from harming you. And the costs that I may be required to bear to refrain from harming you are considerably greater than the costs that I may be required to bear to save you (2020).

Frowe argues that instead of considering the cost that I can be required to bear to *save* others to assess lockdowns, we must consider the cost that I can be required to bear to *avoid harming others.*

As Frowe argues, we are usually expected to bear greater costs to avoid harming others than to save others. Frowe considers a pair of examples. In the first case, Alice is caught in a sluice gate in a river. Betty can save Alice, but would probably lose her own arm in the process. In the second case, Betty is being chased by an attacker who wants to chop off her arm. Betty can only save her arm by lethally trampling over Alice, an innocent passer-by who happens to be in the way. Frowe appeals to our intuitions about the two cases: we should think that Betty is not morally required to sacrifice her arm to save Alice from drowning in the sluice gate, but *is* morally required to suffer the loss of the arm to avoid killing Alice (Frowe 2020).

Frowe argues that we should compare the loosening of anti-COVID-19 restrictions to other risk-imposing activities:

> ... activities that pose higher risks of serious harm, such as driving, are tightly regulated. And even typically low-risk activities are subject to moral, if not legal, constraints. If the park is crowded, I may not persist in kicking about my football. If I know my horse is a frequent kicker, I should not be riding her on busy public bridleways (2020).

I've responded to Frowe's article elsewhere, arguing that she is partly but not completely right (Woollard 2020). Frowe is right that if you go out and infect someone with COVID-19, you have *done* harm to them and not merely allowed them to suffer harm. So, she is correct that staying at home to avoid spreading COVID-19 is avoiding doing harm. Nonetheless, some lockdown measures are not standard cases of avoiding doing harm, but instead belong to a strange type of case which involves both saving and refraining from doing harm. They are cases where, for reasons outside the control of either agent or victim, in order to avoid doing harm, you have to *do* something, to perform some action. These cases are morally distinct from both standard cases of doing harm and standard cases of saving. This means that neither analogies with standard cases of saving others nor standard cases of avoiding harming others are appropriate when working out whether to impose or maintain a lockdown.

I argue that some lockdown measures place such significant restrictions on my movements that they require me to make a positive fact about my behavior hold. For example, they require me to stay at home. Let us suppose, for example, that I live at 29 Acacia Road. That I am at 29 Acacia Road is a positive fact about my location. It tells you where I am. On my analysis of the doing/allowing distinction (Woollard 2015), making a positive fact about one's location hold is doing something.[3] If a lockdown measure is restrictive enough that it requires me to make a positive fact about my location hold, complying with it will be doing something to prevent deaths. If we are doing something to prevent deaths, then we can think of ourselves as saving lives. With other anti-COVID-19 measures, like mask-wearing or getting vaccinated, it is even clearer that avoiding putting others at risk of harm requires each of us actively to do something. These are cases of both saving and avoiding doing harm.

On my view, cases where agents are both saving and avoiding doing harm are a delicate balancing act. Governments may be permitted, or even required, to protect those who would have harm done to them. So anti-COVID-19 regulations are often legitimate. Nonetheless, when such restrictions require the agent to do something and when it is not her fault she is in this situation, governments may have extra strong duties to compensate the agent for the burdens this imposes on her.

Frowe and I are not Libertarians. We both hold that it can be permissible for the government to coerce individuals to bear costs to save the lives of others. But as important as the differences are between the two of us and Libertarians, we do all have something important in common. Like Frowe and me, Libertarians draw a key moral distinction between doing harm and merely allowing harm. Libertarians have to do this, otherwise their theory just doesn't make sense. Unless you recognize a robust distinction between doing harm and merely allowing harm, you cannot hold a theory of minimal government interference that sees preventing a citizen from harming others as the only legitimate ground for coercing them. If you think there is no difference between doing and allowing harm, then you have to think that whenever government coercion would be legitimate to preventing someone from doing harm then they could also legitimately prevent someone from allowing the same harm.

---

3. My analysis draws on Jonathan Bennett's (1995) account of what it is for a fact to be positive rather than negative. I thank Daniel Elstein whose question to Frowe about whether staying home might count as positive on Bennett's account prompted my realisation that my own account had interesting implications for this type of case.

That leaves us with two quite different approaches. The first recognizes it as legitimate for government to interfere with Bob to prevent him from killing James, but also recognizes it as legitimate for government to force Bob to save James's life. That is not a theory of minimal government interference. The second approach doesn't recognize it as legitimate for government to force Bob to save James' life, but also does not recognize it as legitimate for government to interfere to prevent Bob from killing James. That approach doesn't fit the bill either – it doesn't see preventing a citizen from harming others as a legitimate ground for coercing them. It is only if we treat doing and allowing as morally different that we can have a theory of minimal government interference which protects us from others doing harm to us.[4]

Like Frowe and me, Libertarians should recognize that it matters that anti-COVID-19 regulations are aimed at preventing individuals from doing harm. Libertarianism recognizes that it is permissible for the government to coerce citizens to prevent them from doing harm to others. To make the Freedom Objection stick, they need to show that the regulations to prevent the agent doing harm are illegitimate in this case. They would need to argue, for example, that the risk/ burden profile doesn't add up i.e., that the burden is so large that we cannot expect someone to bear that burden to avoid imposing that risk of harm on others. For at least some anti-COVID-19 regulations, such as masks, that seems like a hard argument to make. The burden of wearing a mask is relatively small and the risk of harm is significant (at least when highly transmissible and dangerous variants of COVID are widespread).

---

4. This is a bit of an oversimplification. On the face of it the Libertarian could appeal to other distinctions, such as the distinction between strictly intended harm and merely foreseen harm. They could say that governments can legitimately interfere to prevent strictly intended harm but not merely foreseen harm. That could give them a theory of minimal government interference which still provides some protection against harming. I argue elsewhere that any attempt to draw a distinction between different ways of countenancing harm to others needs to appeal to both the doing/ allowing distinction and something that explains the same set of cases which the intended/ foreseen distinction was introduced to try to explain. I have my doubts that the intended/foreseen distinction is the one that we are looking for, but we need something that does the same job. Embracing either distinction on its own leads to deeply implausible verdicts about cases. See Woollard 2017, pp. 142-158.

The Appeal to Responsible Face Owners

The Freedom Objection to anti-COVID-19 regulations has links to an objection to restrictions on gun ownership. It is no accident that many of the anti-mask protestors in the US were visibly armed. Both anti-maskers and the pro-gun lobby object strenuously to regulations designed to save lives by arguing that they are a violation of freedom. I want to finish by considering a common move in debates about gun regulation—I call this move 'the appeal to responsible gun owners'. A very similar move is seen in discussion of mask mandates. Let's call this 'the appeal to responsible face owners.' I'm skeptical of the appeal to responsible gun owners. However, I will show that whatever force such an appeal has in the context of gun control, the analogous 'appeal to responsible face owners' doesn't work because of asymptomatic and pre-symptomatic spread. The same will be true of versions of this move used against other anti-COVID-19 regulations.

The appeal to responsible gun owners argues that restrictions on gun ownership cast too wide a net. They do not only coerce those who would otherwise do harm. They place restrictions on many, many responsible gun owners. These responsible gun owners, or so the argument goes, would only ever use their guns for legitimate reasons. They use them to hunt for game to feed their families. Or they use them at the shooting range, developing impressive skill and accuracy. Sometimes the list of legitimate reasons to use a gun includes protecting oneself or one's family against violent criminals.

According to the appeal to responsible gun owners, it is unjust to restrict the behavior of these responsible gun owners in order to prevent other people from doing harm with guns. Responsible gun owners do not harm others or even put others at risk of harm. According to Libertarianism, it is only permissible to coerce an individual to prevent *that individual* from doing harm. We can coerce Bob to prevent him from killing James. That's legitimate under Libertarianism. But we cannot coerce Bob to prevent Mary from killing James. That is not legitimate under Libertarianism.

As I said, I have my doubts about the appeal to responsible gun owners when it comes to the debate about gun control. I am very definitely not a Libertarian. But we can put that issue aside for the purposes of this paper. I'm interested in looking at the version of the appeal to responsible gun owners that I have seen in the context of anti-mask protests: the appeal to responsible face owners.

According to the appeal to responsible face owners, most people do not harm others or put them at risk of harm when they go shopping without a mask. Fred only puts others at risk by shopping without a mask if Fred has COVID-19. But, the argument continues, no one who has COVID-19 should be out shopping anyway. Fred is a responsible face owner. If he had COVID-19, he would stay at home in isolation.

The problem with this argument is that it assumes that people can know whether or not they have COVID-19. But the reason why COVID-19 has become a global pandemic is precisely because of the high rates of asymptomatic and pre-symptomatic spread. Fred might have COVID-19 and never develop symptoms. He might have COVID-19 and be shedding the virus for several days before developing symptoms. So Fred cannot know whether or not he has COVID-19. And given that he does not know whether or not he had COVID-19, Fred *is* putting others at risk of harm by going shopping without a mask. In a global pandemic, with a virus with high rates of asymptomatic and pre-symptomatic spread, any person who does not *know* that they do not have COVID-19 could have the virus. And you count as being put at risk if you are exposed to droplets from the breath of someone who could have the virus. The level of risk will depend upon many factors including the levels of infection in the local community and what that particular person has been doing recently. Nonetheless, there is still a risk.

Some might be tempted to respond that the risk is not very significant due to the very fact that I appealed to earlier: COVID-19 has high levels of asymptomatic spread. Those who object to anti-COVID measures often argue that for those who are healthy, the likelihood of serious harm from COVID-19 is very low. Even ignoring the fact that healthy people can die from COVID-19 and that many others suffer from the devastating effects of 'long COVID', this argument does not work. Suppose Fred does not wear his mask to the supermarket. Everyone else at the supermarket is healthy. Fred expects those who are vulnerable to stay at home for the duration of the pandemic—he cannot be expected to change his behavior to help others avoid risks that are due to their own vulnerabilities.[5] But the people at the supermarket pass the virus on to others. Those others pass it on to more people. As the numbers of people infected through Fred grows,

---

5. The reader may detect that the author disagrees with Fred's stance here.

the likelihood that someone will suffer serious harm or death becomes significant.

Summary

In this essay, I have explored the Freedom Objection to anti-COVID regulations such as requirements to wear masks in public places: the objection that such regulations violate citizen's freedom. I have argued that, even assuming Libertarianism, the approach to political philosophy which places most importance on freedom from government coercion, the Freedom Objection does not work. Libertarians recognize an exception to the illegitimacy of government coercion. They recognize that governments may legitimately coerce an individual to prevent that individual from doing harm to others or from putting others at significant risk of harm. Failure to comply with anti-COVID regulations does involve that individual putting others at significant risk of harm. Such regulations are not a violation of individual freedom. They are a legitimate limit on individuals' freedom to harm others.

References

Bennett, Jonathan. 1995. *The Act Itself.* Oxford: Oxford University Press.
Frowe, Helen. 2020. "Is staying at home really about 'saving lives?" *CapX,* December 14, 2020. https://capx.co/is-staying-at-home-really-about-saving-lives
Howard, Jeremy, Austin Huang, Zhiyuan Li, Zeynep Tufekci, Vladimir Zdimal, Helene-Mari van der Westhuizen, Arne von Delft, et al. 2021. "An Evidence Review of Face Masks against COVID-19." *Proceedings of the National Academy of Sciences* 118 (4): e2014564118. https://doi.org/10.1073/pnas.2014564118.
Mill, John. 1977. *The Collected Works of John Stuart Mill, Volume XVIII - Essays on Politics and Society Part I.* Toronto: University of Toronto Press, London: Routledge and Kegan Paul. Pp. 213-310.
Narveson, Jan. 1988. *The Libertarian Idea.* Philadelphia, PA: Temple University Press.
Nozick, Robert. 1974. *Anarchy, State, and Utopia.* New York: Basic Books.
Quote Investigator. 2011. "Your Liberty to Swing Your Fist Ends Just Where My Nose Begins." *Quote Investigator,* October 14, 2011. https://quoteinvestigator.com/2011/10/15/liberty-fist-nose

Walen, Alec, and Bashshar Haydar. 2020. The ethics of a pandemic are not those of a 'new normal'. *CapX*. https://capx.co/the-ethics-of-a-pandemic-are-not-those-of-a-new-normal

Woollard, Fiona. 2015. *Doing and Allowing Harm*. Oxford, Oxford University.

Woollard, Fiona. 2017. "Double Effect, Doing and Allowing, and the Relaxed Nonconsequentialist." *Philosophical Explorations* 20 (sup2): 142–58. https://doi.org/10.1080/13869795.2017.1356355.

Woollard Fiona. 2020. "Can Staying at Home be Saving Lives and Avoiding Killing? COVID-19, Lockdowns and the Doing/Allowing Distinction." *Ethics and International Affairs*. https://www.ethicsandinternationalaffairs.org/online-exclusives/can-staying-at-home-be-saving-lives-and-avoiding-killing-covid-19-lockdowns-and-the-doing-allowing-distinction

Fiona Woollard is a professor of philosophy at the University of Southampton. Her research interests include normative ethics, applied ethics, the philosophy of sex, and the philosophy of pregnancy, birth and early motherhood. Her monograph, *Doing and Allowing Harm*, is available from Oxford University Press.

Prayer to St. Roch, Patron of Plague Sufferers
By Jack Coulehan

Originally submitted on September 25, 2020

Please take your work to the next step,
St. Roch, beyond being a friendly ghost
to the lost. Bring us back from the edge.

Pour out the healing grace of your touch
at a distance, if possible. We beg you.
Believe me, the people are skeptical.

Continue making the sign of the cross
to heal us, but add Islam's crescent,
David's star, the mudra of compassion.

It won't be easy for many of us
to trust the intervention of a saint.
We've embraced the lure of miracles

like medications and vaccines
since you did yours, but if you try,
if you open your arms to all of us

without distinction – to the frightened
and weak, the sturdy and confident,
the traumatized and sick –

the blessing might come back,
and the plague succumb.

Jack Coulehan is an Emeritus Professor of Medicine and former Director of the Center for Medical Humanities, Compassionate Care, and Bioethics at Stony Brook Renaissance School of Medicine. Jack's essays, poems and stories appear frequently in healthcare journals and literary magazines, and his work is widely anthologized. He is the author of seven collections of poetry, including *The Talking Cure: New and Selected Poems* (2020). His other books include *Blood & Bone* and *Primary Care*, two anthologies of poems by physicians; *Chekhov's Doctors*, a collection of Anton Chekhov's medical tales; and an award-winning textbook *The Medical Interview: Mastering Skills for Clinical Practice*.

The Great Matter of Life and Death (or Morning in Kilauea)
By Craig D. Blinderman

Originally submitted September 30, 2021

A red crested cardinal sings a quiet song
not far from the magic dragon's home
where myth and sky are held in stillness
and leaves curl with the touch of a toe
sensing fleshy solidity.

The palm tree in a storm.
The oaks burning all alone.
The blessed worm toiling on.

O' these haunted days
behind masks and mandala covered walls
caring for those who will not survive.

The gurgling last breaths
witness bodily struggle
and our collective sin.

What must we do
before the matter ends
and life returns
to its vastness?

Behold the songbird!

For words are not permitted
in that incomprehensible space
between mourning
and restoration.

Craig D. Blinderman, MD, MA, FAAHPM, is a national leader in palliative medicine. At the time of submission of this poem, he was the director of the Adult Palliative Care Service and an Associate Professor of Medicine at Columbia University Irving Medical Center/New York-Presbyterian Hospital. His academic interests include decision-making at the end of life, the role of palliative care in public and global health, medical ethics, narrative medicine, and the integration of contemplative care and meditation in clinical practice. He also has a strong interest in teaching and developing programs to improve medical trainees' skills in communication and care for the dying.

Early Pandemic Reporting from New York City: A Journalist's Reflections
By Sheri Fink

Originally submitted October 9, 2022

The following is a reflection written in October 2022 prefacing a reprint of the author's April 2020 New York Times article 'Code Blue': A Brooklyn I.C.U. Fights for Each Life in a Coronavirus Surge.

At the time I began reporting from the Brooklyn Hospital Center in March of 2020, hospitals overwhelmed by an influx of novel coronavirus patients were the exception in the United States. Until then, these conditions had existed mostly in China, Iran and Italy, and many American hospitals were operating as if we would be immune. Not enough was being done to get ready.

Cases in the US had begun their upward march, evident to clinicians even in the absence of sufficient molecular testing tools. Public health experts argued that surges in illnesses and deaths could be blunted if people radically reduced contact with one another. But that required once unthinkable societal sacrifices. The virus appeared to be mild in the majority of people, and not everyone was convinced.

The strain on the healthcare system in New York City, where the virus was taking off, was an important piece of the equation. At the time, awareness of the conditions was limited primarily to those who worked in hospitals treating coronavirus patients. My editor at the *New York Times*, Rebecca Corbett, asked if I could report from one of them. I had been a journalist covering healthcare for many years. I also have a medical degree and had trained in infection prevention and control measures prior to going to West Africa in 2014 to embed with an Ebola treatment unit.

This article was the second dispatch that photographer Victor Blue and I sent from the Brooklyn Hospital Center while most New Yorkers were being told to stay at home. What left the biggest impression was the workforce's spirit and creativity. Even though staff members were laboring long hours, undertaking risks to themselves and their families – even experiencing personal tragedies – workers did not run around in a panic. They flexed. They improvised. They substituted when resources fell short. I wanted to show these adaptations because I had seen similar reactions help save lives in previous emergencies. In addition to raising public awareness, the information would be useful to medical providers in other places.

What is painful re-reading this now is knowing how many more waves of this virus remained in store, how many parts of our country and the world experienced a similar overwhelming. How many more precious individuals died. How long families couldn't visit loved ones. Most of all, what is clear is that the sacrifices these medical pioneers on the American coronavirus front lines were making would not be an exception. They would become the norm.

'Code Blue': A Brooklyn I.C.U. Fights for Each Life in a Coronavirus Surge
By Sheri Fink

Originally published April 4, 2020 in The New York Times.
Reprinted, with permission by The New York Times.
Associated photographs and related video reporting for this article are available at: https://www.nytimes.com/2020/04/04/nyregion/coronavirus-hospital-brooklyn.html

The night had been particularly tough. Patient after patient had to be intubated and put on a ventilator to breathe. At one point, three "codes" – emergency interventions when someone is on the brink of death – occurred at once.

Dr. Joshua Rosenberg, a critical care doctor, arrived the next morning at the Brooklyn Hospital Center. Within hours, he was racing down the stairwell from the main intensive care unit on the sixth floor to a temporary one on the third, where he passed one of his favorite medical students.

"Shouldn't you be home?" he asked, registering surprise. Clinical rotations for students had been halted to avoid exposing them to the coronavirus. "My mom's here," the student replied.

Dr. Rosenberg, 45, let out an expletive and asked which bed she was in. "I'm rounding there now," he said and made sure the student had his cellphone number.

Earlier, residents from the ICU had presented their cases to Dr. Rosenberg and others, speaking in shorthand and at auctioneer-like speed. There were so many patients to get through last Monday:

"Admitted for acute hypoxic respiratory failure secondary to likely COVID-19."

"Admitted for acute hypoxic respiratory failure secondary to confirmed COVID-19."

"Admitted for acute hypoxic respiratory failure, high suspicion of COVID-19."

Nearly every person lying in a bed in the new intensive care unit, just as in the main one, was breathing with the help of a mechanical ventilator.

There were patients in their 80s and in their 30s. Patients whose asthma and diabetes helped explain their serious illness. And patients who seemed to have no risk factors at all. Patients from nursing homes. Patients who had no homes. Pregnant women, some of whom would not be conscious when their babies were delivered to increase their odds of surviving to raise their children.

This was the week that the coronavirus crisis pummeled the Brooklyn hospital, just as it did others throughout New York City, where the death toll reached more than 2,000, as the governor warned that vital equipment and supplies would run short in just a few days, as the mayor pleaded for more doctors and as hospital officials and political leaders alike acknowledged that the situation would get even worse.

At the Brooklyn center – a medium-size independent community hospital – that misery was evident. Deaths attributed to the virus more than quintupled from the previous week. The number of inpatients confirmed to have COVID-19, the disease caused by the virus, grew from 15 to 105, with 48 more awaiting results. Hospital leaders estimated that about a third of doctors and nurses were out sick. The hospital temporarily ran out of protective plastic gowns, of the main sedative for patients on ventilators, of a key blood pressure medication. The sense of urgency and tragedy was heightened by a video, circulating online, showing a forklift hoisting a body into a refrigerated trailer outside the hospital.

Amid the unfolding disaster, in a week in which he would see more deaths, counsel some families to let loved ones go and scramble to save others, a weary Dr. Rosenberg paused to watch his team tend to their patients. "It's making the best of what you can do," he said.

A Crisis Gathers Strength

Dr. Rosenberg had to stay home the previous week, battling a fever and intense fatigue from what he assumed was COVID-19 (a test, taken after he felt better, later came back negative). He could barely climb the stairs to his bedroom. Returning to work this past Monday, he told a reporter, was like walking into a storm.

"This is insanity," Dr. Rosenberg said to a colleague that day.

Before he left, the intensive care unit had its usual 18 beds. The surge was then hitting the emergency department, leading the hospital to construct a tent outside and screen scores of people a day. Many, mildly ill, were reassured and sent home.

But during the time he was gone, the number of people progressing to severe illness skyrocketed, and the ICU had to expand, then expand again, effectively doubling. "In a week's time, we've transitioned from a crowding outside to a crowding inside," said Lenny Singletary, the hospital's senior vice president for external affairs.

Even before the ICU's morning report had started, Dr. Rosenberg and other staff members had to rush to an outpatient unit. A middle-aged man had come to the hospital for dialysis but was sweating profusely. Staff members were about to help him breathe using a mask with pressurized air, known as a BiPAP machine.

But Dr. Rosenberg, chair of the hospital's infection control committee, thought it was a poor idea. There was no way to know right then whether the man's illness might be caused by the coronavirus, and there were fears that the device could release virus particles into the air, potentially spreading the disease. The patient was moved to the emergency room. "He has a high chance of getting tubed" and needing a ventilator, Dr. Rosenberg told colleagues.

In the new ICU, a repurposed chemotherapy infusion unit, blue plastic gowns fluttered from door hinges, drying after being wiped down for reuse. A patient bed, tilted up like a slide, held pink plastic bins overflowing with patient supplies. Dr. Rosenberg's critical care team assembled in mismatched clothing, masks and protective eyewear, hair and foot coverings—wearing much of the scarce equipment all day, not changing between patients.

With so many staff members out and so many new patients, the array of doctors, nurses, pharmacists, and respiratory therapists who were accustomed to working in the ICU needed reinforcements. Dr. Rosenberg welcomed a podiatrist and two of her resident trainees, a neurosurgery physician assistant, surgery residents, and a nurse anesthetist. "All people who are good with knives and big needles," Dr. Rosenberg quipped.

Now, some nurses were caring for five critically ill patients at a time, a ratio he called "crazy." The norm for experienced ICU nurses at the hospital was just two.

At 10 a.m., Dr. Rosenberg and Dr. James Gasperino, chief of medicine and critical care, jumped on a call with the hospital leadership about challenges the center was facing and how it was coping with them.

The chief medical officer, Dr. Vasantha Kondamudi, later summed it up: Staff was short, medical residents were falling ill every day, and the number of patients with suspected or confirmed COVID-19 was ballooning in nearly every area of the hospital. Yet the crisis had not peaked.

Nurses and others from departments that had cut back on services, like elective surgery and outpatient clinics, were being trained and redeployed. "You're working completely differently," said Judy McLaughlin, senior vice president and chief nursing executive. But even that wasn't enough: The hospital had requested more than 100 volunteer doctors and nurses from the city's Medical Reserve Corps and was rapidly working to vet them.

After the call, Dr. Gasperino conferred in the hallway with the director of respiratory therapy. The hospital had 98 ventilators, many acquired in recent days, including small portable devices from the national stockpile. Employees were running simulations to practice how they might use each ventilator to treat two patients, a difficult and risky proposition. "We're doing this because the alternative is death," Dr. Gasperino said.

An alert sounded on the loudspeaker, interrupting the conversation:

"Code blue, 6B. Code blue, 6B."

The critical care team was designed to respond to emergencies anywhere in the hospital. Although he was supposed to be on his way home after an overnight shift, Dr. Gasperino joined more than a dozen others pouring into the patient's room.

"COVID?" someone asked.

"No, not COVID," came the answer.

Young residents stood on either side of the man's bed and took turns doing chest compressions. Nurses ran out of the room and back in with supplies. Dr. Gasperino threaded a catheter into a large vein to infuse medication into the patient's body. The man's pulse returned.

At about the same time, one of the pregnant patients was wheeled from the intensive care unit and into an operating room for a cesarean section. She was in her early 30s, and her baby was being delivered nearly two months early in an effort to save the mother's life. Over the past day, doctors had ordered two doses of steroid medication to help the infant's lungs mature.

During rounds earlier that morning, a resident presented the woman's case. She had been put on a ventilator and sedated the previous evening. Dr. Rosenberg cursed under his breath: This disease was cruel.

Grasping for Solutions

As Dr. Rosenberg walked down the corridor, nearly every door he passed had a neon colored sticker warning that personal protective equipment must be worn inside. "COVID" was handwritten on many of them.

Staff members had separated control boards from some of the ventilators, so they could adjust their settings and monitor patients without going inside their rooms unless necessary, reducing exposure to the virus. Nurses were making a similar adjustment with the pumps that delivered intravenous medications, adding extension tubing that snaked across floors into hallways.

Workers rushed in and out of the rooms preparing for procedures. "Watch out, don't trip!" Dr. Rosenberg warned a colleague. Moments later, he had to repeat the warning. "Watch out, don't trip!"

Later that day, when a patient became unstable, Dr. Rosenberg passed out masks with a face shield – "they're clean, save them, they're gold" – to staff members before they entered the man's room. Dr. Rosenberg put on a sterile gown and ski goggles, which he said he preferred because they didn't fog up. He inserted a narrow tube into a patient's artery to better monitor his vital signs. Procedures performed inside the room, close to the patient, posed the greatest risk of exposure.

Amid the grimness, Dr. Rosenberg tried to keep the mood positive, his energy fueled by espresso from an automatic machine in his office. He called his colleagues "dude," made sports analogies to explain his points and sometimes asked how their families were dealing with the stress. Even in the thick of a crisis, he directed questions to trainees that forced them to think hard about the next step in care for each patient.

Being a teacher came easily to him. He had studied science at Wesleyan

– earning his degree in three years to save on tuition costs – and then taught it to first graders at the Choir Academy of Harlem, a now shuttered public school that was the home of the famous Boys Choir. He went on to medical school in Israel, later returning to New York, where he now lives with his wife and two daughters.

Dr. Rosenberg and his team reviewed the status of one of the many patients who were receiving a "COVID cocktail" of the antimalarial drug hydroxychloroquine, held up by President Trump as a potential cure, and the antibiotic azithromycin. Dr. Rosenberg referred to it as a "maybe-maybe-this-will-work cocktail," because only a couple of tiny studies supported its effectiveness against COVID-19. Still, the doctors were prescribing it aggressively now, early in the course of hospitalization, in the hopes that it could prevent the lung damage that led patients to need ventilators.

The cocktail is generally considered safe, though it may have serious side effects in certain patients. One man in the ICU developed a deadly arrhythmia and had to be shocked back to life the night before Dr. Rosenberg's Monday shift. The doctor told his residents that the patient should not go back on the drug.

"I don't think the public realizes how often we don't really know" whether something works, Dr. Rosenberg said. Different coronaviruses can cause the common cold, which "affects all of us," he said. "There's no medicine to get better from it—it's just time, patience." What scared him with this new coronavirus, though, was the thought that "time and patience when somebody's on a ventilator is different from time and patience when someone has the sniffles."

His team had also begun treating some patients with another medication, an experimental antiviral drug called remdesivir. But the hospital had to apply to the manufacturer, Gilead, for emergency permission to use it on each patient, who had to have a confirmed diagnosis of COVID-19.

"Do we have a positive test?" Dr. Rosenberg asked about one patient. A colleague replied, "Not yet." Test results from a Quest commercial laboratory in California had been taking about a week, making it harder to isolate infected patients within the building, provide certain treatments and even discharge people. Laboratory workers at the Brooklyn hospital managed to retrofit equipment and start their own testing last weekend, which doctors considered a game changer.

But with one problem resolved, another arose. This past week, there were days when the hospital ran short of a drug to treat life-threatening low blood pressure in many of Dr. Rosenberg's ICU patients, as well as a sedative that many were receiving to relieve the distress of being on a ventilator. The doctors ordered substitutes.

The chief pharmacist at the Brooklyn hospital, Robert DiGregorio, worked until after 2 a.m. on Thursday to try to source more of one drug. Going forward, Dr. Rosenberg predicted, "the biggest threat will be medication shortages."

Painful Conversations

Dr. Rosenberg was struck by the range of the patients felled by this illness—various ages, ethnicities, and medical histories. Some who had been critically ill, most of them younger, were starting to recover enough to be taken off a ventilator and breathe on their own.

But as he and his team stopped outside each room, they saw many who were from nursing homes and had multiple medical problems — the type of patients who filled the intensive care unit during flu season. Now some were extremely sick, with failing organs.

"Very poor prognosis," Dr. Rosenberg said about one man, in his 70s, who had developed kidney damage. "He's going to pass from this."

"Has anyone been in contact with the patient's family?" he asked. He asked a variation of that in front of other rooms. "All of these patients need a palliative care" consultation, the physician said of the seriously ill.

The patients were alone. Visitors were no longer allowed into the hospital, and doctors had to call family members to update them, get their permission for doing procedures and – for many – discuss end-of-life care.

That day and continuing through the week, Dr. Rosenberg had many difficult conversations, on the phone and often through translators, about shifting from trying to extend life to withdrawing life support and focusing on comfort.

"A lot of family members don't realize how sick the patients are or how bad the prognosis is with this disease if you develop respiratory failure," he said, particularly in the context of advanced age and other health conditions. "The families really want to see their loved ones." The team was using iPads and smartphones to connect them.

He said that the state's laws governing withdrawing patients from ventilators were complicated. The default, generally, is for doctors to initiate and continue providing life support unless the patient or proxy has clear directives otherwise. "It reflects on the need for these conversations in primary care well before somebody gets sick and for that information to be disseminated to family members."

He added, "There are an awful lot of really young patients in their 50s and 60s who I'm sure never thought about this."

There were fears throughout the week that New York's hospitals would soon run out of ventilators and be forced to ration them, but doctors at the Brooklyn center said they had enough for now. Dr. Rosenberg worried more about having enough staff members and medications.

Still, Dr. Rosenberg said that he and his colleagues were looking at protocols for how to ration care, developed by intensive care doctors at other medical centers, in case conditions worsened.

The goal was to expand capacity to avoid the need to limit treatment. Gary G. Terrinoni, the hospital's president and chief executive, said he had received donations of food and supplies, but was appealing to the city and state for physical beds, equipment and funds to "ensure we can serve the community" as his clinical colleagues fought "the good fight."

But even discharging those who no longer needed hospital care to make space for new patients was sometimes proving difficult. Dr. Rosenberg worried about getting one of his patients, ready to leave the ICU, accepted back into a nursing home, where across the city staffing had fallen short. Government officials were working on sites to accept released patients, but those had not yet opened.

Even death did not always guarantee an exit. By the end of the week, the hospital had accepted two refrigerated trailers from the city's medical examiner. Workers were building shelves in one of them to make space for more bodies, as overwhelmed funeral homes were failing in some cases to retrieve them. A tent discouraged onlookers from recording more cellphone videos.

Meanwhile, patients continued to arrive at the ICU—some of them with ties to the 175-year-old institution, near Fort Greene. "It's like home for us," said Dr. Kondamudi, the chief medical officer.

Dr. Antonio Mendez, the vice chair of the emergency department, was born at the hospital, and his mother, Josefina, was admitted as an ICU patient. "She is a fighter and so are her doctors," he said.

On his first day back, Dr. Rosenberg checked her blood gas, a measure of the effectiveness of her breathing support. It "looks pretty darn skippy," he said and praised his team for their management of her care.

Late in that long day, Dr. Rosenberg learned that one of the hospital's own medical residents, whom he knew well, was in the emergency room, with symptoms of COVID-19 and a worrisome chest X-ray.

"He comes right up," he told his team, "because he's at high risk of getting intubated."

To admit the physician to the ICU, however, Dr. Rosenberg had to get more staff. "We need more nurses," he said. Given how overwhelmed they are, "they're getting killed."

Soon after, two nurses who normally worked in the cardiac catheterization lab walked into the unit to offer their assistance. Dr. Rosenberg applauded. "This is the cavalry," he said.

Dr. Sheri Fink is at work on a book about the global COVID-19 pandemic. She wrote the New York Times bestselling book *Five Days at Memorial: Life and Death in a Storm-Ravaged Hospital* and was a producer of the eponymous limited series on Apple TV+. Her ProPublica/New York Times Magazine article on Memorial won a Pulitzer Prize and National Magazine Award. Fink's coverage of the COVID pandemic and an Ebola outbreak in West Africa shared Pulitzer Prizes with New York Times colleagues. She also co-created the Emmy-nominated Netflix series *Pandemic: How to Prevent an Outbreak* (2020), filmed prior to COVID-19.

Spiked Cetus
By Richard Donze

Originally published in the Journal of the American Medical Association on March 28, 2023.
Reproduced with permission from JAMA. 2023. 329(12):1035.
Copyright©2023 American Medical Association. All rights reserved.

When considering the virus
(if otherwise unnamed the
definite article modifier in

the 2020s can only mean
one) and stepping back
briefly from managing masks

munizations and meds may-
be summon that sophomore
American lit man-v-nature

discussion around Melville's
classic but imagine a different
outcome after Starbuck (in

the movie version you may
have also watched in class
as we did) says, to the effect,

"Sure, he's a big whale, I get
that, but we're whaling men,
so let's have at him" and then

instead of the Pequod going
down that pin-cushioned
cetacean spiked with spear-

avir or harpoonimab at whom
Ahab for hate's sake spit his
last breath whirlpools below

the great shroud of the sea
and so many more besides
Ishmael escape to tell thee.

Richard Donze's individual poems have appeared in the *Journal of the American Medical Association*, the *Annals of Internal Medicine* and in three physician poetry anthologies (*Blood and Bone*, *Primary Care* and *Uncharted Lines*). Finishing Line Press published his first poetry collection, *The Natural Order of Things*, in November 2021. Dr. Donze is a practicing board certified Occupational Medicine physician, has spoken/presented regionally and nationally on topics in his specialty, written essays for trade publications and participated in local poetry readings. He was recently named Poet Laureate of East Goshen Township in Chester County, southeastern Pennsylvania.

Digital Health Revolution
By Pracha Eamranond

Originally submitted November 5, 2021

Introduction

Digital health has been rapidly evolving for decades yet has accelerated even more so during the COVID-19 pandemic. Our global healthcare system has recently been challenged with implementing innovation to further health, including data sharing and newer technologies such as artificial intelligence (AI). Once the COVID-19 pandemic hit, digital strategies such as patient portals, health apps, and online bookings became much more prevalent. As an example, telemedicine became the automatic default almost overnight to provide care across large swaths of the world (Ali et al. 2020). Lockdowns, followed by varying degrees of social distancing, led to a several-fold increase in telemedicine utilization compared to the pre-COVID-19 era (Bestsennyy et al. 2021). Similarly, the internet, already booming with health information online prior to COVID-19, experienced even more instantaneous popularity around all things COVID-19.

The internet's growth as a health information tool is evidenced by online searches via Google as well as social media platforms such as Instagram (Rovetta and Bhagavathula 2020). Such immense progress generated unintended adverse consequences, including misinformation, depersonalized care, as well as disparities in access to reliable health information. One of our principal challenges in improving healthcare delivery and health outcomes will entail combating misinformation while also ensuring equitable distribution of evidenced-based digital care strategies. Since such misinformation, as well as genuinely useful information about health, only became possible with an expanded internet, it is worth pausing to reflect on the history of this information engine.

History of the Digital Era

The Digital Era started in the 1970s with the advent of personal computers, which enabled large volumes of information to be transferred quickly and more seamlessly than through any other past medium. Many actors in the healthcare industry were clearly reluctant to embrace technology as a means of providing care since it represented such a revolutionary break from convention. At a foundational level, physicians were often skeptical of using a computer as a basis of interacting with a patient. I recall early in my medical training using pen and paper to write notes and prescriptions, often ignoring the advent of anything electronic such as electronic health records (EHRs) or e-prescribing. Conversations were fraught with how technology was taking away valuable face-to-face time with patients and inserting metal hardware into a sacred provider-patient relationship. Clinicians across the world were lamenting the fall of the Golden Age in medicine when no digital technology intruded upon the patient-physician relationship (O'Mahony 2019).

The Golden Age in medicine is generally considered to be from the middle of the 20th century to the end of the 1970s. During this time, huge advances in medicine occurred. The first randomized trial published in 1948 demonstrated the efficacy of streptomycin against tuberculosis (Medical Research Council 1948). The first successful organ transplantation in 1954 at the Peter Bent Brigham Hospital (Merrill et al. 1956) was performed. Working at Brigham & Women's Hospital (renamed, in 1980, from Peter Bent Brigham Hospital), I witnessed how digital technologies can be developed and rolled out with relative ease in well-funded healthcare institutions (Tseng et al. 2018).

While technology is creating opportunities and reshaping outdated healthcare paradigms, it is unintentionally erecting barriers between cutting-edge care and a vast number of patients who need it. Even in an environment that embraces innovation like Brigham and Women's Hospital, questions abound how technology might be a double-edged sword where high-cost advances disproportionately disenfranchise disadvantaged populations. Clinical trials are largely sponsored by industry players who promote high-cost medications. This process often generates cost-prohibitive medications that illustrate how a myopic emphasis on modernization can outstrip practical considerations of access and affordability.

Similar to the influx of newer medications, the remote monitoring of vital signs with the data uploading of blood sugars, blood pressure, and oxygen saturations has been readily implemented over years; yet studies including disadvantaged patients were far rarer, which was partially attributed to lack of access and ability of these patients to install, manage, and fully-leverage sophisticated devices remotely. Access to digital technologies has been improving over time yet the digital divide still persists, e.g., access to basic tools including internet; tech-enabled innovation like wearable monitors; and access to digitally-enabled health networks due to geography, local infrastructure, and other factors that more privileged populations take for granted.

By the turn of the 21st century, advances in network interconnectivity and political reform across the world had helped catapult EHRs and other technologies into mainstream healthcare. From the clinical knowledge side, I have seen the transition from reading seminal textbooks (such as Harrisons Principles of Internal Medicine – a.k.a. "the bible" of internal medicine) to e-learning. UpToDate® (an online resource covering almost all aspects of medicine, that is continually reviewed and updated by experts in their fields) has revolutionized how clinicians around the world access new health information and guidelines at the point of care. Founder Dr. Bud Rose started with the idea in the 1980's and was able to put his medical knowledge onto floppy disks in 1992 (Sax 2020).

This digital innovation has been so successful because rapidly changing medical information and recommendations are efficiently disseminated digitally in real time across the web. This is in stark contrast to traditional medical journals and textbooks that are constantly months to years out-of-date by the time they are published due to the constant churn of discovery that far outpaces the slow schedule of print media.

The 21st century saw the advent of patient-facing online platforms that provide a seemingly limitless number of options through which one can access healthcare. Patients can look for guidance about their health issues via search engines, engage in social media groups related to their interests/conditions, utilize health apps to manage their chronic diseases, and interact directly with their care teams through patient portals rather than phone calls or in-person visits. These are some of the clear advantages to tapping into health expertise digitally over traditional in-person visits with a doctor.

Furthermore, technology in healthcare led to the introduction of newer ways to manage healthcare such as using AI, machine learning (ML), personalized medicine, and robotics for microsurgery or remote procedures. As an example, many healthcare systems are utilizing AI/ML processes to provide care, unbeknownst to most patients and clinicians. AI can be used to diagnose and treat several specific conditions more quickly. By utilizing information within the medical record as well as other discrete data, an AI-based program can more accurately read imaging studies, interpret laboratory testing, and determine optimal treatment options far more efficiently than humans alone (Peek et al. 2020). Since IBM Watson first showed that computers can beat human champions in Jeopardy (Best 2013), there has been high expectation that AI could aid healthcare delivery by overcoming the default limitations inherent in manually collecting, analyzing, and sharing data feeds to intervene in healthcare. Blood transfusions are a prime example of this benefit.

A simple blood transfusion which has the propensity to lead to potentially fatal transfusion reactions can be ordered and given now with a much lower likelihood of such a reaction. AI contributes to this decrease in reaction risks by determining when a patient truly needs a transfusion (Levi et al. 2021). Another key example is early detection and treatment of life-threatening infections (Yuan et al. 2020). Newer technologies such as precision medicine can apply AI to patients' genetic characteristics, environmental factors, and individual behaviors/lifestyle. Depending on the situation, AI can yield other discrete data including pathogen-antibiotic resistance profiles, cancer cell subtypes, and specific study characteristics that might apply only in unique situations. Many of the complexities of introducing newer technologies such as AI, including more mundane aspects like data privacy and lack of consent, have gone under the radar for the most part but continue to challenge health systems to ensure healthcare technologies are appropriately implemented with the patient in mind.

Impacts of the COVID-19 Pandemic During the Digital Era

Many pandemics have raged during the Digital Era including HIV/AIDS, SARS, MERS-CoV, and Ebola. However, no infectious agent in the modern era has had such an immediate impact on the digital space like the SARS CoV-2 virus with the COVID-19 disease. Unlike previous pandemics in recent history (e.g., after the Spanish Flu pandemic of 1918), the spread of COVID-19 was immediate, with cases in every corner of the world within weeks. It is worth noting that at the time of this writing, HIV/AIDS has led to far more recorded deaths in aggregate (WHO n.d.a) but its preventable transmission and much slower pace did not earn the burning platform globally that COVID-19 quickly attained.

Since the beginning of the COVID-19 pandemic in 2019, telemedicine and EHRs still appear to be the most widely used technologies by the public, but AI, big data, and the Internet of Things are other commonly used digital strategies being implemented broadly in healthcare (Tilahun et al. 2021). On an individual level, digital technologies on computers and mobile devices engage patients successfully in physical exercise, dietary modification, and lifestyle changes such as smoking cessation and alcohol reduction (Mclaughlin et al. 2021; Gold 2021). Digital interventions can be used with good effect on a variety of conditions, including improving mental health and reducing suicide risk (Dimeff et al. 2021).

However, the downside effects of digital technologies leading to adverse outcomes, such as social isolation and mental health problems, are also prevalent (Marciano et al. 2022). The deluge of information, also termed "infodemic," may be harmful in and of itself (Calleja et al. 2021). This uncontrollable data dump, not all of which is accurate, tends to occur during a public health pandemic which can lead to confusion, risk-taking, and behaviors that can harm health and lead to erosion of trust in health authorities and public health responses. Further downstream adverse events such as erroneous data, data breaches, and privacy infringement entail other ethical considerations not previously envisioned when creating digital tools to manage health (Di Giovanni, Cochrane, and Lewis 2022).

AI technology has already been leveraged to manage different workflows at the patient and system levels (Yin, Ngiam, and Teo 2021). Rather than rely on an individual clinician or operationalizing lab testing alone, AI is used to glean epidemiologic data to predict those at risk, who should be tested, and which symptoms are indicative of COVID-19 in the context of other available data such as imaging and lab results (Rasheed et al. 2021). Deep learning, which is a layered version of AI/ML, has been increasingly used during the pandemic for assessment of COVID-19 as well as other disease entities (Nayak et al. 2022). Broadly speaking, deep learning is machine learning based on artificial neural networks that traverse multiple layers of deep data feeds for more complex data digestion (Kriegeskorte and Golan 2019). Deep learning has applications in natural language processing/speech recognition, interpreting complex images more efficiently than humans, and non-patient-facing processes such as drug development. Extracting vast quantities of data across the internet earns new-found efficiencies for the discovery and optimization of drugs, devices, and other technologies.

While AI is just one of many individual innovations spurred on by the pandemic, there is a global stimulus to apply digital technologies to propel a host of medical advances (Bernardo et al. 2021). Digital capabilities allow unprecedented sharing of data across countries and organizations that enables dissemination of expertise on a broad range of innovative topics such as collection of COVID-19 data, pandemic transmission predictions, as well as crowdsourcing to jumpstart nascent technologies in software and hardware (e.g., COVID testing, ventilators). Perhaps the most significant technological advance to help save lives was the COVID messenger RNA (mRNA) vaccines.

The mRNA vaccines represent significant progress in terms of rapid development, standardization, and distribution of inoculation technology. The remarkable advances required to go from bench to booster for vaccines included integrated exploration of the underlying SARS-CoV-2 immunological science via academia and pharmaceutical industries, rapid clinical trial implementation, record-pace regulatory approvals through emergency use authorizations, and dissemination of mRNA vaccines at lightning speed across borders (Barrett et al. 2022).

Post-pandemic Considerations

While there have been multiple pandemics affecting global communities, the COVID-19 pandemic has brought unprecedented challenges to healthcare delivery. Clearly no other infectious agent has disrupted so much of modern society as SARS CoV-2. With so much continuing uncertainty as to how long the COVID-19 pandemic will go on, telemedicine has become a necessity in health systems around the world while simultaneously leveraging digital health to deliver safe care for patients in person (e.g., triaging patients with variable risk for COVID-19). The interaction of AI/ML, precision medicine, deep learning, other technologies, and emerging innovations will continue to have serious ramifications for health outcomes globally.

This essay is not meant to catalogue all new digital technologies but rather to point out that innovative, diverging technologies are being scaled to intersect with patients at an unprecedented pace. Different perspectives exist on which digital technologies are most influential in healthcare. In one study, most of the hospital leaders polled intend to expand virtual care in the years after the COVID-19 pandemic (Beckers Hospital Review 2021). Among market experts, AI does seem to be one of the most important technologies, but there are many other advances including electronic billing, 3D printing, nanotechnology, blockchain, robotics, wearable devices, augmented/virtual reality (AR/VR), and chatbots just to name a few (Majdi 2017; Beckers Hospital Review 2021; Meskó 2020).

The arrival of the metaverse has taken AR/VR a step further by creating a collective virtual shared space, otherwise defined as a convergence of 3D virtual spaces to provide an enhanced physical reality. The metaverse is being explored within medical education, particularly given the pandemic challenges of educating trainees without exposing them to COVID-19 infection (Kye et al. 2021). Exploration into the metaverse has gone even further by allowing surgeons to train for complex surgery beyond traditional robotic technologies (Koo 2021). AR stereotactic spine navigation platforms are currently enabling neurosurgeons to more precisely visualize spine anatomy in real-time while performing surgery successfully, akin to having 3D global positioning systems while operating (Molina et al. 2021).

The ultimate impact of these technologies has yet to be seen and will likely be difficult to measure as diverse societies differentially apply new technologies at varying degrees. With the ability of health systems to provide care remotely during the pandemic, some sicker patients have been managed more efficiently outside the hospital system, particularly at home. Newer types of data feeds and analytic dashboards allowing real-time decisions have led to the opportunity to provide a higher level of care, e.g., non-invasive mechanical ventilation, critical care medication infusions, intensive care monitoring of clinical conditions, and better distribution of medical staff to support hospital-at-home interventions (Johns Hopkins Medicine). Using digital technologies (e.g., organ-sustaining machines for heart, lung and/or kidney failure) for acutely ill as well as ambulatory patients (e.g., managing hypertension or diabetes with real time sensors), these programs have led to improved clinical outcomes and patient satisfaction at a lower cost (Cryer et al. 2012). At the same time, such improvements in digital, remote healthcare help prevent unnecessary exposure to COVID-19, which remains a major goal since the beginning of the pandemic.

While there is much to celebrate in terms of advances in digital technologies, there are clear concerning trends in online "misinformation", which can be defined as the promulgation of false information without the malicious intent to mislead (Watson and Tsuyuki 2021). In contrast, "disinformation" is narrative that intentionally misleads or manipulates the truth. Disinformation has been used by governments, militaries, organizations, and individuals to foster a desired result. With the widespread use of social media during the pandemic, more misinformation and disinformation are being spread through such platforms as Twitter, Facebook, YouTube and others (Suarez-Lledo and Alvarez-Galvez 2021). Many "fake news" stories, i.e., stories manufactured to simulate *bona fide* news stories from accredited and traditionally reputable news sources, are being distributed via posts, instant messaging, and chatrooms. Furthermore, many of these disinformation posts are being propagated by relatively few individuals who are highly unlikely to be working in groups that deliver evidence-based guidelines by reliable, known experts.

Combating misinformation is exceedingly challenging given how diffuse such networks have become in the context of an immense and global infrastructure that is the Internet. Understanding the diffusion techniques of misinformation and creating campaigns geared at re-adjusting mindsets will be critical for fighting rampant disinformation particularly as it becomes more sophisticated digitally. It is estimated that up to 80% of people are seeking health information online, and some do not know how to differentiate between health mis/disinformation and facts (Rodgers and Massac 2021). It may be surprising to some that there is such a high degree of misunderstanding of the health literature regarding the widespread risk to one's health and that of others. This is certainly the case for the COVID-19 vaccine where mis/disinformation has led to lower vaccination rates globally. The US surgeon general, Vivek Murthy, has declared misinformation a global threat to public health (Office of the Surgeon General 2021).

There are specific ways that the WHO has recommended we all combat misinformation: (1) Access the source, (2) Go beyond the headlines, (3) Identify authors, (4) Check dates, (5) Examine supporting evidence, (6) Check your biases, and (7) Turn to fact-checkers (n.d.b). At a very simple level, one needs to know where to turn for trusted, evidence-based content that does not distort or misrepresent facts. A majority of people are using social media to obtain information making it imperative that social media platforms increase the oversight and control of accounts that are spreading misinformation (Berg 2021). Facebook has removed or restricted several accounts from Facebook or Instagram, which includes preventing them from being recommended to other users, reducing the reach of their posts, and blocking flagged accounts from promoting themselves through paid ads (Wong 2021).

However, many argue that social media platforms are not doing enough to level the playing field but are allowing bad actors too much freedom to provide biased health information. While it is important that larger organizations have the ability to regulate health misinformation, ultimately the social media users are responsible for verifying the information they are consuming and for finding qualified sources of information for corroboration. Unfortunately, similar to the distrust of computers storing health information or EHRs managing patient workflows, many express a significant skepticism of health information channels, no matter how grounded they are in evidence-based medicine. Time and digital health interventions will determine how effective digital education can be in informing the public and driving health-seeking behavior.

Well-known health disparities have disproportionately impacted populations of racial and ethnic minorities (CDC 2021) amongst whom disinformation campaigns are exceedingly persuasive, since these patients frequently have a low health literacy which is related to worse health outcomes (Howard, Sentell, and Gazmararian 2006; Naeem and Kamel 2021). Common areas of misinformation include medications, non-communicable diseases, eating disorders, and other forms of medical treatment (Suarez-Lledo and Alvarez-Galvez 2021). With regard to COVID-19, misinformation about vaccines can lead to dangerous consequences, i.e., vaccine hesitancy and downstream COVID-19 infections and mortality (Suarez-Lledo and Alvarez-Galvez 2021). Numerous studies have demonstrated that COVID-19 leads to more hospitalizations and deaths in racial and ethnic minorities (CDC 2021). Addressing disparities in healthcare access and outcomes in a systematic way to provide equitable high-quality care to all will ultimately be a determining factor in mitigating the mortality differential for disadvantaged populations (Wen and Sadeghi 2021).

There are other areas of misinformation around masking, disease burden, and treatments which have also contributed to preventable COVID-19-related deaths. There are many groups (including physicians) spreading misinformation and disinformation, and their actions can hamper efforts to vaccinate the public (Rubin). Policing these groups, particularly physicians, has been challenging for governing boards in the context of free speech in relation to its potentially adverse health impacts (Baron and Ejnes 2022). When such erroneous information overtakes factual health information, it not only creates vaccine hesitancy where consumers are skeptical of vaccine benefits, but also vaccine apathy where consumers simply do not care anymore (Wood and Schulman 2021). Many of these misinformation campaigns flood the media such that true health information gets overlooked, lost, or framed as just one opinion among a chorus of other apparently equivalently valid perspectives, leading to apathy and misperceptions.

Conclusions

Emerging technologies and the diffusion of their applications remain an exciting area within healthcare that will assuredly continue to blossom. These digital technologies, from navigating a patient's electronic record to AI/ML-based interventions to guide therapies across populations, have already led to phenomenal advances in data-sharing, capacity-building, and improvement in health outcomes. Systematic approaches to providing all patients equal access to appropriate technologies will continue to challenge our global health system in the decades to come. Inevitably this type of progress also leads to unintended, undesirable consequences including misinformation and health disparities for underprivileged populations.

Among our duties as patients, family members, friends, and healthcare professionals is the obligation to be proactive in preventing and managing downstream adverse events while continuing to leverage digital tools to promote well-being. Our ability to be good caretakers of digital tools will enable us to improve health outcomes while minimizing the risks that misinformed health behaviors and maldistributed care can bring.

References

Arshad Ali, Shajeea, Taha Bin Arif, Hira Maab, Mariam Baloch, Sana Manazir, Fatima Jawed, and Rohan Kumar Ochani. 2020. "Global Interest in Telehealth During COVID-19 Pandemic: An Analysis of Google TrendsTM." *Cureus* 12 (9): e10487. https://doi.org/10.7759/cureus.10487.

Baron, Richard J, and Yul D Ejnes. 2022. "Physicians Spreading Misinformation on Social Media — Do Right and Wrong Answers Still Exist in Medicine?" *New England Journal of Medicine* 387 (1): 1–3. https://doi.org/10.1056/NEJMp2204813.

Barrett, Alan D T, Richard W Titball, Paul A MacAry, Richard E Rupp, Veronika von Messling, David H Walker, and Nicolas V J Fanget.

2022. "The Rapid Progress in COVID Vaccine Development and Implementation." *Npj Vaccines* 7 (1): 20. https://doi.org/10.1038/s41541-022-00442-8.

Beckers Hospital Review. 2021. "Hospital execs eye expanded virtual care and streamline platforms in years ahead." Accessed October 26, 2021. https://www.beckershospitalreview.com/hospital-execs-eye-expanded-virtual-care-and-streamlined-platforms-in-years-ahead-2.html?oly_enc_id=9741H0807612C9D.

Berg, Sara. "Social media networks must crack down on misinformation." American Medical Association. June 15, 2021. https://www.ama-assn.org/delivering-care/public-health/social-media-networks-must-crack-down-medical-misinformation.

Bernardo, Theresa, Kurtis Edward Sobkowich, Russell Othmer Forrest, Luke Silva Stewart, Marcelo D'Agostino, Enrique Perez Gutierrez, and Daniel Gillis. 2021. "Collaborating in the Time of COVID-19: The Scope and Scale of Innovative Responses to a Global Pandemic." *JMIR Public Health Surveill* 7 (2): e25935. https://doi.org/10.2196/25935.

Best, Jo. 2013. "IBM Watson: The inside story of how the Jeopardy-winning supercomputer was born, and what it wants to do next." Tech Republic. September 9, 2013. Accessed March 17, 2022. https://www.techrepublic.com/article/ibm-watson-the-inside-story-of-how-the-jeopardy-winning-supercomputer-was-born-and-what-it-wants-to-do-next/

Bestsennyy Oleg, Greg Gilbert, Alex Harris, and Jennifer Rost. "Telehealth: A Quarter-Trillion-Dollar Post-COVID-19 Reality?" McKinsey & Company. July 9, 2021. Accessed October 26, 2021 https://www.mckinsey.com/industries/healthcare-systems-and-services/our-insights/telehealth-a-quarter-trillion-dollar-post-COVID-19-reality.

Calleja, Neville, AbdelHalim AbdAllah, Neetu Abad, Naglaa Ahmed, Dolores Albarracin, Elena Altieri, Julienne N Anoko, et al. 2021. "A Public Health Research Agenda for Managing Infodemics: Methods and Results of the First WHO Infodemiology Conference." *JMIR Infodemiology* 1 (1): e30979. https://doi.org/10.2196/30979.

Center for Disease Control. 2021. "Health Equity Considerations and Racial and Ethnic Minority Groups." CDC. April 19, 2021. Accessed October 26, 2021. https://www.cdc.gov/coronavirus/2019-ncov/community/health-equity/race-ethnicity.html.

Cryer, Lesley, Scott B Shannon, Melanie Van Amsterdam, and Bruce Leff.

2012. "Costs For 'Hospital At Home' Patients Were 19 Percent Lower, With Equal Or Better Outcomes Compared To Similar Inpatients." *Health Affairs* 31 (6): 1237–43. https://doi.org/10.1377/hlthaff.2011.1132.

Dimeff, Linda A, David A Jobes, Kelly Koerner, Nadia Kako, Topher Jerome, Angela Kelley-Brimer, Edwin D Boudreaux, et al. 2021. "Using a Tablet-Based App to Deliver Evidence-Based Practices for Suicidal Patients in the Emergency Department: Pilot Randomized Controlled Trial." *JMIR Ment Health* 8 (3): e23022. https://doi.org/10.2196/23022.

Giovanni, Robert Di, Andrew Cochrane, and David J Lewis. 2022. "Adverse Events in the Digital Age: Finding the Sharpest Tool in the Box." *Therapeutic Innovation & Regulatory Science* 56 (1): 23–37. https://doi.org/10.1007/s43441-021-00337-1.

Gold, Natalie, Amy Yau, Benjamin Rigby, Chris Dyke, Elizabeth Alice Remfry, and Tim Chadborn. 2021. "Effectiveness of Digital Interventions for Reducing Behavioral Risks of Cardiovascular Disease in Nonclinical Adult Populations: Systematic Review of Reviews." *J Med Internet Res* 23 (5): e19688. https://doi.org/10.2196/19688.

Howard, David H, Tetine Sentell, and Julie A Gazmararian. 2006. "Impact of Health Literacy on Socioeconomic and Racial Differences in Health in an Elderly Population." *Journal of General Internal Medicine* 21 (8): 857–61. https://doi.org/10.1111/j.1525-1497.2006.00530.x.

Johns Hopkins Medicine. n.d. "Hospital at Home." Accessed October 26, 2021. https://www.johnshopkinssolutions.com/solution/hospital-at-home/

Koo, Hullyung. 2021. "Training in lung cancer surgery through the metaverse, including extended reality, in the smart operating room of Seoul National University Bundang Hospital, Korea." *Journal of Educational Evaluation for Health Professions* 18 (33). https://doi.org/10.3352/jeehp.2021.18.33

Kriegeskorte, Nikolaus, and Tal Golan. 2019. "Neural Network Models and Deep Learning." *Current Biology* 29 (7): R231–36. https://doi.org/10.1016/j.cub.2019.02.034.

Kye, Bokyung, Nara Han, Eunji Kim, Yeonjeong Parks, and Soyoung Jo. 2021. "Educational applications of metaverse: possibilities and limitations." *Journal of Educational Evaluation for Health Professions* 18 (32).

Levi, Riccardo, Francesco Carli, Aldo Robles Arévalo, Yuksel Altinel, Daniel J Stein, Matteo Maria Naldini, Federica Grassi, et al. 2021. "Artificial Intelligence-Based Prediction of Transfusion in the Intensive Care Unit in Patients with Gastrointestinal Bleeding." *BMJ Health &Amp; Care Informatics* 28 (1): e100245. https://doi.org/10.1136/bmjhci-2020-100245.

Majdi, Lisa. 2017. "17 Technology Innovations That Will Influence the Future of Digital Healthcare." Cox Blue. October 4, 2017. Accessed October 26, 2021. https://www.coxblue.com/17-technology-advances-that-will-influence-the-future-of-digital-healthcare/.

Marciano, Laura, Michelle Ostroumova, Peter Johannes Schulz, and Anne-Linda Camerini. 2022. "Digital Media Use and Adolescents' Mental Health During the Covid-19 Pandemic: A Systematic Review and Meta-Analysis." *Frontiers in Public Health*. https://www.frontiersin.org/articles/10.3389/fpubh.2021.793868.

Mclaughlin, Matthew, Tessa Delaney, Alix Hall, Judith Byaruhanga, Paul Mackie, Alice Grady, Kathryn Reilly, et al. 2021. "Associations Between Digital Health Intervention Engagement, Physical Activity, and Sedentary Behavior: Systematic Review and Meta-Analysis." *J Med Internet Res* 23 (2): e23180. https://doi.org/10.2196/23180.

Medical Research Council Streptomycin in Tuberculosis Trials Committee. 1948. "Streptomycin treatment of pulmonary tuberculosis." *British Medical Journal* 2(4582): 769-782. https://www.ncbi.nlm.nih.gov/pmc/articles/PMC2091872/

Merrill, John P, Joseph E Murray, J Hartwell Harrison, Warren R Guild, and John M Barry. 2002. "Successful Homotransplantation of the Human Kidney between Identical Twins." The Journal of Urology 167 (2, Part 2): 830. https://doi.org/https://doi.org/10.1016/S0022-5347(02)80268-3.

Meskó, Bertalan. 2020. "Ten Ways Technology is Changing Healthcare." The Medical Futurist. March 3, 2020. Accessed October 26, 2021. https://medicalfuturist.com/ten-ways-technology-changing-healthcare/

Molina, Camilo A, Daniel M Sciubba, Jacob K Greenberg, Majid Khan, and Timothy Witham. 2021. "Clinical Accuracy, Technical Precision, and Workflow of the First in Human Use of an Augmented-Reality Head-Mounted Display Stereotactic Navigation System for Spine Surgery." *Operative Neurosurgery* 20 (3). https://journals.lww.com/onsonline/Fulltext/2021/03000/Clinical_Accuracy,_Technical_

Precision,_and.9.aspx.

Naeem, Salman B, and Maged N. Kamel Boulos. 2021. "COVID-19 Misinformation Online and Health Literacy: A Brief Overview" *International Journal of Environmental Research and Public Health* 18, no. 15: 8091. https://doi.org/10.3390/ijerph18158091

Nayak, Janmenjoy, Bighnaraj Naik, Paidi Dinesh, Kanithi Vakula, Pandit Byomakesha Dash, and Danilo Pelusi. 2022. "Significance of Deep Learning for Covid-19: State-of-the-Art Review." *Research on Biomedical Engineering* 38 (1): 243–66. https://doi.org/10.1007/s42600-021-00135-6.

Office of the Surgeon General. 2021. "Confronting Health Misinformation: The U.S. Surgeon General's Advisory on Building a Healthy Information Environment." Current Priorities of the U.S. Surgeon General. July 15, 2021. Accessed October 26, 2021. https://www.hhs.gov/surgeongeneral/reports-and-publications/health-misinformation/index.html

O'Mahony, Seamus. 2019. "After the Golden Age: What Is Medicine For?" *The Lancet* 393 (May): 1798–99. https://doi.org/10.1016/S0140-6736(19)30901-8.

Peek, Niels, Mark Sujan, and Philip Scott. 2020. "Digital Health and Care in Pandemic Times: Impact of COVID-19." *BMJ Health &Amp; Care Informatics* 27 (1): e100166. https://doi.org/10.1136/bmjhci-2020-100166.

Rasheed, Jawad, Akhtar Jamil, Alaa Ali Hameed, Fadi Al-Turjman, and Ahmad Rasheed. 2021. "COVID-19 in the Age of Artificial Intelligence: A Comprehensive Review." *Interdisciplinary Sciences: Computational Life Sciences* 13 (2): 153–75. https://doi.org/10.1007/s12539-021-00431-w.

Rodgers, Kimberly, and Nnandi Massac. 2020. "Misinformation: A Threat to the Public's Health and the Public Health System." *Journal of public health management and practice* 26, 3(2020): 294-296. https://doi.org/10.1097/PHH.0000000000001163

Rovetta, Alessandro, and Akshaya Srikanth Bhagavathula. 2020. "Global Infodemiology of COVID-19: Analysis of Google Web Searches and Instagram Hashtags." *J Med Internet Res* 22 (8): e20673. https://doi.org/10.2196/20673.

Rubin, Rita. 2022. "When Physicians Spread Unscientific Information About COVID-19." *JAMA* 327 (10): 904–6. https://doi.org/10.1001/jama.2022.1083.

Sax, Paul E. 2020. "Early Memories of Burton 'Bud' Rose, Founder of UpToDate — and Medical Education Visionary." HIV and ID Observations. *NEJM Journal Watch*. 6 May 2020. https://blogs.jwatch.org/hiv-id-observations/index.php/early-memories-of-burton-bud-rose-founder-of-uptodate-and-medical-education-visionary/2020/05/06/

Suarez-Lledo, Victor, and Javier Alvarez-Galvez. 2021. "Prevalence of Health Misinformation on Social Media: Systematic Review." *J Med Internet Res* 23 (1): e17187. https://doi.org/10.2196/17187.

Tilahun Kassahun Dessie; Mekonnen, Zeleke Abebaw; Endehabtu, Berhanu Fikadie; Angaw, Dessie Abebaw, Binyam; Gashu. 2021. "Mapping the Role of Digital Health Technologies in Prevention and Control of COVID-19 Pandemic: Review of the Literature." *Yearbook of Medical Informatics* 30 (01): 26–37. https://doi.org/10.1055/s-0041-1726505.

Tseng, Jocelyn, Sonia Samagh, Donna Fraser, and Adam B Landman. 2018. "Catalyzing Healthcare Transformation with Digital Health: Performance Indicators and Lessons Learned from a Digital Health Innovation Group." *Healthcare* 6 (2): 150–55. https://doi.org/https://doi.org/10.1016/j.hjdsi.2017.09.003.

Watson, Kaitlyn E, and Ross T Tsuyuki. 2021. "Pharmacists Must Combat Mis/Disinformation!" *Canadian Pharmacists Journal* / Revue Des Pharmaciens Du Canada 154 (2): 68–69. https://doi.org/10.1177/1715163521992037.

Wen, Leana S. and Nakissa B. Sadeghi. 2020. "Addressing Racial Health Disparities In The COVID-19 Pandemic: Immediate And Long-Term Policy Solutions." Health Affairs Blog. July 20, 2020. Accessed October 26, 2021. https://www.healthaffairs.org/do/10.1377/hblog20200716.620294/full/

WHO. n.d. "The Global Health Observatory." Accessed March 17, 2022. https://www.who.int/data/gho/data/themes/hiv-aids

WHO. 2022. "Let's flatten the infodemic curve." WHO Newsroom. Accessed March 17, 2022. https://www.who.int/news-room/spotlight/let-s-flatten-the-infodemic-curve

Wong, Queenie. 2021. "Facebook removed more than 20 million posts for COVID-19 misinformation." CNET. August 18, 2021. https://www.cnet.com/news/social-media/facebook-removed-more-than-20-million-posts-for-COVID-19-misinformation/

Wood, Stacy, and Kevin Schulman. 2021. "When Vaccine Apathy, Not

Hesitancy, Drives Vaccine Disinterest." *JAMA* 325 (24): 2435–36. https://doi.org/10.1001/jama.2021.7707.

Yin, Jiamin, Kee Yuan Ngiam, and Hock Hai Teo. 2021. "Role of Artificial Intelligence Applications in Real-Life Clinical Practice: Systematic Review." *J Med Internet Res* 23 (4): e25759. https://doi.org/10.2196/25759.

Yuan, Kuo-Ching, Lung-Wen Tsai, Ko-Han Lee, Yi-Wei Cheng, Shou-Chieh Hsu, Yu-Sheng Lo, and Ray-Jade Chen. 2020. "The Development an Artificial Intelligence Algorithm for Early Sepsis Diagnosis in the Intensive Care Unit." *International Journal of Medical Informatics* 141: 104176. https://doi.org/10.1016/j.ijmedinf.2020.104176

Dr. Pracha Eamranond has dedicated his career to furthering the health of underprivileged populations. Dr. Eamranond teaches the Social Medicine and Practice of Medicine courses at Harvard Medical School. He cares for patients with complex psychosocial and medical issues at Brigham and Women's Hospital in Boston, MA.

Family Legends: Physicians and Pandemics Across Millennia
By Kenneth V. Iserson

Originally submitted July 17, 2020

As most of us encounter a global pandemic for the first time, physicians on the front lines share their bravery and bewilderment with the earliest physicians who encountered deadly untreatable diseases. In this paper I have imagined myself as only the latest in a long line of physicians present for these devastating historic events. In each instance, I detail an imagined ancestor who brushes up against the more famous and historically very real physicians of the day. My imagined physician ancestors – Assarakos, William Kuklinsky, David Swerdlow, Abraham Buzin, and Luis Proshler – represent physicians of their times but were not real people. These written chronicles and eyewitness accounts provide a useful mirror on the pandemic that the world is now experiencing.

The Plague of Athens in 430 BCE

Let's begin with Assarakos, the first physician of my imagined lineage, who experienced the Plague of Athens in 430 BCE, during the Peloponnesian War. Although its origin was obscure, the citizenry believed that the pestilence had arrived in Athens from Ethiopia by way of Egypt and Libya (Thucydides 1956). It is said that, unlike many of his peers, Assarakos stayed to treat those who fell ill. But his nostrums were limited, and the illness took the lives of nearly 100,000 people. He could, however, provide public health advice and comfort sufferers and survivors. As Thucydides, who himself contracted the disease, wrote:

> And the most dreadful thing about the whole malady was not only the despondency of the victims, when they once became aware that they were sick, for their minds straightway yielded to despair and they gave themselves up for lost instead of resisting, but also the fact that they became infected by nursing one another and died like sheep ... Athenians suffered further hardship owing to the crowding into the city of the people from the country districts ... since no houses were available for them and they had to live in huts that were stifling in the

hot season, they perished in wild disorder. Bodies of dying men lay one upon another, and half-dead people rolled about in the streets (Thucydides 1956, 349-351).

As happened during subsequent plagues, myths and magical thinking surrounded supposed causes and cures. Noted clinicians such as Hippocrates advocated the use of fire in the form of bonfires to fight the plague (Pinault 1992). To explain the etiology of epidemic diseases, Pinault writes that Aëtius of Ameda "attributed their cause to a common factor, such as air tainted by a putrefying vapor caused by a great number of corpses, which happens in war, or the unhealthy miasma released by swamps, marshes, or drainage ditches" (Pinault 1992, 55). Based on this mythical belief, Aëtius used alternative medicine techniques to keep, in his own words, "people healthy by applying opposites, and sometimes used cooling techniques, if this should be the case, and sometimes heating. And by kindling a great fire one should be able to turn the air hot and dry as it is becoming moist and cold, just as they say Hippocrates did among the Athenians and also Acron of Acragas" (Pinault 1992, 55).

These curatives were of no help and the plague devastated Athenian society. People abandoned their gods as useless, disregarded harsh laws designed to control the population, and participated in a huge shift in wealth when many aristocrats died. As Thucydides wrote, "the catastrophe was so overwhelming that men, not knowing what would happen next to them, became indifferent to every rule of religion or law" (Thucydides 1916, 126). After two more waves (429 BCE and 427/426 BCE), the plague subsided. However, with no leadership (Athens' leader, Pericles, also perished), Athenian society and its military were permanently damaged, markedly diminishing its subsequent status. Our family's physician, Assarakos, survived, continued practicing medicine, and was said to have sired many children, three of whom became physicians.

Smallpox in Seventeenth-Century England

Smallpox, initially confused with measles, flared up intermittently in England. In late seventeenth-century England, William Kuklinsky, another in our fictional physician ancestry, read the following treatise (written in early English) to learn about the disease while a physician-apprentice:

The signes when one is infected are these, first hee is taken with a hoate feauer, and sometime with a delirium great paine in the back, furring and stopping of the nose, beating of the heart, hoarsenesse, rednesse of the eies and full of teares, with heauinesse and payne in the head, great beating in the foreheade and temples, heauines and pricking in all the body, drynes in the mouth, the face verie red, paine in the throate and breast: difficulty in breathing, and shaking of the handes and feete, with spitting thicke matter.

When they doe soone or in short time appeare, and that in their comming out they doe looke red, and that after they are come forth they doe looke white and spéedily grow to maturation, that he draweth his breath easily, and doth find himselfe eased of his paine, and that his feauer doeth leaue him, these are good and laudable signes of recouery ...

Auicen [original emphasis] saieth there are two speciall causes which produce death vnto those that haue this disease: either for that they are choked with great inflammation and swelling in the throate called Angina, or hauing a flixe or laske which doeth so weaken and ouerthrow the vitall spirits, that thereby the disease is encreased, and so death followeth (Kellwaye 1593).

Dr. Kuklinsky visited a woman named Alice Thornton while she was tending to her daughter Katherine, who was ill with smallpox in 1666. Ms. Thornton later detailed the event in her autobiography:

Uppon the 29th of September, when I was yett very weake, began my daughter Katte with a violent and extreme pain in the backe and head, with such scrikes and torments that shee was deprived of reason, wanting sleepe, nor could she eate anything. For three daies she contineued, to my great affliction, not knoweing what this distemper would be. At last the smale pox appeared, breaking out abundantly all over; but in her unguidablenesse stroke in againe, soe that my brother Portington used many cordialls to save her life, afftter which they appeared, and then we had more hopes, but was in great danger of losseing her sight. She was all over her face in one scurfe, they running into each other. But loe, by the goodnesse of God, for which I humbly blesse and praise His holy name, she passed the danger of death, beginning to heale. Her extreamity beeing soe great, crieing night and day, that I was forced to be removed, though very weake, as before, into the scarlett chamber, for want of rest (Thornton 1875, 157).

On occasion, apprentice physician Kuklinsky was privy to heroic leadership that saved many from the dreadful disease, most notably when he accompanied physician John Radcliffe to consult for Queen Mary II of England, wife of William of Orange. King William:

had but too good reason to be uneasy. His wife had, during two or three days, been poorly; and on the preceding evening grave symptoms had appeared. Sir Thomas Millington, who was physician in ordinary to the king, thought that she had the measles. But Radcliffe, who, with coarse manners and little book learning, had raised himself to the first practice in London chiefly by his rare skill in diagnostics, uttered the more alarming words, small pox ... the most terrible of all the ministers of death ... filling the churchyards with corpses, tormenting with constant fears all whom it had not yet stricken ... Towards the end of the year 1694, this pestilence was more than usually severe. At length the infection spread to the palace, and reached the young and blooming Queen. She received the intimation of her danger with true greatness of soul. She gave orders that every lady of her bedchamber, every maid of honour, nay, every menial servant, who had not had the small pox, should instantly leave Kensington House. She locked herself up during a short time in her closet, burned some papers, arranged others, and then calmly awaited her fate (Macaulay 1884, 575).

Queen Mary, age 32, died shortly thereafter. In contrast to many other rulers, before and since, she cared for all the people she ruled and endeavored to keep them from the horrors of disease that awaited her. William Kuklinsky, who had survived smallpox as a child, was immune. He went on to have a successful medical career and, eventually, his own students.

Yellow Fever in Philadelphia, 1793

In 1794, our ancestor Dr. David Swerdlow joined the new medical faculty in Montpellier, France. He carried on an extensive correspondence with his medical colleagues in the new United States. Best known among them was Benjamin Rush, a University of Pennsylvania professor of medical theory and clinical practice, signer of the Declaration of Independence, and founder of the College of Physicians of Philadelphia. Dr. Swerdlow was astonished to hear that, in 1793, Dr. Rush had diagnosed the disease devastating the new nation's capital as "bilious remitting, yellow fever." Dr. Rush wrote that he diagnosed the illness in several patients on August 19 (Rush 1794, 11). Within two weeks, a majority of residents had fled the city, including the governor, Rush's wife and children, and some of the city's 80 doctors. The mostly poor people who remained tried to protect themselves by wearing camphor bags or tarred rope around their necks, putting garlic in their pockets and shoes, covering themselves in vinegar (which may have had some mosquito repellent activity) (Kiarie-Makara 2010), and lighting bonfires in the street (Rush 1794, 23), harkening back to Galen's and Aëtius's mention of bonfires to treat epidemic illnesses.

The medical community was deeply divided about the epidemic's origin between those who advocated a local cause (which was true, due to the city's ample supply of Anopheles mosquitoes) and those who believed that it had arrived with the 2,000 immigrants from the slave revolution in Haiti (also probably true) (Gum 2010; Pernick 1972). Politicians spurred this division, stirring animosity toward the refugees for political gain.

Describing the epidemic, the medical community's differing views, and Philadelphia's sad state, Philip Freneau, a well-known poet and the editor of the *National Gazette*, wrote:

Pestilence

Hot, dry winds forever blowing,
Dead men to the grave-yards going:
> Constant hearses,
> Funeral verses;
Oh! What plagues—there is no knowing!

Priests retreating from their pulpits! -
Some in hot, and some in cold fits
> In bad temper,
> Off they scamper,
Leaving us - unhappy culprits!

> Doctors raving and disputing,
> Death's pale army still recruiting -
> > What a pother,
> > One with t'other!
> Some a-writing, some a-shooting.
>
> Nature's poisons here collected,
> Water, earth, and air infected -
> > O, what pity,
> > Such a city,
> Was in such a place erected! (Powell - Bring Out Your Dead)

Society descended into chaos and, with the governor in hiding, the city mayor was left to handle the crisis. Commercial activity and churches ceased functioning. As Rush wrote, the panic was so great that "Many people thrust their parents into the streets, as soon as they complain of a headache" (Biddle et al. 1892, 32). By the end of August, he wrote, about 325 people had died and the city's hospitals closed to new yellow fever patients. The city appropriated a building outside the city limits to house impoverished victims. Despite the efforts of many gallant volunteers, the conditions there were horrendous:

> It exhibited as wretched a picture of human misery as ever existed. … The sick, the dying and the dead, were indiscriminately mingled together. The ordure [excrement], and other evacuations of the sick, were allowed to remain in the most offensive state imaginable. … It was, in fact, a great human slaughterhouse, where numerous victims were immolated at the altar of riot and intemperance (Carey 1830, 40)

Rush believed the disease stemmed from impure air, especially decaying vegetable matter. Known for his somewhat antiquated techniques, he advocated treating patients by rebalancing the four bodily humors (blood, phlegm, black bile, and yellow bile). Rush treated up to 120 patients a day, even when he was ill, by administering laxatives and emetics, doing phlebotomy, and inducing diaphoresis. Along with 20 grams of calomel (mercurous chloride) four times a day, he prescribed jalap (another purgative) and massive bloodletting. He wrote,

I preferred frequent and small, to large bleedings in the beginning of September; but towards the height and close of the epidemic, I saw no inconvenience from the loss of a pint, and even twenty ounces of blood at a time. I drew from many persons seventy and eighty ounces in five days; and from a few, a much larger quantity (Rush 1794, 271-2).

Dr. Swerdlow agreed with neither Rush's proposed cause of the yellow fever nor his approach to treatment. He wrote that he concurred with those advocating strict quarantines (which occurred) and preferred the "French" method of treatment, which included bedrest, cleanliness, wine, and Peruvian bark (quinine) administration. (Neither treatment was effective, and there is still no treatment for yellow fever.)

Several months later, Dr. Swerdlow received a reply that included the same phrase that Dr. Rush had directed toward his Philadelphia colleagues who disagreed with him: "Dr. Rush is extremely sorry to differ from his friend Dr. Currie, in his opinion respecting the prevailing epidemic, published in the Federal Gazette of last evening" (Rush 1794, 234).

When November's frosts killed the mosquitoes, the epidemic dissipated. One person wrote to the Philadelphia papers praising those "intrepid sons of Galen who have not deserted their posts" and "begged a tear for the [ten] physicians who had died" (Powell 1993, 148-9). It is estimated that more than 5,000 people in a population of 45,000, including Dr. Rush's sister, died, and as many as 20,000 fled the city. Dr. Rush went on to become the Treasurer of the US Mint, continuing to practice medicine at the Pennsylvania Hospital, and acted as medical tutor for Meriwether Lewis before the Lewis and Clark Expedition. Dr. Swerdlow, due to his political views, was forced to flee France just ahead of the Revolutionists' guillotine.

The 1918 "Spanish" Flu

When the 1918 influenza pandemic erupted during World War I, US military service allowed one of my imagined doctor ancestors, Dr. Abraham Buzin, to observe the disease both in the United States and Europe. At least 50, and as many as 100, million people died worldwide, more than in any other pandemic. Most died between mid-September and mid-December of 1918. In the United States, the very poor died at twice the rate of that of the rich, and more young men than young women died, although they contracted the flu about equally (Sydenstricker 1931; Frost

1920). It is still unclear where the disease originated, but the "Spanish" flu, as it was called, quickly devastated every army in Europe.

Posted at Camp Devens, a training base just outside Boston, Capt. Buzin was only two years out of medical school and suddenly overwhelmed with critically ill patients. Between September 8 and the end of the month, they had diagnosed 14,000 cases of flu, about one-fourth of the Camp population. Of these, 757 died, resulting in an alarming case-fatality rate of more than 5%; the rate would not improve throughout the pandemic (Byerly 2005, 75; Wever and van Bergen 2014, 541). One of Buzin's colleagues wrote a letter (with original spelling and syntax) describing both the overall situation and the typical cases:

> These men start with what appears to be an ordinary attack of LaGrippe or Influenza, and when brought to the Hosp. they very rapidly develop the most viscious [sic] type of Pneumonia that has ever been seen. Two hours after admission they have the Mahogony spots over the cheek bones, and a few hours later you can begin to see the Cyanosis extending from their ears and spreading all over the face, until it is hard to distinguish the colored men from the white. It is only a matter of a few hours then until death comes, and it is simply a struggle for air until they suffocate ... We have been averaging about 100 deaths per day ...
>
> The normal number of resident Drs. here is about 25 and that has been increased to over 250 ...
>
> We have lost an outrageous number of Nurses and Drs. ... It takes Special trains to carry away the dead. For several days there were no coffins and the bodies piled up something fierce ... An extra long barracks has been vacated for the use of the Morgue, and it would make any man sit up and take notice to walk down the long lines of dead soldiers all dressed and laid out in double rows. We have no relief here, you get up in the morning at 5.30 and work steady till about 9.30 P.M., sleep, then go at it again. Some of the men of course have been here all the time, and they are TIRED ...
>
> We eat it live it, sleep it, and dream it, to say nothing of breathing it 16 hours a day (Grist 1979, 1632-3).

Dr. Buzin was soon sent to Europe and initially posted to the St. Marylebone Infirmary in London, where the infirmary's medical superintendent, Dr. Basil Hood, explained that the large hospital had already sent half its nurses to war. Dr. Hood later wrote,

> All training, and indeed every sort of trimming, went by the board. The staff fought like Trojans to feed the patients, scramble as best they could through the most elementary nursing and keep the delirious in bed! ...
>
> Each day the difficulties became more pronounced as the patients increased and the nurses decreased, going down like ninepins themselves.

Although he required that nurses wear lint masks and keep their distance from coughing patients, they ignored the directions when tending to fellow nurses. "Sad to relate some of these gallant girls lost their lives in this never-to-be-forgotten scourge and as I write I can see some of them now literally fighting to save their friends then going down and dying themselves."

Despite Hood's advice "not to interpose their faces too near the blast of those coughing," he wrote that in the case of one nurse,

> Nothing I could do or say had the slightest effect in influencing her to diminish the risks to herself. She was consumed with a burning desire to save her ... inevitably, the nurse developed a lung infection, dying soon after the woman she had been nursing.

In another case,

> One poor nurse, I remember, with a terribly acute influenzal pneumonia, became so distressed she could not stay in bed and insisted on being propped up against the wall by her bed until she was finally drowned in her profuse, thin blood-stained sputum (Honigsbaum 2020).

The Army soon sent Dr. Buzin to mainland Europe where, because of his experience, he was "seconded" to the British Army medical unit (RAMC). All the armies fighting in Europe were devastated by the flu, although the Americans suffered the worst. He heard that the RAMC was so short-handed that Dr. (later Sir) Alexander Fleming, who was serving in the RAMC primarily to study wound infections, ended up carrying the corpses of influenza victims to the improvised cemetery after the orderlies had gotten ill (Wever and van Bergen 2014; Maurois 1959). (In 1945, Dr. Fleming won the Nobel Prize for discovering penicillin.) Dr. Buzin also met Dr. Geoffrey Keynes (later knighted for his early work in transfusing blood), who had been shocked at seeing "rows of corpses, absolutely rows [sic] of them, hundreds of them, dying from something quite different. It was a ghastly sight, to see them lying there dead of something I didn't have the treatment for" (Macdonald 1980, 287).

Even peace could not halt the onslaught of influenza victims. Reflecting on Armistice Day, November 11, 1918, Sister Catherine Macfie, a nurse at a nearby casualty station, wrote about treating many wounded soldiers:

> who had Spanish influenza as well. ...The boys were coming in with colds and a headache and they were dead within two or three days. Great big handsome fellows, healthy men, just came in and died. There was no rejoicing in Lille the night of the Armistice. There was no rejoicing (Macdonald 1980, 297).

After the war, Dr. Buzin took surgical training and occasionally worked with Dr. Franklin Martin, later the head of the American College of Surgeons, who related his own experience as a patient:

> About 12 o'clock I began to feel hot. I was so feverish I was afraid I would ignite the clothing. I had a cough that tore my very innards out when I could not suppress it. It was dark; I surely had pneumonia and I never was so forlorn and uncomfortable in my life. ... Then I found that I was breaking into a deluge of perspiration and while I should have been more comfortable, I was more miserable than ever. ...When the light did finally come I was some specimen of misery—couldn't breathe without an excruciating cough and there was no hope in me (Solly 2020).

Dr. Martin survived and continued his leadership as a surgeon, founding what is now the *Journal of the American College of Surgeons*. Dr. Buzin had a long career as a surgeon, medical historian, and community leader.

Typhus in the Concentration Camps, 1940s

A respected Dutch ophthalmologist until the Nazi invasion in 1940, Dr. Luis Proshler, another fictional ancestor, was sent to the Breendonk concentration camp. Sometime afterwards he escaped and joined the Groupe G resistance movement, working as both a doctor and a guide for the Comet Line that smuggled Allied servicemen to safety. At the end of 1944, he again fell into German hands, eventually landing in Dachau Concentration Camp, probably in early March 1945, during a typhus epidemic. After that, we have only sparse information; the following is therefore abstracted from camp survivors' recollections. As a former inmate, Floris Bakels, described:

> Lice were present everywhere, even on your crust of bread ... The kraut was terrified of epidemics. He installed a barrack as a quarantine zone and did not ever show up there; the patients were tended by Jewish doctors and their assistants ... it was the gateway behind the hill above the camp ... (Bakels 1993, p. 188-9).

Typhus is a dreadful disease. As Sir John W.D. Megaw described it in 1942:

> [Typhus] is conveyed from man to man by human lice. In most of the cases there is high fever lasting from 10 to 16 days, with early and pronounced nervous symptoms and a characteristic rash. ... [The incubation period] is usually 8 to 12 days. ... The chief features of cases seen in adults [are a sudden onset of] chill, shivering, or rigor (60 to 80%), severe frontal headache (90%), and pains in the back and limbs. Vomiting frequently occurs (25 to 50%). ... At first drowsiness or mental confusion is present, succeeded by stupor or delirium in many of the severe cases. ... The temperature rises rapidly, reaching its maximum of 103° to 105° F. within two or three days and then remaining high ... for 8 to 12 days. ...The pulse soon becomes feeble, it may be slow in proportion to the temperature; the blood pressure falls ... The breathing is usually hurried ... mental disturbance and physical weakness are conspicuous. ... [Mortality] is almost negligible in children and is seldom more than 5% below the age of 20. It rises slowly till about the age of 40, when it is from 10 to 15%. It then rises somewhat steeply, reaching about 50% at the age of 50. Few patients of 60 and over recover (Megaw 1942, p 401-3).

In the camps, sick prisoners endured horrendous conditions.

> The surest prophylactic against typhus was mass delousing: the disinfection of the persons, their clothes, and their accommodations. ... Disinfection was an integral component of the dictatorial camp code, and was accompanied by harassment, excess, and humiliation. Inmates were forced to wait naked in the cold for hours for clean wash from the laundry. As in the induction ceremony, their hair was shaved and their private parts were wiped with dirty rags or sprayed with disinfectants. A number of prisoners were submerged and drowned in the vats containing the viscous liquid. If a louse was found on a prisoner, he or she was beaten or killed by the SS, the medical attendants, or the block leaders. The procedure was anything but efficient. Generally, cleaning was only superficial. ...
>
> If the epidemic appeared to be serious, the SS set up special infirmaries or infection blocks. This procedure fell back on the model of spatial separation. The epidemic was combated by isolating the sick prisoners in a closed area. ... The sole purpose of the block was to isolate the sick, not to cure them. ... It was a jail for the sick, one whose inmates had been written off (Sofsky 1999, p 211-2).

French physician Dr. André Lettich later described a similar situation at the Birkenau concentration camp where he had been imprisoned:

> Block 7 was a wooden barracks like the others. Over the door there was this cynical inscription: "Infection Department." If one opened the door, one's first spontaneous reaction was to step back and hold one's nose, the air was that repulsive, biting, stifling, and unfit for breathing. Everything was full of screams and moans. Eight or ten patients were lying on bunks that barely had enough room for five, and thus most of them had to sit up. In this jail for patients, all illnesses and every conceivable injury were represented. Typhoid fever, pneumonia, cachexia, edemas, broken arms and legs, fractured skulls, all helter-skelter. How could the physicians have treated these poor wretches even if they had been given a chance to do so— without medications and with paper bandages? It was impossible. Sometimes there were ten or fifteen aspirin tablets for 800 or 900 patients. And why tend to them and put on bandages when twice a week the nurses had to

load all patients on trucks that took them to the gas chambers? The German method was the wholesale liquidation of the human material that only took up space (Langbein 2004, p. 206).

Post-war researcher Wolfgang Sofsky later wrote:

> Like other invalids, those ill with infectious diseases were a preferred target for deliberate liquidation actions. For the SS, killing was the simplest means to combat an epidemic. In this way, it saved on food, space, and medical and other care, and rid itself of the burden of time-consuming permanent supervision. ...
>
> If the epidemic could no longer be contained, there was one last-ditch resort. The SS sealed off the entire camp and fled from the infected area. ... The way now stood clear for the epidemic to rage unchecked. ... The hungry, ill, and dying lay packed together in the bursting blocks. Separation and isolation were virtually impossible. ... Piles of corpses amassed in the camp streets and along the paths, since the body carriers and the crematorium could not keep up with the headlong pace of dying. ... Courage and pity, a sense of responsibility and readiness to sacrifice, the mustering of the last ounce of physical energy and willpower—these were the final resources available in the battle against the epidemic. ... Because of the lack of medical supplies, doctors who were found in the newly arriving prisoner transports were able only to institute administrative measures. They classified the sick, attempting to divide them into separate groups. Dysentery patients were placed near the latrines. ... Purification squads were organized, and, in a risky move, brushes and brooms were gathered to clean the blocks. ... By burning down the legs broken off from wooden chairs, charcoal was prepared as a treatment for diarrhea. Sick patients were given a "diet soup" made of water mixed with a bit of flour or groats (Sofsky 1999, 212 - 3).

Despite taking as much care as he could while tending to patients, Dr. Luis Proshler succumbed to typhus on April 29, 1945, hours before the camp was liberated. In the interest of public health, his body was quickly buried in a mass grave. He had no survivors.

COVID-19

As the COVID-19 pandemic rages I, like most of my older and experienced colleagues, find myself sidelined. After a 50-plus-year career in academic emergency medicine, participating in multiple disaster responses around the world, and spending considerable time working and teaching internationally, I have been told that I am too old to work on the front lines. I must stand back, eligible only to work at an indigent care clinic.

I never expected my dynamic and exciting clinical career to end on a whimper. COVID-19 struck just as I was departing Guyana where, for a decade, I have been teaching, supervising clinical research, and practicing emergency medicine as a licensed member of their residency faculty. In that resource-limited setting, I could help train the country's first and future medical leaders. Physically taxing but mentally stimulating, it was worth every ounce of effort.

Tragically, clinical work and teaching during the COVID-19 and future pandemics will no longer be my responsibility, but that of my younger colleagues and their descendants.

References

Bakels, Floris B. 1993. *Nacht Und Nebel: Night and Fog.* Translated by Herman Friedhoff. Cambridge, England: Lutterworth Press.

Biddle, Alexander, John Adams, Thomas Jefferson and Benjamin Rush. 1892. *Old Family Letters Relating to the Yellow Fever.* Series B. Philadelphia: J.B. Lippincott Co.

Byerly, Carol R. 2005. *Fever of War: The Influenza Epidemic in the U.S. Army during World War I.* New York, NY: New York University Press.

Carey, Mathew. 1830. *Miscellaneous Essays.* New York, NY: Carey and Hart.

Frost, Wade Hampton. 1920. "Statistics of Influenza Morbidity: With Special Reference to Certain Factors in Case Incidence and Case Fatality." *Public Health Reports* (1896-1970) 35 (11): 584–97. https://doi.org/10.2307/4575511

Grist, Norman Roy. 1979. "Pandemic Influenza 1918." *British Medical Journal* 2 (6205): 1632 –33. https://doi.org/10.1136/bmj.2.6205.1632

Gum, Samuel A. 2010. "Philadelphia Under Siege: The Yellow Fever of 1793." Pennsylvania Center for the Book. https://web.archive.org/web/20220804001159/https://www.pabook.libraries.psu.edu/

literary-cultural-heritage-map-pa/feature-articles/philadelphia-under-siege-yellow-fever-1793

Honigsbaum, Mark. 2020. "'Nurses Fell Like Ninepins': Death and Bravery in the 1918 Flu Pandemic." *The Guardian*. April 5, 2020. https://www.theguardian.com/world/2020/apr/05/nurses-fell-like-ninepins-death-and-bravery-in-the-1918-flu-pandemic

Kellwaye, Simon. 1593. "A defensatiue against the plague contayning two partes or treatises: the first, shewing the meanes how to preserue vs from the dangerous contagion thereof: the second, how to cure those that are infected therewith. Whereunto is annexed a short treatise of the small poxe: shewing how to gouerne and helpe those that are infected therewith. Published for the loue and benefit of his countrie by Simon Kellwaye Gentleman." London: John Windet, 1593; Ann Arbor: Early English Books Online Text Creation Partnership, 2011. https://quod.lib.umich.edu/e/eebo/A04785.0001.001/1:10?rgn=div1;view=fulltext

Kiarie-Makara, Martha W, Hae-Soon Yoon, and Dong-Kyu Lee. 2010. "Repellent Efficacy of Wood Vinegar Against Culex Pipiens Pallens and Aedes Togoi (Diptera: Culicidae) Under Laboratory and Semi-Field Conditions." *Entomological Research* 40 (2): 97–103. https://doi.org/10.1111/j.1748-5967.2010.00265.x

Langbein, Hermann. 2004. *People in Auschwitz*. Translated by Harry Zohn. Chapel Hill, NC: University of North Carolina Press.

Macaulay, Thomas B. 1884. *History of England from the Accession of James II*. Vol IV. Chicago: Belford, Clarke & Co.

Macdonald, Lyn. 1980. *The Roses of No Man's Land*. London: Michael Joseph Ltd.

Maurois, Andre. 1959. *The Life of Sir Alexander Fleming: Discoverer of Penicillin*. New York, NY: Dutton.

Megaw, J. W. D. 1942. "Typhus Fever." *British Medical Journal* 2 (4265): 401–3. https://doi.org/10.1136/bmj.2.4265.401

Pernick, M. S. 1972. "Politics, Parties, and Pestilence: Epidemic Yellow Fever in Philadelphia and the Rise of the First Party System." *The William and Mary Quarterly* 29 (4): 559–86.

Pinault, Jody Rubin 1992. *Hippocratic Lives and Legends. Studies in Ancient Medicine*. Leiden, Netherlands: E.J. Brill.

Powell, John Harvey. 1993. *Bring Out Your Dead: The Great Plague of Yellow Fever in Philadelphia in 1793*. Philadelphia: University of Pennsylvania Press.

Rush, Benjamin. 1794. *An Account of the Bilious Remitting Yellow Fever, as it Appeared in the City of Philadelphia, in the Year 1793*. 2nd ed. Philadelphia: Thomas Dobson.

Sofsky, Wolfgang. 1999. *The Order of Terror: The Concentration Camp*. Translated by William Templer. Princeton, NJ: Princeton University Press.

Solly, Meilan. 2020. "What We Can Learn From 1918 Influenza Diaries." *Smithsonian Magazine*, April 13, 2020. https://www.smithsonianmag.com/history/what-we-can-learn-1918-influenza-diaries-180974614/

Sydenstricker, Edgar. 1931. "The Incidence of Influenza among Persons of Different Economic Status during the Epidemic of 1918." *Public Health Reports* 46 (4): 154–170. https://doi.org/10.2307/4579923

Thornton, Alice. 1875. *The Autobiography of Mrs. Alice Thornton, of East Newton, Co. York*. Edited by Charles Jackson. Durham, NC: Andrews and Co.

Thucydides. 1956. *History of the Peloponnesian War, Books I and II*. Translated by Charles Forster Smith. Cambridge, MA: Harvard University Press.

Thucydides. 1916. *History of the Peloponnesian War*. Translated by Rex Warner. Harmondsworth, Middlesex: Penguin.

Wever, Peter C., and Leo van Bergen. 2014. "Death from 1918 Pandemic Influenza during the First World War: A Perspective from Personal and Anecdotal Evidence." *Influenza and Other Respiratory Viruses* 8 (5): 538–46. https://doi.org/10.1111/irv.12267

One of the world's first residency trained emergency physicians, Dr. Iserson practiced and taught for nearly three decades at the University of Arizona's ED/Level 1 Trauma Center. Chair of the medical center's Bioethics Committee for 25 years, he was a founding member of the Society for Academic Emergency Medicine and the American College of Emergency Physicians Ethics Committees. Having authored hundreds of scientific articles and a dozen books, he now practices global and disaster medicine and at local indigent-care clinics. His practice on all seven continents included 16 months as the US Antarctic Program's Lead Physician and as an NGO physician in Central and South America, Asia, and Sub-Saharan Africa.

On Witnessing: Photojournalism and Visualized Trauma
By Ryan Christopher Jones

Originally submitted March 10, 2022

The following reflection includes names of patients. The names have not been altered as they appear – with permission – in the publicly-available article "The Last Anointing" in the New York Times, published on June 6, 2020. Mr. Jones was the photographer for that article, and his additional photographs from that experience follow this essay.

For three weeks in April and May 2020, I photographed a team of Boston-area priests as they administered the sacrament of *last rites* to Catholic patients dying from COVID-19 in local hospitals. On the morning of May 5, 2020, I was granted access to photograph two men at St. Elizabeth's Medical Center and it was the first time I witnessed what this new disease did to a human body. Trying to make sense of what I saw just a few hours before, that evening at around 9 p.m., I wrote the following in my notebook:

I had two minutes to photograph in each of the two rooms. I wasn't told the names of the men but I overheard the first man's name was Otto, the other was Mr. Dempsey. Both had COVID-19 and were near the end of their life and Fr. Ryan Connors came in to give them both last rites. Otto looked worse than I ever could have imagined. Sores and lesions on his face, his eyes kept alive only by medicine—and even that was waning. They were both intubated and the only hope that seemed to exist in those rooms was spiritual; hope for a physical healing is gone.

I had no idea what the priest was saying. My brain could only focus on not stepping on the tubes on the ground and trying to not photograph my reflection in the windows and making sure my pictures were in focus. I couldn't think about the life this man led prior to me showing up to photograph his death. I couldn't think about his family who couldn't be there to hold his hand. I couldn't think about the truncated 'anointing of the sick' prayer the Catholic Church had to put in place so their priests limited their exposure in administering the sacrament to the dying. I couldn't think of all that in the moment, but I can think of it now.

Looking at the pictures is tough. I can see the pain and the loss of life in slow motion—far slower than in the moment. I wish I could say there was an element of beauty to this moment but I can't. It's brutal and tragic and lonely and inconceivable. But it is the truth, and in this case that's more important than beauty.

Otto Barrios died three weeks and one day later. Skip Dempsey survived, disproving my earlier declaration that hope for physical healing was impossible. At the time I saw them, both men were intubated and unconscious as they lay in their hospital beds surrounded by a fortress of expensive machines, but no family. They were not allowed. Despite this, however, those same families who could not be present with their loved ones allowed me to document the scenes in their absence.

I was on assignment for *The New York Times* with *Times* religion reporter, Elizabeth Dias. I was physically present in Boston to photograph the story while Elizabeth reported remotely to minimize exposure for all parties. We were first granted access to the priests by the Catholic Archdiocese of Boston. Then, both St. Elizabeth's Medical Center and Newton-Wellesley Hospital granted us access to their COVID wards. But to report this story as a human one and not just an abstract idea, access to the isolated patients themselves was crucial. Because of HIPAA privacy laws, neither Elizabeth nor I could speak to the patients' next of kin until *after* they had allowed me to be present in the rooms. So the communications teams at both hospitals pitched the story to these families with grace and delicacy, and five families ultimately agreed to be a part of the story that was published online as "The Last Anointing" on June 6, 2020. I am forever grateful to the families who trusted in me to be present in those sacred and despairing moments.

For three weeks I was holed up, alone in a Homewood Suites in Brookline, waiting for people to die. It's a hard sentence to write, but brutal self-reflections are needed to make sense of the sometimes extractive elements of photography and photojournalism. I wrestle with it constantly: how does one tell an honest and humane story of human suffering without resorting to tropes and exploitation? In my experience, that happens when I can connect with and really listen to the people I photograph. But how does that happen in a COVID ward where meaningful access is restricted by layers of PPE, HIPAA, limited time and proximity, and even unconsciousness?

For most of my career I have struggled with the moral quandary of how to document suffering responsibly, and in 2018 I wrote an op-ed for *The New York Times* called "How Photography Exploits the Vulnerable" (Jones 2018). In it, I call on myself, my colleagues and the photojournalism industry at large to re-evaluate how we often resort to troublesome and stereotypical depictions of vulnerable people simply because it's how we've conditioned our visual language. The unhoused, immigrants, refugees, and people struggling from drug addiction are often visually depicted in the single dimension of pain and suffering, as if they are incapable of experiencing anything else.

Despite my mission to be an ethical photojournalist, was this *last rites* story, in and of itself, unethical? Was my mere presence harming the families who weren't even allowed to be present at their family member's last days? Was my position as photographer for *The New York Times* one of unfair and inequitable privilege? When feeling confused or conflicted I often return to Arthur and Joan Kleinman's "The Appeal of Experience; The Dismay of Images: Cultural Appropriations of Suffering in Our Times." In it, they meditate on the ways that news images and visual media have a nasty tendency to exploit abstract suffering for entertainment. It is reassuring that I am not alone in my conflict, as the Kleinmans write that:

> This globalization of suffering is one of the more troubling signs of the cultural transformations of the current era: troubling because experience is being used as a commodity, and through this cultural representation of suffering, experience is being remade, thinned out, and distorted (Kleinman and Kleinman 1996, 2).

But was my presence in this story harmful? One that contributed to this distorted and commodified representation of suffering? The subsequent years after reporting "The Last Anointing" have shaken my foundation of what it means to be a witness to a cruel world, and my feelings on this career often vacillate between historical recorder and grimy voyeur.

I never planned on being a photojournalist, and especially the archetypal kind that parachutes into foreign countries to take photos of war-torn 'over there' for American consumption. This is not a value judgment because working as a foreign correspondent is an arduous and important job, but personally I was always more interested in the mostly local stories that affected my own cities, communities, and country. I mention all this because local and domestic photojournalists aren't usually trained to manage acute trauma in the ways that foreign correspondents are. So when Northeast metropolises found themselves at the center of a new and terrifying contagion, as a photojournalist based in New York City, I found myself responding to not just a global pandemic, but a local one that devastated the city and the region I called home. This virus affected the five boroughs with a swift and furious brutality that even the notoriously resilient city couldn't fathom, and photojournalists across the Eastern seaboard were asked to document the trauma in real time.

After leaving Boston and upon returning to New York, I immediately had to cover the erupting George Floyd protests. Next, I traveled to California and Iowa for more COVID coverage throughout the summer. Then I documented the tumultuous 2020 presidential elections in Houston and Los Angeles. Along with many of my colleagues across the country, I felt an intense whiplash in needing to be physically present amidst so much social transformation. It was existentially exhausting, but I didn't realize it because this job requires an emotional blockade in order to get the hard work done and published. It's why so many photojournalists return from war with acute post-traumatic stress disorder (Newman, Simpson, and Handschuh 2003).

In December 2020 I was invited to speak to a class at Harvard taught by Arthur Kleinman, Davíd Carrasco, Michael Puett, and Stephanie Paulsell called "Quests for Wisdom: Religious, Moral, and Aesthetic Searches for the Art of Living in Perilous Times." Throughout the semester the class and faculty engaged "with the problems of danger, uncertainty, failure, and suffering that led the founders of the social sciences and humanities to ask fundamental questions about meaning, imagination, aesthetics, social life, and subjective experience." Professors Carrasco and Kleinman are mentors and advisors of mine, and they asked me to present a gallery of my 2020 photos from January to December, knowing the tremendous arc of suffering that accompanied both my year as a photojournalist but also the many losses suffered by the whole world. In the middle of the presentation, while discussing the reporting of "The Last Anointing," I felt something strange well up in me. I tried to suppress it but it kept coming back. Stronger. Stronger. It was grief.

In the middle of that presentation I realized for the first time I hadn't processed any of what I had witnessed in 2020. Throughout the year I kept suppressing any reconciliation in order to push on, to make more work, to cover the next cataclysmic news event to befall 2020. I had focused so much of my energy on being a photojournalist I had completely ignored just being a person, and that class of 150 people watched in silence as I started to tear up, unexpectedly, while responding to a question about sharing space with the Boston priests. As anthropologist Michael Jackson writes in *The Politics of Storytelling*, "the act of sharing stories helps us create a world that is more than the sum of its individual parts" (Jackson 2013, 58). There was something quite intimate and powerful about making my private experience public, and for the first time in 2020 I was not a witness, but I was *being* witnessed.

To be seen is a gift, and it's one that journalists are rarely privy to while they focus their gaze onto others. Through all my struggles with the ethics of documenting trauma in "The Last Anointing," I can only hope that in some small way, those painful stories can bring peace to the families who couldn't be there: to know that someone, anyone, was physically there in those final moments, as a witness to life lived and life lost.

References

Jackson, Michael. 2013. *The Politics of Storytelling: Violence, Transgression and Intersubjectivity*. Copenhagen: Museum Tusculanum Press, 58.

Jones, Ryan Christopher. 2018. "How Photography Exploits the Vulnerable." *New York Times*, August 31, 2018. https://www.nytimes.com/2018/08/31/opinion/photography-exploitation-opioid.html

Kleinman, Arthur and Joan Kleinman. 1996. "The Appeal of Experience; The Dismay of Images: Cultural Appropriations of Suffering in Our Times." *Daedalus* 125 (February): 2. https://www.jstor.org/stable/20027351.

Newman, Elana, Simpson, Roger, and David Handschuh. 2003. "Trauma Exposure and Post-Traumatic Stress Disorder Among Photojournalists." *Visual Communication Quarterly* 10 (1): 4–13. https://doi.org/10.1080/15551390309363497

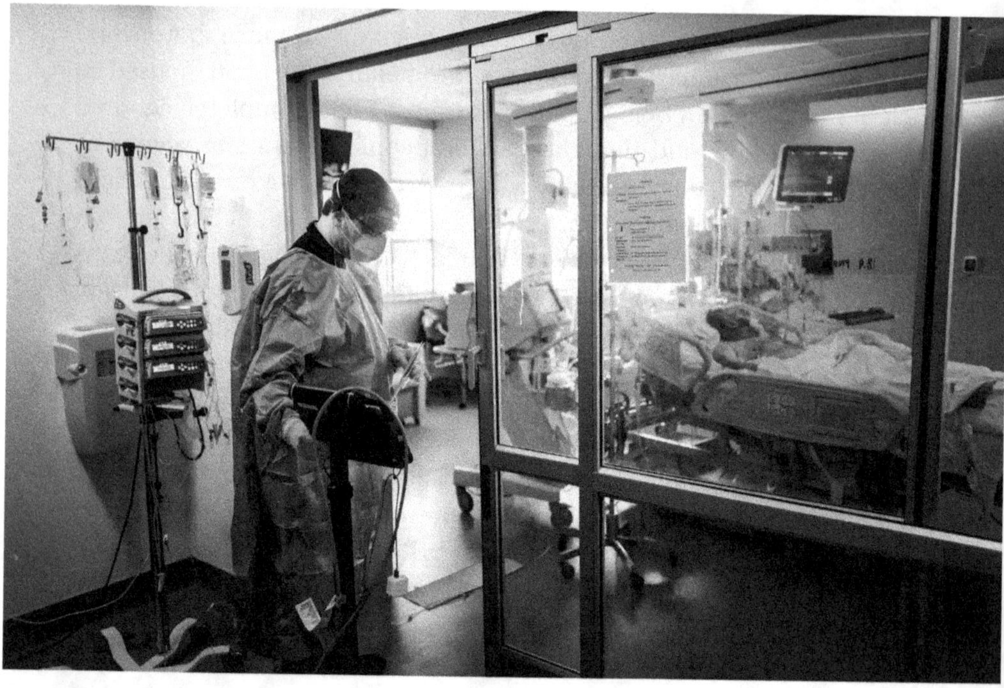

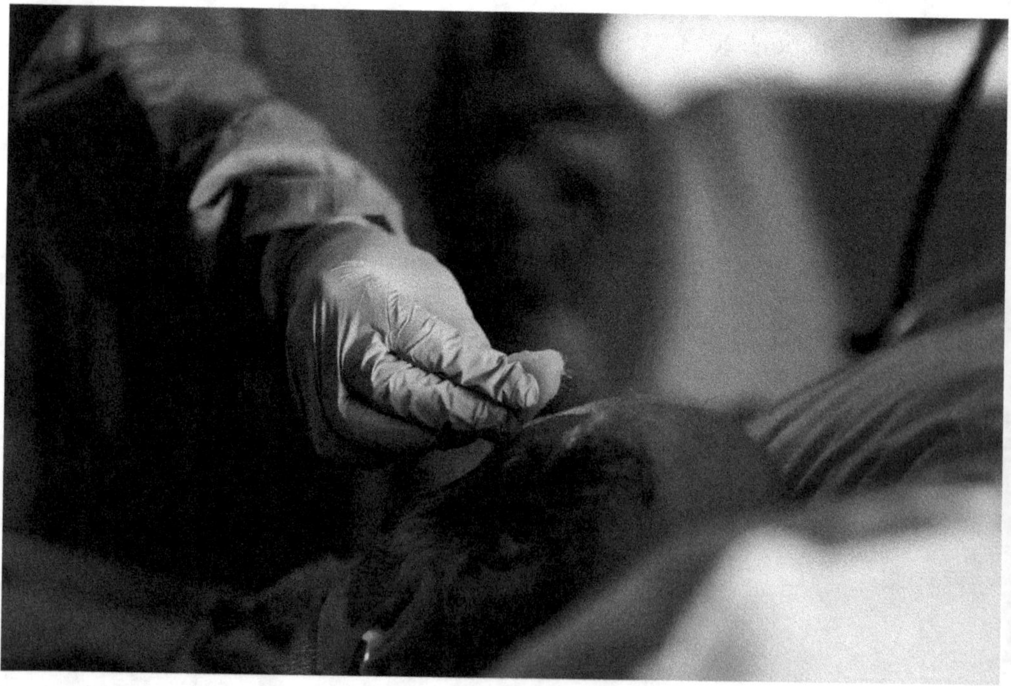

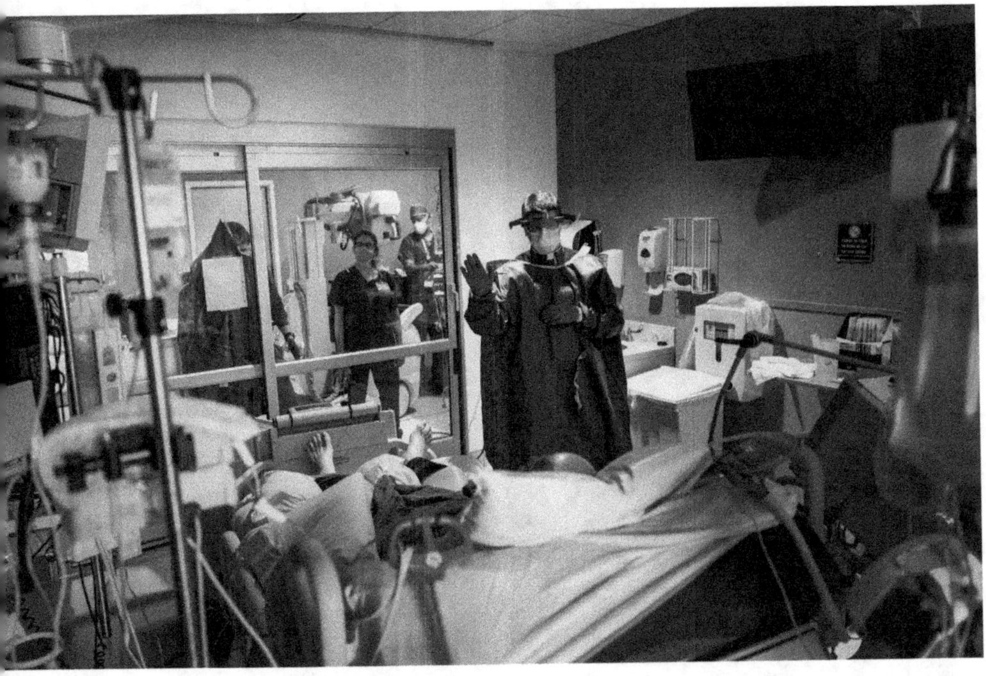

The Pandemic and the Humanities

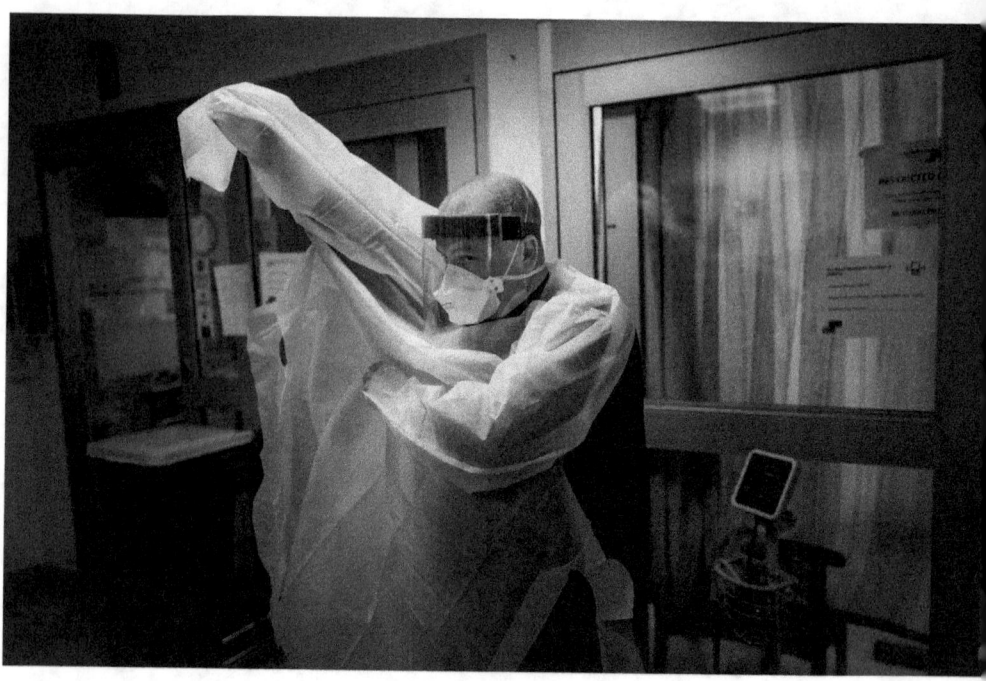

Photographs from the sacrament of last rites in Boston hospitals Spring 2020

Ryan Christopher Jones is currently a PhD student in Social Anthropology at Harvard University, where he is studying the political ecology of water in Central California. Prior to starting the doctoral program, Ryan worked as an independent photojournalist for *The New York Times*, *The Washington Post*, *ProPublica*, and others, focusing on issues of migration, labor, and the environment. In 2022, Ryan was awarded the 2022 American Mosaic Journalism Prize for his reporting on Mexican-American communities in California and New York, and he also served on the jury for the Pulitzer Prizes for Photojournalism.

www.ingramcontent.com/pod-product-compliance
Lightning Source LLC
Chambersburg PA
CBHW070749230426
43665CB00017B/2303